Images of the Present Time

The Seminars of Alain Badiou

The Seminars of Alain Badiou

Kenneth Reinhard, General Editor

Alain Badiou is widely considered to be one of the most important Continental philosophers of our time. Badiou has developed much of his thinking in his annual seminars, which he delivered in Paris from the late 1970s to 2017. These seminars include discussions that inform his major books, including *Being and Event*, *Logics of Worlds*, and *The Immanence of Truths*, as well as presentations of many ideas and topics that are not part of his published work. Some volumes of the seminar investigate individual thinkers and writers such as Parmenides, Plato, Nietzsche, Heidegger, Beckett, and Mallarmé. Others examine concepts such as infinity, truth, the subject, the present, evil, love, and the nature of change. These seminars constitute an essential part of Badiou's thinking, one that remains largely unknown to the non-Francophone world. Their translation is a major event for philosophers and other scholars and students in the humanities and social sciences and for the artists, writers, political theorists, and engaged intellectuals for whom Badiou's work has rapidly become a generative and inspiring resource.

For a complete list of seminars, see page 431.

Images of the Present Time

2001–2004

Alain Badiou

Translated by
Susan Spitzer

Introduction by Kenneth Reinhard

Columbia University Press
New York

Columbia University Press gratefully acknowledges the generous
contribution to this book provided by the Florence Gould
Foundation Endowment Fund for French Translation.

Columbia University Press
Publishers Since 1893
New York   Chichester, West Sussex
cup.columbia.edu

First published in French as *Images du temps présent* (2001-2004)
© 2014 Librairie Arthème Fayard
English translation copyright © 2023 Columbia University Press
Paperback edition, 2024

Library of Congress Cataloging-in-Publication Data
Names: Badiou, Alain, author. | Spitzer, Susan L., translator.
Title: Images of the present time, 2001-2004 / translated by Susan Spitzer;
introduction by Kenneth Reinhard.
Other titles: Images du temps présent. English
Description: New York : Columbia University Press, 2023. | Includes index.
Identifiers: LCCN 2022014887 | ISBN 9780231176064 (hardback) |
ISBN 9780231216692 (pbk.) | ISBN 9780231548526 (ebook)
Subjects: LCSH: Philosophy, French—20th century. | Time.
Classification: LCC B2430.B274 A5 2024 | DDC 194—dc23/eng/20220614
LC record available at https://lccn.loc.gov/2022014887

Cover design: Julia Kushnirsky

Contents

Year One: Contemporary Nihilism

Year Two: The Logic of Exceptions

Year Three: What Does it Mean to Live?

Editors' Introduction to the English Edition of the Seminars of Alain Badiou

KENNETH REINHARD, SUSAN SPITZER, AND JASON E. SMITH

With the publication in English of Alain Badiou's seminars, we believe that a new phase of his reception in the Anglophone world will open up, one that bridges the often formidable gap between the two main forms in which his published work has so far appeared. On the one hand, there is the tetralogy of his difficult and lengthy major works of systematic philosophy, beginning with a sort of prelude, *Theory of the Subject*, and continuing with the three parts of *Being and Event*, *Logics of Worlds*, and the *Immanence of Truths*. On the other hand, there are his numerous shorter and occasional pieces on topics such as ethics, contemporary politics, film, literature, and art. Badiou's "big books" are often built on rather daunting mathematical ideas and formulations: *Being and Event* relies primarily on set theory and the innovations introduced by Paul Cohen; *Logics of Worlds* adds category, topos, and sheaf theory; and *The Immanence of Truths* expands into the mathematics of large cardinals. Each of these great works is written in its own distinctive, and often rather dense, style: *Theory of the Subject* echoes the dramatic tone and form of a Lacanian seminar; *Being and Event* presents a fundamental ontology in the form of a series of Cartesian "meditations"; *Logics of Worlds* is organized in formal theories and "Greater Logics," and expressed in richly developed concrete examples, phenomenological descriptions, and scholia; and for reading the *Immanence of Truths*, Badiou suggests two distinct paths: one short and "absolutely necessary," the other long and "more elaborate or illustrative, more free-ranging." Because of the difficulty of these longer books, and their highly compact formulations, Badiou's shorter writings—such as the books on ethics and Saint Paul—often serve as a reader's first point of entry into his ideas. But this less steep path of induction brings its own problems, insofar as these more topical and occasional works often take for granted their relationship to the fundamental architecture of Badiou's thinking and thus may appear to have a greater (or smaller) role in it than they actually do. Hence the publication of Badiou's seminars from 1983 through (at least) 2012 makes available a middle path, one in which the major lines of Badiou's thinking—as well as its many extraordinary detours—are displayed with the remarkable clarity and the generous explications and exemplifications that always characterize his oral presentations.[1] It is extraordinarily exciting to see the genesis of Badiou's ideas in the experimental and performative context of his seminars, and there is a great deal in the seminars that doesn't appear at all in his existing published writings.

The first volume of the seminars to be published in English, on Lacan, constitutes part of a four-year sequence on "anti-philosophy" which also includes volumes on Nietzsche, Wittgenstein, and Saint Paul. The second volume, on Malebranche, is part of a similar cluster on being, which also involves years dedicated to Parmenides and Heidegger. And the later volumes, beginning in 1996, gather material from multiple years of the seminars, as in the case of *Axiomatic Theory of the Subject* (which is based on the sessions from the years 1996–97 and 1997–98), and *Images of the Present Time* (which was delivered in sessions over three years, from 2001 to 2004).

Isabelle Vodoz and Véronique Pineau are establishing the French text of the seminar on the basis of audio recordings and notes, with the intention of remaining as close as possible to Badiou's delivery while eliminating unnecessary repetitions and other minor artifacts. In reviewing and approving the texts of the seminars (sometimes as long as thirty years after having delivered them), Badiou decided not to revise or reformulate them, but to let them speak for themselves, without the benefit of self-critical hindsight. Given this decision, it is remarkable to see how consistent his thinking has been over the years. Moreover, each volume of the seminars includes a preface by Badiou that offers an extremely valuable account of the political and intellectual context of the seminars, as well as a sort of retrospective reflection on the process of his thought's emergence. In our translations of the seminars into English, we have tried to preserve the oral quality of the French edition in order to give the reader the impression of listening to the original recordings. We hope that the publication of Badiou's seminars will allow more readers to encounter the full scope of his ideas, and will allow those readers who are already familiar with his work to discover a new sense of its depths, its range, and its implications—perhaps almost as if reading Badiou for the first time.

The Seminars of Alain Badiou (1983–2016): General Preface

ALAIN BADIOU

The Seminars in English

It is a great pleasure for me to write this preface to the English-language edition of the entire collection of thirty years of my seminars. The information below is intended simply to shed some light on what these thirty years of public speaking have meant, to me and my various audiences, and why there may be some interest, or even pleasure, to be found in reading the seminars.

I. A Few Historical Reference Points

The word "seminar" should, in principle, refer to collective work around a particular problem. Instead, where these seminars are concerned, it refers to my own individual, albeit public, work on many different problems, all of which were nonetheless united by a philosophical apparatus explicitly claiming to be systematic.

Admittedly, the word "seminar" was already used in the latter sense with reference to Lacan's famous seminar, which, for me and many other people, has raised the bar very high when it comes to this sort of thing.

That a large part of my teaching took the form of such a seminar—whose ongoing publication in French, and now in English and Spanish, will show that it remained virtually free from any institutional authority—was originally due to pure chance.

At the beginning of the academic year 1966–67, while I was the senior class teacher at the boys' high school in Reims, I was appointed lecturer in an establishment that had just been created and that testified to the rapid expansion of higher education in the supremely Gaullist France of those years: the Collège universitaire de Reims, affiliated with the University of Nancy. Initially, only so-called propaedeutic [i.e., college preparatory] teaching was to be provided there (at the time, there was a first year of studies with that name, validated by a final exam that, if successfully passed, allowed students to begin their first year of university). So I was asked to teach the philosophy option in this preparatory year. But all of a sudden, thanks to one of those nasty betrayals so typical of academic life, the University of Nancy announced that, for the time being, it couldn't relinquish its philosophical powers to Reims and that there wouldn't be any philosophy option for the preparatory program to which my position was attached.

So there I was, a teacher of a nonexistent discipline. Given these circumstances, what else was there to do but hold an open seminar? And that's what I did for two years (1966–67 and 1967–68), before—I have to brag a bit here—an increasingly large audience and, what was even more flattering to me, one that was there out of pure interest since there was no final exam to reward their faithful attendance.

If I'd had the energy to look for my notes from that time long ago (when no one had either the idea or the means to bring in one of those big, clunky tape recorders to record my improvisations) and to revise those notes and turn them into a written text, I could have proudly begun this edition of the seminars with the one from 1966–67—fifty years of free speech!—, the year devoted to Schopenhauer, and then continued with the 1967–68 seminar, when my syllabus was focused on Mallarmé, Rimbaud, and Lautréamont, in that order. The *Chants de Maldoror*, however, which I had intended to begin dealing with in early May, was sacrificed on the altar of the mass movement.

And then, as a result of that May upheaval, which was to drastically change my life and my thinking about many issues other than academic appointments, I was appointed (since those appointments continued to be made nonetheless) Assistant Professor at the Experimental University of Vincennes, which soon became Paris 8.

The context in which I began teaching courses there was so feverish and politically so intense, the actions afoot there so radical, that the government decided that the philosophy degrees granted by Paris 8 would have no national accreditation! So there I was again, forced to give an open seminar since there was no state validation of our teaching efforts, despite the fact that they were highly innovative, to say the least.

This marginalization lasted for years. So—if, once again, the documentation really allowed for it—I could give an account of the free and open seminars of the 1970s, which, when all the exciting, frenetic collective action going on at the time allowed them to take place, were devoted in particular to the Hegelian dialectic, to Mallarmé again, to my beloved Plato, and to Lacan, always before audiences that were there out of pure interest alone, since there was no exam and therefore no academic credit to validate their attendance.

Actually, a synthetic account of that period does exist: my book *Theory of the Subject*, published by Seuil in 1982 under the editorship of François Wahl (English translation published by Continuum, 2009). It provides an admittedly very freely rewritten account of the seminars that were held between January 1975 and June 1979.

Beginning in those years, as a result of the so-called political normalization, things calmed down in the universities, even in the one in Vincennes, which had incidentally been moved to Saint-Denis. In the early 1980s, the government authorities decided that we of the glorious Department of Philosophy—where you could hear lectures by Michel Foucault, Michel Serres, François Châtelet, Gilles Deleuze, Jean-François Lyotard, and Jacques Rancière—deserved to have the national accreditation we'd lost gradually restored. It was from that time on, too, that the seminars began to be systematically recorded by several different attendees. Little wonder, then, that I decided to publish all of the seminars between 1983 and the present: for these thirty-odd years, abundant, continuous documentation exists.

Not that the locations, the institutions, and the frequency didn't change. Indeed, starting in 1987 the seminar moved to the Collège international de philosophie, which owed its creation in large part to the determined efforts of everyone in "living [i.e. non-traditional] philosophy" who felt put down and badmouthed by the University, Lyotard and

Derrida being the two most emblematic names at the time. In that setting, I rediscovered the innocence of teaching without exams or validation: the seminar was now officially open and free of charge to everyone (for the reasons I mentioned above, it had actually always been so). It was held in the locales that the Collège secured or bargained hard to secure for its activities: the old École polytechnique on the rue Descartes, the École normale supérieure on the boulevard Jourdan, an industrial institution on the rue de Varenne, the Institut catholique on the rue d'Assas, and the main auditorium of the University of Paris 7 at Jussieu.

In 1998, when my seminar had been held under the auspices of the Collège international de philosophie for ten years, a crisis of sorts erupted: one faction of the Collège's administration viewed with suspicion both the form and the content of what I was doing. As far as the form was concerned, my status in the Collège was an exceptional one since, although I'd initially been properly inducted into it under Philippe Lacoue-Labarthe's presidency, I had never been officially re-elected as a member of the Collège. The content was viewed with suspicion because in those times dominated by the antitotalitarian ideology of human rights, rumors were going around that my teaching was "fascist." As I was unwilling to put up with such an atmosphere, I broke off my seminar midyear, thereby causing a lot of confusion.

I set it up the following fall at the École normale supérieure, where I'd been appointed professor. It remained there for fifteen years, which is pretty good, after all.

But this seminar was fated to always end up antagonizing institutions. I had to use the largest lecture halls at the ENS due to the sizeable audiences the seminar attracted, but at the start of the 2014 school year there was a dark plot afoot to deny me all access to those rooms and recommend that I accommodate around 250 people in a room that held only 80! After driving Lacan out, the prestigious ENS drove me out too! But, after all, I told myself, to suffer the same fate as Lacan was in its own way a glorious destiny. What happened to me next, however, can literally be called a "coup de théâtre," a dramatic turn of events. My friend Marie-José Malis, the outstanding theater artist and great renovator of the art of directing, was appointed artistic director of the Théâtre de la Commune in the Paris suburb of Aubervilliers. She offered to let me hold my seminar there, and I enthusiastically accepted. For two and a half years, in the heart of a working-class suburb, I stood on the stage before a full house and interspersed my final seminars, which were connected with the writing of my last "big" book, *L'Immanence des vérités*, with actual theatrical presentations. I was generously assisted in this by Didier Galas, who created the role of Ahmed in my four-play cycle, written in the 1980s and 1990s for the artistic and stage director Christian Schiaretti: *Ahmed the Subtle, Ahmed Gets Angry, Ahmed the Philosopher,* and *The Pumpkins*. On January 16, 2017, my Final Seminar took place in the Théâtre de la Commune in Aubervilliers, where pure philosophy, congratulatory messages, anecdotes, and theatrical productions all combined to celebrate the seminar's long history for one last time.

I'd always wanted the seminar to be for people who worked. That's why, for a very long time, it took place between 8 and 10 PM, on Tuesdays for a few years, on Wednesdays for probably twenty years, if not more, and on Mondays between 2014 and the time it ended in 2017, because theaters are dark on Mondays . . .

In these various places, there was a first period—five years, from 1987 to 1992—when the seminar had a feeling of spontaneity to it as it ran through philosophy's "conditions," as they're called in my doctrine: poetry, the history of philosophy (the first seminar on Plato's *Republic* dates back to 1989–90), politics, and love. It was over the course of those years, especially during the sessions on the rue de Varenne, that the size of the audience increased dramatically.

From 1992 on, I began putting together large conceptual or historical ensembles, which I treated over several consecutive years: antiphilosophy, between 1992 and 1996; the Subject, between 1996 and 1998; the twentieth century, between 1998 and 2001; images of the present time, between 2001 and 2004; the question of subjective orientation, in thought and in life, from 2004 to 2007. I dealt with Plato, from 2007 to 2010; then with the phrase "changing the world," from 2010 to 2012. The final seminar, which was held, as I mentioned above, in a theater, was entitled "The Immanence of Truths."

I should point out that, although it was a more or less weekly seminar at the beginning, it was a monthly one for all of the final years of its existence.

II. The Seminar's Form

As I mentioned at the outset, my seminar ultimately took the form of an ex cathedra lesson, the venerable old form known as the "formal lecture" [*cours magistral*]. But this was the outcome of a long evolution. Between 1969 and, let's say, the late 1980s, there were questions from the audience. It was obviously a lot easier to entertain questions in a room with 40 people at Vincennes than in a theater with 300. But it was also a matter of the time period. Initially at Vincennes, every "class" was a sort of steeplechase in which the hedges, which had to be jumped over elegantly and efficiently, were the constant hail of questions. It was there, as well as in the tumultuous political meetings I attended, that I learned how to stay unfailingly focused on my own thinking while agreeing with perfect equanimity to answer any question calmly, even if it was clearly a side issue. Like Claudel's God, I took crooked paths to reach my goal.

I must admit that, little by little, with the "normalization," I was able to rely on the audience's increasing unwillingness to listen to overly subjective rambling, rants with no connection to the subject under discussion, biased ideological assaults, complaints about not understanding or boasts about already knowing it all. Ultimately, it was the dictatorship of the masses that silenced the frenzied dialectic of interruptions without my having to change, on my own, my relationship with the audience. In the Jules Ferry auditorium at the ENS or in the Théâtre de la Commune, nobody interrupted anymore, or even, I believe, considered doing so, not out of fear of a stern refusal on my part but because the ambient opinion was no longer in favor of it.

I never ruled out having someone else come and speak, and thus, over time, I extended invitations to a number of people: François Regnault, to speak on theater; Jean-Claude Milner, to speak on Lacan; Monique Canto, to speak on Plato; Slavoj Žižek, to speak on orientation in life, etc. These examples give you a sense of my eclecticism.

But in the final analysis, the seminar's form, solidly in place for about twenty-five years, remained by and large that of a one-man show. Session by session, I began with careful preparation, resulting in a set of lecture notes—I never really wrote out a seminar—that provided the basic outline, a few summary sentences, and the quotations or references used. Often, I gave out a handout containing the texts that I would read and comment on. I did this because my material was nothing like philosophical references in the traditional sense of the term. In particular, I had frequent recourse to the intellectual concentration that poetry allows for. Naturally, I also engaged in logico-mathematical formalism. However, it's very difficult to make extensive use of that resource before large audiences. I usually reserved it for another seminar, one that could be called arcane, which I held for a long time on Saturday afternoons and which contributed directly to my densest—and philosophically most important—books: *Being and Event* and *Logics of Worlds*. But for the time being there are no plans to publish these "other" seminars.

III. What Purpose Did the Seminar Serve?

It's hard for me to say in what respect my seminar was useful for people other than myself. What I noticed, however, was that its transmission of sometimes very complex subjects was of a different sort from that of my writings on these same subjects. Should it be said that the seminar was easier? That's not exactly the point. Clearly, philosophy has always combined oral activity and writing and has often privileged the oral over the written, as did its legendary founder, namely, Socrates. Even those—like Derrida—who promoted the primacy of writing were very careful never to overlook physical presence and the opportunities oral presentation provides for transference love, which Plato already theorized in his *Symposium*.

But I think that the oral presentation, as far as I myself and no doubt many attendees were concerned, conveyed the movement of thought, the trajectory of the investigation, the surprise of discovery, without having to subject them to the pre-established discipline of exposition, which is largely necessary whenever you write. It had the musical power of improvisation, since my seminar was not in fact written out. I met many seminar attendees who hadn't read my books. I could hardly commend them for it, obviously. But I understood that the thinking-on-the-spot effect of the oral presentation had become the most important thing to them. Because if the seminar "worked" as it should—which was naturally not guaranteed—the audience felt almost as if they themselves had thought up what I was talking to them about. It was as though all I'd done, in Platonic parlance, was trigger a recollection in them, whereas philosophical writing per se demanded sustained and sometimes unrewarding effort. In this respect, the seminar was certainly easy, but such easiness also left traces, often unconscious ones, of which attendees who thought they'd understood everything would have been wise to be wary.

For me, there's no question that the seminar served as a laboratory. I tested out ideas in it, either already established ones or even ones that emerged during my public improvisations, by presenting them from a variety of perspectives and seeing what happened when they came in contact with texts, other ideas, or even examples from contemporary situations in politics, art and public opinion. One of the great advantages of oral presentation is to be able to repeat without really boring your audience—which would be very difficult to do in writing—because intonation, movements, gestures, slight accentuations, and changes in tone give repetition enough charm to make it not just acceptable but even retroactively necessary. So the seminar went hand in hand with the inner construction of my thought, something Deleuze would have called the moment of invention of the concept, and it was like a partly anarchic process whose energy could later be captured by prose in order to discipline it and incorporate it into the philosophical system I've created, whose final, and I daresay eternal, form, is nonetheless the written form.

Thus, some of the seminars directly became books, sometimes almost immediately, sometimes later. For example, *Saint Paul: The Foundation of Universalism* (the 1995–96 seminar, published by Presses Universitaires de France in 1997; English translation published by Stanford University Press in 2006); *Wittgenstein's Antiphilosophy* (the 1993–94 seminar, published by Nous in 2009; English translation published by Verso in 2011); *The Century* (the 1998–2001 seminar, published by Seuil in 2005; English translation published by Polity in 2007). In all three of these cases, the content of the books is too similar to that of the seminars for there to be any need for the latter to be published for the foreseeable future.

But all the seminars are in a dialectic with books, sometimes because they exploit their effects, sometimes because they anticipate their writing. I often told my seminar attendees that I was without a doubt throwing myself on the mercy of their attention span (a two-hour seminar before such an audience is truly a performance), but that their presence, their degree of concentration, the need to really address my remarks to them, their immediate reaction to my improvisations—all of that was profoundly useful to my system-building efforts.

The complete set of volumes of the seminar may, in the long term, be the true heart of my work, in a dialectical relationship between the oral and the written. Only the readers of that complete set will be able to say. It's up to you now, dear reader, to whom every philosopher addresses himself or herself, to decide and pronounce your verdict.

Introduction to the Seminar *Images of the Present Time*

KENNETH REINHARD

Badiou delivered the series of lectures entitled *Images of the Present Time* at the Collège international de philosophie in Paris over three years, between 2001 and 2004, although the third year was suspended after only four sessions.[1] After having spent the previous three years examining the waning twentieth century, Badiou entered the twenty-first century by posing the question of "the present": what does it mean to be present to one's own time, to be one's own contemporary? In what sense might one *not* be present to the present? Is being in the present a question of cutting through the symbolic and imaginary wrappings of reality and seeking an immediate encounter with something real? The twentieth century was "the century of the hypothesis of the absolute beginning," according to Badiou; does an authentic experience of the present require such a radical break with the past?[2] Or is being present a question of keeping pace with the fleeting "now" in the temporal flow of subjective or chronological instants? What is the relationship of the present with the future? Finally, can any philosophy be adequate to its own time? For Hegel, we recall, "the owl of Minerva only takes flight at dusk"—that is, wisdom is blind to its own moment as it unfolds; it can only be retrospective, a reconstruction after the fact.[3] For Badiou the question will be, as he puts it, can we think a philosophical bird that flies at dawn? How can thinking be adequate to the contemporary moment?

During the years in which he delivered this seminar, Badiou was writing *Logics of Worlds*, the second of the three volumes of *Being and Event*, in which his emphasis shifts from an ontological account of situations to the logics that determine the degree to which something may or may not appear in a world—that is, be registered not only in its simple being but also as being *there*, as *counting*. The primary obstacle that we face in reflecting on our present time is the fact that we are effectively world-less; as Badiou writes, "we are in an in-between period, between a worn-out, deteriorating, exhausted world and a world that is not yet either calculable or foreseeable."[4] Badiou follows Plato in defining a "world" as a situation in which "justice [is] done to the visible."[5] When a vast quantity of the elements (above all, the people) in a situation do not show up, do not count as significant, do not receive justice, we are in default of a world. And this lack of a world is also the lack of a present time: our worldless experience of temporality is no more, Badiou writes, than a "stagnant restlessness, or a restless stagnation," the unspooling of a flickering reel of static images that produce only the illusion of movement and change.[6]

In *Logics of Worlds*, Badiou names the general consensus that describes the contemporary liberal West "democratic materialism," which he defines as the belief that a world is made up of nothing other than bodies and languages—*bodies* meaning human beings as well as all other material entities and *languages* implying the contingent cultural systems of meaning and value through which those bodies are named, situated, and put into relation with each other. When Badiou introduces the expression "democratic materialism" in this seminar, he calls it a proposition defined by the question of "what is meant by a body being seized by a language," a question that could also describe intersectional cultural studies today.[7] Democratic materialism is indeed a "materialism" in its refusal of the existence of gods, spirits, angels, or any other "nonmaterial bodies." It is "democratic" insofar as it considers all systems of value and meaning to be equal, as well as historically and geographically local, with none regarded as intrinsically superior to any others. Its only universal value is the belief that values are relative, that any claims to an absolute must be rejected out of hand. One of Badiou's central arguments in *Images of the Present Time* is that the primary "emblem" of our time is democracy itself, which is generally regarded as the only legitimate political ideal and the only alternative to the various disastrous historical totalitarianisms, left and right, of the past century. Although Badiou does not equate emblems such as democracy with ideology, they do involve some classic ideological functions, such as suturing contradictory beliefs into an apparently consistent whole.[8] But if ideology is understood to mean the use of ideas to obscure reality, for Badiou the essential role of emblems is to defend against ideas, to block thinking as such.[9] Democratic materialism regards beliefs that do not conform to its underlying capitalist structure and its emblems with suspicion, and is especially allergic to claims of truth. The implicit imperative of democratic materialism, enacted and displayed in its emblems, is to "live without any ideas."[10]

Yet while Badiou agrees with democratic materialism's claim that there is nothing other than bodies and languages—no third "noumenal" element—he argues that human beings are capable of producing exceptions to the totality of bodies and languages. Badiou opposes to democratic materialism what he calls "the materialist dialectic," which will supplement those liberal beliefs with the exceptional possibility of *truths*.[11] Hence the opposition that matters here is not between materialism and idealism but a scission within materialism itself. So, what is a truth? For Badiou, a truth is something singular with a possibly universal value that human beings are capable of producing. Truths are not generated by philosophy, according to Badiou, but through the four types of truth procedures that he distinguishes: politics, science, art, and love. Those procedures involve the identification of exceptions to what is normative or generally believed to be possible in a world—anomalies that Badiou calls *events*—and the practical elaboration of the novel consequences of those events as new truths. Hence in Badiou's usage, truths are not statements defined by their internal coherence or their correspondence to existing things; rather, they are *new* things that poets and artists, scientists and mathematicians, political activists and revolutionaries, and lovers of all kinds create in relation to the void of an exceptional event. The inclusion of truths in the dialectic has a retroactive effect on the meaning of both bodies and languages: the bodies that matter, so to speak, in the materialist dialectic are not simply those that are given by nature, but new bodies created in the unfolding of a truth; and the meaning of languages will split to mean both the conventions of communication and language as a creative act, which Badiou calls a "subject-language."[12] The work of *Images of the Present Time* is both to show how the dominant images or emblems of our day suppress the possibility of a real present in a real world and to demonstrate how exceptions that allow new truths to appear may nevertheless emerge, on occasion, and reconstitute the bodies and languages of a world.

In *Logics of Worlds*, Badiou distinguishes three modes of the human experience of a present in terms of three types of subject: faithful, reactionary, and obscure. The "faithful" subject is defined by its fidelity to an event and its commitment to the exploration of possible truths opened up by that event: "The product of this fidelity is the *new present* which welcomes, point by point, the new truth" (53, emphasis added). The "reactive" subject, on the other hand, refuses to incorporate itself into the unfolding present of a truth and argues that the best we can hope for is "a present 'a little less worse' than the past, if only because it resisted the catastrophic temptation which the reactive subject declares is contained in the event" (56). For the reactive subject, the danger represented by the event has been "extinguished," but like a still smoldering fire, it threatens to burst into flames once again. This subject sees the possibility of the new present, but fights against it and instead calls for the restoration of (an improved version of) the past. Finally, the "obscure" subject neither produces a new present nor calls for a return to the past, but occludes the past and allows the present to descend "into the night of non-exposition." Badiou's example is that of political Islamism, which he understands as the call for something like a pseudo-present, one based not on tradition but on "the paradox of an occultation of the present which is itself in the present" (60). Whereas the reactive subject insists that no evental rupture is necessary—that the past can simply be extended into the present—the obscure subject ignores the past and attempts to replace the present with a phantasmatic, totalized, and atemporal body such as God or the Folk. If the reactive subject rejects the evental break and calls for historical continuity, and the obscure subject declares an eternal present into which both past and future dissolve, the faithful subject creates a new present that imbricates elements of both the past and the future. The seminar on *Images of the Present Time* anticipates this typology of subjects.

Each year of *Images of the Present Time* has its own topical focus and subtitle: the first, "Contemporary Nihilism," anticipates Badiou's discussion of the reactive subject (and to a lesser extent the obscure subject), while the second, "The Logic of Exceptions," and the truncated third, "What Does It Mean to Live?," establish the conditions for what Badiou will call the faithful subject. The first year opens with a reading of Jean Genet's 1956 play, *The Balcony*, which Badiou regards as an allegory of the images that dominate our worldless time as well as the possibility of exceptions to their rule. Jacques Lacan had discussed the play in a session of his 1958 seminar, *Formations of the Unconscious*, as an exemplary comedy of the phallus, and Badiou's reading of *The Balcony* expands on Lacan's insights. The piece is set in a brothel where the prostitutes and their clients engage in sexual play dressed in the costumes of figures of authority (Judge, General, Bishop, etc.), while outside in the streets a violent revolution is raging. The brothel represents the contemporary world as pure simulacrum, a closed hall of performative illusion and fantasy; and a central function of comedy, according to Lacan, is to reveal and ridicule phallic authority—represented in Genet's play by the Chief of Police, who finally discovers his authentic costume, the image of images par excellence, when he makes his appearance in the brothel in the costume of a giant penis. In Badiou's reading, *The Balcony* represents the relationship between the dominant images of our time and the will to "dis-image" embodied by the revolutionaries, who are unsure whether they should destroy all images or replace the old images with new ones. For Badiou, the play asks the question, can there be a desire—sexual or political—that is not phantasmatic, that is not based on the phallus or other such signifiers and images? Can we break free from our so-called society of spectacle? Can there be a *real present* that is not merely absorbed into the specular world of the imaginary, and if so, how can we encounter it?

Badiou describes four primary moments or approaches to the analysis of the dominant images of our time.[13] First, and most briefly defined, is what he refers to as the "systemic stage," which clarifies the *structure* or underlying law of our historical moment. In Genet's play, it is the well-ordered world of the brothel, under the supervision of the madam and the protection of the Chief of Police, but this can be generalized as what Badiou calls the "prostitutional" matrix of social relations today, understood as "the reduction of every norm to the commercial potentialities of bodies—of which sex is but one variation—through the twin procedures of commercial validation and biological valuation." "The prostitutional," Badiou writes, "is the democratization of prostitution."[14] The fundamental logic of our prostitutional times, in the broadest sense, is global capitalism, but other aspects of contemporary society could also be understood in these structural terms: the system of nation states, for example, or the embedded architectures of class, race, and gender, all of which operate under the emblem of democracy.

The second stage of analysis is the identification of what Badiou calls the "real tracings" or *exceptions* to the structure of the time; in *The Balcony*, the primary exception is the revolution—however precarious and liable to fall into new modes of the prostitutional it may be. Moments of exception to capitalism, the state, and the police have emerged on occasion in the modern world: the great revolutionary movements, the Paris Commune in 1871 and those that followed in Mexico, Shanghai, and all over the world, as well as the many other autonomous zones and experiments in autopoetic social and political organization that have arisen despite the underlying capitalist structure. Badiou urges us to create an "encyclopedia" of such exceptions in order to take stock of the resources we will need to counter the images that dominate today. The vulnerabilities of capitalism and the emblems that cloak it can be discovered in the traces of those exceptions. Such exceptions may constitute events, as the seeds of new truth procedures and new modes of subjectivity. Of course, the truths elaborated in relation to those exceptions are not exclusively political, but also occur in the realms of science, art, and love. If politics, according to Badiou, involves the "tracing of the collective," science is "the tracing of the letter in its appearing," through the inscription of symbolic elements and functions in their materiality (similar to Lacan's account of what he calls "mathemes"). Art is "the real tracing of the infinite resources of the finitude of the sensible world," and love is "the real tracing of the Two," that is, of difference as such.[15]

The third moment of analysis (although often the initial point of interpretation) is determining the *emblem*, the "images" that give the underlying structure its ideological coherence, its apparent consistency, and that guarantee its circulation; again, for Badiou, the key image of our present time is emblematized in the word "democracy." Badiou writes that an emblem expresses the "spiritual community" of a time in the way that what Lacan calls a "master signifier" does, as a shared point of attachment "that both unites and rallies people."[16] Hence we must identify the primary emblems that mask the contradictions of the underlying system, as well as the secondary emblems constellated around them. For example, the emblem of "democracy" works hand in hand with that of "freedom" to support global capitalism. The primary motto of freedom implied by American democratic materialism is the "pursuit of happiness"—the freedom to enjoy the variety of pleasures that stock the shelves of generalized prostitution. The subject of democracy is negatively defined by the objects it consumes, all interchangeable and all available through the general equivalent of money. Such freedom, Badiou points out, is actually "the harshest and bitterest of servitudes," in which the subject is no more than a passive consumer, the empty point through which an endless conveyer belt of commodities circulates. For Badiou, "freedom to enjoy" is the nihilist core of democracy.

The fourth stage of analysis involves the identification of the *naked power* that defends the emblems, emerging in reaction to the exceptions that oppose them. Although at one time the primary power summoned to counteract exceptional truths was the state (and perhaps in many cases it still is), today the locus of naked power is less clear, perhaps less "naked." Badiou criticizes two recent accounts of such power: Foucault's theory of "biopower" (and its elaboration by Agamben) and the analysis of technology proposed by Heidegger and his followers. For Badiou, naked power today, on its most fundamental level, does not act through the state's forceful regulation of living bodies or the imposition of *techne* onto *physis*, but through the democratic materialist imperative to separate the body from *ideas*: to be a recognizable individual under the emblem of democracy, we must continue to passively receive and consume its commodities, material and symbolic, without trying to think about their means of production or distribution. Hence naked power in democratic materialism takes the form of the imperative to pursue our freedom to *enjoy without thinking*. We should note that this is very close to how Lacan describes the force of the superego, which exerts its coercive power not as a law of prohibition but, on the contrary, as an obscene injunction to *jouissance*. In Badiou's analysis, there are two modes of naked power's imperative to enjoy: the "libertarian" (and perhaps libertine) compulsion to be consumed by enjoyment and the "liberal" promises of satisfaction through the serial consumption of commodities. In the first case, Badiou's model is the use of recreational drugs for the sake of detaching from the world, thereby equating enjoyment with nothingness, under the imperative to *become* the waste product left over from enjoyment; in the second case, the drive to be a good citizen-consumer is to reduce the world to a garbage heap of the empty husks of transient pleasures.[17] The function of naked power today, whether its agents are subjective or objective, is to separate us from our infinite capacity for making works of truth. And this power is first of all simply *political* (rather than biopolitical or technopolitical), insofar as it requires our consent, under the guise of personal freedom and the illusion of autonomy. It is not, however, a question of our consent to any particular emblem, any fixed ideological point, but consent to the belief that the underlying structure of capitalism and the emblems that grant it consistency are simply the irrecusable nature of things. Badiou writes, "In other words, the essence of power isn't alienation, even though alienation is an absolutely fundamental operation. The essence of naked power is ultimately the belief that alienation is necessary, in one way or another. We have to be forced, not so much to go along with images as not to be able to claim that we can do without them."[18] Finally, naked power is a kind of violence, under the guise of consent, that persuades us that limitations are objectively necessary, that submission to the "natural" structure of consumer capitalism and its emblems is our only choice—and no choice at all.

In the second year of the seminar, Badiou focuses on the question of how a true present can be constructed by following the "tracings" or inscriptions of real exceptions across the surface of emblems. If there is no present today, it is because we are doubly alienated by what Badiou calls "repetition" and "projection." When we become too caught up in history and tradition, we are liable to simply repeat the past, which becomes a deadweight on the possibility of creating a present. Repetition can also take the form of constant novelty, the endless marketing of minor differences as real innovations; as Badiou writes, "change can be just as repetitive as immobility."[19] In both cases, the present is reduced to nothing more than the empty place for repetition. But we can also fail to construct a real present by the radical destruction of the past in the name of the glorious "projection" of a future ex nihilo, as was the case at times for both the Russian and Chinese revolutions. These modes of alienation by means of repetition and projection correspond not only to the positions of the reactive and obscure subjects but also to what twenty years earlier, in *Theory of the Subject*, Badiou called the "two deviations": the "deviation to the right," which sees the place of the subject as predetermined and its static repetition as necessary and salutary, and the "deviation to the left," which mercilessly destroys tradition and thrusts itself into a future unconnected to any past. Between these two modes of temporal alienation, the present is reduced to nothing more than a gap, the empty point of transition between past and future, with no consistency of its own. A real present, Badiou argues, is not something that we can simply inhabit, according to either orientation (or their nihilistic conjunction) but is something that must be actively *constructed*. A real present requires what Badiou calls (in another central term from *Theory of the Subject*) the "torsion" of past and future, through which the past has not fully passed and the future, in some sense, is already here; that is, something from tradition must be transformed and sublimated to the status of the future. This is not simply the preservation of those parts of the past that we value, but the rewriting or reinflection of some precise points into the anticipation of something new.

We can understand this torsion of past and future in terms of the two key modes of the production of change that Badiou describes in *Being and Event*: fidelity and forcing. On the one hand, a truth procedure involves fidelity to an event as something that is always in the past. Fidelity is the work of insisting that there *was* an event and, by following its implications and consequences, of bringing it into the present. On the other hand, Badiou uses the concept of forcing—a mathematical technique for the production of unprecedented new sets that he borrows from Paul Cohen—to describe how the projection of a truth procedure into the future when it *will have been* completed can be used to generate useful knowledge in the present. To borrow a term that Badiou borrows from Deleuze, the "disjunctive synthesis" of *fidelity* to something in the past (repetition) and *forcing* of something in the future (projection) is required for the construction of a real present.

Badiou uses a passage from Mallarmé's 1895 essay "L'Action restreinte" ("Restricted Action") as a kind of motto or counter-emblem for the production of a real present: "there is no Present, no—a present does not exist. . . . For lack of the Crowd's declaring itself."[20] In Badiou's reading, Mallarmé sees the bloody massacre in which the Paris Commune was liquidated as having destroyed both the present and the possibility of any future revolution. Badiou does not agree about the future, but what especially interests him here is Mallarmé's understanding of the nonexistence of the present as the result of a collective failure to "declare." According to Badiou, the crowd *does* on occasion declare itself, and it does so precisely as an *exception*. But what does Mallarmé mean by a declaration? For Badiou, *declaration* should be understood, first of all, in opposition to communication: a declaration is not the transmission of knowledge or a message, it is not an utterance governed by a common set of rules and practices—it is not, strictly speaking, language, although it may take a linguistic form—but the *interruption* of communication, and the announcement of a present. A declaration is what holds together a repetition of something from the past and a projection into the future, creating the present in which they conjoin. Badiou writes, "the present contained in the declaration, in what the Crowd declares, is something that raises repetition to the level of projection." Through the declaration, projection becomes something like the sublation or sublimation of repetition, rather than its opposite; and this is precisely what Badiou means by the "torsion" of past and future:

> A true declaration always involves a skewing of tradition, not a pure separation from it. I think the word that best describes this is "torsion." It is a matter of putting tradition into torsion so as to connect it to projection, an occasionally violent torsion that's exerted on tradition but doesn't separate from it altogether. It's not a disjunction. It is this movement of torsion that will go through the heart of the situation, its perplexed, entangled, ambiguous, and complicated heart, to produce what will be called the complexity of the present.[21]

Badiou describes four modes of such a declaration, corresponding to the four types of truth procedure: in the case of *science*, the declaration is a "demonstration," which in its purest form is a mathematical proof. A proof is not an argument that can be rebutted, an opinion that can be countered by another point of view. If it is wrong, if some error in reasoning has been made, then it has failed to be a proof. A scientific declaration of this kind is not limited by its historical or geographical context; it is addressed to everyone and to all times, even if it may be absorbed into some larger declaration at a later point. A scientific demonstration has consequences that unfold in the present by finding its future in the transformative sublation of some element of its past. Our subjective access to the declaration in *art* is what Badiou calls "contemplation": to be arrested by the experience of an object in "the crystallization of a changeless duration," a present that is also "the recapitulation of an enormously long past." To contemplate a piece of art is to withdraw it from the realm of objective judgment, in the sense of comparison or evaluation, as well as from valuation and exchange in the art market. A *political* declaration takes the form of an "action": in a protest or a revolution, one is subjectively taken over by the creative and violent intensity of a heterogeneous present. Such action is not "the orderly or rational management" of acts but "an upsurge that creates its own present" by means of "a collective, unpredictable, incalculable, really present linkage of something that reorients the elements of the past." And finally, perhaps the paradigmatic case of declaration is the declaration of *love*. To really say "I love you" is not to state a fact, to communicate a piece of information, but to profess a "passion" that comes into the present in the act of being uttered, unexpectedly, and without calculation or guarantee of return. It is noneconomic, a pure expenditure without reciprocity; in the sense that it is not about circulation and consumption, the declaration of love is *objectless*, a purely subjective experience of the present.

Each of these modes of declaration functions by constituting a point of the present, a moment that is isolated from the ordinary temporality of capitalist circulation, a point of exception and concentration where some element of the past is elevated to the status of the future perfect. But such a declaration of the present is itself transitory; the goal is not to remain in its ecstatic eternity but to bring it *back* into the quotidian world of static repetition in order to make the invisible visible—to *justify*, if you will, the elements of a world. This is Badiou's version of the final moment in Plato's allegory of the cave, when the escaped prisoner who has seen the light of reason decides to return into the darkness, in order to bring that new experience of a truth into the present time.

In the third, interrupted, year of the seminar, Badiou begins to address the "timeworn" philosophical question "What does it mean to live?" by surveying some key classical philosophical responses to this question, from Plato, Aristotle, and Saint Paul to Hegel and Nietzsche. Democratic materialism takes up the issue in the vitalism that passes from Nietzsche and Bergson to Foucault and (to a certain extent) Deleuze: the category of life is understood as "simultaneously ontological and normative" insofar as a true life is one that simply "affirms life," that sees life as both means and end.[22] For democratic materialism, the answer is restricted to the *finitism* of bodies and languages: living well means that bodies should be allowed as much enjoyment as possible with as little restriction as necessary from authoritarian languages and laws. The materialist dialectic, on the other hand, emphasizes the *infinite* possibilities that the subject of a truth discovers in what at first seemed impossible: "We're no longer dealing with the finitude of the action of sensory bodies as marked or instrumentalized by languages but with the shift to an infinite capacity made possible by an event."[23] The final sessions of the seminar anticipate Badiou's remarkably original account in *Logics of Worlds* of the nature of a new "body" in the materialist dialectic, one based on the event and the participation of a faithful subject in a truth procedure, hence in excess of the dichotomy of bodies and languages: "The evental rupture makes possible the emergence of new bodies, bodies that can be the materiality, the material support, for the new subjective form, which also includes the subject-language."[24] This new body includes the biological concept of a body, but is not limited to its natural and vitalist assumptions; ultimately, the new concept of body that Badiou introduces potentially includes whatever can be the ground for a truth procedure, whether it is organic or inorganic. Such a body is never simply born but always *reborn*, as a new constellation of preexisting bodies—a new *crowd*—that is capable of supporting the subject of a truth.

Badiou will develop many (but not all) of the ideas from the four sessions of this third year of the seminar in *Logics of Worlds*. Its final chapter is dedicated to the question of what it is to live. He writes:

> Life is a subjective category. A body is the materiality that life requires, but the becoming of the present depends on the disposition of this body in a subjective formalism, whether it be produced (the formalism is faithful, the body is directly placed "under" the evental trace), erased (the formalism is reactive, the body is held at a double distance by the negation of the trace), or occulted (the body is denied). Neither the reactive deletion of the present, which denies the value of the event, nor, a fortiori, its mortifying occultation, which presupposes a "body" transcendent to the world, sanction the affirmation of life, which is the incorporation, point by point, to the present. To live is thus an incorporation into the present under the faithful form of a subject. (508)

To live in the empty present of democratic materialism is not our fate; it requires our consent—which we can withhold. In the final line of *Logics of Worlds*, Badiou offers the assurance that "we are shielded from this consent by the Idea, the secret of the pure present" (514). We can agree with the premise that there are only bodies and languages and still believe that occasionally, and as an exception, a truth too is possible, and that such truths transform how we think about both bodies and languages. We do not need to consent to the inevitability of emblems and the images that conceal from us our own capacity for becoming faithful subjects of a truth. We can live in a present that is woven from fibers drawn from evental ruptures in the past and the projections of a future that will have been.

About the 2001–2004 Seminar

ALAIN BADIOU

This hefty volume, representing two and a half years of monthly lectures, is, for a number of reasons, a sort of turning point in the general history of my seminar. First of all, following on the heels of the venture attempted by *The Century*, it was really the first of the series of seminars that deal with a single subject for several years in a row. Second, it was probably beginning with this seminar that it became common to see a large and diverse audience of all ages and from very different backgrounds, with increasingly weak ties to any specific institution, in attendance. Third, it was with this seminar that a method of circulation between philosophy per se and its conditions was settled on: poetry and theater were referred to quite often, while the political commentary was more specific and more frequent. There are extensive references to Brecht, Rimbaud, Saint-John Perse, Valéry, and Hölderlin in this seminar, but also to Genet and Pierre Guyotat, as well as an ongoing analysis of the American military invasion of Iraq. Fourth, this seminar marked the end of my collaboration with the Collège international de philosophie, which it had been a part of for a good fifteen years. This cessation, which was quite sudden given that it was announced in February 2004 as the suspension of the 2003–2004 seminar, was motivated by the reasons I spelled out in a letter read to the audience on the very day it ended (see the document that takes the place of the fifth session) but also by my no longer feeling comfortable, as time went on, in that institutional setting. What may have contributed to this feeling were the mixed opinions expressed here and there about a fifth feature of the seminar of those years, namely that one of its running themes was the radical critique of parliamentary democracy. Hence—and this is the sixth point—the seminar's relocation the following year to the École Normale Supérieure, within the Centre International d'Étude de la Philosophie Française Contemporaine (CIEPFC), where it is still located at the time of the writing of this introduction.[1]

The seventh virtual point might be as follows: those who have read *Logics of Worlds*, which was published in 2006 [English translation, 2009], will readily see how this seminar goes hand in hand with its writing and therefore with a movement of thought that goes beyond the ontological abstractness of *Being and Event* toward a thinking of appearing, of what an object is, and of the actual multiplicity of worlds.

The twenty sessions of "Images of the Present Time" bring together elements that may seem unrelated but whose unity lies in the philosophical question of the present, the present time, and the conditions under which philosophy may be truly contemporary with its own time. This is why there is an overall arc that goes from an analytic of our present, dominated in actual fact by its retreat or absence ("a present is lacking," as Mallarmé says), to the principles of the construction of a real present and of the features of a Subject subordinated to it.

This trajectory is organized around three approaches, corresponding to the years 2001–2002, 2002–2003, and 2003–2004, which was interrupted.

In the first year, we start off with the emblems of the present time ("democracy," for example, but also "human rights," or "respect for others"), then work our way back to the naked power that determines their use, and finally uncover the vulnerability in which the principle of a thinking that is neither servile nor condemned to semblance can be embedded. This approach could be subtitled "contemporary nihilism."

In the second year, we examine the effects of the subject's appearance before the market, of the universal reduction of every popular, state, or intellectual consistency to a formless multitude, by the most violent means (the war in Iraq), if need be. All the evidence shows that the essence of liberalism is destruction. But the most important thing is to identify the heterogeneous sites, the subjective possibilities for maintaining a distance from the destruction. I propose in this connection the quartet of demonstration, contemplation, action, and passion. On that basis, I was able to set the task: to construct a present, so that there might be a present again. I define it as a projection toward the future that still preserves, in torsion, something of the repetitive dimension of the past. This approach could be subtitled "the logic of exceptions."

The third year interrogates what it means to inhabit a true present. It tackles the classic philosophical question of the true life, since philosophers have for the most part thought, well before Rimbaud, that the true life is certainly absent. "Life" will be understood in a sense opposite to that given it, based on Nietzsche's or Bergson's work, and in the wake of Foucault, Deleuze, and Agamben, by the theorists of "biopolitics." Indeed, I will argue that life begins for the human animal when what it is concerned with, what it is faithful to, is indifferent to the body, indifferent to any "self-expression," and, more fundamentally, eradicates all finitude. "To live" is in fact simply to inscribe in any material the sign that the infinite is indeed there, or, in other words, as Hegel said of the Absolute, "with us." The difficulty is to be aware of it. "To live" is thus always to discover, in oneself and in the world, the innermost kernel of what we are capable of in terms of the infinite. Whence the title of this final section, "What does it mean to live?"

Alain Badiou, January 2014

Images of the
Present Time

Year One

Contemporary
Nihilism

Session 1

November 21, 2001

Before coming to see you, I was thinking about what I had done over the past ten years, here or elsewhere, in my yearly seminars. Is what I'm going to do now, in just a moment, a consequence of that? Does any meaning emerge from it?

For four years I studied anti-philosophy, which is something that was remote from my own thinking. It was an education by distance. Each year I spoke about the thinkers I considered to be the three great contemporary anti-philosophers, one after the other: Nietzsche, then Wittgenstein, then Lacan, and finally I spoke about Saint Paul. I educated philosophy, or educated myself, with what is explicitly opposed to it: the trilogy of contemporary anti-philosophy and the foundational, and partly mythical, anti-philosophy that Saint Paul represents.

Then—and this is certainly one of the lessons I learned from that investigation—between 1996 and 1998, over a period of two years, I reformulated the building blocks of a theory of the subject. A theory of the subject is an old topic in itself and an old topic for me as well, but this was a reworking of it, a reworking in a very specific sense. What an anti-philosophy always claims is that philosophy ignores subjective singularity. This obliteration of singularity in favor of an empty rhetoric of mastery is the main charge the anti-philosopher levels against the philosopher. The anti-philosopher points out that the singularity of existence, of life, is such that any operation of erasure of that singularity creates a mastery based on forgetting and censorship. So you might say that to return to the theory of the subject after allowing oneself to be educated by the anti-philosophers is to give a considered answer to the following question: Is it possible to think subjective singularity philosophically after being exposed for four years to those great writers who, from Saint Paul (against the Athenian philosophers) to Pascal (against Descartes), from Pascal to Rousseau (against Voltaire and Hume), from Rousseau to Kierkegaard (against Hegel), from Kierkegaard to Nietzsche (against everyone), from Nietzsche to Wittgenstein (against everyone), and from Wittgenstein to Lacan (against Hontology[1]), have contended, not without vehemence, that the philosopher's alleged conceptual mastery is a censoring of personal faith, of the voice of conscience, of the pure fact of existing, of life, of the ineffable, or of *jouissance*? As you might expect, I have maintained, as best I could, but unwaveringly, that yes, the philosopher can emerge victorious from this ordeal.

Having thus attempted, between 1992 and 1998, to stand up to the anti-philosophical challenge, I next dealt with the twentieth century for three years. There was of course a simple anniversary effect about this, of which there's no reason to be particularly proud. But I think something else was involved as well. There was the idea, or the question, which has long haunted me, as to whether philosophy, with its tradition and its renewal, its continuity and its discontinuity, is really capable of meeting the challenge of the present time. Is it capable, with its own creativity, of withstanding the intensity of the present? This is a question it has asked itself for a very long time. And central to this concern is Hegel's statement to the effect that philosophy always comes "after"; it declares the meaning, the concept, of what, in actuality, has already taken place. The owl of Minerva only takes flight at dusk. You know the aphorism, which induces what might be called philosophical melancholy. Not that Hegel himself dwelled on it; he was sufficiently aware of being able to define his time as the time when Absolute Knowledge is attained. Nevertheless, in the statement itself, in the silent flight of this late-flying owl, the melancholy of someone who is not entirely present in the present can be sensed. Isn't there always something backwards-looking about philosophy, something retrospective? Of course, the retrospective aspect is a strength in its own way, but there's a price to be paid for it. Far from meeting the challenge of the life of the present, philosophy, owing to a kind of endless introspection, often seems out of sync with its own time. It speaks about it, of course, but always in an out-of-sync way. It only starts speaking about its own time from the delayed perspective when that time is no longer exactly what it was.

This question, which is very important to me, is none other than the question of what contemporaneity is. What is philosophy contemporary with? Is it really contemporary with its own time? Or is it ultimately always very slightly nostalgic? In short, always in search of lost time?

One of the tendencies of contemporary philosophy is to say that there's something forgotten, lost, erased, or absent. It is typical of contemporary thought to assess the present not on the basis of the traces of the present alone but on the basis of what it lacks, or even on the basis of the thesis that "a present is lacking." That's Mallarmé's thesis, though it's been reformulated by many philosophers. It is also Rimbaud's "We are not in the world." This means that contemporaneity itself has been lost. Is philosophy condemned to take off only from the standpoint of such a loss? Is philosophy, today, essentially nostalgic, so to speak, forever asserting the dimension of a loss? In other words, is it philosophy's destiny to be in mourning mode? In mourning for being, in mourning for truth, in mourning for metaphysics, in mourning for the present, in mourning for meaning, in mourning for thought?

When you come right down to it—to adopt Nietzsche's bluntness—isn't this nostalgic, mourning dimension a pathological trait of philosophy? As though philosophy were too old, really sclerotic, afflicted with an incurable hardening of the arteries? As though something in it had slowed the circulation of its blood? To be sure, philosophy is old, very old. And the question of just how old and sick it is, is very real: after all, there are so many philosophical statements about the end of philosophy, statements like "Metaphysics is over" or "From now on we should devote ourselves to simple finitude," or "It's time for the grammar of statements and brain physiology!" It's as though philosophy could no longer walk very fast, as though it needed a cane or even crutches. This is a personal, crucial question for me.

When, in 1998, I turned to the twentieth century, to what philosophy could say or think about it, it was with the aim of taking stock of the present. The task was to at least constitute the present of the twentieth century—before it completely disappeared—as a category of philosophy. My intention was to determine to what extent philosophy could make the twentieth century a living category and therefore think its present as a present.

I've said a number of things about this. But you could say that doesn't prove anything since I was talking about the century only as it was ending. I was still at dusk. The owl hadn't taken flight any sooner than usual. I had had to wait till the century was over to talk about it—further proof that philosophy was only able to assess the present in the past. So I said to myself: "I need to go further; I need to really talk about the present." That's the reason for the seminar I'm proposing, which I've called "Images of the Present Time." With a title like that, you have no choice but to talk about the present time. I already told you this would take three years! So I'm already not looking backwards, not being weighed down by the nocturnal weight of the past, but reckoning with the future of this present. I'm offering you three years in the present.

———

I'd like to say a few words today about the approach to this undertaking. The aim is to take the risk of the present, to formulate hypotheses about the present that may well be disproved by circumstances, by an event, by something that might happen. The question will nevertheless remain as follows: What is our present? What is the present to which philosophy bears witness? I'm going to try to change our iconic bird into a bird that takes flight at dawn! With this image of the anti-owl, the challenge is quite simply to explain the concept of "the present." It's a meditation on time, approached from the present: Of what present are we the living contemporaries in philosophy?

I'd like to begin with two questions that immediately arise when you read my title:

- Why did I choose this title, "Images of the Present Time," and not just "The Present Time"?
- What approach or figure of thought will be used to get into this question?

I'm going to make a detour, because the question is quite complex. The detour will consist in my turning to a remarkable passage of Lacan's, which can be found in his March 5, 1958 lecture. This lecture was reprinted in *The Seminar, Book V*, the title of which is *The Formations of the Unconscious*. The authorized version of the seminar was published [in French] in 1998. It contains an analysis by Lacan of Jean Genet's play *The Balcony*. We're going to see what the real subject of the play is. I encourage you to read the whole play right away, in case you haven't already read it. It's a very complicated play. But one thing is certain: it's a play that explicitly asks what becomes of images when the present is one of uprising or revolution. It could be summarized that way. So it's a play about the relationship between images and the present.

A brief historical aside: on May 13, 1958 there was a military coup d'état in Algiers, which, after various incidents, would lead to General De Gaulle's return to power. Genet's play is from 1956, so it's already in the context of the Algerian War. Lacan analyzed it in March 1958, just before the coup and De Gaulle's return to power. So we're dealing with a historicity that needs to be kept in mind. It wasn't as if nothing was happening. Around the same years there was a dispute between Merleau-Ponty and Sartre about the following issue. Merleau-Ponty had said: "History never confesses," and Sartre had replied: "That's not so, the truth of History always comes out eventually."

As you know, the Algerian War is making a tentative "remembrance" (as they like to say) comeback these days. The last old men of the war, the decrepit torturers, are starting to speak the truth. The confession of the true present of that horrific war is coming out right about now, roughly fifty years after the fact. Maybe there's a really simple rule, namely that history confesses when those who were involved in that history are dying off. So we might say: Sartre and Merleau-Ponty were both right. Merleau-Ponty was right in saying that there's no spontaneous confession of history. History conceals its own present. When will the war that's going on in Iraq, for example, come clean about the true nature of its present? We know nothing about it. Maybe we'll know a little more about it fifty years from now, or maybe some of us will know a little more about it.

This is something we'll have to discuss again. At any rate, one of the problems with the present is that the present doesn't present itself as present. The present is shrouded in the obscurity of its presence, at least when it's a live, enigmatic present, a question-filled present. Although in 1956, in 1958, the present was the Algerian War, we're far from having access to the confession of that present, to the clear and distinct presence of the present, despite the tremendous efforts of a number of people. In that sense, Merleau-Ponty was right. But Sartre was right, too, because, in the final analysis, something like a confession is always eventually wrung from history. Not in the form of the presence of the present but in the form whereby the present re-creates the past and makes it happen again, in a new rendition of the past. Today there's a new rendition—tentative and limited in scope—of the Algerian War. Back then, it was the present. When Lacan discussed Genet, when Genet wrote *The Balcony*, they did so in the largely unpresented figure of the present that was the war, military affairs.

On May 13, the military coup occurred, and there was a session of Lacan's seminar on May 14. The session, the day after the military coup in Algiers, was entitled "Le désir de l'autre" [The other's desire]. Well, the other's desire had sure manifested itself in Algeria! But on March 5 Lacan discussed *The Balcony*. What did he say? He began by saying that it was a comedy and went on to compare it with Aristophanes's plays. He gave a definition of comedy that will be of interest to us. "Comedy embraces, takes in, and enjoys the relationship with an effect . . . namely, the appearance of this signified called the phallus."[2] I would say that the most important word in this definition may be "appearance"; in any case, that's the one I'm going to focus on. Comedy is always the comedy of the present. This is something that has long been noted: tragedy is always backwards-looking, while comedy is in the present. Comedy is the comedy of the present in the sense that it makes the phallus, dare I say, of that present appear. Let's say that it exposes the comic appearance of that aspect of power that's in the present. That's its subversive function, which has long been recognized. Comedy is a thinking of the present, not just any thinking of the present but the thinking that makes the phallus appear. The phallus isn't some unspecified element but rather that aspect of power that will appear in the present. It is also the mockery of it, which is why it's comic. It could be said that each individual comedy is unique in identifying power in the present, in the ludicrous form of its appearance as the phallus. This means the procession of power with its antics, its solemnity, its chaos, its undertaker aspect. The President of the Republic, found dead in the Élysée Palace in the arms of a prostitute, and who they would say "died in action," is really the ideal comedy.[3] But, in a deeper sense, it means the signifying foundation of power itself, the foundation in the present in the derision of its exhibition.

My aim in this respect—this is one of the first meanings I'll ascribe to "image"—will be to identify the register of the philosophical comedy of the present, in the sense I just mentioned, in the sense of the real appearance of the present or of that aspect of power that is in the present. However, what will appear is the utter emptiness of this power. Once power is exposed or exhibited as the phallus, that is, in its signification, the comedy will show that it is actually powerlessness, that it's nothing like power. This is the register of showing.

The aim of comedy is both to expose what, in the present, is power and to show that no sooner has it been exposed, no sooner has it appeared, than this power disintegrates and displays its nothingness, its emptiness. In short, one of the problems in understanding the present is that all real power is secret and operates in the deepest shadows. And so what we see of it, its image, is only farcical nothingness.

Of course, comedy is also the denunciation of the emptiness of a number of names: the names under which power appears.

To give a simple example, countless comedies are aimed at exposing the emptiness of the name of the father, the emptiness of paternity, of paternal authority. This is an inexhaustible subject of comedy. What presents itself as the agency of paternal authority in the phallic signified of phallic mockery is exhibited, exposed, revealed, to actually be totally empty. This, says comedy, is a stroke of luck for the happiness of the young couple, who will be able to get married despite the father's opposition. This is the simplest of plots. It already illustrates the mechanism by which comedy, in exposing the phallic signifier of power in the present, immediately dethrones it. It is a dethroning of the name: in this case, that of the father figure. But it can also be the figure of the Church, the state, finance, or the great lord. It can be all kinds of figures. Consequently, it is true that comedy is the opposite of tragedy: tragedy is the melancholy acceptance of the signifiers of power, while comedy is the gleeful dethroning of them. All this is ultimately pretty simple.

Let's answer our second question now: which names in the present will be exposed as the phallus and dethroned by the phallic comedy of the present? I'm going to tell you right away what I think the main name will be, because I'd like to be able to state the hypotheses. The main name, I'm a little sorry to say, will be "democracy." Thus, I intend to write the comedy of democracy, that is, to make the word "democracy" serve as the key name of contemporaneity, in the sense that it's the phallic name of the present. And since *The Balcony* will be a preliminary operator in this production of the philosophical comedy of the present, as the comedy of the signifier "democracy," let me remind you now of the play's dramatic structure.

It begins with a figure of order as an order of images: images and order are closely interrelated. This figure of order is a brothel. The brothel is obviously the exemplary figure of something that is strictly ordered. It is under the control of a strong, shrewd madam, Irma, who organizes its rituals. So it's a completely closed world with its own laws and is completely governed by a legislation of the imaginary: clients come to the brothel to get off on an image.

Is there a congruence between this figure of the brothel and today's world? I think that in many respects there is. To claim that our world is a brothel, in the sense I just mentioned, wouldn't be an utterly absurd thesis, on two accounts—provided, of course, that we're talking about Genet's brothel, *The Balcony*'s brothel, which is a metaphysical brothel, the most sublimated brothel in the history of literature. First, on account of the closure aspect: the brothel is a closed space, but one that is closed up on the infinity of images. Basically, a brothel is a closed mirror, a mirror in which clients look at the simulacrum on offer. This combination of the limitlessness of the images, on the one hand, and their closure, on the other, is a possible metaphor of some aspects of our world. That's because this combination touches on a major problem, which we'll come back to later, namely: how does our world combine infinity and closure? *The Balcony*'s brothel is something like that. People come there to get off, in the attire of the triple figure of power (judge, general, and bishop). They come disguised as a judge, a general, or a bishop, and the sexual scene takes place imaginarily in these costumes. It's a place of order, and it's a place where people get off; they get off on the images of order.

On closer inspection, there are three levels of reflections: they are images of images of images.

First, it's an image because the person disguised as a judge, a general, or a bishop is neither a judge, nor a general, nor a bishop, but he appears in this guise. Second, he has this image reflected back to him by the other person, the woman, the prostitute, since she will treat him as though the image were real. Thus, there's the image in the clothing—the disguise—and then the image in the gaze of the prostitute. And third of all, these emblems of authority are themselves historical images. In 1956, the year the play was written, the sabre and the holy water sprinkler [standing for the alliance of the Army and the Church] were no longer the emblem of power. That emblem dated from earlier times. So we've got a historical image; the reflection of the historical image in the mirror of *jouissance*; and finally the imaginary materiality of the disguise. There's a childlike figure (dressing up), a historical figure (the fact that these are old, well-documented emblems), and a figure of *jouissance* (the prostitute's gaze and ritual). Childhood, history, and *jouissance*: these are the three levels of the brothel imaginary.

Today, and this may be one of the challenges of staging the play, the historical element is somewhat lifeless. There aren't enough people still going to brothels to dress up as a bishop before being taken charge of by the prostitute. It's something a bit esoteric. You could take a show business personality, for example (to return to democracy), or a finance apparatchik, or a human rights celebrity. That would get the point across faster. But then the problem is that you don't know how to dress up! Let's say you want to dress up as a human rights celebrity, but how do you do so? It's not easy. By putting on a white shirt, perhaps? I'm giving a humorous twist to this question, but it's a real question, because it leads to another one, which is to what extent these are images. Can you get off on the human rights activist's white shirt or the banker's attaché case? Democratic rule means there are no more costumes. Our world is extremely unequal, but inequality is no longer in costume. This seems like a trivial point, but it's in fact very important: costumes are the sign of a regime of collective acceptance of inegalitarian difference. The latter is costumed, staged, emblematized, and is part of accepted social inter-action. Having costumed inequalities is not the same as having inequal-ities without costumes, inequalities that are, so to speak, secularized. In the case of the figure of order represented by Genet's brothel, this is a real issue. And that's probably why Genet himself remained in the realm of the image of images of images, the realm of emblems that had connotations but were old ones, predating the democratic present. So much for the first figure of Genet's play: the brothel as the figure of the order of images.

Next, outside the brothel, there's a second figure, which can be called the figure of the real, or the figure of life. This is the pure present, the pure present as evanescence or as an explosion of rage. Indeed, it just so happens that there's an uprising going on outside, a revolutionary upris-ing, with militants of this revolutionary uprising, and among them a key character named Roger, whom Genet describes in the sixth scene as "the model of the proletarian leader." The situation is thus perfect for a stage production: you've got a space of official closure of images and, outside, a classic space of revolution. The whole problem is what relationship there is between these two spaces. What relationship (or what non-relationship) will be established between the pure eventual figure and the field of images, which is also the field of desire and *jouissance*? The prob-lem posed by the play is what the desire for revolution can possibly be if it refuses any projection into the closed space of images. In other words, can there be a vital desire that is non-fantasmatic? This will be expressed through the dramatization of the relationship between the revolution-aries' camp and the interior of the brothel. Ultimately, the very simple question is whether it's possible to break free from images. This is a ques-tion about the present, and it's for this reason that it will concern us. Can a real present, a vital present, avoid dying from absorption into the form of the image? Here's what Genet says about it in the preface to the play, a preface that is incidentally repeated almost word for word in the text of the play itself:

> A few poets, these days, go in for a very curious operation: they sing
> the praises of the People, of Liberty, of the Revolution, etc., which,
> when sung, are rocketed up into an abstract sky and then stuck there,

discomfited and deflated, to figure in deformed constellations. Disembodied, they become untouchable. How can we approach them, love them, live them, if they are dispatched so magnificently far away? When written—sometimes sumptuously—they become the constituent signs of a poem, and as poetry is nostalgia and the song destroys its pretext, our poets kill what they wanted to bring to life.[4]

As you can see, the problem is the relationship between the present and poetry. Can poetry be made out of what is the very life of the present? The analogy of this question, in the play, is the relationship between the revolution and the brothel. How can the present resist images? Genet's thesis is merciless: it maintains that, as soon as it is captured by the image, and especially the most beautiful image—the poem, the work of art—the real is murdered. To give a twist to something Lacan once said, Genet's thesis is that the image is the murder of the thing.[5] No real can survive being shown in an image.

Genet is suggesting a rule here: to venture into the images of the present time (since it's the general title I'm discussing) will be in large part to attempt to grasp *what has no image*. The present of the present is what has no image, what breaks free from images. The real of the present is dis-imaged. And this real is to an even greater extent the dis-imaging agent, something that has dis-imaging power.

We should learn from our adversaries in this regard. I myself am amazed at the power of the people in charge of these wars to suppress images in wartime. It's an extraordinary ability, if you think about it, given that we're also told, as a law of our world, as the basis of the media's omnipotence, that images of everything have increased ad infinitum and that we live amid the circulation of images. In wartime, oddly enough, there are no more of them. All of a sudden everything goes dark.

It might of course be objected that there has always been propaganda based on total censorship during war. Sure! But people didn't live in a world that claimed to be a "society of the spectacle," a world in which the real itself is made up of images. The ability to suddenly and absolutely suppress any image is now an ability we must be concerned about. It is clear that our times are just as able to suppress images as to disseminate them all over the world. And, since the powers-that-be can propagate images but can just as easily suppress them, the conclusion is that these powers-that-be are the masters of the images, not their slaves. So it's incorrect to claim that the essence of our society has been grasped when we say that it's a society of the spectacle.

This is why what really matters is, and ultimately remains, what does not itself have an image, what is itself dis-imaging. Ultimately, the problem for the investigation of the present time, of which Genet's play *The Balcony* is an allegory, can be formulated as follows: What is the relationship between the supremacy of images on which the powers-that-be pride themselves and the will to dis-image? Contrasting the rules of image supremacy with the pursuit of fundamental dis-imaging is a key issue in the speculative or philosophical investigation of the present time.

In *The Balcony*, this is precisely the issue that divides the revolutionaries. The revolutionaries, outside the brothel, hesitate: should they use images for themselves, devise their own images? Or should they exemplify dis-imaging, the pure will that is not based on any image? This will be the drama of the real outside the brothel, outside the official ritual of images. There will be those who say: "We should produce our own emblems, which won't be the Judge, the General, or the Bishop but will be like the Republic in Delacroix's painting or the proletarian hero with the red flag. We'll be defeated if we ourselves don't come up with images whose force and power are comparable to the ones cooked up in the hell of the brothel." And then on the other hand there are those who say: "No, our difference, our truth, is to be dis-imaging and never to trust images."

Let me read you a short excerpt from the play. It's an argument between Roger and Louis.

LOUIS: Did you ask for the bazookas?
ROGER: Again? Bazookas, bazookas! That's the magic word, it's a regular fetish! Bazookas for everyone!
LOUIS: We've got to take advantage of youthful enthusiasm. And youngsters can't fight unless they adorn themselves with war cries. They try to get wounded so as to show their scars. They want bazookas . . .

ROGER (*bluntly*): No bazookas.

LOUIS (*irritably*): Then according to you we should be fighting hand-to-hand?

ROGER: As the word implies, hand-to-hand fighting eliminates distance.

LOUIS: Do you distrust enthusiasm?

ROGER: I distrust nervousness. The rebellion's riding high, and the people are having a carnival. They're shooting for the fun of it.

LUKE: They're right. Damn it, let them have their fling! I've never seen such excitement: one hand on the trigger, the other on the fly. They shoot and screw.

ROGER: Must you use such language! (*With sudden anger.*) What exactly is it that you're after? If I yanked Chantal from the brothel . . . [*Chantal does in fact come from the brothel: she's the woman the revolutionaries intend to transform into the generic image of the revolution, as the female emblem of the insurrection.*] [6] . . . it wasn't to plant her in another—or in the same one—that's a mockery of the old one. Carnival! Carnival! You know well enough we ought to beware of it like the plague, since its logical conclusion is death. You know well enough that a carnival that goes to the limit is suicide!

LOUIS: Without the people's anger there'd be no revolt. And the people's anger is a carnival.

GEORGETTE: Then we must fight without anger. Reason should be enough.

ROGER: The enemy's losses are high; ours are incalculable. We've got to win at any cost. These gentlemen on the other side are as happy as can be about our war. Because of it they'll be able to attain, as they put it, even greater renown. The people mustn't enjoy themselves. And they mustn't play. Starting now they've got to be in dead earnest.[7]

Here we have the two platters of a theatrical scale, and you can see that the question will be our question, too. In the matrix that is Genet's *The Balcony*, the question of images insists outside the brothel even though the brothel is their proper place. The question always comes back; it insists, because it may well be that there can be no desire without images. That is in fact exactly what Roger's opponents in the popular camp, the camp of the uprising, maintain. At this point in the play we've got two figures: the brothel, united, and the revolutionaries, divided. But there is a third figure for Genet, a shared element, which serves to maintain the imaginary order and yet has no image itself. On the one hand, this third element circulates freely in the world of fantasy, the world of deceitful desire, the world of the emblems of power, but, on the other hand, it has no image, in the way that the Judge, the General, and the Bishop all have one.

Genet affirms the existence of something that's in complete collusion with the official power of images but that, strictly speaking, has no image in the sense of an emblem. This thing is the police, the Chief of Police. He's the key figure of power but in a way that's different from that of images.

Ultimately, the Chief of Police is the phallus. What Lacan identified in his teaching as the function of the phallus Genet identifies as the real key to the power of images, precisely because this power of images has no image itself. In other words, central to the investigation of the present (Genet's question is: What happens to the present when it is tested by images?) we need to find what, despite reflecting the power of images, nevertheless has no image and yet doesn't belong, as do Roger and the revolutionaries, to the dis-imaging outside.

In other words, there is a moment when we come across the real of power as the unrepresented real. This is what Genet calls "the chief of police." As this is a play, it has to be a character. "Chief of Police" denotes someone who, even though fully complicit with the power of images, nevertheless has no image.

This is expressed in a very humorous way: as the Chief of Police is the key accomplice of those who do have an image, he'd like to be like them. In the play, he anxiously asks Irma, the brothel's madam: "Has a client dressed up as the chief of police finally come in?" And as this is never the case, he goes away disappointed. He would so like to have an image, which proves that he doesn't exemplify authentic dis-imaging. He's not like the revolutionary. The revolutionary, exposed to the danger of images, seeks the non-image, while the police chief, dis-imaged because of his position, seeks the image. But he can't find it.

The artistic and intuitive proof of this—the power of the fantasy based on the unrepresentable—is the phallus, which is for Lacan the key to signification in general. The key to the potential power of images is not itself able to be either represented or symbolized.

The theatrical metaphor of this connection that Genet proposes is that, at the end of the play, when, after a series of complicated twists and turns, circumstances have taken a favorable turn for the powers-that-be, the Chief of Police, in search of formal attire, will announce that his outfit will be . . . a phallus costume. That's what the Chief of Police will wear—he'll dress up as a phallus!

A few preliminary remarks are in order before I read you the end of the play. The action is at an end, and it is here that the play becomes melancholy in its own way. Roger says: "Outside, in what you call life, everything has crashed, no truth was possible" (391). This is a question that we, too, will have to ask about our own present. Must we speak like the defeated revolutionary, Roger? Has everything outside crashed? Was no truth possible? Does the present, our present, produce a sort of incapacity for truth? Does the present, as the imageless law of images, always end up giving rise to the impossibility of any truth?

At any rate, by the time Roger pronounces his verdict on the present, the Chief of Police has long since arrived and announced: "I've found my costume." He has found his costume, and this costume is the phallus.

Let me read you a passage from this crucial scene. It should be noted that the woman who's called the Queen is none other than Irma, the brothel's madam, who has become the queen so as to beguile the rebellious masses with a dream and appease them:

THE CHIEF OF POLICE (*trying to smile*): I think that . . . victory . . .
    we've won the day . . . May I sit down?
He sits down. Then he looks about as if questioning everyone.
THE ENVOY (*ironically*): No, nobody's come yet. Nobody's yet felt
    the need to abolish himself in your fascinating image.

THE CHIEF OF POLICE: That means the projects you submitted to me aren't very effective. (*to* THE QUEEN) Nothing?

THE QUEEN (*very gently*): Nobody. And yet the blinds have been drawn again. The men ought to be coming in. Besides, the apparatus has been set up; so we'll be informed by a full peal of bells.

THE ENVOY (*to* THE CHIEF OF POLICE): You didn't care for the project I submitted to you this morning. Yet that's the image that haunts you and that ought to haunt others.

THE CHIEF OF POLICE: Ineffectual.

THE ENVOY (*showing a photographic negative*): The executioner's red coat and his axe. I suggested amaranth red and the steel axe.

THE QUEEN (*testily*): Studio 14, known as the Studio of Executions. Already been done.

THE CHIEF OF POLICE (*to* THE ENVOY): You see. These masquerades prove how unimaginative you are. Maybe you're exhausted? As a matter of fact, you look anemic to me. No. I want my image to be both legendary and human. It should, of course, accord with eternal principles, but my face should be recognizable in it.

THE JUDGE (*making himself agreeable*): Yet you're feared. You're dreaded. You're envied. The people's hymns of love are proofs of it.

THE CHIEF OF POLICE: I'm afraid that they fear and envy a man, but . . . (*groping for words*) . . . not a wrinkle, for example, or a curl . . . or a cigar . . . or a whip. The latest image that was proposed to me . . . I hardly dare mention it to you.

THE JUDGE: Was it . . . very audacious?

THE CHIEF OF POLICE: Very. Too audacious. I'd never tell you what it was. (*Suddenly, he seems to make up his mind.*) Gentlemen, I have sufficient confidence in your judgment and devotion. After all, I want to carry on the fight by boldness of ideas as well. But the fact is—I don't know where to turn first. It was this: I've been advised to appear in the form of a gigantic phallus. A prick of great stature . . .

THE THREE FIGURES *and* THE QUEEN *are dumfounded.*

THE QUEEN: George! You?

THE CHIEF OF POLICE: What do you expect? If I'm to symbolize the nation, your joint . . .

THE ENVOY (*to* THE QUEEN): Allow him, Madame. It's the tone
of the age.

THE JUDGE: A phallus? Of great stature? You mean—enormous?

THE CHIEF OF POLICE: Of my stature.

THE JUDGE: That'll be very difficult to bring off.

THE CHIEF OF POLICE: Not so very. What with new techniques
and our rubber industry, remarkable things can be worked out. No,
I'm not worried about that, but rather . . . (*turning to* THE BISHOP)
. . . what the Church will think of it.

THE BISHOP (*after reflection, shrugging his shoulders*): No definite pro-
nouncement can be made this evening. To be sure, the idea is a bold
one. (*to* THE CHIEF OF POLICE) But if your case is desperate, we
shall have to examine the matter. For . . . it would be a formidable
figurehead, and if you were to transmit yourself in that guise, from
generation to generation . . .

THE QUEEN (*alarmed*): No room's been provided for it. No studio's equipped. . . . After all, though my house is reputed for its
imaginativeness, it's known for its decency, and for a certain tone
as well.

THE CHIEF OF POLICE (*gently*): Would you like to see the model?
(373–75)

When he gets to this point in his analysis of the play, Lacan, taking
off from Genet's intuition, will try to say what the phallus is all about,
apart from its comedic appearance. He will analyze comedy. Comedy
is the farce of the phallus; its function is to reveal its ridiculous aspect.
And for Lacan—in his own terminology—the phallus is the signifier of
signification, the signifier of that which circulates as capable of signifying. So the man of circulation, the Chief of Police, will be the emblem
of the phallus thus defined by Lacan. I quote: "This something that can
be given or withheld, conferred or not conferred by the one who is thus
confused, in the most explicit way, with the image of the creator of the
signifier, the 'Our Father,' the 'Our Father who art in heaven.'"[8] Here we
have the distinctive feature of all circulation in the figure of the absolute
Other, in the figure of the "Our Father."

My own intention is different, since we're dealing with the thinking of the present. I'll use the matrix—*The Balcony*—in the way I'll now explain. Remember that we have four elements:

- The brothel, the place of the law of images
- The revolution, pure externality
- The Chief of Police
- The ultimate emblem of the Chief of Police, which is the phallus, the phallic disguise appropriate to naked power, the power that underlies any representation only to the extent that it is not itself represented

On the basis of these four elements, I will ask four questions:

1.   What is the facticity of the present? What is our brothel? There is its commercial instantiation and/or its political pornography. What type of association is there between closure and infinity today? How are closure and infinity associated in what we (perhaps mistakenly) call our "world"?

2.   This time the question has to do with the outside. What are the real tracings of what breaks free from images, from imagery? In the order in which these tracings originate, are truths, contrary to what Roger says, possible? For him, no truth is possible; everything must come under the law of images. But if some truths are dis-imaging, is dis-imaging itself possible?

We will thus have the equivalent of the inside and the outside in Genet's drama.

3.   This is the question about the Chief of Police. What is it that, when confronted with truths (which we assume are possible and real), safeguards the present's facticity? That's what the Chief of Police is. He's the one who ultimately enables the brothel to continue to exist despite the uprising. That's also why he fails to become a character in the brothel: he's the one thanks to whom the brothel withstands the test of the outside, not someone who belongs to the world of reflections, images, the interiority of the mirror. Therefore, my third question becomes: What is it, today,

that when confronted with a truth of any sort nonetheless preserves most of the present's facticity—its commercial instantiation, its political pornography, and so on? What is the anonymous name of power, the name of naked power? Is it the state of the situation, the state *tout court*, nations or the transnational? Is it what Negri calls "empire"? Is it still local authorities, like the Chief of Police? Is it the axiomatic of capital, the American military? What exactly is our Chief of Police? The question isn't about the law of the world but about the obscure, anonymous guarantor of that law, the one that's not visible in the law of visibility, the one that's the guarantor of circulation and that therefore doesn't circulate.

4.   Assuming we have identified it, what is the emblem that symbolizes its preservation? What is its intended, albeit absent, imagery? The Chief of Police realizes that only one costume is right for him, the phallic costume. What is the emblem under which the naked power of the present time can attain its own representation?

"Images of the Present Time," the general title of this seminar, will be the compilation of the answers to these four questions, provided we find them. It will be the writing of the philosophical comedy of the present in four acts, which I'll sum up in reverse order:

• Act 4: What is the ultimate emblem of the meaning of the present, i.e., of that under which it is recognized as the guarantor of general circulation? As I already told you, my proposition will be that it is democracy. That's why I will accept the common assumption that we are in the age of democracy, in the exact same sense that the Chief of Police wants to embody the age of the phallus. Hence, in the sense that that's the attire, the only attire, in which the circulating power can be widely identified.

• Act 3: Presentation of the element to which this costume is ultimately suited, namely, naked power, of which "democracy" is merely the emblem.

• Act 2: A power—what I call naked power—only really reveals itself, only really shows what it's capable of, when tested by what is different from it. Naked power is not the law of preservation of what there is; it's the law of defense of what there is against the heterogeneous. The Chief of Police only exists because there's the revolution. Without the revolution he would serve no purpose; the brothel wouldn't need him. The question of naked power is that of a paradoxical element that can be defined as follows: a world only holds together when tested by what is different from it.Yet this issue has now become unclear. The question of naked power used to be clearly defined: it was the state, the state apparatus, which was the chief of police of the ruling class, of the bourgeoisie. But today the definition of the term, and even the question as to whether there's really a ruling class, is not at all self-evident, even though, through the greatest of paradoxes, its emblem—democracy—is. Indeed, "democracy" is consensual: people are democrats in the exact same way as everyone is subject to the law of the phallus. But what the emblem is the emblem *of*, the naked power operating beneath the emblem, remains an unclear question. And so, since this element only exists when confronted with what is different, we will have to ask: *Is* there anything different? Is there anything other than what there is? Is there anything noncommercial, nonpornographic? Is there an outside of the brothel? Does anything happen? Are there events, subjects?

- Act 1: Presentation of the law of what there is, as self-persistence.

I gave the four questions in forward, then backward, order to show how they work. If we're able to connect them in an intelligible way, we'll have the image of our times. How do we begin: with the foundation or with the emblem? It's debatable. Do we begin with what appears or with the law, with the structure? In Genet's play, the order is fairly classical. He begins with the law and how it works, then he presents the outside, then the Chief of Police, and then the phallus. He begins with the structure; then, having established what the structure is, he examines the exception; then, having established what the exception is, he examines what circulates between the structure and the exception; and then he tries to find the ultimate name for it all. For Genet, the phallus is the ultimate concept. For us, "democracy" will in a way be the ultimate concept. With this approach, you have a very effective classical order. It's the order of Genet's drama, of classical comedy, of Molière's comedies (especially *Tartuffe*).

As for myself, I am not going to use this classical order. I'll begin with the emblem. I'll ask what the meaning of the consensual nature of the word "democracy" is in today's world. This is a virtually formal question, a question of conditions. What conditions must be met by a present for "democracy" to be an iconic word? Incidentally, Lacan might also be asked on what conditions the word "phallus" can be the signifier of signification. But he asks it very well himself. *We* are going to proceed from the bottom up, and thus construct the image of the present time from its emblem. This could also be formulated, more ontologically, as: we'll begin with appearing in its very appearance. Not with the structure. The present is what is there, what appears. We are going to take the present as it is there, in contemporary subjectivity.

I think everyone is aware that today is an "in-between" today. We're between two worlds, but neither of their boundaries is really clear, neither what is coming nor what we've come from. I make the assumption that democracy, too, is an in-between signifier. It connotes something that doesn't know where it comes from or where it is going. And I'll conclude with a literary reference. When he was young, Ibsen wrote an enormously long play, *Emperor and Galilean*. Later he wrote important bourgeois social dramas, but when he was young he wrote world historical dramas. This play tells the story of the emperor Julian the Apostate, who, after Constantine, when the empire had become Christian, sought to reinstate paganism. He wanted to restore the dead gods. At one point in Ibsen's play he says: "The old beauty [*which should be understood to mean the beauty of the Greek gods, of the pagan imaginary*] is no longer beautiful, and the new truth is not yet true."[9]

The present time is something that no longer has a predictable predicate. It might be said, not that the old beauty is no longer beautiful but that the revolution is no longer revolutionary. And isn't it possible that the new "truth," which is that there's no such thing as truth, is perhaps not true? Yes, we can sense as much: what we're told is the truth—the democracy of capital—isn't true. So we're between a predicate that's no longer appropriate and a predicate that's not yet appropriate. We're in an age without predicates. That's why I am using the method of images. Otherwise, I'd just tell you what the concept is. Since our truth is uncertain, we're going to try to enter into the present time via the emblem. Since our own desire is unclear, we're going to begin with the Chief of Police's desire.

Session 2

December 3, 2001

L ast time I told you that I was beginning a three-year seminar entitled "Images of the Present Time," and I essentially asked two questions.

My first question was: Why this title? And more specifically: What does the word "image" have to do with it?

My second question was: What will the seminar's overall approach be? What will our method of development be?

I devoted the first session to the first question, using Jean Genet's play *The Balcony* as a guide. I'd like to inform you that this play will be performed in a new production at the Théâtre Gérard Philipe in Saint-Denis, from April 15 to May 12. Prior to that, from March 4 to 31, *The Blacks*, one of Genet's other two major plays (the third being *The Screens*), will also be performed at the same theater. I don't know whether these productions will be any good, but I'm convinced that these plays by Genet are significant contemporary landmarks, even if they date from the 1950s.

—————

The analysis of *The Balcony* allowed me to establish a method, which I'll briefly review, concerning what it means to think the image of a historical moment. How can thinking be oriented toward capturing the image of a historical moment, in the sense of the title "Images of the Present Time"? Thinking the image of a historical moment basically means compiling four different constructions, four different approaches. Generalizing what I found in *The Balcony*, I identified four stages that I'll give a more abstract version of now:

1. Thinking the structure of the historical moment: this is what could be called the systemic stage.

2. Identifying the real tracings that, although on the surface of the structure, i.e., located there and nowhere else, are nevertheless exceptions to this structure. The objective is to identify the tracings of exception, which can be viewed either as internal externalities (what happens in Genet's *The Balcony*), local externalities, or perhaps as superficial scratches, scratches on the surface, marks on the surface constituting exceptions to the law of this surface. I, for one, call them "truths," but the question of names isn't important for now. The important thing is knowing that the objective is to identify the real tracing of what the structure of the historical moment does not allow to be thought. One might also say that it's the identification of a structural inexistent that nevertheless exists as a tracing.

For me, as you know, these tracings are always to a greater or lesser extent one of the four canonical categories: art, science, politics, and love. I'm convinced that this list is neither arbitrary nor incomplete. So let me remind you of my definition of these four categories, as tracings of exception.

*   Science is the real tracing of the letter in its appearing. It is an exceptional tracing, an emergence that treats the play of letters inscribing it as real.
*   Politics is the tracing of the collective (not in the sociological sense), the collective as the real irruption of what counts it as such.
*   Love is the real tracing of the Two or of difference.
*   Art is the real tracing of the infinite resources of the finitude of the sensible world.

We are in the second stage here, the stage of identifying the real tracing that, from within one of these four categories, is able to call forth, despite being inexistent with respect to the structure, something that is an exception to it.

3.   This is what safeguards the structure when it's confronted with the exceptions. It's the third stage of this linkage. It's the pivotal point of the investigation. In a thinking that is too one-sidedly structural, or shall we say too one-sidedly systemic, there has always been the risk of thinking the structure's consistency only as continuity. What is attributed as strength to the structure is its insistence, its capacity for repetition. What fails to be seen is that it is necessary to think that which, from outside a given structure, safeguards it with respect to the exceptions, not just with respect to the continuity of preservation. There is an important effect to be thought: the structural countereffect of the exceptions, which is actually the real point of any structure. Yet this—how a given order preserves itself, not just as an order but when tested by what is an exception to it—is something that the mere description of the structure doesn't include.

This is in my view a very important point. The safeguarding of the structure is itself coeval with the exceptions. It is neither a consequence, nor a mere nodal point, nor a crux of the structural figure concerned. In other words, every order is tested by its exceptions, and this testing of an order by its exceptions constitutes its real, its historicity, its point of real contingency. So what is important in an order, in the strategically creative guise of an order, is the countereffect, not the effect.

I have suggested calling this countereffect "naked power," power as the nakedness of the order. You can't deduce it from the order alone but rather from the order grasped through the countereffect of what is an exception to it. It is always a point of obscurity of the order. It must therefore be accepted that the real power of an order is not exactly transitive to that order itself. The description of an order won't suffice to reveal the secret of its power to you. Usually, historico-sociologico-politico-, etc. thought considers, on the contrary, that the description of the order will reveal the secret of its power. But the secret lies in the countereffect: what is it capable of with regard to the exception? This point always has to be reclaimed, because it is itself always partly contingent on the exceptions. So you can call this point the effect of chance on the preservation of the order, the effect of chance of the exceptions.

I'm going to use a somewhat anecdotal yet instructive example. It's an exception in the realm of artistic innovation: Schoenberg's invention of a new musical system, the breakthrough of a musical art that was unprecedented because it was no longer based on the interplay of tonalities. Tonal music is the figure of the order here, the structural figure. But the true nature of this order would be revealed in what it was capable of doing as a countereffect of the innovation, of the creation of twelve-tone, and later, serial music. Let's call art's order "academism." What is the power in art? Is it the power of repeating what there is? Not really: that's just a superficial description of academism. You can gauge academism's power when you're dealing with the question: What is it capable of with respect to what is attempting to be an exception to it? The essence of academism is always expressed as *neo*-academism, because the countereffect will naturally always be called "neo-something." Whenever you see "neo," you can be sure you're hot on the trail of real power. Power presents itself as the "neo" figure of the order. Thus, in Genet's play, there's a new Chief of Police. He's the same one, but the same one as a new one. That's why he has to find new emblems and why he must become the prick-headed police chief. The essence of this third stage, the order tested by the exceptions, is the figure of the "new order." Remember that "New Order" [*Ordre Nouveau*] was the name of a fascist group. This is how we should understand the meaning of the slogan of Bush, the chief of police of the U.S. brothel: his phallus is called "the new world order." We have since seen that it was the name of the old order, grasped in the countereffect of its exceptions. This is a crucial determination point of the linkage as a whole.

4.   This is the stage of the emblem, as what actually ensures the concealment and preservation of naked power. It's what represents the order, tested by its exceptions, in a figure of the ideal or of preservation. It's a somewhat intricate yet simple mechanism, with a great analytical and descriptive capacity with regard to a given situation. The emblem exists to conceal not the order in general but the aspect of the order that has been tested by its exception. We're really dealing with what controls images. The law of images resides in what regulates the emblems responsible for presenting as ideal and preservation what is actually the countereffect of the exception.

Ultimately, the production of a thinking of the images of the present time occurs in four stages:

- The systemic stage
- The exception stage
- The naked power stage
- The emblem stage

If we can manage to combine all four in a figure of linkage, then we'll have a thinking of the images of the present time. Genet's play, as a drama, is a living allegory of all this, and I'd like to come back to it briefly for one last time. The arrangement of the four stages can be seen in it in a particularly clear way:

- The systemic figure is the brothel (Madame Irma, who is also the Queen).
- The figure of the real tracing is the revolution (Roger and his comrades).
- The naked power is the police chief.
- The ultimate emblem is the phallus.

Last time, I identified the various components, but now what is the dramatic linkage the play proposes? *The Balcony* sets up the following linkage: the manipulation of the emblems by the powers that be leads to the dissipation of the exception into the structure. That's why it's a tragedy, even if it's a comedy. Ultimately, by manipulating the emblems, the Chief of Police will end up getting the revolutionary, Roger, himself to become a figure in the brothel. There is the idea that, as a result of the manipulation of the emblems by the powers that be, the exception becomes illegible: the fact that it is swallowed up in the structure results in its illegibility. It is no longer legible as an exception on the surface.

I'd like to say one more thing about this. The apparent trajectory is 1, 2, 3, 4, namely, brothel, exception, the Chief of Police's entrance, and emblems. But in reality, the trajectory in thought, the true dramatic trajectory, is the opposite. We begin with the emblems (including those of the Judge, the General, and the Bishop), we next show

how these emblems are linked to the powers that be, then we show the exception (the revolutionaries), and, by the end, we're able to think the element of order, the system, completely, because we've seen it tested by the exception. I told you that this was kind of what I was proposing to do here, in keeping with the idea that beginning with the systemic won't take us very far. We've got to begin somewhere else. Nor do we have to begin with the emblems. We can try to begin with the Chief of Police, the naked power, who is the testing of the order through its exception. But we're soon faced with the question of the manipulation of the images.

Regarding the question of the sequence (1, 2, 3, 4 or 4, 3, 2, 1), these are things you experiment with when you're trying to solve a problem: you try to find the form, you try to figure out what's not working, the reason it's not working . . . and then how it crystallizes in a signifier, an image. These are ordinary thought processes. But isn't the 4, 3, 2, 1 sequence at risk of becoming circular? The move from the system to the emblems can also be from the emblems to the system, which means that the linkage might always be more or less circular. What you recognize here is the idea that affirmative thought (eternity) may appear as circularity. This is the debate with Nietzsche, with the question of the eternal recurrence. But let's not forget that what we're seeking is a way of thinking and of life that is not in thrall to modern nihilism. Are we doomed from now on to the instantaneousness of modern nihilism, or will we be able to affirm, in opposition to it, a figure of infinity? For Nietzsche, as we know, the approach that effectively combats nihilism involves affirming the eternal recurrence. There's a connection between the two in his thought. We might say, to use Deleuze's vocabulary, that nihilism and eternal recurrence really constitute a disjunctive synthesis. On that score, I'm going to read you the very end of *The Balcony* so that you understand what happens in this respect. It ends with Madame Irma, the brothel's madam. She has been playing the role of the Queen for a while. A burst of machine-gun fire is heard. It's the ambiguous outside world, the exception that has become unclear:

THE QUEEN: Who is it? . . . Our side. . . . Or rebels? . . . Or? . . .
THE ENVOY: Someone dreaming, Madame . . .

THE QUEEN *goes to various parts of the room and presses buttons. Each time, a light goes out.*

THE QUEEN (*continuing to extinguish lights*): . . . Irma . . . Call me Mme Irma and go home. Good night, sir.

THE ENVOY: Good night, Mme Irma.

THE ENVOY *exits.*

[*You think: How about that: the image is done away with when she shuts the lights out. Mme Irma, who was the Queen, doesn't even want to be called "Madame" anymore. She turns back into Mme Irma. She does away with the image, the emblem.*]

IRMA (*alone, and continuing to extinguish lights*): It took so much light . . . two pounds' worth of electricity a day! Thirty-eight studios! Every one of them gilded, and all of them rigged with machinery so as to be able to fit into and combine with each other. . . . And all these performances so that I can remain alone, mistress and assistant mistress of this house and of myself. (*She pushes in a button, then pushes it out again.*) Oh no, that's the tomb. He needs light, for two thousand years! . . . and food for two thousand years. . . . (*She shrugs her shoulders.*) Oh well, everything's in working order, and dishes have been prepared. Glory means descending into the grave with tons of victuals! . . . (*She calls out, facing the wings.*) Carmen? Carmen? . . . Bolt the doors, my dear, and put the furniture-covers on . . . (*She continues extinguishing.*) In a little while, I'll have to start all over again . . . put all the lights on again . . . dress up . . . (*A cock crows.*) Dress up . . . ah, the disguises! Distribute roles again . . . assume my own . . . (*She stops in the middle of the stage, facing the audience.*) . . . Prepare yours . . . judges, generals, bishops, chamberlains, rebels who allow the revolt to congeal, I'm going to prepare my costumes and studios for tomorrow. . . . You must now go home, where everything—you can be quite sure—will be falser than here. . . . You must go now. You'll leave by the right, through the alley. . . . (*She extinguishes the last light.*) It's morning already.

(*A burst of machine-gun fire.*)

That's Genet's version of the thesis that, ultimately, the image of a historical moment is only thinkable as a recurrence. This could be called his Nietzscheanism: eternity as circularity. As you can see, it ultimately ends with the repeated ambivalence between costumes and machine guns. It will all start over again the same way, with the costume as the law of the order of images and with the machine gun symbolizing the rebels' exteriority. It will all be reaffirmed—the order, the exception, the connection between the two, the Chief of Police who will emerge from his tomb—and finally the emblems will be reaffirmed. This is a possible thinking of a historical moment as affirmation. The historical moment is neither the passage nor the destruction nor the flight of time: it is reaffirmable, and that's what gives it its consistency. What is reaffirmable isn't the historical moment as a moment; it's the linkage of the four figures. This is what I call the disjunctive linkage of nihilism and the eternal recurrence. It is a thesis about the image of a historical moment, about what the thinking of a historical moment is. To think a historical moment is to think what can be reaffirmed in it, or, in other words, what can return.

The effort I'm asking you to make is to try to undo this disjunction: nihilism does not necessarily have to be connected with the eternal recurrence. Or, to put it another way, to think a historical moment we don't have to imagine its recurrence, its reaffirmation. A historical moment can really be thought of as an unrepeatable singularity, which means that it proposes a path from the order to the emblem that does not have to be reversible, that's not a circular path. But I'm convinced that we're essentially dealing with their connection today. Genet's thesis, which is at bottom a Nietzschean thesis, is a dominant thesis, given that it's based on the belief that, assuming we try to be exceptions to the order again, we'll end up playing the same scene again. This is a belief, and deep-rooted propaganda as well, but it's propaganda that we ourselves create, true propaganda, ultimately: the belief that if we commit ourselves again to the figure of the intelligibility of the exception and the consequences that follow from it, we'll be performing the same play again, the play of the twentieth century, as it were. And that we shouldn't perform it again because—and this is the second aspect of the propaganda—it was a bad play. It was disastrous, devastating, bloody, horrible. This is a frank opinion, and it's the critic's right to express it. But that's not the essence of the matter. The essence of the verdict—and we need to look into ourselves to see how much we buy into it—is the belief that that particular play is actually the only one there is. That's the paradox of contemporary propaganda. The most important thing is not to say that the play, the play of the communist revolution, was bad. OK, it wasn't always good; it may have been bad, very bad, but it happened, and let's leave it in its grave. But what the propaganda says and wants us to do is *not* to leave this bad play in its grave. No, no! It must always be remembered, it must be remembered for all time. That's what the famous "duty of remembrance" is all about. Usually, we're quick to forget a bad play. Here, the order is never to forget it, so that it should never be performed again. But why would it be performed again? Because, says the propaganda of the eternal recurrence, it may be part of the banned repertoire, but it's the repertoire nonetheless. There's no other play in the revolutionary genre. So the only precaution is to remember for all time that the play is bad so as to never perform it or perform it again.

The linkage of the four components that I was talking about is accomplished as if there were only the systemic, the comprehensive stage. Contained in the verdict on the twentieth century is the belief that there's only one play and that this play will ineluctably be performed again if anything at all is performed. So let's take off our costumes, remove our makeup, and, above all, not perform anything anymore. This issue, which I think is extremely important in the contemporary context, is a new one. And it can only be understood through the logic I'm suggesting to you, which connects the four stages. Now you can understand why I came back to my first question: What does "images of the present time" mean?

This brings me to the second question: our approach. What will the successive stages, the real sequence of this undertaking, be?

First, the diagnosis. The diagnosis will begin with the emblem, not the systemic. I will contend that the most important emblem is contained in the word "democracy." Of course, we're dealing here—as usual when it comes to emblems—with the name, with the word. This doesn't mean that we'll do away with all possible uses of the word. We're using "democracy" here in the sense of its function as an emblem, in the sense of something that serves as the ideal figure for an obscure naked power, in the sense of something that collects indiscriminately around the obscurity of naked power. Something that the Chief of Police disguises himself as. The contemporary Chief of Police is disguised as democracy. That isn't a judgment on democracy in general or on other, completely different uses of the word that have occurred and will continue to occur. It is essentially about what collects around an obscure power. Obscure in the sense that it's an order tested by the contingency of its exception. And beneath this name, this emblem—this phallus, if you will—there is something like the present of a power. That's the initial hypothesis.

Here is where I'll attempt to define what should be understood by "contemporary nihilism," which is the focus of this year's seminar. Contemporary nihilism must necessarily be analyzed via the figures of positivity of the present time. You haven't successfully accomplished the analysis of a nihilism if you haven't accomplished the analysis of its ideals. The critique of nihilism shouldn't be the starting point. In "Images of the Present Time," I'm going to present contemporary nihilism's positive, ideal figure, because the key to understanding it is the deciphering of its emblems, not the deciphering of its system. To think that the key to understanding contemporary nihilism lies in economic alienation, in economic horror, and so on, is to bark up the wrong tree.[1] That only explains the systemic, which is of course indispensable for understanding what there is, but the subjective key to nihilism can only be grasped where the idealized figure of the time occurs, not in the overall, manifest system of alienation. Today, when there is only capitalism, you'll find that no one is really in favor of it. There's no longer any need to be in favor in of it. No one says it's a fundamental ideality. The subjective key to nihilism cannot be capitalism, condemned on all sides as an "economic horror." The key is democracy; there is no other. It is in its name that all real action is taken. And its extreme ambiguity, typical of all genuine emblems, makes our own enterprise very complicated. You can't give a concealing function to a word that is not ambiguous. It has to have a rallying force, some real pizzazz. So we need to get away from this ambiguity. That's the only possible starting point if we want to think contemporary nihilism in terms of its subjective figure, the figure that enables it to win people over. Propaganda against the obvious bogeyman (capitalism as such, its generic monstrousness) is necessary, but it doesn't get at the subjective functioning.

After examining contemporary nihilism, I'll ask the question that Kant already asked: How can we orient ourselves in thinking, or, in other words, how can we place ourselves under the authority of the non-image-creating, of what is not under the democratic emblem of the present time? How can we place thinking somewhere other than under this emblem? Since the emblem operates under the name "democracy," I have no hesitation in saying that this endeavor is aristocratic. I'll propose an oxymoron and describe this approach as "proletarian aristocratism."

- "Aristocratism" denotes the fact, which many people have intuited and which was thought through by Deleuze and Guattari, that exceptions are carried by what they, Deleuze and Guattari and others, call minorities. "Aristocratism" thus refers simply to the idea that truth is conveyed by minorities, possibly very small ones.
- "Proletarian" means two things. First, that it is "working" (in the sense of "the worker"), i.e., that it's in the form or the demand of the work, whatever the sphere of the work may be. Second, that it's addressed to everyone. I'll explain this oxymoron in greater detail later on. For now, I've given you a brief overview of what breaking free from emblems means.

The third stage will be to assess the resources. Once this approach, proletarian aristocratism, has been settled on, an inventory will need to be taken: what resources do we have to counteract the images of the present time? I think this hinges on the relationship between philosophy and nonphilosophy, or false philosophy (the so-called New Philosophy, for example). How do we get to the exceptions? How do we get to the real tracings? This is an encyclopedic investigation. It's the old philosophical project of the encyclopedia of truths, of exceptions, of the order confronted by exceptions to the order.

Just as an aside, one of the great refrains of modernity is that an encyclopedia is impossible. "It's impossible to know everything anymore. We need to specialize, we need to share the work among ourselves, split the work up, work in teams, subteams, etc." Such unanimity is suspect! Ultimately, in what sense was it less true, or more true, in Plato's or Hegel's day? The quantitative is deceptive: we're dealing with an encyclopedia of exceptions, with what is in a figure of appearing, emerging, novelty. Is trying to make an inventory of it impossible? I don't think so. I think that the thesis that an encyclopedia is impossible is nothing but the bourgeois thesis of the division of labor projected onto the order of knowledge. It's an oppressive thesis. We need to try to accept the conditions of a modern encyclopedia and identify what is important for thought. For starters, we should try to show that there's no impossibility per se involved. The idea that it would be intrinsically impossible must be vigorously refuted. We need to restore the philosophical objective of an encyclopedia of exceptional truths. We need to examine why the thesis of the impossibility of the encyclopedia, the imperious thesis of specialization and the division of labor, is so widespread, obsessive, and incessantly repeated.

So far, we have three stages: the diagnosis (or the emblem), the approach (how to orient ourselves), and the encyclopedia.

The fourth stage will be focused on the question "What does it mean to live?" In the final analysis, the purpose of all this is only to ask under what conditions living is possible, other than as a systemic position, as an assignment of places in any given system. What is a subjectivation that has its own emblems? The drama of Genet's *The Balcony*, the tragedy of its comedy, is that, ultimately, the revolutionaries fail to find their own emblems. They take the others' emblems. Roger, the consummate revolutionary, ends up being emblematized in the brothel itself. There is a failure of emblem creation. The question comes down to whether one can invent one's own emblems or whether one is subject to the law of the dominant emblem system, the established emblem system. It's also the restoration of the vocation of philosophy as wisdom, in the sense that the possibility of not being under the dominant emblems and therefore being in a diagonal relationship to the order might be called wisdom. "Is this the way men live?"[2] "This way": that's Aragon's question. How can we live *this way*?

The result is a reconnection with something ancient. The question of wisdom, the question of what it means to live, the question of whether we're capable of living under our own emblems, is indeed an ancient question. In fact, what is being called for is a new renaissance. Every renaissance is a return to the ancient. Every (re)birth presupposes a birth. And I think that that's what our priority should be. Or else we'll have total barbarism. With the question of philosophy conceived of in this way, it's a new birth that's involved, a new ability to ask the most fundamental questions of existence as relevant questions, even though they are regarded as absurd or impossible questions.

It is striking that, in the 1950s, this was what Lacan intended psychoanalytic treatment for. Lacan proposed an ascetic ideal of psychoanalytic treatment, an affirmative ascesis. The year was 1954, a few months before the outbreak of the Algerian War, and the session of May 19, 1954 of Seminar 1 (a very fine seminar, this Seminar 1, with a very ancient-sounding tone) ends this way:

> Should we push analytic intervention to the point of becoming fundamental dialogues on justice and courage, in the great dialectical tradition? That is a question. It is not easy to answer, because, in truth, modern man has become singularly incapable of tackling these great issues. He prefers to resolve things in terms of behavior, adjustment, group ethics, and other such nonsense. Hence the gravity of the problem posed by the analyst's humane education.[3]

This is a remarkable passage. Here, too, you have the diagnosis, namely that the dialectical dimension of the ancient thought tradition, that capacity, has been lost. Basically, what Lacan was saying already back then is that, faced with these questions, we need to recover an aptitude, a capacity, for engaging in dialogue—although engaging in dialogue means thinking dialectically—about justice and courage. This injunction (as well as that incapacity, for that matter) is rooted in the interplay among what he calls the three fundamental passions: love, hate, and ignorance. It was a stroke of genius, a contribution to philosophy, to have posited as a fundamental dimension of experience that ignorance is a passion. Ignorance is not a lack; it's a passion for not knowing, a passion for remaining ignorant. And when modern man sees things in terms of group ethics, adjustment, and other such nonsense, it's because he's making the passion for ignorance predominate in himself. This is another way of describing a characteristic of contemporary nihilism.

A little later, on June 30, when the question of these three passions and the purpose of analysis came up, Lacan would say: "It is only in the dimension of being and not in that of the real that the three fundamental passions can be inscribed" (271). "Real" should be understood here in the sense of "reality," not in the sense of what he would later call "the real." It might also be said that the question "What does it mean to live?", which is ultimately the question of how we organize the three fundamental passions, has to do with a dimension of being. "This revelation of speech," Lacan would also say, "is the realisation of being" (271). As you can see, the inscription of the three fundamental passions that define modern man, with his incapacity to talk about justice and courage, has to do with being, and the revelation of speech—the rebirth, in the sense I mentioned—the rebirth through psychoanalytic treatment, is tantamount to the realization of being.

The question "What does it mean to live?" is thus in the dimension of being and in the dimension of the revelation of being. It's this conjunction that needs to be examined. The passions must be inscribed in the dimension of being and must be traversed by speech that is a realization of being. How is it possible to be simultaneously in a dimension and in a realization? To put it more simply: how is it possible to be there, in this world, and yet to be in the realization of something other than this world? How is it possible to be of the world (the dimension of being) and yet to be the revelation (the realizing revelation and not just the inhabiting of being)? Is being there only an inhabiting? If you are capable of justice and courage, you are not only in the dimension of being but also in the revelation, in the realization. You don't just inhabit the world, even poetically; you experience its creation.

We could attempt to frame the question as follows:

- The dimension of being is the dimension of the organization of the fundamental passions. It is the predominance of love over hatred and ignorance. That really sounds like a Christian idea, but what does it mean today? At any rate, it means the predominance of the Two, that is, the predominance of difference, or of a gap. How can something like a gap be created or a distance or a gap be established? To live, to really live, is to live at a distance from how we're instructed to live.

- The realization is something like hard work. You have to be an aristocrat as to the dimension and a proletarian as to the realization. That is the real approach to being. Last time, I referred to that phrase spoken by one of Ibsen's characters: "The old beauty is no longer beautiful, but the new truth is not yet true." Our world is a bit like that, a bit "in-between": the old project is no longer feasible and the new project is not yet visible. We should take our cue from what Lacan said half a century ago. A world that's between two things requires a particular discipline of thought because you're not supported by any structure. Since you're in an in-between space, a gap, you are your only reference point. So you need a discipline. You can rethink such a discipline through the four protocols of the images of the time.

As regards the emblem system, since we're beginning with the emblems, the discipline will be the act by which we accept to break away from the dominant democratic emblem. That's the first kind of discipline, the one I've called a proletarian aristocratism. The second kind consists in keeping at a distance the naked power that this emblem conceals. Once the act of distancing ourselves from the emblem has been accomplished, we still have to keep our distance from naked power, which is revealed in all its obscenity when its emblem is torn away. The obscenity is fascinating, as the play clearly shows. Once the emblem is gone, the obscene remains, and what's more, nowadays, the obscene flaunts itself. So the Two of love needs to be used against the jointure of ignorance and hatred, which is a possible definition of the obscene, of naked power: a particular jointure of ignorance and hatred. The third type of discipline requires us to extol the exceptions, to keep the encyclopedia of truths up to date. To that end, we need to remain as indifferent as possible to the media. We need to rely solely on what we ourselves experience. What is shown doesn't matter. The encyclopedia is one for nomads, not for sedentary people glued to the news on TV. It is not easily accessible through the internet, through connectivity. It's experienced more than it's connected to. Connectivity, or communication, is also a source of fascination, just like the obscene and the emblem. Taking our distance from it, cutting ourselves off from it and keeping the encyclopedia up to date will require a discipline, a nomadization. The exceptions aren't what we're shown, so we need to experience them. All this will take us back to the order, but from the standpoint of its weaknesses, its vulnerability. However, in an in-between order it's difficult to identify the weaknesses, whereas it's easy to do so when an order is an established one. Endeavoring to find the real weaknesses in nihilism is the fourth type of discipline.

We thus have the disciplinary guidelines leading to "What does it mean to live?": the discipline of the act, the discipline of distance, the discipline of experience, and the discipline of weaknesses or flaws. On this basis, we'll be able to live. And I'll conclude by giving the final word to poetry. You're going to hear the four points again:

- The order, referred to as "exploitation" (this is an old poem!)
- The exception called "we," we the vanquished of appearances, those who, to go by mere appearances, are nothing but losers
- Naked power, referred to as "oppression"
- The emblem of power, which is necessity, the promiseless promise of necessity, which proclaims that things will always stay this way

How does the linkage occur? The linkage will be the balance, at the linking point, between "never" and "today."

Injustice today walks with a confident step.
The oppressors settle in for ten thousand years.
Power proclaims: This is how things are, and how they'll stay.
The only voice that can be heard is the government's.
And on the markets exploitation declares loud and clear:
I've only just begun. But many of those oppressed now say
What we want will never be.

Whoever is still alive should never say never!
What is certain is not certain.
Things will not stay as they are.
Once the rulers have spoken
The ruled will speak.
Who dares say: never?
On whom does it depend if oppression remains? On us.
On whom does it depend if its thrall is broken? Also on us.
Whoever has been beaten down must rise up!
Whoever is lost must fight back!
Whoever has recognized his condition—how can anyone stop him?
For the vanquished of today are the victors of tomorrow
And "Never" becomes: already today![4]

Session 3

January 16, 2002

Jean-Luc Nancy, who will be the focus of a conference at the end of this week, is receiving special recognition. He is a great survivor: he underwent a heart transplant, so he has someone else's heart. One of his finest essays, "The Heart of Things," in *A Finite Thinking*, sums up his thinking and will provide me with an introduction to my subject. Nancy wanted to take on one of the challenges of philosophical modernity by attempting to respond directly to a provocation on the part of the psychoanalysts regarding philosophy. A provocation, or perhaps a conviction. As you know, Lacan professed what he called an "anti-philosophy," thus inscribing psychoanalysis in a very profound but also extremely tense relationship with philosophy. I devoted my seminar six or seven years ago to that tension. One of the tenets of Lacanian anti-philosophy is that there is something that philosophy doesn't want to know about, namely, enjoyment. This is a thesis that immediately brands psychoanalysis as anti-philosophy, since psychoanalysis, quite obviously, cannot be unaware of enjoyment.

Why, in the opinion of many psychoanalysts, doesn't philosophy want to know anything about enjoyment? Because enjoyment is connected to what cannot be symbolized, to what is not related to any symbol or concept (as philosophers would say), i.e., the Thing, the unspeakable Thing, which, in psychoanalytic orthodoxy, inevitably refers to the mother's body. Enjoyment is intrinsically linked to this primal unspeakable Thing. Yet philosophy, say the psychoanalysts, is based on not having to take that primal unspeakable Thing into account. This is, moreover, what allows it to say that anything can be raised to a concept. But if philosophy proposes to say that anything can be raised to a concept, then it must excise, so to speak, the Thing, excise the primal Thing, the unspeakable Thing that ultimately serves as material for or as a summons to enjoyment, since all enjoyment, in the final analysis, is enjoyment of this Thing. Anti-philosophy thrives on the accusation that philosophy has to turn away from the Thing, all the while claiming that it will turn toward the Thing itself, or, as Husserl put it, that it will "return to things themselves." But psychoanalysts won't fall for that claim: if philosophers say they will return to it, to the Thing they turned away from originally, it's because they don't want to know anything about it.

This is a possible reason for the very ancient connection between philosophy and asceticism, which can be interpreted in many ways. It is, as we know, one of Nietzsche's pathways for establishing himself, too, as an anti-philosopher. Nietzsche was someone who said quite simply, and I quote, "the philosopher is the criminal of criminals,"[1] because, through the fundamental connection between philosophy and asceticism, hence ultimately between philosophy and Christianity, philosophy merely gives free rein to *ressentiment*, to the reactive forces. There's a sort of meeting of minds here between Nietzsche and Lacan, between Nietzsche and psychoanalysis. Their systems are naturally not the same, but there's a sort of convergence between them at the point where the idea that it is the very essence of philosophy to be ascetic, to disdain—by arranging to ignore it—the fact of enjoyment, is pronounced, and denounced. As far as the anti-philosopher is concerned, this isn't some odd philosophical orientation. Rather, it is in its very essence that philosophy forecloses anything that has to do with enjoyment. You could say that philosophy is built as a sort of "de-joicing" [*dé-jouir*] instead of being based on a rejoicing [*réjouir*]. De-joicing means that philosophy doesn't just speak out or preach against enjoyment, it's deeper than that: philosophy is a discipline of thought that is based—says the psychoanalyst anti-philosopher—on not taking enjoyment into account, on not seeing that this issue may be central to thought. As a result, philosophy, which claims to be a thinking, is a sham, precisely because it doesn't see that enjoyment may be at the very heart of thought.

All this has a lot to do with our subject, because the present moment, our present moment, our current context, is undeniably under the emblem of enjoyment. I would even say that it has become our sole imperative: "Enjoy!" The emblem of enjoyment is what is called, in journalese, "modern hedonism." Viewed more dramatically, hedonism is enjoyment that has emerged as the key concern of the nihilism of our time. This is what must be understood when people talk about the death of ideologies. For if ideologies are dead, then of course there is only enjoyment, enjoyment and the paths of enjoyment. From a strictly governmental point of view, the question is what is consistent with the greatest enjoyment. It could be argued, moreover, that what is consistent with the greatest enjoyment is, given the circumstances, the least enjoyment. Enjoy as little as possible and you'll increase your chances of enjoying as much as possible. That kind of agenda is very common in politics. But even if cutting down on enjoyment is recommended, you're still under its emblem. You're in the economy of enjoyment.

That said, the famous modern hedonism, which Plato actually already identified in the ideology of democracy more than two thousand years ago, takes two opposite forms, the libertarian form and the liberal one.

First, there's the libertarian version, which presents itself as emancipatory and has roots that go way back. It is epitomized by one of the slogans of May '68, "Enjoy without restraint." The whole question is whether it's possible to enjoy without restraint, and what that means exactly. It's clearly about experiencing an enjoyment that would be free from all attachments, an enjoyment that would be characterized by detachment. "Without restraint" means no attachments, and therefore, of course, "no law." But it's more radical than "no law": no attachments, no obstacles, is the idea of an enjoyment that unfolds immanently. It's not a polemical but an obvious point that this is a drug-oriented conception of existence. Drugs are not just substances, poisons, and so on. They're a metaphysics, a metaphysics of detachment. Drugs undo attachment, temporarily of course but also effectively, at any rate for the subject concerned. Drugs provide, perhaps artificially, an enjoying without restraint, in the literal sense of the term: drugs remove all restraint from enjoying. You get high.

"Getting high" is a good way of describing what, I insist, is not just intoxication but is instead, because of the imperative connected to it ("Enjoy
without restraint"), a metaphysics of detachment. But since the real
world is nothing but attachments and can be defined by the system of
attachments it presents, it could be said that enjoying is the negation of
the world, precisely because it is under the ideal of the absolute suspension of attachments. In this sense, it is really a nihilism. The metaphysics
of drugs is nihilistic, and nihilism is a powerful tendency of thought. We
could say that, in the libertarian vision, enjoying, or the imperative of
enjoyment, is itself nihilistic. What is it ultimately about if not turning
yourself into the world's waste product? Radical hedonism, for anyone
who knows or has been acquainted with the metaphysics of drugs, is a
radical nihilism, which involves turning yourself into the world's waste
product for deep reasons, not just because you're addicted to drugs. The
crucial point isn't addiction; it's the metaphysical subjectivity that lies
behind it and that equates enjoying and the nothingness of the world
through the breaking away from all attachments.

I should point out that this imperative, to turn yourself into the world's
waste product, can in its own way be an imperative of saintliness—in the
sense of the well-known connection between saintliness and abjection—
an imperative of utter disdain for the world for the sake of something
other than the world. The saint, too, disdains worldly attachments. He
or she devalues and denies the world and becomes its waste product, as a
holy waste product. Consequently, you could say that, in the most radical,
exemplary versions of the drug-oriented conception, it's a case of what
could be called a saintliness without God or a sacredness without God.
The links among intoxication, the sacred, and drugs have been explored,
moreover, time and again in literature and poetry. That's the first version
of the question of enjoyment, which I call the libertarian version.

Then there's the liberal version. It's something else altogether: it's
about buying enjoyment. That's the imperative. This is actually how the
world works, with the pervasive suggestion that it's always possible to
buy at least a small bag of enjoyment, a small quantity of something
that releases you for a little while. The problem with this imperative is
that it's meaningless, because enjoyment can't be bought: inasmuch as
it is the Thing, is connected to the Thing, it has no equivalent. It can't

be integrated into financial circulation. When it comes to buying enjoyment—and we all go along with this imperative; no one's completely exempt from it—we always buy empty shells, mismatched pieces, and we always get ripped off. Whether you're buying a car, a prostitute, or a vibrator, ultimately, buying enjoyment is only ever buying its packaging. The liberal imperative of enjoying is a subtle doctrine of packaging. It's the opportunity to buy a packaging of enjoyment, which, unlike enjoyment itself, can be changed and substituted and is endlessly interchangeable, surrounding a missing, absent enjoyment. The packaging, at least, will have been sold. This is also a kind of nihilism because, as regards the promise of enjoyment, what is sold is only the packaging of nothing, and clearly, as a result of selling packagings in which nothingness is wrapped and which must then be thrown away, the world itself is turned into a waste product. The imperative of liberal enjoying aims to turn the world into a waste product, into a heap of garbage, of packagings of empty or missing enjoyment.

We're talking about our world, about the images of the present time. It's important to see that we're dealing with the constant blurring between two different figures of enjoying: one of them takes it upon itself to become the waste product of the world, in the drug-oriented vision of existence, while the other, through the selling of vanished enjoyment, turns the world into a waste product. The only thing the packaging retains of enjoyment is its garbage aspect, its trashy aspect. And I include advertising, which is one of its main forms, in packaging.

I'm going to say something that may seem provocative and rather biased, namely that a large swath of the environmental movement wants packaging, waste, to be biodegradable and the packaging's contents, if any, to be organic themselves. The organic within the biodegradable, or, in other words, a healthy enjoyment, a natural enjoyment, in nonpolluting packaging. I'm not sure this is the solution. I'm exaggerating, no doubt, but I don't think what I'm saying is entirely wrong. I really believe that something about the environmental subjectivity involves grappling with this issue of enjoyment, which, it is hoped, is not so deadly and is steeped in neither the extreme nihilism of the drug-oriented vision of existence nor the liberal nihilism of the predominance of packaging over the thing itself. But it's not as easy as all that. In order not to share in these nihilisms, a radicalism of a different sort is needed. It's not enough to keep saying "Let's try to make sure that a real enjoyment is sold"—this is the "nature" aspect, i.e., meadows should be real meadows, fish should be real fish, jam should be real jam, and so on—and "Let's make sure that the packaging doesn't suffocate the visible world, doesn't turn the world into a garbage heap." These feelings are understandable but already too internal to nihilism, since what is hoped for is a rectified nihilism, a reform of nihilism, a reform of nothingness. But nothingness is hard to reform. I'll just finish this digression with this thought: nobody is comfortable with contemporary nihilism.

So let's keep the imperatives in mind: on the question of nihilism and its connection to enjoying, the first type of connection involves turning oneself into the world's waste product and the second type, turning the world into a waste product. The synthesis of the two would be turning oneself into the waste product of a waste product. If the world is a waste product and you turn yourself into the world's waste product, then you're turning yourself into the waste product of a waste product. This is the cutting edge of contemporary nihilism, which establishes the element of subjectivity as the waste product of a waste product via the complex circulation between libertarian nihilism and liberal nihilism—all of it, I repeat, under the injunction of enjoyment, as though there were no more serious human endeavor than to enjoy. That's the primary imperative and the true meaning of the death of ideologies: let's not kid ourselves, what the human animal wants is to enjoy, and that's how you get it, with the result that it turns the world into a waste product and turns itself into the waste product of a garbage heap.

Given all this, we might be inclined to think that philosophy is really right not to want to know anything about enjoying! The imperative of enjoyment is particularly deadly and leads to our becoming the Thing ourselves, garbage, either in the order of the world or in the order of self. So it is ultimately quite true that if you're under the emblem of enjoyment, something like thinking or philosophy becomes impossible. And it's only now that we know how right the ancient figure, the Greek figure that connected philosophy with asceticism, was, and to what extent enjoyment, in that form, is deadly and incompatible with thinking. So we need to reactivate, find strong new figures of philosophical asceticism and propose a modern asceticism. There is an asceticism in Deleuze's work, for example. In any thinking that is the least bit self-respecting today, there is a proposition of asceticism. This doesn't mean putting on a crown of thorns or hiding in a hole. It just means detaching oneself a bit from the imperative of enjoyment in its twin, libertarian and liberal, forms.

That's one possible conclusion. But it's also possible to come to a different conclusion and say that enjoyment should be thought, from within philosophy, in another way. It can be argued that, in its nihilistic figure, enjoying is a false concept, a false experience, and that right from the start what is being proposed is a bad kind of enjoyment. That's why its consequences are so disastrous. So, rather than rehabilitate asceticism, we need to rehabilitate enjoyment, to think it otherwise. This is how Jean-Luc Nancy has attempted to respond to the challenge posed by psychoanalysis, by proposing an affirmative theory or thinking of enjoyment. He returns to this a number of times in his work, but perhaps the most striking of his essays is one from 1986, "L'Amour en éclats," which was reprinted, in somewhat revised form, in *Une Pensée finie* in 1990 [translated as "Shattered Love" in *The Inoperative Community*, 1991; reprinted in *A Finite Thinking*, 2003]. It is a very interesting philosophical essay on the question of love, part of which is devoted to the question: "What does it mean to enjoy?" This question is not pursued all that often in traditional philosophy. Nancy's position could be summed up as another attempt to get away from hedonism, from contemporary pleasure-seeking individualism, not through a form of asceticism but through a reformulation of the question of enjoyment. To that end, he puts forward three propositions that I think are very important.

The first proposition is: "To joy [*jouir*][2] is no more impossible, as Lacan had it, than possible, as the sexologists would have it."[3] Let's leave aside the issue of whether Lacan actually said that "joying" was impossible. This statement means, in any event, that both of the nihilisms of enjoyment must be rejected. Clearly, the idea that "joying" is impossible is the libertarian, extremist, radical conception, in which "joying" is beyond all bounds and all ties to the world. In the end, "joying" is connected in one way or another to death. Only what is impossible is worthwhile: that is the contention of libertarian "joying." Only this impossibility is real, only "joying" is truly real. But, for Nancy, that's not right. As the sexologists would have it, enjoyment is possible: this is liberal enjoyment, enjoyment that you'll buy from sexologists or from anyone selling it. Nancy's proposition, according to which "joying" is not impossible but not possible either, simply means that he will keep enjoyment out of both the nihilisms that have become attached to it, the radical, deadly nihilism of drug-oriented existence and the convivial, commodified nihilism of liberalism. In other words, "joying" neither requires death nor can it be bought. That's what this first negative proposition tells us.

So it will be necessary to say what "joying" *is*. Nancy then offers a second proposition: "Joying is the traversal of the Other" (106, trans. modified). "Joying" is indeed a touching, a traversal, a movement of being itself but of being as Other, as Other in itself, as Other that is itself capable of being other than self. So "joying"—which Nancy obviously connects very strongly to joy, playing on the similarity of sound between *jouir* ["to joy"] and *joie* ["joy"]—is the joy of being insofar as it is the traversal of the Other. But what exactly is this traversal of being as "joying"?

Then comes the third, key proposition: "To joy is an extremity of presence,[4] *self* exposed, presence *of self* joying outside itself, in a presence that no present absorbs and that does not (re)present, but that offers itself endlessly" (107). This is a very deliberate definition. A few remarks are in order.

We can see clearly what Nancy's attempt, or temptation, is: it is to say that "joying," enjoyment, is neither narcissistic nor selfless. It is not a purely self-centered relationship, a relationship of absorption of self by the self, a submersion of the subject in itself. But neither is it pure devotion to the Other, absorption into the Other, fusion with the Other, or, in its degraded form, a contract with the Other. This is how Nancy maneuvers between two nihilisms: enjoyment is not self-annihilation nor is it a negotiation with the Other. It is neither mystical nor commercial; it belongs to neither libertarian nihilism nor liberal nihilism. To "joy" is to establish a relationship with self outside of self: it is an ex-position of self, a self exposed, which is in-itself-outside-itself. It's not a representation, it's not a theater; it's a presentation. This presentation that doesn't represent is an offering.

In Nancy's essay, there are two crucial words: "offering" and "exposition." I would basically say that his whole ontology, which derives from Heidegger but inflects Heidegger toward an ethics of alterity, consists in understanding how exposition can be an offering. To expose oneself is to be required by an offering. That's the basic framework.

As regards "joying," something of self must of course be involved, something Nancy calls the absolute singularity of enjoyment. No one can deny that enjoyment lies in the singularity of the person "joying." However, we shouldn't think that the essence of "joying" lies in oneself, in self-enclosure. It is important to grasp the outside-itself of the "joying" self: it is the traversal of the Other, to such an extent that the self is also the Other. Where it can expose itself absolutely in "joying," the "I's" singularity has the potential to be other, to be outside itself. At the same time, as an offering, it begins again; it can offer itself endlessly, it is not closed up in the unicity of a representation. As a result, enjoyment becomes an experience of being itself. This is how Nancy attempts to respond to the challenge imposed on us by the most extreme contemporaneity regarding this issue of enjoyment, through both the exorbitant emphasis on the issue of enjoyment and the nihilistic impasse in which it is stuck. In an admirable effort, he attempts to propose, expose, and offer a way forward.

That said, I don't share this point of view. I admire the definition, but I think it's completely wrong. An enjoyment of that kind can only be the enjoyment of angels. So I'm going to take up Nancy's third statement and discuss it point by point.

1.   "Joying" is never an extremity, an extremity of presence. It's never something that's reached the way an extremity is, let alone an extremity of presence. It's the extraction of a section or slice, captured in discontinuity. That's why recovering from enjoyment is rather disconcerting: the aspect of rupture is more prominent than that of extremity.

2.   "Joying" is not an exposition; it's not a self exposed. That's too "soft" a version. "Joying" is an *imposition*, not an exposition. More specifically, I'd be willing to say that it's the exposition of an imposition, and it's impossible to eliminate that dimension. We're all well aware that the question of enjoyment, as it's experienced sexually, is always the question

as to what the moment of imposition is. Basically, it's impossible to ignore the dimension of violence in all enjoyment inasmuch as it's violence done to oneself first and foremost, a wresting of enjoyment from oneself, which results, moreover, from a certain kind of hard work. In this regard, we need to stay close to the sweat of bodies, or else, as I said, we'll be talking, like the Byzantine theologians, about the enjoyment of angels. There is hard work and violence, the exposition of an imposition, in enjoyment, for a discontinuity that is not an extremity but a rupture.

3. "Self joying outside itself": I understand the tension, but it's only intelligible in the sexuated position. If you want to think through this "self outside itself," you have to connect enjoyment to the question of sex, as a difference of position, not necessarily of biological sex. "Self outside itself" is not thinkable as if self and outside itself had to do with the same self: the self of the outside itself isn't the self of the self. A complex transfer is involved, which effectively means that something has to be shifted from oneself by relying on an outside-itself that is a sexuated outside-itself. There's no such thing as an indeterminate outside-itself.

This is where the disagreement lies between Nancy and Lacan. For Lacan, the outside-itself is so "outside" that there's no relationship at all. In sex, the self has no relationship with the outside-itself. Of course, we don't have to agree with Lacan about this, but the fact remains that he is asking the real question, namely, to what extent the outside-itself of the sexed relationship—or of enjoyment as traversal of the Other—calls forth a self that is not a self in regard to which there is an outside-itself. Even if you don't necessarily agree with the Lacanian axiom that "there's no such thing as a sexual relationship," it is still undeniable that there is no transitivity between the self and the outside-itself.

4. "Presence that no present absorbs": I would turn the statement around and say that enjoyment is a present that no presence absorbs. It's a present wrested from time, in such a way that it isn't presence. Enjoyment is a pure present, which may be a long-lasting present but which, for the whole time, remains a present that does not present any presence. It is, if you like, a present that is embedded in the pure present of the traversal of the Other but that brings forth no presence. We know full well that presence only returns post-enjoyment. This is

the role traditionally assigned to tenderness. Tenderness after orgasm is the present giving way to presence. In orgasm, on the other hand, there is a demonic or ecstatic present, something that happens in the order of the pure present where presence fades away. You're happy afterward, with a different kind of happiness—which is not enjoyment—to recover something like presence. You're glad to see that the other person is there. This is presence, but only insofar as it has been eradicated by the present, by the violence of the present. Nancy's statement overlooks the influence of fantasy in enjoyment, an influence that is complicated, and variable depending on the positions of the sexes. Something like a representation adheres or sticks to enjoyment. It's not true that it doesn't represent: it also represents, it's also dependent in a certain sense on representation.

5. "Offers itself endlessly." I'm not sure "offer" is the right word. The truth is, there's something about enjoyment that's like repetition, something that is constantly called to repeat itself, to want or need to repeat itself, since there's nothing else you can do with enjoyment but repeat it. Enjoyment is by definition something that has no use, no purpose other than itself. This something may return: that's the most you can hope for it. "Offer" weakens the insistent nature of the question, which is inherent in the useless consummation that enjoyment is, useless because it has no purpose or end other than itself.

So I disagree with every word of the text, but I admire it and can see it as a remarkable and necessary attempt to find a way forward in the effort to detach the question of enjoyment from its contemporary alienation. However, I don't think we can address the question of nihilism directly by way of the question of enjoyment. What I mean by this is that we need to return to enjoyment but from a different angle than itself. Enjoyment can't be dealt with on the basis of enjoyment: in trying to release it from the grip of nihilism, we fall back into an Edenic conception. Yet that is precisely the conception Nancy proposes: that of an enjoyment cut off from its real, of a power detached from its real obliteration. But its real is much more than the contemporary influence of the propaganda promoting enjoyment.

Accordingly, I think we have to partly, and at least temporarily, accept psychoanalysis's anti-philosophical verdict that philosophy doesn't want to know anything about enjoyment. In any case, philosophy, when put to the test, which I'm proposing to it here, of thinking the contemporary, won't begin with enjoyment. It will methodically turn away from it but still in the hopes of being able to return to it. Methodically turning away from it will point to a way that won't make enjoyment the prime authority for the understanding of the contemporary. Because in that case thinking falls under the jurisdiction of nihilism.

This quarrel with Nancy was thus an enormous preamble to our question.

Now—since we're not beginning with enjoyment, even if we hope to come back to it—I'd like to remind you of the four maxims of thought that will serve as our real starting point:

1. We must oppose the democratic emblem.

Just as an aside, I'd like to emphatically repeat that it is not my intention to abandon the word "democracy." For the time being, "democracy" will be taken to mean the contemporary fetish, but there are other possible and real meanings and uses of the word, which I'll also try to reconstruct. "Democracy" is understood here as a constitutional fetish, as a figure of state representation. It is used as a noun, as, for example, when people talk about "the democracies." But I think that there's no legitimate use of it except in the adjective form: this or that can be said to be democratic. There are democratic processes, decisions, and subjectivities. But there is no such thing as *democracy*—that's a fetish of the state—any more than it's acceptable to speak of *the* democracies, let alone the Western democracies. But there *is* such a thing as the democratic, and I'd say that part of the problem is to free it from its capture, its monopolization, by the noun "democracy." So, if we oppose the democratic emblem, it's in the sense of democracy or the democracies, of everything our societies pride themselves on. We won't concede the word to them. Instead, we'll recover the adjective's power, which has been wiped out by the noun.

2. We must try to distance ourselves from the naked power behind this emblem.

3. We must identify the exceptions.

4. We must find the vulnerabilities in the in-between order, that figure of transition, which is a figure of confusion.

Let's begin with the first maxim. What is the democratic emblem? How does it function as an emblem? The planetary expansion of the democratic would supposedly represent a possible peaceful order, a new world. This means that those who, for the time being, are impeding this peaceful order or making it impossible are the nondemocrats. If there were only democrats, we'd already have this peaceful order, but there are bad guys. Who knows why there are bad guys? . . . It's odd, if you think about it, but that's the way it is. Without these bad guys, we'd have a peaceful, consensual world. And it's this world that is globalizing.

To digress for a moment, "globalization" means that there's no world yet. The democratic emblem is the emblem of a world that has already found its principle, i.e., the democratic principle. The only problem is that a number of contrarians are preventing this principle from spreading and organizing the whole earth, which is infinitely perfectible, into a world. What the emblem is about is, first, that the principle has already been found, so there is no question of bringing a different world into being, and, second, that its expansion is underway, in keeping with a principle of infinite perfectibility. Despite the obstacles, democracy will spread throughout the whole world, although the bad guys will have to be bashed from time to time and things put right. This is why Fukuyama could say that it was the end of history: history had found its ultimate principle, democracy, as a matter of fact. The end of history—which Hegel sought and which he saw in Napoleon or in the Prussian state; which Kojève sought and which he saw in the fact that capitalism had spread all the way to Japan and that history had therefore conquered its own Orient—this end was finally found and formulated by Fukuyama in a thesis that many people subjectively agree with: we've reached the end of history in the sense that the world has its principle, the principle I've called capitalo-parliamentarianism. Now it's only a matter of this principle finally operating in places where it has not yet gained control over actual situations. So a world is assumed whose principle and immanent perfectibility we know, a world that does not have to become fundamentally different but only has to perfect itself in its own order, the democratic order.

I, for one—and this is the basis of my critique of the emblem—believe that we're living at a time when there's no world at all, not even, and especially not, in the form of the ongoing globalization of a world principle. It is misleading, or even tantamount to a sham, to say that there's a world. This doesn't mean there are no situations, capital flows, deaths, and so on, but it leads to introducing a new distinction into the nihilism concerning the world.

- The first figure of nihilism is: There is a world, but this world is meaningless. This is the most common thesis, the absurdist thesis. There is a world, but in people's minds this world is absolutely devoid of meaning. This is existential nihilism: the world exists, and we exist in the world, in the world and for the world, but this world has no meaning.
- The second figure of nihilism is: There is no world. This thesis means that the nihilism isn't existential but ontological. It is the being of the world that is lacking; there is no being of the world as such. There is not a lack of meaning in what there is but a radical incoherence. There is only an inconsistent multiplicity.

With that, we could resume the discussion with Jean-Luc Nancy. In his 1990 essay collection, *A Finite Thinking*, the introduction includes a long note about the world. For Nancy, the world is the expansion of existence beyond human reality alone. It's the application of the category of existence to more than just humanity. It's a meditation on animals, stones, stars, and so on. It's the answer to the question "Why is there what there is, all there is, and nothing but what there is?"[5] I personally disagree with this formulation. First of all, "all there is" doesn't mean anything. What there is isn't all there is, and whether it constitutes a world is a different question. Second of all, I don't think that there is only what there is. There isn't all there is, and there isn't nothing but what there is. That's a Leibnizian conception of the world:

why is there something rather than nothing? Why this world rather than another? Leibniz is the philosopher of the question of the world in the sense Nancy asks it: "World" is a category of existence, which authorizes asking the question of existence with regard to all there is. Jean-Luc Nancy's world is the locus of the event of the "there is," of existence as existence that surpasses human existence. It's a category of the meaning of being, the locus of a meaning of being.

For me, "world" cannot be a category of the meaning of being. I understand "world" in a different way. "World" is a category of the contingent arrangement of being-there. There is a world when there is a logic of being-there, of appearing, a logic of contingency, if you will. And, consequently, there is a plurality of worlds, a plurality of logics, a multiplicity of possible and real worlds, and it may be that there is no world. All it takes is for the "there is" to be devoid of logic, to be illogical, or between two different logics. That is indeed what I would say about our world inasmuch as there isn't any: it is between two logics. So there are, and have always been, two meanings of the word "world." Either the world is the source of meaning, the locus of the source of meaning (Nancy), or the world is just a logical, possibly ambiguous or indeterminate, figure of appearing.

Given this, things must be seen in their historical perspective. These two meanings of the word "world"—the world as an answer in terms of meaning to the question of what there is, and the world as a multifaceted logical figure of appearing—arose at the same time. Plato keeps both together. He keeps the source of meaning and the transitory logical figure of appearing stuck together, as it were. His great work on the world is the *Timaeus*. The *Timaeus* is an account of the cosmos, that is to say, of the world. In this account, Plato, without ever clearly naming them, subtly plays on the two possible meanings of the world, the world as the totality of meaning and the world as a construction, as a figure, or even as a machine. He tries to keep both these senses of the word "world" together. This is what you hear at the very end of the *Timaeus*. It's one of the rare conclusions of a Platonic dialogue in which Plato seems perfectly pleased with what he's accomplished. Often, the dialogues kind of fizzle out: "We weren't successful, we'll have to try again, see you tomorrow . . ." But here Socrates-Plato is clearly very pleased, and the closing lines are dedicated to the world:

> Let us now declare that our account of the universe has reached its end. For our world has received mortal and immortal living beings and has been completed in this way: as a visible living creature containing all creatures that are visible, a perceptible god which is an image of the intelligible, as the greatest and best, the most beautiful and most perfect, this heaven, being one and unique in kind, has come into being.[6]

This is a beautiful and mysterious passage that has two possible meanings.

On the one hand, the world is in the perfection of meaning. It is in this respect that it is a very great, very good, very beautiful, perfect god. For it is (I'm translating it again, staying close to the Greek) "a sensible god that is the icon of the intelligible god." This means that the world is the source of meaning: although sensible, it is in the light of the intelligible. It is a visible icon of the intelligible god. But it is also a visible living creature that, as I'm retranslating it, "situates all visible living creatures in accordance with their container." It is a logic of visibility, the general container of the visible, a topological logic of the visible world. This is superb, for in this conclusion, Plato, contented and lyrical, attempts to glue together the two meanings, the world (why is there this rather than something else?) and the question of a harmony of appearing (the topology of visibility).

I will take "world" in its second sense, because you have to choose between them. Nancy chooses the first sense in its secularized, post-Heideggerian form: the world should be the icon of the intelligible god, but since there is no creator god, it will settle for being the existential icon of meaning. *I* would say: what is meant by "world" is the visible living creatures' situation, ultimately humanity's situation. And given the situation of the visible living creatures, I would say that today there is no world. Indeed, the world isn't the container of all the visible living creatures; on the contrary, it deprives the overwhelming majority of human beings of their visibility. It isn't a container but an expulsion. It is a protocol of exclusion from the visible, not one of situation in the visible. Hence the cardinal importance of the category of the excluded.

Let me just mention a couple of things about this, quickly, because I'm not really going to elaborate on it. The question of the existence of the world isn't the question of objective wealth; it's the question of names. What constitutes a world is who is named and who isn't, and therefore who is counted and who isn't. I will argue that in the old world, the world that probably stopped existing in the years 1970–1980, there was a world. This doesn't mean that that world was perfect. It wasn't the cosmos of the *Timaeus*; it might have been horrible in many respects. But the existence of the world and the assessment of the world are two different things. In the old days—about thirty years ago; we age fast—there was a world, in the sense that any worker or peasant farmer had a potential political name, an inscription in class and national liberation struggles, and so on. Nobody lacked a potential name. This world gave out the names and inscribed them in different camps. There were names and a distribution of names. What I call a world is, in a way, when, however remote from any figure of power someone may be, they are nevertheless not precluded from receiving a name. This name creates a future for them—which may be said to be false or illusory—but having a future, even a fragile or illusory one, is not the same thing as not having one at all. But we are in an in-between period when a huge number of people have no names. That's what democracy is in its emblematic sense: it's the acceptance of non-naming. There's no need for names since we're all equal before commodities! Most people have no name other than being excluded from the advantages of the false world. "Excluded" is the name of those who have no name. No name, no future. Nowadays, a peasant farmer has no name. In the past he could have the name of "Third World peasant farmer," which connected him to a historical process. That's all over now. As a result, he has no name, no future, no hope. Hope is a vague imaginary; a name inscribes you in the symbolic. The overwhelming majority of people are not inscribed. They count for nothing. As their only model, they're offered the societies that are not theirs, a vague promise, to which nothing connects them except being excluded from wealth, from democracy, from the West, and so on. "Market" and "globalization" are the names of what is not a world. "The market" is truly the symmetrical opposite of "excluded," because the excluded are excluded from the market. "The market" is the name of those who have no world.

Next time, I'd like to explore this issue and examine how the relationship between the lack of a world and the democratic emblem works, because I'm going to argue that there's a relationship between the two. We'll proceed by way of a reinterpretation of Plato's critique of democracy. This text, Book 8 of the *Republic*, is frowned upon and frequently characterized as totalitarian. Whatever the case may be, we'll see that there's one thing Plato touches upon, which is the connection between a certain image of democracy and the lack of a world. This is the relationship that I'll attempt to bring to light next time.

Session 4

January 30, 2002

At our last session, I introduced the hypothesis that the distinctive feature of the present time is that there is, strictly speaking, no world. Needless to say, in so doing I had to make a decision about the word "world," which has two principal meanings: on the one hand, the world as the source of meaning, the world as the horizon of meaning for all experience, and, on the other hand, the world as a logical figure, the consistent distribution of appearing, in terms of what is counted, accounted for, and thought in its exact place. I told you that it was striking that in the *Timaeus* "cosmos" still meant both things at once. Indeed, Plato holds together both meanings of what he understands by "cosmos," and later a division, a separation, occurs, with the result that there are valid, coherent, but conflicting interpretations of the *Timaeus*. As for us, we're going to take "world" in the second sense: the world as justice done to the visible realm, or, in Plato's words, the cosmos as "container of visible living beings," as that which does justice to existents in the fullness of their visibility. This is why I claim that there is no world and that we are in an in-between period, in the time between the absence of one figure of the world and the creation of a figure yet to come that is still obscure. This is, of course, a question that has to do with the problem of time. What time are we in? This should be understood as: What is our fundamental temporality? I think that our temporality is an in-between one, too. It's a temporality concentrated or focused entirely on itself. We can therefore assume that there is no world, in the sense that we are in an in-between period, between a worn-out, deteriorating, exhausted world and a world that is not yet either calculable or foreseeable. One of the signs of this absence is the extreme uncertainty over naming. I suggested that the world today is the market that's in fact called "the world market" and that, ultimately, the distribution of names either includes or excludes. In the end, there are those who benefit from the market, whose lives can feed off the market, and those who don't benefit from it, whose lives are actually foreclosed or excluded by the market. These are rough but fundamental categories. Indeed, "excluded" is not a name; it's the word for the absence of name, just as "the market" is the word for a world that's not a world. "Globalization," moreover, means that there's a process that will, perhaps, lead to a world, or that is trying to constitute a world, but that no world, strictly speaking, is present in our present.

On that basis, we will transform the question of democracy by asking what relationship there is between the absence of world and the democratic emblem. What makes democracy the emblematic political name of an age that is in-between with respect to the question of the world? This is a precise, almost technical, observation. Behind it, there is a very interesting problem that can be formulated as follows: Of what world is democracy the democracy? What is the world that's configured under that name, the world of which that name claims to be the positive emblem?

It is in this connection that I'd like to reread Book 8 of Plato's *Republic* in a somewhat new way. There's an obviously hostile presentation of democracy in this book. It's a well-known, very controversial text. Of course, for Plato as for us, democracy is a system of government. So "democracy" is taken not in terms of real politics, politics practiced by the masses—besides, in that case, it's called "mass democracy"—but as a form of government, with constitutional freedoms, a general regulation of the issue of opinions, an elected government, etc. Plato's approach is one of the founding texts on the issue, and there's clearly a reactionary aspect to it. There's no denying it. It's not true that it's a persuasive and

profound analytical text from start to finish. The politically reactionary aspect is related to Plato's conviction that democracy won't be able
to prevent the overall collapse of the Greek city-state. Plato is basically
the thinker of the decline of the Greek city-state, which he intends to
save. But he thinks democracy is incapable of maintaining or preserving
this historical configuration, the Greek city-state, so he will advocate
a figure—this is the reactionary aspect—that he himself says predates
democracy, and even predates any form of state, a bit like the way Rousseau's social contract fictitiously predated any political configuration.

This issue of reactionism concerns us, too, because in our world—
which is not a world—we encounter a great many reactionary positions,
positions that might be called nostalgic. The most typical of these is
republican nostalgia. Like all true nostalgia, this nostalgia amounts to
wistfully longing for a state of affairs that never was. Nostalgia constructs its object, which it adorns with the real virtues of an imaginary
past. Was the French Republic admirable during the colonial period, in
the 1950s? At the time of the surrender to the Germans, in the 1940s?
At the time of the all-out repression of the workers' movement, in the
1920s? During the period of the bloody nationalism of World War I?
When it arose from the "final solution" of the problem of working-class
politics, i.e., the repression of the Paris Commune? Of course, you can go
back as far as Robespierre and Saint-Just, but you've got to have what it
takes and master the intense dialectic of Terror and Virtue in the service
of the public good! If it's just to go back to General MacMahon[1] or to
what Henri Guillemin called "the Republic of the Juleses"[2] (Jules Simon,
Jules Favre, Jules Ferry), well, forget about it. I'm saying this to point out
that this nostalgic position is actually a construct in the present. A construct in the present that's nevertheless reactionary because it invokes a
putative past as a more or less activatable norm of this present. There's
something like this in Plato, in the figure of aristocratism that he advo-
cates, that world of order and hierarchy in which everyone has their
place, and so on. Nostalgias are in actual fact almost always nostalgias for
order. Rarely do you find anyone who's nostalgic for disorder—although
that would be a much more interesting idea! And these nostalgias usually describe the present as the abandonment, repudiation, disintegration of that order, or, in other words, as decline. This isn't a criticism.

Any worldview is a dialectic of order and disorder. When I say that there's a world provided that there's an acceptable distribution of names, all I'm doing, after all, is evoking a figure of order, a figure of order in the names. Plato's aristocratic classifying theory is an ordered and hierarchical theory of classes, of groups. It is a meditation on the collapse, on the end, hence on a lost order. That is an indisputably reactionary aspect.

Let me just make a brief digression here. I've pointed out on several occasions that when Plato asks what is ultimately the reason that an order, however excellent it may be, at some point enters its twilight phase or its decline, he extends this inquiry to include his own proposition. Within Plato's political utopia, there's a theory of the inevitable decline that overwhelms the utopian figure itself. In the political field, the breakdown of the will is inescapable, even in the best of cases. Yet the really extraordinary thing is that Plato assigns the collapse of his aristocratic communism to a very specific point in time. At a given moment in the citizens' education, a disruption occurs in the requisite balance between gymnastics and music, and this disruption of harmony occurs to the detriment of music (which, for Plato, it's true, also includes poetry). The cause of the decline is thus the overemphasis on sports. That's food for thought—although it could be argued that, in today's world, there's also an overemphasis on music. And with the spread of mass phenomena, in this case music and sports, it is indeed a problem related to the constitutive imagery of the contemporary world. I've always been struck by the fact that Plato focused on this sort of thing, that is to say, education, culture. For him, the decline isn't connected with military defeats or the forgetting of philosophy but rather with the immanent balance between mass cultural phenomena related to the general education of citizens. To conclude on this point, let's recognize, then, in Plato's nostalgia for the aristocratic order and its stable hierarchy, as well as in this meditation on the inevitability of decline, the bleak political pessimism typical of all reactionary views.

That said, we're left with a question where this text is concerned. It has a conceptual aspect to it that can't be reduced to its critical, reactionary disposition and is linked to some reflections on the type of world formalized by democracy. Democracy, not just as a formal principle but as a figure of formalization of the world, raises the question of the subject that is connected to this world. And ultimately the main point will be: What is the world of democracy? What is the subject that is constituted within it? What description can be given of the democratic individual? We need to read the text without forgetting its reactionary dimension but taking it literally. We can then identify two theses:

1. The democratic world is not really a world. The world is a nonworld.
2. In the nonworld, the subject is only constituted by the relationship to its enjoyment, a relationship that has two forms: Dionysian abandon (that of the young democrat) and the indistinction between pleasures (that of the old democrat).

1.   Why isn't the democratic world a world? Well, because it's a world in which everything is assumed to be equivalent to everything else, and this, in Plato's eyes, precludes the configuration of a world. Let me remind you of this well-known sentence: "[Democracy] is an enjoyable kind of regime [*The first predicate! He doesn't deny that democracy is enjoyable.*][3]—anarchic, colorful, and granting equality of a sort to equals and unequals alike."[4] This actually means that democracy, albeit enjoyable—but being enjoyable isn't the only virtue possible—doesn't constitute a world because it doesn't establish an equality of Subjects but rather a possible equivalence of everything with everything else. Transposing this, we could say that what lies behind modern democracy is the general equivalent, the monetary principle of general exchange, which creates a potential zone of equivalence of everything with everything else through its monetary presentation. That's not what Plato is talking about, but there is still the intuition that democracy's general configuration of the world equates the equal and the unequal and therefore subsumes inequality under equality, an equality that can only be abstract, or formal, precisely because it incorporates inequality. Let's say that the democratic world is the world of universal substitutability. In a certain sense, anything can be substituted for anything else. It's a world that is not configured in the logic of its appearing. That's the meaning of its anarchy: "Anarchic" doesn't mean "lawless"; it means "universal substitutability."

2.   As for the subject, the democratic man, you've got to hear how Plato describes him when he examines the way he lives:

> From then on, I imagine, a young man of this sort lives his life spend-
> ing at least as much money, effort and time on unnecessary as on nec-
> essary desires. If he is lucky, he may not get too carried away with his
> orgy. As he grows older and the first flush of excitement fades, he may
> accept back some element of the party he exiled, and avoid complete
> surrender to the usurpers. Putting all his pleasures on an equal foot-
> ing, he grants power over himself to the pleasure of the moment, as
> if it were a magistrate chosen by lot. And when he has had his fill of
> it, he surrenders himself in turn to another pleasure. He rejects none
> of them, but gives sustenance to all alike. . . . And so he lives out his
> life from day to day, gratifying the desire of the moment. One day he
> drinks himself under the table to the sound of the pipes, the next day
> he is on a diet of plain water. Now he is taking exercise, but other days
> he is lazing around and taking no interest in anything. And sometimes
> he passes the time in what he calls philosophy. Much of his time is
> spent in politics, where he leaps to his feet and says and does whatever
> comes into his head. Or if he comes to admire the military, then that
> is the way he goes. Or if it's businessmen, then that way [in other words,
> start-ups!]. There is no controlling order or necessity in his life. As far
> as he is concerned, it is pleasant, free and blessed, and he sticks to it
> his whole life through. (274)

This description of the democratic man is all the more remarkable in that it is, on the whole, absolutely spot-on phenomenologically. What defines him is the interchangeability of desires and pleasures. With, I repeat, a certain abandon when he's young and, when he's old, a unique kind of wisdom, which consists in thinking that, at the end of the day, pleasures are all the same, just as everything in the world ends up being the same as everything else. This is the principle of construction of the democratic subject: a subject that accepts a complete indeterminacy of objects. This means that he bases his subjectivity on the interchange-ability of objects and is nothing but a disparate succession of desires attached to substitutable objects.

The thesis that will be of particular interest to me, because of the conclusions Plato draws from it, is that, basically, this is a world tailor-made for youth, a world whose main imaginary figure is and can only be youth. Even if those pulling the strings are often old men, they have to be young old men, so to speak. Concerning democracy, Plato speaks about this "form of government . . . so attractive and so youthful" (277, trans. slightly modified). Democracy's attributes are its pleasantness, attractiveness, and happiness. Note the hedonistic aspect of this political figure (it's the substitutability of pleasures). So there is something essentially youthful about the democratic system in terms of its norm. This doesn't preclude very respectable old men from being in charge. "Youthful" doesn't mean a government under the control of young people; rather, it indicates an inherent trait of democratic governments when it comes to the substitutability of pleasures. In another passage, we read: "The old descend to the level of the young. They pepper everything with wit and humor, trying to be like the young, because they don't want to be thought harsh or dictatorial" (276). In that sense, there's something about democracy that necessarily sets youth up as a norm. It's of course an internal norm, a living subjective norm, not a principle of government. Democracy's norm of life is the paradigmatic young man and the old man in sweats running after him. Plato ties this to the fact that the person best suited to the indiscriminate substitutability of pleasures is the young man. The old man takes what comes, while the young man is Dionysian as regards substitutability and perhaps more tempted by nihilistic practices. But, in any case, the old man follows suit. For Plato, this is pathological: in his orderly aristocratic eyes, it's the young man who ought to imitate the old man. We don't necessarily have to go along with him on this, but he was surely the first to have discovered what the press today calls "the cult of youth." He astutely diagnosed the fact that at the heart of democratic representation, of its doctrine of existence, there was this social phenomenon of promoting the young person as a paradigm of modern vitality. He correctly observed that the cult of youthful desire was inherent in this emblem and that, ultimately, the main imperative was to "get moving." Thus, the old man himself, crippled with arthritis, "gets moving" and tries to dance what everyone's dancing, to make people believe for as long as possible that he has remained very youthful. You can't help but admire how insightful the connection was that Plato established between youth and the democratic emblem.

The question we need to ask is: "What happens when a society's emblem is uniquely youth?" Well, there's a constant need to adapt, retrain, retire, or put people out to pasture. A fifty-year-old executive is considered too old. Thus, the contemporary buzz phrases are, for example: modernity at any cost, constant modernization, out with the old. And all this is at work in the figure of an eternal youth of the world, which has to be pursued as a norm and an ideal.

But what happens when there's no longer, or at any rate seemingly no longer, any positive use for old age in the emblems? I see two alternatives.

- First, the terrorist alternative of this figure. From the Dionysian essence of youth, the valorization of brutality, senseless brutality, of which young people are perfectly capable due to the uncontrollability of their actions, is abstracted as a political alternative. This is what happened with the Red Guards in China during the Cultural Revolution and with the adventure of the Khmer Rouge in Cambodia. In both cases, the active masses were made up of very young people. Likewise today, in some African countries, there are armed troops made up of twelve-year-old children, who have proven to be real savages.

- The other figure is the one I'd call cultural triviality, which is actually a figure of entertainment as a social paradigm.

The two can easily coexist. If you look, here and now, at the ordinary image of youth, you can see something of both. On the one hand, we're shown the nice young people of cultural entertainment, the reality shows like *Loft Story* [a toned-down version of *Big Brother*], for example, which show something like youth left to its sphere of musical flirtation, of diatonic sex, along with, if I may venture this oxymoron, a sort of commercial innocence. But behind it are the terrible thugs of the *banlieue*, armed to the teeth, those delinquents profiled in the statistics, on whom it's imperative to crack down. This is the interlocking of a twin figure of fascination, which can be either attractive or repulsive, depending on the circumstances. The first figure is essentially associated with triviality and general entertainment (it's the one the old man or the future old man will run after), as presented by the TV host, who is himself already a little past his prime. But we also know that in any TV series there's always the urban terrorist figure of the frightening young thug who terrorizes people. The norm of youth is actually the general social norm, with that ambiguity of the norms that makes the fascination appear as either positive or repulsive.

As a matter of fact, every emblem ends up being nihilistic, since it's a cover for nothingness, the play of nonthought. This is what Plato means, even if he doesn't use the word. If youth is the sole norm of a society, it necessarily means that something like a vacuousness or a nothingness is shaping that society from within. And democracy controls this vacuousness because, once again, democracy means that youth is the sole norm. In a sense, youth *has* to be a norm, if only because it's the future. But being a norm in terms of the future and being a norm in terms of the actuality itself of the present of that future are not the same thing. Needless to say, I'm not arguing against young people. Youth is the time of the future, sure. But we're talking about a completely different phenomenon here, that of "the young person" as emblem and normative fascination affecting society as a whole. This is nihilistic because it leads to the denial of the idea of a *shaping* of the future, of the idea that the future isn't some random interval but must in some way be shaped, planned for, anticipated. It is tantamount to eliminating the idea that society is immanently accountable for its future. If youth becomes emblematic, society is reduced to being no more than its present, its immediacy, and there's no longer the idea of an educational process. Let's not take "educational" here in its most minimal sense: "educational" is taken in the sense in which "youth" does indeed mean the future, but from the standpoint of its shaping, of its purposeful, carefully considered shaping. Even in a project of total revolution, of subversion of society, it remains a shaping, something that, as the future, derives from the present. The idealizing promotion of youth as a norm goes hand in hand with that singular figure of nihilism that amounts to eradicating the fact that a society must shape its future, whatever its dominant representation. Ultimately, this is really the meaning of Plato's description: we have nihilism because we have a conception of time as immediacy, as the unilateral promotion of the present. Long-term forecasts in our society are becoming increasingly shorter. They follow election or commodity cycles, and little by little they end up being like weather forecasts.

What we have here is the correlation of three terms: the absence of world, the democratic emblem, and the youthful imaginary, and these three terms are essentially correlated around a deformed conception of time, which has no temporal discipline other than the discipline of nature, the discipline of the primitive state of things. Plato's thesis is that this combination is a recipe for disaster. The future is like the return of the repressed: if it isn't shaped, it returns in the form of disaster. Disaster, says Plato, occurs when the people have "jumped out of the frying pan of subjection to free men into the fire of a despotism of slaves, exchanged their excessive and untimely freedom for the harshest and bitterest of servitudes, where the slave is the master."[5]

The whole point is to determine what's meant by "subjection to free men." We've got a new thesis here: "real" democracy consists in remaining in subjection to free men. "Free subjection" is an oxymoron whose meaning is as follows: subjection to freedom is subjection to freedom as the thinking or shaping (the immanent shaping) of the future. This, for Plato, is merely a relative danger—the frying pan of free subjection, which is opposed to the fire of a despotism of slaves—because such subjection prevents the absolute substitutability of pleasures. Freedom calls for a discipline that, as the shaping of the future, is opposed to the immediate substitutability of pleasures. This is really a "frying pan": a voluntary obedience. But in jumping out of that frying pan, you fall under the control of something whose nature, in Plato's eyes, is related to slavery.

Transposed to the modern world, that would mean: in trying to avoid subjection to a coherent political project of emancipation, you fall into the despotism of the slaves of Capital. In the guise of excessive and untimely freedom (the freedom of the substitutability of pleasures), you have the harshest and bitterest of servitudes. This reveals the secretly tyrannical essence of democracy: it lies precisely in seemingly "anarchic" insubordination, which affords the illusion that in this, and this alone, the unrestrained freedom of the substitutability of pleasures is enjoyed. But the substitutability of pleasures is only one particular form of freedom and by no means the definition of freedom as such. Freedom may be something completely different: the discipline of the project in its shaping, in its expansion, or in one's idea of a future. It then involves a certain amount of subjection: there is no project without a discipline of that project. The whole point is how the discipline will confront the freedom promoted by democracy, that of the substitutability of pleasures and the authority of the present. Because, sooner or later, democracy will reveal its despotic essence, the fact that it is, in and of itself, subjected to the despotism of pleasures, which has been called by an apt name: pure *consumption*, of both the false world and the self.

Thus, following in Plato's footsteps, we've established the connection between democracy and nihilism, a correlation that hinges on the question of the world and the question of time. For the nonworld is time as flight, as passage. Time as consumption, or consummation. And my thesis is that this is precisely what full-fledged democracy requires. What do people in a democracy wait for, other than for the economy to get better or worse? It's really meteorological: tomorrow the weather will be nice, or clouds are gathering, the weather will be bad.[6] It's all quantified, standardized, and totally unpredictable. The experts talk about cycles, but the average citizen couldn't care less; it's no consolation to be laid off because the weather's bad. That's what globalization is all about! Why isn't he happy? Being laid off is modern; the opposite would be old-fashioned. As he's Dionysian and young, he ought to be happy! Now there's finally a chance to get retrained, to change up the routine! To participate, if only by being unemployed, in the indispensable, constant "reforms"! I'm hardly exaggerating. I must stress this conception of time, according to which an erratically regulated present time is the time of modern life. This time retains nothing, no shaping of the future but not the past either, since the past, by definition, isn't modern. The prescribed time is the time of nihilism itself, a time that lets no time remain. It's a time without retention, "retention" to be understood in the sense of a dam retaining water. Retention is not necessarily old-fashioned or reactionary. It's a quasi-ontological disposition, which can take a variety of forms. There can be no creative project without a retention of time. But ours is a time of the squandering of life, of life as squandered or ruined. Youth, or the fabricated image of youth, is the emblem of this time without retention. It is, moreover, a construct, because the idol of "youth" has been constructed around three features:

- Immediacy, entertainment, or, in other words, the principle that everyday life without a future can be regarded as the figure itself of life
- Fashion as the succession, as the substitutability, of presents
- Movement in place, the "Let's get moving!" Rather than movement, it is actually constant restlessness. Movement is its own norm; from a qualitative point of view, there's no difference between it and immobility. Other societies have valued immobility and extolled slowness as the highest norm. Here, it's a peculiar kind of movement, one that is absolutely in place, not a movement of transformation of the totality as such, or a call to change the world, to make new suns come up. . . . You have to run, to run in place, because anyone who doesn't move will be eliminated, since the place is none other than the place of the race.

These features—immediacy, fashion consciousness, the imperative of movement in place—have been isolated as emblems that can be summed up with the word "youth," which explains why youth is the norm of it all. An ever-changing vacuousness—a mutable nothingness, another oxymoron—can thus be the transient, even televised, iconic image of the democratic process. This constant display of ever-changing vacuousness is incidentally not without its charms. I admit that I myself can sit there mesmerized before it, in a semicomatose state. And if so many people watch all this, in all its forms, it's because they see in it an image of the present time, an image that combines vacuousness and movement, that is, the inner changeability of nothingness, in a nondialectical way. What's more, it is rather cleverly contrived: there need to be standards; it has to be a respectable kind of vacuousness. This nothingness mustn't be a stationary one. So there's a kind of ultimately quite sophisticated drive, which, as everyone knows, is calculated and carefully thought out, to obtain this peculiar thing, a busy triviality. Often, the triviality is stuck in the inertia of its stupidity, and it's therefore not easy to make it mobile, to ensure that we can expect something from it. Shows require suspense. But what kind of suspense can there be in triviality? Movement thus requires complex processes, such as voting processes, for example. For a long time, I voted. I even ran for office once, but for ages now I've had trouble understanding how voting as a political process survives these exercises in changeable vacuousness! It's like going from voting for Loana and Christophe [the Season 1 winners of the TV reality show *Loft Story*] to voting for Jospin and Chirac. . . . What I'm interested in is the power of the imagery, because it works. There's something extremely grotesque about it, which I can scarcely believe isn't obvious. This is not a question of intellectual elitism. *Everyone* sees how grotesque it is. But that doesn't stop it from going on; the grotesqueness is part of its very nature. This is so in the context of nihilism, where it's appropriate for there to be a changeable vacuousness. It's a real image of the present time. You can't dismiss it as if it were of no importance: it's the present itself and has all the force of the present. It's impossible to negate the present in its very presence. It's only natural: everyone wants to live. Basically, there's this belief that life in nothingness is better than nonlife, better than death. But what we're told is that we have to choose between them. There's no third alternative. Either there's the norm of ever-changing vacuousness, of busy triviality, or—no one really knows why—things are inevitably deathly, totalitarian, fanatic, and so on. Ultimately, better nihilism than death. And everyone constantly rejoices, with a rather obscene and vulgar rejoicing, at the sight of all this, that is, at the fact that vacuousness is still preferable to nothingness. This has always been nihilism's power. Nietzsche knew as much when he remarked that nihilism's power stems from a single principle: Living for nothing is better than not living at all. So we arrive at this astonishing thing: "youth" is the name for all this, this busy triviality, this power of nothingness. When you think about it, it's an extraordinary figure, because there were eras when youth meant the power of something, the daring force of the future, not of nothingness. So we're witnessing a sort of reversal.

This first approach leads to the following conclusion: The contemporary world's emblem is the democratic emblem, and, in a certain sense, youth is the emblem of this emblem; it is really its image. Remember that youth, as the emblem of the emblem, is a construct, an image, an imaginary. It's a purely contextual word that does not refer to empirical youth but instead functions as a construct. Insofar as any construct requires bodies, it could be said that this is the way consumer society uses the youthful body. Maybe that's better, after all, than sending young people off to war, fired up as they are by the morbid passion of nationalism!

Youth as the emblem of ever-changing vacuousness has introduced us to an idea that would spread and become very important, namely that, like any emblem, this one crystallizes a conception of time. The conception at work here is that of time without retention. Clearly, if you want a doctrine of time *with* retention you need to seek out emblems other than youth as it's constructed today.

Our method, let me remind you, consists, first, in examining the emblem and then in distancing ourselves from naked power so as to identify the exceptions, to see whether there's any weakness in contemporary domination. But how can we distance ourselves from the power behind the emblem? How can we break free from the emblematic system and begin to get some distance? Since the figures of fascination are everywhere at work, what can "the place and the formula" of the distancing be?[7]

There is a reactionary approach—as we saw with Plato—that amounts to a peevish hostility toward youth, on the grounds that in the past, things were better. This is to turn the emblem, preserving it by reversal, into a reactionary symptom. I suspect Jean-Pierre Chevènement of having a penchant for the reactionary interpretation of the emblem![8] The campaign against the "little savages," his announcement that special youth detention centers were to be built: none of that strikes me as being the right approach. There is indeed a nihilistic cult of youth in contemporary society, but when it comes to actual young people, something different is involved. Thinking that the emblem of youth has to be violently destroyed in order for a time with retention to be restored is a trap some people have proposed. They indulge in nostalgia for repression, as if the young were responsible for the construction of the emblem, which is quite simply something our world has constructed. There's a lot less reason to blame the young than to blame the TV executives or the big financiers. Hostility toward youth is a reactionary approach we need to be wary of. The great Plato himself verges on this sort of reactionary grumbling in his critique of democracy.

So we should neither adopt a hostile attitude toward the predicate "youth" as such nor fetishize youth as an emblem. Instead, we need to maintain an egalitarian indifference to that predicate and push for its elimination as a normative predicate. It's certainly not great to be young, but it's not so bad either. De-emblematizing won't happen with the hostile or repressive reactionary approach, which is an absolute dead end. What's needed is a specific effort to eliminate the predicate, consisting of a certain kind of deconstruction of the notion of modernization or modernity. Perhaps we should work toward de-presentifying or de-fetishizing the present. But there, too, the danger lies in the overvaluing of the past, in reactionary nostalgia. The problem is, rather, determining what the future means, what a shaping of the future might mean. I'm absolutely convinced that the first step, where this emblem system is concerned, is to break with the dominant conception of time. We can't attain even a minimal resistance to the emblems of the present time without breaking with what youth is the emblem of, namely, the triplet of instant entertainment, the interchangeability of fashions, and movement in place. How can we make this break with the conception of time? We're not going to get very far into that today: it will be the second important step in our investigation. It is at any rate a problem of slowing down, because the pure present's principle of busyness is in fact speed. We're always being told that the world is changing at a dizzying pace and that we have to run to keep up with it. Predication on speed is the norm of movement in place. We've got to find a new figure of slowness. It can't be the old figures; we've got to come up with a new one. If you think about it, it's remarkably difficult to be slow. There's very little leeway. The problem is how to achieve a creative slowness, at the very heart of the hectic present. Movement itself, the present itself, needs to be slowed down. But we'll see that, then, the tragic temptation is to introduce an artificial slowness, which I'd call an ecstatic slowness, and it would be deadly because it's the slowness of stupor. In "stupor," the slowness of a narcotic [*stupéfiant*] should be understood. This is, once again, the possible norm of another type of nihilism, the nihilism that arises from a sort of desire to stop or suspend the temporal restlessness, but to do so through evasion. Let's beware of drug-induced slowness. We need to be able to invent a nonnarcotic slowing down that's not an artificial slowing down of normal competitive activity either. Philosophy has something to say about this. The history of this question began with Plato, when he said that philosophy is a long detour. The time of the long detour involves bypassing something or being willing to take a roundabout route rather than rushing right to the thing itself. Philosophy has thus had experience in how to circumvent time, how to impose detours on it. This is what we'll be dealing with next time.

Session 5

March 13, 2002

We had begun to examine what I proposed to call "the democratic emblem" insofar as, in the present time, it signifies a political capture of subjects and ultimately their incorporation into the consensus of the dominant powers. We reread Plato's famous text (Book 8 of the *Republic*) about the democratic state and its corresponding subjective character type. While I took into account the reactive, indeed reactionary, aspect of Plato's position, I showed that he had clearly seen that the substitutability of pleasures is a fundamental figure of capture and that it is central to the democratic emblem's subjective functioning. On that basis, I showed that democracy, in its contemporary sense, is directly related to the nonexistence of the world, to a nonworld situation. There is no world, which explains why some proclaim a new world order while others combat globalization. Whatever the case, this is the issue on which the debate is focused. The nonworld of contemporary democracy is a temporal flight, that is to say, an instance of planetary time as a substitutable, empty, and deferred present. It is substitutable because every moment is equal to every other one, none being declared strategic or decisive, and it is empty because these moments aren't incorporated into a representation of the future. They comprise a sort of vanishing present, which constitutes the dominant temporality.

Finally, I attempted to say that there was a combination—very interesting, philosophically speaking—of vacuousness and change, something that grounds change in nothingness itself. I called this a stagnant restlessness, or a restless stagnation, insofar as it combines, in a nondialectical relationship, a principle of universal mobility and a principle of stagnation. On the basis of this nihilism of time, I showed that a certain representation of youth functioned as an emblem and that if there was a contemporary cult of youth, it was ultimately because the word "youth" could be the obvious emblem of this vanishing temporality, of this ever-changing vacuousness. The emblem of the present time, or its fetish, is, as I said, first and foremost democracy, but the emblem of this emblem is an idea of this youth, of this youth of the nonworld, which is nowadays called its modernity or its modernization. The world, according to the propaganda, is constantly younger than its inhabitants, and all are required to meet the challenge of the modernity of the world, as the absolute figure of a primordial youth, which is, in a sense, always lost or irretrievable.

The provisional conclusion is that if we want to distance ourselves from what's behind the emblem, which is actually an extremely ferocious naked power, and therefore keep away from this ferocity underlying the emblem exhibited in its essential seductiveness, we absolutely must not adopt the sort of reactionary hostility to the young that, under the pretext of concerns about security, fuels electoral debates. That's an absurd approach, especially since the young are not to blame. On the contrary, we should adopt an attitude of indifference to the predicates associated with youth. These predicates include immediacy, entertainment, fashion, brands, shoes, innovation, modernity, team and entrepreneurial spirit, nonstop communication, conspicuous sexuality, sports, looks, roller skating, music playing in your ears, coolness, availability—you can come up with many as you like! That's what's called the youth of the world. I'm not saying we should systematically steer clear of them, but the most important thing is to acquire a certain indifference to these predicates attributed to the representation, deemed wonderful, of the youth of the world. The key to achieving this lies in the question of the representation of time. Indeed, we need to be able to propose what Plato called the long detour of thought, i.e., the possibility of slowing time down, of retreating from the uncontrollable speed of the world. Remember that it's speed with no direction, with no obvious motive. It's the speed at which the world must move, so to speak, motionlessly, if it wants to be true to its image.

Let me suggest a different approach. It is, I believe, impossible to be under the democratic emblem, and therefore under the emblem of this emblem, the youth of the world, other than under the assumption that the most important thing is the body. "Youth" also means that the contemporary democratic order is a democratic order of bodies, in a twofold sense. It is the bodies that are counted and valued. But, in addition, the body is the real meaning of the subject. A subject is above all a body. Some will say: "Congratulations! That's a really materialist doctrine!" After all, I myself concede that, in some respects, it's very true that there are only bodies. But it would be a mistake to think that, in the contemporary world, the subject is assigned to the body in a materialist sense. Far from being a basic given, or the simple fact that every subject is embodied, the democratic body itself is a construct, a construct appropriate for anyone who's able to live under the democratic emblem as a body. It is the body of the interests of the body, a specific, codified, constructed body, once the democratic individual has been identified as such. This can be formulated in two ways:

1. The individual corresponding to the democratic emblem is attested to by their encounter with commodities. This is what is counted as the contemporary principle of equality, as abstract equality. We know, moreover, that those who, for one reason or another, are not counted in this encounter are given the name "excluded." They are in a way excluded from this supposedly egalitarian encounter with commodities, and this is why they cease to be "real" democratic subjects. Because what attests to a really democratic subject is its correct, consumerist appearance before the glittering market.

2. This subject, for the reasons I mentioned, is valued for the visible signs of youth. In this sense, too, the subject is a body, a body valued for its preservation or survival beneath the visible signs of youth. I am purposely using the phrase "visible signs of youth," because people usually talk about the visible signs of age or illness. But that's just it: emblems are in this sense always

old things, because they're kept alive artificially. Who can fail
to see that, today, "democracy" is a stuffed fetish, a mummy, or
a sort of old lady being kept alive in an artificial coma? But it's
she, this dying old lady, who's snickering beneath the manifest
"youthfulness" of the executive who keeps fit with jogging,
organic food, the tanning booth, skiing, and tennis.

Basically, to be a body qualified to live under the emblem is first and
foremost to be neither excluded nor obsolete. That's the imperative of
the times. If you're excluded, your case will be examined with touching
sympathy, and if you're obsolete, you'll be urged to retrain. Those are
negative determinations, but this could also be expressed with different
predicate determinations. For example, you've got to be productive and
modern, or, to put it another way, competitive and "in the loop." As for
life itself, you've got to "have a good plan" when it comes to the body
that you are, with its willingness both to be validated by the encounter
with commodities and to be valued for the visible signs of modernity.
"Validation" means it's not excluded. "Valuation" means it's "in the loop."
Validation is commercial: to be always available for the encounter with
commodities, to be the eternal equivalent of a consumer, the customer
body, the kingly body ("the customer is king"!). As for valuation, it is
formally biologizing. Whence the extreme importance of physical fitness
for society's leaders. Entire journals have been devoted to this one single
issue, the extreme difficulty of keeping fit and having the requisite body.
Through validation and valuation, the democratic individual becomes
identical to their body.

This brings us back to something I already approached by a different route: enjoyment. The body is at the heart of my analysis because it
is central to the images of the contemporary world. The images of the
present are body images. Earlier, I said that what we were required to
do was join our bodies to the unspeakable Thing, to connect them with
enjoyment. And that almost familial injunction "Enjoy yourself however you can, enjoy yourself however you want!" is an essential kind of
joining of the body with the Thing, which is involved in all enjoyment.
But ultimately, the typology of the Thing (the Thing of enjoyment) has,
as I said, two visible signs, two identifiable features. On the one hand,

it's the Thing of detachment, something like a drug. And, on the other hand, it's the Thing of substitutability, of general equivalence, and that means money. Ultimately, the contemporary body, as formalized by the imperative of enjoyment, therefore consists, in the radical extremity of its composition, of drugs and/or money, and the circulation or permeability between them. One of you pointed out to me that this explains why nothing is more emblematic of the present time than the Mafia, because it's the very site where drugs and money are exchanged. That's why it's at the heart of the image of the present time. You just have to go to the movies to see this. The Mafia is the key social organization, the quintessential body, the collective body, with the particular element of cruelty that attaches to this substitutability when it's pervasive. The Mafia is drugs and money, with no intermediate body. From this perspective, our society could be said to be the society of the omnipresence of bodies as commodified bodies or as detached, substitutable, anaesthetized bodies, with all of this under a Mafia-like control. And this analysis, which enters into the question of the contemporary by way of the imperative of enjoyment, is confirmed by the regression analysis of the emblem, with which we come back to the fact that, at the heart of everything, there is the body. This is a first linkage between drugs and money. More generally speaking, we could say: commercial validation and biological valuation. Except that the combination of body value and market value has a name. It's even the generic name for it. Commercial validation and biological valuation with a linkage between the two is called "prostitution." So it might be vigorously argued that under the democratic emblem there is an ideal of social relations, a sinister ideal, which we'll say is of a prostitutional type. Basically, the prostitutional—as was clearly seen by Genet, with whom we began this seminar—is the emblematic figure of the emblem itself. We will therefore say that, in the major images of the present time, we discover the prostitutional identity of social relations in general.

Three objections, which I am going to examine, can nevertheless be raised to this hypothesis.

The first is that, overall, the trend in modern democracies has instead been to crack down on prostitution per se, to make it illegal. Prostitution has long been a public and established profession. For decades, the brothel was a remarkable French institution, a leading republican institution. The Third Republic was a republic of the brothel. That's where the politicians all went after the big conventions. They went as a group to the brothel. Read Maupassant. It was a major social function. You might say: it's not like that anymore; there was the Marthe Richard law [1946], the outlawing of brothels. The trend is not toward an expansion or an official recognition of prostitution but rather toward restricting it, making it illegal, and cracking down on it.

That argument is actually pretty weak. All it does is bring prostitution into line with another obscure fetish of our societies, drugs. Prohibition, its increase or decrease, isn't significant at the level we're dealing with. A reasonable case could be made that the real of the democratic emblem—what, at some point, produces a figure of it so real that it's obscene—is precisely what is supposed to remain hidden. Since what is presented under the democratic emblem, what its real is, is naked force, it's clear why it has to remain hidden. What must especially remain hidden is the fact that the naked force behind democracies has a very special tendency to be savagely exerted on the weakest bodies. Given that there are bodies, there are some that are weaker than others. We'll see that the naked force exerted on the weakest bodies is a crucial fact, as is shown by a simplistic but very important question: How is it that the leading world power can bomb Afghanistan and say that it wants to do the same to Somalia? Afghanistan and Somalia are two of the weakest, poorest countries in the world! And they are precisely the ones that the democratic imperial power has been hitting mercilessly for decades. Not England, or Germany, no! Not China, even if it probably would like to do the same thing. A colossus and its democratic cronies drop bombs on Afghanistan, Somalia, and maybe Iraq someday, after they've bled it dry. I know all the justifications (fear of the Islamists, etc.). But let's stick with the image for a moment: the United States mercilessly bombing the poorest people on the planet. This is not like the interimperial wars of the last century, when at least the French, the English, the Americans, and the Germans, all civilized people and democratic for the most part, killed one another, with millions of casualties that were civilized and democratic bodies. Why is there today the doctrine of war with zero casualties on the powerful country's side and a huge body count on the other country's side? It's because you're making war on zeroes! It's easy to avoid being killed when the people you're up against have only got sticks and a few guns! If it were war against a real medium-sized power it wouldn't be zero casualties. What's the connection with what I've been saying? It's the fact that here again is found, as a basic rule, the use of naked force perpetrated on the weakest bodies. There's something like this about prostitution in the strict sense of the word, which is why its suppression is also a complicit maintenance of it. So this is an important argument for making the prostitutional matrix in our societies the generic figure of exchange between valued bodies and commercial validation.

Now for the second objection. The legal normalization of prostitution, brought into line with salaried, unionized employment, has been proposed. Prostitutes will no longer be called "prostitutes" but "sex workers," who will be put back into the circuits of the ordinary salaried workforce, with unions, taxation, paying of income taxes, and so on. I, for one, would say that the wage normalization of this occupation strikes me as confirming its homogeneity with the general system rather than its heterogeneity. There's something about it that can be recognized as a legitimate occupation, but involving what, exactly? Involving what, if not the exchange of bodies and money? This is not the first time that legalization and unionization would serve to reveal an integration rather than an opposition. That's what happened with the worker revolts. The supporters of a fair unionization of the sex trade prove that selling one's sexual body for money is the ultimate symbol of there being only the body = money equivalence under the democratic emblem.

By the way, I've never liked the supposedly feminist slogan "My body belongs to me." It obviously underlies the fact that I can sell it. But what does private property, which has been at the very heart of every kind of oppression for thousands of years, have to do with it?

The third objection that could be raised is that, in one country or another, they've begun to criminalize the clients. This is the case in the Scandinavian countries. The client is the guilty party. But what does criminalizing the client prove? It ultimately proves that prostitution as a professional sector, as a dedicated site of the monetary exchange of bodies, may have actually outlived its usefulness. It is supposedly an old, obsolete figure, as compared with the generalized prostitutional. I'd see this as the shift from small- to large-scale industry. If the prostitutional is secretly an all-pervasive universal matrix of the trade in bodies, of the summons to appear in the encounter between commodities and the valuation of bodies, then prostitution, the oldest profession in the world, becomes archaic, outmoded. The prostitutional, on the other hand, becomes paradigmatic.

What does "prostitutional" mean, then? Well, that it's a figure of the reduction of every norm to the commercial potentialities of bodies—of which sex is but one variation—through the twin procedures of commercial validation and biological valuation. I'll let you find other examples of this. The suppression of a single, more or less illegal occupation doesn't mean that the general significance of that occupation is disappearing—quite the contrary. Instead, we'd better get used to the fact that the suppression of a single occupation in a particular sector isn't a sign that that that occupation is going to disappear but rather the sign that its mode of existence is expansionary and part of a generality of a different sort. It could be said (this way of putting it is a bit extreme) that the prostitutional is the democratization of prostitution—not in the sense of prostitution for all but in the sense that the nodal element of prostitution (namely, the equating of everything with a space reduced to the exchange of bodies and money) is a general figure that can't be equated with the particular form it has in prostitution strictly speaking. It can therefore be said that the prostitutional is perfectly compatible with the sectorial suppression of prostitution.

In this connection, I'd like to address in passing a taboo subject, the issue of pedophilia. What I think has to be said, at any rate, is that there's a forced involvement of children and adolescents in visual pornography today. Nobody can deny it. Visual pornography is forced on everyone. I'm not playing the stickler for morality or the prudish moron. We've got to face facts, accept the objective statement that visual pornography is increasingly forced on children, in a pervasive way—think of the computer as the gateway to porn sites . . . I contend that this forced (in the sense that it happens without any particular mediation) involvement of children in visual pornography is directly related to pedophilia as an obsession of public opinion. They're two sides of the same coin. If you don't understand the first point, then you won't understand the second one either, and vice versa.

I'd like to say a word about this depressing emblem of our times, the obsession with pedophilia. There should certainly be laws, inasmuch as every society, in one way or another, defines what a child is. I don't think anyone, apart from the perverts themselves, and even then, would dispute this. What is at issue isn't the unquestionable need to shield children from adult sexuality. The point is, how does that relate to forced exposure to visual pornography? If, on the one hand, you constantly insist on child protection legislation and go on and on about children's innocence, while at the same time these same children are exposed to the prostitutional commercialized world, the result will be a symptom that, I fear, will take the form of an obsession with pedophilia. In my view, this is also a sign of the pervasive prostitutional figure of contemporary society, with this mind-boggling coexistence of a commercialized visual exposure, of a tolerated pornographic nature, and totally obscurantist theories about innocent childhood. Here we are, a century after Freud, after all, and we know that the sexual curiosity of children exists. There is no such thing as the innocence of children. Or rather: it has no meaning other than a legal one. The law must specify who, by virtue of being a child, must not be a sexual object available to adults. That's necessary, but it has nothing to do with the popular notions of innocence needing protection. I think that the secret behind this distortion is the exposure and simultaneous concealment of the prostitutional heart of society as a whole. What can't be commercialized doesn't exist; everyone agrees about that. The child's "innocence" is their nonexistence as a body available for exchange. And since there are only bodies and their encounter with commodities, there is ultimately a legitimacy to sex traders, except in cases of supposed innocence, which is merely absence from the market. As long as individuals are subject to commercial validation and the valuation of their bodies, with a prostitutional linkage between them, you can expect to see a series of symptoms attesting to this type of configuration in the life of the society. The security-related obsession with pedophilia is one of those symptoms.

At the beginning of this seminar, we saw that Genet used the brothel as a metaphor for circulation. Today, I'd like to turn to a great French writer who anticipated the figure of prostitutional materialism as the secret figure of modern social relations. This writer is Pierre Guyotat. His work is extremely powerful. I can't put forward the thesis of the paradigmatically prostitutional nature of the contemporary body without thinking of him. His greatest book, in my opinion, was published in 1967, though it was really written between 1963 and 1965 (the dates are significant). It's called *Tomb for 500,000 Soldiers*. So we're going to go through this book a bit.

In Guyotat, the problem of the (completely fantasmatic) prostitutional is linked to an earlier figure of what we're talking about, namely, the colonial wars. The background of *Tomb for 500,000 Soldiers* is the Algerian War. Since we're at the tenuous beginning today of a return of the repressed as regards the Algerian War—the unimaginable atrocities of that war are starting to be investigated—it is worth examining how, in connection with or through the revisited and imagined material of the Algerian War, Guyotat presents, or proffers, what could be called a prostitutional cosmology. What he proposes is not just a sociology or an obsession. It's a theory of the world, a theory of the universe, that is ultimately a theory of the atomism of bodies. There are bodies, there are only bodies, and these bodies are actually like the atoms of frenzied existence, and I am saying "atomism" in the strictest sense of the word because there's a force of attraction between these bodies. Or rather, there are two distinct, inherent forces of attraction: sex and cruelty. They are by no means psychological or pathological elements but rather what conjoins the bodies in this atomistic cosmology, exacerbated, moreover, by the context of the colonial war. What you've got—and which fits right in with this seminar—is a sort of absence of world. There's the colonial war that lays waste to everything, displaces populations, destroys bodies, and crushes people's will. There's a frenzy of destruction throughout *Tomb*. What this destruction of the world lays bare is precisely an atomistics of bodies, elementally reduced to the flesh of bodies, sex, and cruelty. What I can do with a body, the way I can connect with a body, is related either to the register of sexual capture or to that of assault, annihilation, and so on, in the context of a world destroyed by the colonial war. Because all this—the absence of world caused by war's devastation, the reduction of bodies (the soldier's, the poor person's, the rebel's, and the prostitute's alike) to their corporeal atomic essence, as well as the primitive attraction, represented by sex and cruelty, subsisting among these exposed bodies—all this will take place against the backdrop of the indifferent beauty of the world. Of the world in the sense of nature, a nature completely indifferent to the atomistics of bodies. The subject matter of the book is devastation, the frenzy of destruction, atomistics, and against the backdrop of all that there's a metaphorics of indifferent nature. As a result, it resembles Dante to some extent, because it's an infernal-type violent poetic figure (the metaphor of hell is constantly present), but Lucretius even more so. It's like *De natura rerum*, as a generalized poetics of atomism, with nature's indifference to people's fate and the scattering of corporeal corpuscles, once the world has completely disappeared and the social bond has been broken. The book is organized in chants. Since there are seven chants, I think the reference to Lucretius is therefore a conscious, explicit one.

I'd like to discuss this under three headings, which will just be an introduction to your own eventual reading—a demanding one— of this splendid book. Splendid, written somewhat in the style of Chateaubriand, it is a contemporary book, no question about it, with a passionate loftiness of expression.

To begin with, what is an allegory of the absence of world? How can the fact that there's no world be expressed in literary terms? Next, we'll ask what relationship Guyotat establishes among death of the world, absence of the world, destruction of the world, and disappearance of the gods. This is a hypothesis, a post-Nietzschean hypothesis: if there's no world, it's because there's no God anymore. And the last point is the question of the prostitutional as a force both cosmic, linking everything together, and acosmic (since there's no world). In conclusion, I'll try to show you why we have to keep at a distance or at a remove from these three points.

The first point is the allegory of the absence of world.

What is the literary construction devoted to the allegory of the absence of world? Guyotat's referent, as I mentioned, is the colonial war, which is still relevant to us (and not just because the Algerian War has resurfaced). Indeed, what is the attack on the weakest bodies by the powerful of the day? Colonialism has always been about the destruction of all ties, the disconnection brought about by a temporarily superior race, a race that declares itself superior and *is* superior because it has all the rights over bodies. The book is dedicated to a relative of Guyotat's who died in a Nazi concentration camp. The colonial war is also right behind the Nazi camps (there are several direct references to them in the book). The interesting point is the question of what the destruction of the world is. This is achieved when there is an unleashing of the possibility of having the right over all bodies. If someone has the right over all bodies, then the world is returned to the atomistics of bodies and comes undone, never again to show anything but the attraction of bodies, their destruction, and their prostitutional enslavement. The events in the book will unfold in the universe of a world ravaged by the original principle of an absolute right over all bodies, which, in unraveling the social bond, reveals only two things: the atomistics of bodies, with cruelty and sex as a transient connection, and a timeless essence, a sort of indifferent earthly beauty. The thesis, a very strong one in my opinion, is that *when there is no world, there is nothing but Nature.* Today, owing to environmental alienation, we can see that a cult of Nature, directly related to the absence of world, is gradually developing. When the world comes undone, something remains vaguely glimpsed or desired: the timelessness or the beauty of Nature. Here are two excerpts that deal with the overall vision: the atomistic agitation of bodies as a world undone, and something natural that filters through.

> In the distance, out of the ruts of night, leap starving beasts, they slash the injured storks and the stray children. Human and animal cries then rise from the earth and men watch with indifference the mutilated night. The beasts, heavy, run away, their claws drawn in, toward the top of the hills, jump over ravines, carrying, between their fangs, throbbing prey. Springs gush out, newly born, in the darkness.[1]

And here's another, more lyrical, sample:

> Tonight, the beam lights up the sky, O stars! judgment of the nations, libertarian heavenly bodies, O mother! . . . listen to the footsteps of their astonished fauna; the placards of utopia rustle with the stellar wind; nations of wounded men arrived during the night, are lying

there, ignoring the scenery of flowers and springs where the blazing of
dawn awakens them; earth then covers itself with new tools; in every
ground of different level and colour, a plough, put up, is waiting to be
taken and my hands grip the wood covered with dew. (66)

Look . . . Bali deserted . . . neither cocks nor children cry . . . the
waters held up along the shores among the rushes are made heavy and
dark by blood . . . Vultures and rebels flee, their back pierced by the
sun . . . Look back, look back and while your eyes stirred in vain try to
reconstruct the slaughter uncovered by dawn, let a gentle dagger tear
your loins and the poison fight against your tears. (142)

I've read this to you so that you could hear the literary syntactical blend
of extreme beauty and convulsion—the convulsion of disaster, the convulsion of the nonworld, letting something timeless and unchanging show
through its cracks, like a kind of beauty unfolding behind the atomistics of
bodies. The allegory of the world, the literary challenge, is to express both
the changeability of the crack and what is seen through it. To express at
one and the same time the flaw, the defect, and the timelessness.

The second point is the death of the world and the death of the gods.

There's a hypothesis about the fact that the death of the world can
be symbolized by the death or the flight of the gods. We are in a more
classical, Nietzschean, or Heideggerian register, with the conviction that
there is indeed no world and there is no world because meaning has
withdrawn from it. I said before that "world" had two meanings: it's
either the pure logic of the visible or the distribution of meaning. If you
think that the distribution of meaning is the key to the world, then the
withdrawal of meaning means that there's no world. It is then something
like a withdrawal of the sacred, a withdrawal of the gods or a disappearance of the gods.

Let me read you a few excerpts that deal with this classic hypothesis,
to which Guyotat imparts a particular literary force.

Every day, the beaches below the sea front boulevard were covered
with bodies of young members of the Resistance, who landed at night,
only to be shot by the sea sentries. The victors had overcome easily:
they had conquered a city which was ridding itself of its gods. (11)

That's a beautiful way of saying that if a city rids itself of its gods, then somehow it is subject to being destroyed. There's a direct correlation between the idea of destruction, of defeat, and the idea of the gods' withdrawal.

Here's another excerpt:

> God, who has been at the point of death for three centuries, dies. His priests, in vain, strip the ritual service of his worship, whiten the walls of his temples. God had hidden the secret heart of man, man now sees his bestial heart, his eyes are unsealed, the smell of the beast chokes him, God dies at the moment of man's greatest solitude. (43)

This is an interesting theme. Guyotat links the death of God not to the progress of man's humanity but to man's discovery of his essential animality. Man sees his bestial heart. The definition of God is that God had hidden man's secret heart. When God dies, what man sees is his real heart, the bestial heart. Guyotat doesn't judge. He may even be saying that this is a superior lucidity. What emerges in the gods' withdrawal is the beast. The gods' withdrawal is like the reduction to the atomistics of bodies, because it sets man's bestial heart free. And the smell of the beast chokes him, as though in this withdrawal man was suffocated by his own animal smell. As though the bestiality of the human heart were suffocating man at the moment when the blood drains away and God has disappeared.

Or another one:

> In the intoxication of wine, you call your god, the dumb god, whose absence and silence curb the wrath of men. (114; trans. slightly modified)

The god can still be called, but the god called is the absent god, who alone can still keep anger in check. We've got a literary construction that consists in the invocation of the god as a dead god, for the sole purpose of salvaging what can be salvaged of a devastated world.

The third point has to do with the prostitutional.

Guyotat's text must be read as the only text, to my knowledge, that has ever proposed a sexual cosmology—in the strict sense. It's a theory of the human cosmos as being composed of bodies, between which sexual attraction first, then cruelty, constitute the only remaining figures of connection. It's a world destroyed; the world of the nonworld is like that. This results in a furious, frenetic allegory of a human cosmos abandoned to the random connection between bodies. If that's all there is, we'll have what Guyotat attempts to describe, to express: a nonworld of absolute sexual violence, violence to which everyone clings because it's the last connection, the last atomistic flesh-to-flesh connection.

This is an assessment of the Algerian War, but it's also a prophecy. If there are only bodies and commodities, the only remaining connection is ultimately close combat, sexual or nonsexual close combat. Everything else is monetary transaction. Monetary transaction or close combat, hence the simultaneous development of a vision of the world as driven by financial exchange (contracts) and of a frenzy of close combat as the correlate of contracts. These are the only two possible paradigms.

For us today, the advantage of reading this forty-year-old book (which is therefore about another era) is that it can be read as the description of a world in which the cosmic law is nothing but close combat. It's written with an almost unbearable sort of lyrical intensity. In any case, it can be argued that this is what's coming. I'm not saying what there is but what's coming, by virtue of the fact that, when something is set out axiomatically, there are consequences of it. So if we accept that the two basic laws prevailing are the laws of commercial exchange and close combat, then things will necessarily turn out as follows: first, the contract aspect will be exacerbated, and, second, close combat will be an immediate figure. This is the description of what the nonworld is. So Guyotat will present a prostitutional universe in the cosmic sense of the term, a universe in which bodies have no relationship to other bodies apart from physical or sexual aggression. A universe at the heart of which lies rape. "Rape," moreover, becomes the term for much more than rape. Rape is basically the moment when cruelty and sexuality are the same, the moment when the two connections between the corporeal atoms merge. There is the maximal, completely fatal attraction between atomistic individuals produced by the destruction of the world. I'll read you an excerpt, which is not one of the worst ones in the book. There is without any doubt a modern Sade aspect to it.

> In the evening, soldiers working at these sites return to camp, crammed in the trucks, with burning hot tilts, dazed by weariness and sun, grubby, munching rust. Along the streets of the lower city, the trucks drive at full speed, running over dogs, brushing past old men, women, covering them with dust and grease. The soldiers, tossed about, thrown against each other, excited by those violent contacts and by the sight of women, yell, spit, stand up against the rails, raise their fists, unbutton themselves, tear off, hanging between the barracks, the dried festoons of some ancient feast and tie them around their thighs. When the dust has fallen down again over the spittle, over the pools of blood and the quivering bodies of the dogs, men come out of the houses, drag those fuming remains towards the small gardens and the pits. Later, the forgotten bodies putrefy on the spot and mix with the sand. Cats, dogs, starving children smell out these carrion slabs, exhume them and devour them aside. (52–53)
>
> I sit on the heaped up corpses, blood wets my buttocks, a throat quivers under my cock, two breasts breathe under my thighs and I tilt my head backwards, and my eyes become lost in the starlit sky; the breathing under me weakens, my hard-on points toward the stars, my chest moves up again towards my throat, the jackals' paws claw the flagstones. At the bottom of the valley, the jeeps' and half-track vehicles' headlights dazzle the kingfishers mating on the reeds and on the pink shingles, the monkeys mating inside the ruins of the thermal power station, or playing on the motionless driving belts and gear wheels. At the noise of engines, breaths, moanings have started coming out of the pile of mingled bodies but, under me, the breathing has ceased and I lean back hands joined under the nape and I spread my thighs and I let my cock fall back on my belly and lift my belt. Headlights pierce the smoke. I spring up, I strike the comrades dozing in the vines, throat strangled by the grapes, and we run till morning toward the sea, to purify the harshness of our bodies and of our minds.

In slaughter and in fire, in laughter and relaxation while questioning, we bend forward, we vibrate, we weather like stones. And you love
me, you want to change my sharp-pointed cock into a child's hand,
change my glaring jaw into a casket for your tears; I, stone crushing
thee, my ploughed earth, fire burns all round and does not burn me,
sweat hits us, and here we are wandering in the night sky and suddenly twisted and whirling towards the rising sun, towards the zone
of silence where all the clashes of the battle assemble and sink into the
ground. (105–6; trans. slightly modified)

You can see what I mean by "cosmic atomistics of bodies": little by
little, there is nothing but a sort of jumble of bodies, the most frequent
symbolism of which in the book is embodied by the soldiers, the troop,
in which sex and cruelty merge in a figure of perpetual, immanent rape,
defining a sort of absolute savagery.

I'd now like to explain how Guyotat attempts to conclude, and indicate how *I* think we should continue the path. Once this atomistic fury
of sexual bodies has been described ad infinitum, Guyotat will hesitate
between two conclusions.

The first of these is that the only thing surviving is ultimately the
quasi-solar energy of doubt. All of this, this whole absence of world, this
unleashing of a sexual frenzy of bodies, leads the spirit to commune with
Nature's indifference through a sort of higher doubt. That's Guyotat's
first temptation. There's a beautiful passage about this:

I enter into unbelief with a quivering of joy. My forehead, I want it
crushed and squeezed by the bow of a litter, and my shoulders soiled
by vomit. O doubt, only eternity. (44; trans. slightly modified)

That's the first possible alternative. It's an attitude we could adopt
as we go along our own path: the only thing the world allows for is this
higher doubt, this doubt as the only eternity of a vanished time. If time
has vanished, if time is lost, the only eternity available is that of doubt,
and we enter into unbelief with a quivering of joy. This is a very compel-
ling thesis. Much later on Guyotat will add: "How can I live with a silent
heart?" The question of how to live, which is the question we are moving

toward here, in this seminar, is associated with the fact that if there's no world, then the heart is silent. How can we live with a silent heart? How can we live if we're unable to love? That's what this means. Love is probably impossible; there is nothing but the connection between bodies. In the element of doubt is the first answer. For doubt, at least, matches Nature's indifference, Nature's sublime indifference. The question of man no longer arises. Unbelief is unbelief in man, not in God (he's already dead).

But there's another hypothesis—which sheds full light on the surprising nature of the last chant, the seventh—which is that, when all is said and done, what is coming is a completely new beginning of the world. What is coming amid this devastation is the dawnlike new beginning of the whole world. Amid this sort of atomistic frenzy of sexual and violent bodies and the universal war of all against all, what is coming is a new dawn, which is developing invisibly. Chant 7 presents a new figure of Adam and Eve. After seeing these frenzied, tortured, prostituted bodies in the disgusting universal brothel with the band of soldiers and the impossibility of speech, in chant 7 there then emerges a sort of primal couple, Kment and Giauhare. We had already seen them before, and the way they are now is as if a new humanity had emerged from all of this: Giauhare is expecting a baby. A new humanity that's under a completely different sign, an indecipherable sign, in an emblem that's Christic or redemptive, albeit betokening an obscure redemption, lacking its own language. This is basically Guyotat's version of Heidegger's statement to the effect that only a God can save us. Not in the sense that a God will come, but in the sense that a new humanity will come, miraculously, from out of the utter filth, the universal obscenity. This new truth will be responsible for remaking the world—it will not just come from the world—a little like the way Adam and Eve began the human race. Let me read you the last lines, so you can hear its tone. Kment and Giauhare will have a sort of vision of a defeated God, a fleeting vision, and will understand, through this vision, that they are alone in the world and responsible now for the birth of the world.

> Kment and Giauhare, woken up, walk, knees and fists in the thorns, push the hedge aside: a man bending over the stone, is mating with the

goddess; a mane sticks out of his nape and of his back; on his head a dove and a crown of thorns; his bare legs are vibrating, incandescent; in the distance, on the sea, the sail scuds along towards the island and the fish shoot out, sparkle on the forge, strike the sides of the boat, play in the deep beneath the shadow of the hull; the boat is empty but a beam of light, the first one of dawn, watches and stands by, on the sail. Kment kneels down before Giauhare, and Giauhare before Kment. Fists on the ground, they kiss each other on the knees, on the genitals, on the forehead. (378)

This ending is a sublime new dawn, the re-creation of humanity. We could say this: if we are really in an age when there's no world, and if, therefore, in this period when there's no world, we're doomed, condemned, to this all-pervasive prostitutional figure—the commodified body, the encounter with commodities, on the one hand, and the biological valuation of the body, on the other (this is a possible contemporary interpretation of biopower)—if this is in fact what the situation is, then there are probably three hypotheses, and our thinking wavers among the three:

- There's the hypothesis that doubt is the only attitude that hasn't fallen prey to the world's corruption: "O doubt, the only eternity." This is the attitude I'd call a "higher nihilism," which is neither libertarian nor liberal. It could be called a stoic nihilism: there is no truth possible, but at least we'll remain in the awareness of that absence. It is the singular eternity of the awareness of that absence.
- Then there's the prophetic hypothesis: a world is coming, a God for Heidegger, a new humanity for Guyotat. You've seen how they kneel and face each other, as opposed to a violent confrontation. Facing each other, they acknowledge their own humanity. This is a myth, and it goes along with the vision of the god and the boat sailing on the sea. It's prophetic: it says that the nonworld will take the worst possible course, but that this worst course is pregnant with a new dawn, that something will give birth to a decisively new humanity. This can be formulated in a thousand different ways, but it's a hypothesis of that sort.

I'd like to try to propose a third hypothesis that is not suspended between doubt and the miracle, as are the other two. The first one depicted doubt as the only eternity, while the second declared the paradoxical inevitability of the miracle. The third hypothesis is that in the absence of world there are the lineaments of a world. Not its presence, or even the promise of it, but a sketch of it, or a network of signs that we can explore and link together. While we'll accept something like Guyotat's infernal cosmology (it's relevant to our world, which is also why this is a great literary work), we won't let ourselves be forced into accepting his final position, between the eternity of doubt and the dawn of a miracle. The analysis needs to be pursued, not as an analysis of the emblems of the present but as an effective analysis of what is written on the back of this emblem, on its reverse side, as though we had to read the world not in terms of what it explicitly says but the other way around, in terms of what it seems not to be saying.

Session 6

March 30, 2002

I've been focusing—like Plato in the *Republic*—on the democratic individual, on the subject living under the democratic emblem, and I said that this subject was constructed on the basis of two imperatives. First, it stands before the market stall of goods; the principle of its identity is to be virtually or really a consumer of goods. Second, and for that very reason, it is constructed as a body; it is reducible and equivalent to a body. So the shortest definition of the democratic subject is that it is a commodified body.

That said, I've shown how a body seized by commodified indifference is ultimately a prostitutional body. It follows that the prostitutional is an intrinsic or fundamental characteristic of the emblematic figure of our world, which, as I've already demonstrated, is a nonworld. That's why I turned to the writer who made the prostitutional relationship a general cosmology, namely, Pierre Guyotat. I thus arrived at the idea that, in Guyotat, who is a superlative writer, a dreamer, and a madman, too (but a prophetic madman, a prophet of the sexual cosmology), two solutions or two options were identified on the basis of this nonworld of the sexual cosmology: first, stoical doubt, withdrawal, the attitude of negative indifference to this trafficking of bodies, and second, the advent, at the height of destruction, of a new world, of a dawnlike figure, of a re-creation of the universe on different bases, with the destruction ultimately bringing with it the miracle, as it were, of the assumption of an utterly new world.

I would now like to comment briefly again on these two solutions.

It is important to understand what the first solution is, in terms of our "world," of our absence of world. Guyotat poeticizes the "O doubt, the only eternity" as the allotting, by a dead, absent, inscrutable god, of a "place for eternity," serene and free from chaos. Free from the chaos that is the nonworld as frenzied attraction of bodies, as containing nothing but the attraction of bodies. This is interesting because it is also a contemporary fantasy. Not necessarily detail for detail, but it's a possible contemporary fantasy, i.e., the idea that, through a figure of withdrawal, or some ascetic figure, the world might regain some kind of order. This temptation takes many forms, but it is at any rate not indifferent or unrelated to some aspects of what has been called "the return of religion." What interests me is this deep desire to regain some kind of order, something that's not the democratic individual caught up in the chaos of bodies, something that's like the acceptable grace of a place, even if that place is the result of a negative operation, of a subtraction or a withdrawal, rather than of a commitment or a birth.

I'm going to read you an excerpt in which Guyotat formulates this first option in greater detail. The text shows that this can exist at the very height of the opposite desire and thus be connected with the figures of nihilism: at the height of the nihilism caused by the chaos of bodies, there can come that sort of stoical indifference that puts you in a state of withdrawal, which is also a self-consummation.

> Children, sheathe your swords, men, cover your darts, I rise over you towards the top of the closed valley, suffocated by the smell of pine trees, I run from one end of the stadium to another, the mountain grows covered with soldiers, their spears pierce the tree leaves, I'm going to die, I never changed freedoms, the dry leaves enter my throat, the soldiers nail me with their spears, on the stadium's wet sand, I who dreamed of dying strangled by a boy inside a brothel's toilet, my wounds dry in the mountain air, I die alone by the cries of the birds of the Divinity and I watch my death and my descent to hell; the Divinity does not wait until I am completely dead to allot me a place for eternity, I die honorably, my senses at peace, my mind alone touched by the sun, without revolt, I who wished to die in the confusion of pleasure and despair.[1]

The end of the excerpt is interesting for us: "The Divinity does not wait until I am completely dead to allot me a place for eternity, I die honorably, my senses at peace, my mind alone touched by the sun." In other words, what Guyotat is describing is the absenting of bodies, the retreat from the confusion and frenzy of bodies, the attitude of someone who would like to die in the chaotic nonworld, in the "confusion of pleasure and despair" (this is the nihilistic figure I was talking about). To this person is granted the grace of dying otherwise, the grace of a death that brings forth a mind touched by the sun, in unexpected serenity, which is a way out of the chaos of the world in the form of a spiritual disappearance.

I think this is a subjective attitude that will catch on, that is already catching on, in various ways. It's the figure of a personal abnegation of sorts, which leads to a retreat from the chaos of bodies in exchange for being subject to a sort of disappearance, or death, through which something like a "solar" mind is acquired. It's a figure that is ultimately both serene and sacrificial. It is brought about by the nonworld: it's because you're capable of wanting to die in despair that there comes to you, like an improbable salvation, this nobility of a solar death. This option obsessed Guyotat. It also obsesses the contemporary world, which will provide it with what Bergson would have called mystics, new mystics. We can expect—in fact we are already witnessing—the inevitable emergence of a new mysticism. This doesn't necessarily mean that it's religious in the sense of established religions. It may be, or it may not be. In any case, it considers that since the nonworld is linked to the body, a mind must be acquired through incorporeal laws. This will range from sects to the loftiest, most sophisticated mysticism. There's no need to judge: the spectrum is enormous. But this is one of the images of the present time, an image that inevitably evokes the mystical figure that is capable of freeing itself from the dominion of the body.

The second hypothesis introduced by Guyotat is myth (this is not an attitude like doubt, which ends in mysticism), the myth of a creation of the world, of a new dawn. At the height of the destruction and the chaotic retreat from the world, a new world organically linked to Nature's survival will dawn and unfold. It is also a contemporary characteristic to think that, ultimately, the remedy for, the defense against, the resistance to, the capitalist and industrial destruction of the world is called "Nature." The natural environment, however corrupt and ruined it may be, is still the last resource for something like the re-creation of a world habitable for humanity. It's also an option. An ecological option in the broadest sense, it is practically a metaphysics. It doesn't exactly boil down to the presence of Greens in the government. It's more extreme, more dangerous than that. It's the point where environmentalism intersects with a Heideggerian lineage, a lineage that examines the relationship between *phusis* and *technè*, between nature and technology. I told you that Guyotat's prose, his genius, lies in the way he makes the indestructible beauty of the natural environment shine through the very cracks in the destruction. There's something that remains in the cracks of the chaos of the world as an indifferent and available remedy and that deserves the name "Nature." It's in a reliance on this natural splendor, at once inaccessible and ever-present, that the possibility of a new dawn lies. If we tamper with Nature, it could lead to the height of destruction, and then something like a new world may unfold. This is a mythology in the sense of Genesis, of what would be a second Genesis. What's more, the seventh chant is very similar to Genesis in this regard, since in it we'll see the male, Kment, lift the body of the woman out of a primal mud, an originary mud. Here is the passage:

> On the rock, summit of the new island, mud rises; Kment, leaning on an elbow, straightens himself up, naked, the wounds on his forehead and knees washed, his hair swollen and glossy with mud, his lips red, his mouth filled with sludge; standing, arching his back, hands on his hips, he opens his eyes and looks round; then, squatting down, he searches in the mud with his hands, releases, lifts up Giauhare's body, which he hugs against him, kisses on the lips, on the shoulders and on the breasts. Giauhare wakes up, the silt runs out of her shut eyelids, in the folds of her ears; her cheeks swollen with sludge, Kment kisses them and taking Giauhare's lips between his, he sucks up that silt; thus they mix the sludge of their mouths, their original semen; thus, naked, frozen, they give each other life, and the sun enflames them and places them in its orbit, like two new planets. They rush forward, they dive in the jumble of flowers, foliage, birds and springs. Kment's hand on Giauhare's belly, and hers on the boy's chest; sun sparkles in their hair. (373–74)

This is the mythical construction, like a new Genesis, of what can happen at the height of destruction, when, through the preservation of birds, foliage, and springs, something like a new human race in gestation emerges from Nature.

We are ultimately in a situation that proposes—this is the first option—a kind of mystical wisdom, the wisdom of serene withdrawal, the wisdom of the good death, we might say, the death that isn't death in the despair of bodies but in the sunshine of the mind. This brings us back to an old figure of speculative and mystical wisdom, which is gaining ground in our world. Or else there's the second option, i.e., the dawnlike myth of the creation of a new humanity, at the height of destruction, based on something unchanging that is like Nature. It is a poetic promise, mythical and poetic. So the solutions proposed by Guyotat's novel are either mystical wisdom or poetry with its creative resources, and therefore an esthetic solution in the broadest sense of the term.

You'll note that what is excluded is anything that might seem like a political solution. Not that the book isn't about politics. It actually is, very forcefully so, in many places, and you'll thus find perceptive remarks in it about the France of Pétain, the colonial wars, De Gaulle, and the Nazis. Through its incredible cosmology, the book really does deal with politics but, it maintains negatively, via its very absence, the thesis that, in a nonworld plunged in the chaos of bodies, there is no political solution. That thesis can be transposed to the present context. The nonworld in which we're immersed and which unites us is in the process of uniting the whole planet around its nonworldliness. More generally speaking, it's conceivable that once the world is completed, it's no longer a world. Once something covers the world completely, the world disappears as a world, for there are no longer enough names for people. There are too many people who have been left out in the chaotic anonymity of the world. The thesis is then as follows: when you've reached that point, politics is unthinkable, politics disappears. And even assuming it could be reconstructed, it can only be reconstructed from something other than itself, either from a figure of mystical withdrawal or from an artistic creation. But it can't be rebuilt from itself, because in order for there to be politics, there has to be a world.

I'm not defending this thesis; I'm just saying that it is lurking around. It is definitely lurking in Guyotat's book, but not only there, because today, in the widespread belief in the artificial unity of the nonworld, there lurks the thesis that in such an absence of world, something like politics has lost its powers of rationality, construction, action, or authority. As a result, the pathways of thought or of resistance are not directly political. They might be either spiritual, in the sense of a certain attitude that the sun imparts to the mind, or poetico-artistic. Incidentally, this means that before you think about politics, you need to ask whether there's a world. That question is prior to the possibility of politics. Restoring the world's bonds is a *pre*-political task, even if some people call it a political one. But in its essence—and this is what Guyotat is suggesting—restoring the world's bonds is an artistic task, perhaps a collective artistic task. We need to repair the world's bonds, reforge them, and this task is even more crucial than any politics.

So that's what can be found in the two solutions proposed by Guyotat.

⸺⚬⚬⚬⸺

I'd like to propose a different approach here, and I'm going to try to make a case for it as I go along. I think that the task to which the nonworld calls us—the task imposed on our will by the toxic images of the present time, what is required of us to repair the chaos of the present time—that task is neither spiritual nor artistic. It is really a political task, even if it means seriously renewing the significance of the word "political" and giving it a meaning that differs from its immediacy or its customary usage. "Politics" encapsulates the idea that the task can be formulated, that first its scope and then its practical resources can be determined. This is not exactly the case with spirituality or with artistic creation, which are more in the realm of formal innovation or personal salvation.

You could put it like this: however chaotic or even desperate our situation may be, it is still rational and not the result of a process of disengagement from rationality. Therefore, it's not at all a case of an exceptional subjectivity whose origin is supposedly unknown.

You'll note that Guyotat clearly says that the mystical solution implies a kind of grace. It is only possible, he says, because the dead

God, the absent God, accorded him the grace of dying nobly and in solar spirituality. He who dreamed of dying like Pasolini, strangled by a boy in the toilet of a brothel—that was his utterly nihilistic desire—turned out to have died in solar spirituality. But this is a gift of the dead God; it can't be deduced from the situation in any way. It's a grace. In addition, Kment's and Giauhare's creation of the world is clearly an incalculable figure, a dawn without origin. So it, too, is the fantasy of a pure gift, of a gratuitous grace. For Guyotat, the two solutions—the mystique of solar doubt and noble death, or the solution of withdrawal and the creative solution—are solutions that are intransitive to the chaos. It's impossible to infer them from the nonworld. So they are miraculous in the strictest sense of the word: in the sense that what occurs independently of any possible calculability of the situation of the nonworld is called a "miracle." They are totally improbable, and their beauty stems from the fact that they are either a withdrawal or a grace. The truth is, we are dealing with something like Heidegger's testamentary text: "Only a God can save us." This final word of Heidegger's is also the final word of these two hypotheses. And it means: something has to happen. But this something doesn't happen because of the absence of the world. That's why it's called "God," even if it's a dead god. In Guyotat, something does happen, something that extricates the subject from the chaos of the nonworld but has nothing to do with that chaos itself and is therefore like an external grace. It is an event. As an event, whether of the grace or the creation type, this event only requires a period of waiting, since for the time being you're in a nonworld that is nothing but the chaos of the commodified relationship between bodies.

I'm saying all this because, ultimately, contemporary despair can be observed in a miraculous way of thinking, that is, in a way of thinking that says all you can do is wait for something to happen, something that will either enable you to die a spiritual death or (and this is a lot better!) ensure that a new world is created and unfolds in a dawnlike way. But in both cases, it involves waiting for a miracle to happen. For me, these are solutions that, in a way, are derived not from a consideration of what there is but from the hypothesis of an utterly gratuitous coming of something, which will descend upon humanity abandoned in the nonworld and restore to it either a subjectivity or even a world in harmony with Nature.

I'd now like to suggest, on the basis of these images of the present time, a different solution, a nonmiraculous thesis. It derives from a reasoned conviction, at once empirical and rational, namely that *in the nonworld itself, there are usable traces of something different from it.* Something like a world haunts the nonworld.

We usually speak about the way the nonworld haunts the world. Here, it's the other way around: the traces of a world haunt the nonworld. This way that the figure of a possible world has of haunting the absence of world might be the basis for gaining freedom from the nonworld. We will call "freedom" the fact of not being reduced to no more than a commodified bodily individual. Or, to put it another way, we will call "freedom" the possibility of being in a nonprostitutional generic relationship with humanity as a whole.

I'll add the following: if, on the other hand, a miracle *does* occur, we'll welcome it! Gladly! Under the name of "event," my philosophy is also a secularizing, a rationalizing, of the religious concept of the miracle. In that sense, yes, I do believe in miracles. But I claim that we can believe in miracles without falling prey to the usual gloom of the endless waiting for them to happen. Something creates a trace of a world, which means that we are basically deserving of the miracle. *Only those who do something other than wait for a miracle are deserving of it.* That's a philosophical version of "Heaven helps those who help themselves"! Identify in the nonworld the minute, hard-to-find traces of what proves that it's haunted by a possible world, and that's when something may happen. And if something does happen, you'll be able to recognize it. Those who aren't on the lookout for the traces of the possibility of a world won't be receptive to the miracle. They won't recognize it, or they may even mistake it for one last desperate circumstance. The best approach is to look for something that's in a position of exception in the images of the present time.

Let me remind you that to do this, you have to start by having a completely clear understanding of the workings of the emblems. For the time being, I've defined a four-stage regressive method:

- Analysis of the emblems
- Theory of the naked power behind the emblem in question

- Figure of the exceptions to the order
- Traces of the fallibility of the order, demonstration that this order, which is the order of the nonworld, possesses crucial areas of vulnerability

We had gotten up to the emblems and what the emblem implies in terms of a constitutive subjectivity. So we're going to go back over everything patiently, without rushing ahead to the brilliant poetic figures that lead to the indefinite waiting for a miracle.

—⁓—

The thesis could be as follows: behind the democratic emblem and its corollaries—i.e., bodies—there is a ferocious power that forces people to comply with their subjection to the emblem. As regards democracy (in its ordinary sense, namely, a specific form of state power), the democratic emblem is not itself the cause of its effectiveness. It's an emblem, and, as such, it has the force of images, but it has no more than that. It's a matter of getting people to submit to the emblem, to which they in fact consent. But consent isn't enough. The emblem doesn't just require people to consent to it; it requires them to *submit* to it, to be the market bodies, the commodified bodies, that it demands. Therefore, the question is: What is this power that forces subjects to become commodified bodies? It being understood, moreover, that the form of consent to this submission develops, or crystallizes, around the democratic emblem. There's the form of consent to the submission, and there's the need to identify the power that forces bodies to submit to the role demanded by this consent to the emblem, i.e., the role of commodified bodies or prostitutional substitutability in its metaphorical figure. There is nothing natural about this fate, the universal fate of each of us, in a position of confronting commodities and reducible, as it were, to the vagaries of the body and its enjoyment. We need to get rid of the thesis that there's something natural about this. The problem is that it's a hegemonic thesis. We're all convinced, albeit to different degrees, that humanity is naturally democratic. But it's not naturally democratic, any more than it's naturally antidemocratic. The democratic emblem is a construct that places the individual in the figure of the commodified body and, based on this position, wrests broad areas of consent from them. Only for an individual subjected to this figure is there the possibility of consent to the emblem.

Let's not forget, let's never forget, that this consent and this submission can only be obtained through great violence, because *it is a violence not against bodies as such but against what bodies are capable of beyond themselves.* Violence against bodies exists, and on a vast scale. But that's not what I'm talking about here. Violence against bodies is widely condemned today. It is repudiated and is an object of moral opprobrium. The theory or ideology of human rights is a widespread, organic opposition to violence against bodies, such as torture, physical abuse, and massacres. Our dominant societies condemn such violence. Even though there is much violence against some bodies in exchange for there being no violence against other ones (some bodies, as we know, are worth more than others: some are protected and others aren't), it cannot be said that, in our part of the world, it is primarily a question of violence against bodies. The violence that forces a person to become a commodified body is not exactly a violence against the body. It's a violence against the body's capacity for ideas, its capacity to serve as a support for more than just its own interests, its enjoyment, or its self-preservation. It's a violence that imposes the imperative: "Enjoy yourself however you like, enjoy yourself however you can!" This could be said to be a family imperative, if the family is understood as the ideal site of carefree consumption. And this imperative is opposed to another one, which is: "Live by Ideas." It is important to understand that, in its contemporary form, democracy requires the imperative: "Live without any Ideas." This is exactly what's meant by the ubiquitous notion of the end of ideologies, which I take very seriously since I see that it can be expressed as "Thank God, we're finally living without any Ideas." The classic argument in favor of this animalistic contentment is as follows. "We saw what living with Ideas led to: to violence against bodies. We want to live by life, not by Ideas. Live by life; don't live by Ideas! Live to live, or, in other words, to survive."

This notion of the end of ideologies is crucial. It sounds innocent enough: "Ideologies have done so much harm!" But it's actually a very violent notion. Besides, it's hard to see why ideologies would have been alive at one time and would then be dead. Ideology is not an animal species; it's not like elephants. It's prescriptive. Ideologies are neither alive nor dead. They're not organisms. The notion of the end refers precisely to violence against subjects, violence that attempts to force bodies to be without any Ideas. Because only the body without any Ideas submits obediently to the encounter with commodities, in accordance with the bleak ideal of its enjoyment. Any body that lives under Ideas is a body that is more or less unsuitable for the commodified prostitutional.

Why is there such violence? Because the commodified prostitutional does not accept otherness. It's *a system whose essence is to be uniform.* Any otherness brings Ideas back in. If, when faced with the prevailing imperative "Live without any Ideas," you've got another imperative, of whatever kind, this otherness will necessarily appear as ideal otherness, in one form or another. It can't appear as material otherness, because all the material space is filled with the prescriptions concerning the commodified body. To accept real otherness would mean once again accepting that it's possible, indeed required, to live under the imperative of an Idea. But this is unacceptable, because the violence consists in the injunction: "Live without any Ideas, without any ideologies, without any projects, without any purpose, without any universality." And so—I absolutely insist on this—the system in question, that is, the democratic system, is the only one that expressly deserves the adjective "totalitarian." Soviet totalitarianism wasn't totalitarian at all: it was shot through with dreadful contradictions, to such an extent that the slightest expression of dissent was considered to be an event that merited a trial, a staged show, and an execution. There has been no other regime in which the slightest stirring of an idea has had such a tremendous effect. The slightest sentence was a question of life or death. It was no laughing matter, but that's how it was. It wasn't a smooth-running system as a whole. On closer inspection, you can see that it was anarchic, shot through with incredible turmoil, altering its system every five minutes, changing its language, caught up in chaos, and so on. It was a system that didn't work, that didn't work at all. To think of it as the well-oiled totality of a unified bureaucracy is absurd. I'm not defending that form of state in the least. But it didn't have the capacity to impose a figure of unity that really matched its aim.

That's what led to its downfall: it lacked the capacity it claimed to have. By contrast, the contemporary hegemonic system does have that capacity. It's a system within which the figure of terrible unity is a figure supported by effective built-in material mechanisms. It's not a system with no disorder, far from it, but it's a system that has the absolute capacity to keep otherness out. This can be seen at the level of the emblem by the fact that the democratic emblem is untouchable. It's the only one that is. It's consensual by definition. And, as a result, it attests to a flawless functional unity at the emblematic level, even though that unity is achieved through constant, muted violence. Because getting bodies to submit to being disposed in this way and not otherwise, that is to say, without any Ideas, can of course only be achieved by constant violence perpetrated not so much on the bodies (that's not the issue) as on what they are capable of—I must stress this—beyond themselves.

Let me digress for a moment. This explains why education is such a burning issue in our country (because there's a whole tradition behind it). Never since Plato has this issue of education been so important, never since the Greeks has it had so much urgency. Everyone is aware that it is a critical, confusing, passionate, fraught issue. One of the aspects of the violence I was talking about is the imperative need to destroy the school system. This is easily explained. If there's a need for its destruction, for its transformation into the warehousing of bodies, it's not because the bodies are bad or evil; it's so that they can be trained as quickly as possible to confront commodities in the marketplace. So you can see that it's entirely unnecessary to learn anything in this respect, except what can contribute to the training of the few guardians necessary, on the one hand, and, on the other, what is directly relevant to commercial investments. This is a rather pure and typical example of what I am calling "violence" here. It's striking that people complain about violence in schools. But the violence isn't the violence *in* schools; it's the violence *against* schools, the violence that will sooner or later lead to their systematic, probably near-complete, destruction. I regard this as a strong sign, as a description of what we're dealing with. The violence against schools, the state's destruction of the school system, along with the resistance it also leads to (fortunately), is only one of the processes of the violent dismantling of all subjective otherness. The general line is very clear: above all, bodies must not use any of the potential for Ideas that they are nevertheless capable of. If you look closely at the methods used to destroy schools, you'll see that this is precisely one of the ways the imperative "Live without any Ideas!" is being put into practice. Or, to put it another way: "Rest assured that democracy is only bodies, the disposition of bodies, and nothing beyond it." Children must be turned as soon as possible into commodified bodies. There's no other real imperative.

All this leads to the idea that naked power, the power we're trying to detect behind the democratic emblem, is a power that exerts tremendous violence in what might be called the border zone between bodies and ideas. This violence is perpetrated on anything that might be seen as the body's ability to transcend its immediacy. "Body," let me repeat, is a construct here. It's not the bare biological but the body as a submissive body placed in the commodified figure. This extreme violence inflicts a great deal of devastation, some of which is regarded as perfectly legitimate compared with the constantly invoked bogeyman of totalitarianism, and therefore compared with violence against bodies. But it is important to understand that, under the guise of denouncing real violence against bodies elsewhere than in our own country, the violence done here, which is not violence against bodies but is no less devastating, is simply overlooked. Humanity can't be reduced to bodies. By destroying a school system, a collective mode of being, or anything of the sort, something of humanity is destroyed. Killing people is a crime, but there are many other crimes, many kinds of crimes. In particular, what amounts to getting people to accept, through constant insidious pressure, an irrevocable split between the consumer body, on the one hand, and any form of Idea or thought, on the other, is unquestionably an altogether criminal devastating violence.

Here, too, I think there's something interesting to be found in Plato's old analyses, minus their undeniably reactionary nature. Plato was the first to attempt to conceptualize the relationship between democracy and tyranny. His extremely famous demonstration can be found in Book 8 and at the beginning of Book 9 of the *Republic*. Plato shows how it is in the nature of democracy to turn into tyranny. It's true that, in Plato— and this is not exactly what concerns us here—one follows the other: democracy spawns tyranny. As he says in Book 8, "The chances are that democracy is the ideal place to find the origin of tyranny—the harshest and most complete slavery arising, I guess, from the most extreme freedom."[2] In reality, in his aristocratically oriented genealogical scheme, Plato hints at a deeper truth than the one that defines the move from democracy to tyranny. A truth that *we* experience, which is the tyrannical essence of democracy itself. It's not so much that democracy leads to tyranny because excessive freedom leads to excessive slavery as that there's a tyrannical essence to democracy itself. To be sure, wherever it exists, and only in its own dominant space, it protects the freedom of bodies. But it does so at the price of a harsh and constant restriction, of an extremely narrow definition of what a body is capable of beyond itself. In particular, the contemporary body is a body that must be, that will be forced to be, the body of the death of ideologies, the body without any Ideas. It is this situation that is the true violence of democracy in its present emblem, in the figure of a naked power that is very vigilant in wielding this power over the relationship between bodies and Ideas. And what's fascinating about the present situation is that this violent reduction of bodies to this subjection to the market is called "modernization." What is modern is the body without any Ideas. Take all the texts touting modernization, and you'll see that this is really what it's all about: the more a body without any Ideas you are, the more modern you are. In a certain sense, this means that modernity is a kind of savagery. The essence of naked power shows its ugly face here: modernity is only achieved through savagery. And this savagery is unnatural violence, whatever the consent given the emblems. Because it's very true that many people are glad their bodies are free, particularly since the bogeyman of countries or past eras in which bodies *weren't* free is constantly being brandished before them. But just because there might be something worse elsewhere doesn't mean that what you have is good. I've always thought that argument was pathetic! It's as if, when someone says something stupid, you were to point it out to them and then add: "Yes, but there are some stupid things that are even worse!" It's an idiotic argument that's always being trotted out: "It's not great, but it's better than elsewhere!" Okay, but so what? "You've seen the risks you were running with Ideas, so live without any Ideas!" But what price has to be paid? That mindset plunges us into a sort of commercial animality.

When Plato focuses on the shift or transition from democracy to tyranny and the connection between the two, he describes a political psy-
chology of sorts. Here is what he writes when he depicts the person who,
when called to the free enjoyment of their body, will, in fact, turn back
into a savage. Because it's this that Plato calls the becoming-tyrant. The
tyrant isn't the democrat; he's the democrat who has turned back into a
savage, because there's a latent savagery in his character.

> When the other desires come buzzing around, full of incense, perfume,
> garlands, wine and the dissolute pleasures typical of such gatherings,
> they feed this drone, help it grow to an enormous size, and so plant the
> sting of yearning in it. Then this champion of the soul takes madness
> for its bodyguard, and goes berserk. If it detects in the man any desires
> or opinions which can be regarded as decent and which still feel some
> sense of shame, it kills them off or banishes them from its presence,
> until it has purged the soul of restraint and filled it with foreign mad-
> ness. (287)

This is what I'd like to focus on: I think that naked power, the naked
power of Capital and its lackeys, contemporary naked power, is in fact
like a foreign madness, in Plato's sense. "Foreign madness" means something that's imposed from without, not something that develops immanently, and Plato shows that it begins simply with the substitutability of
desires, which, with us, has become the commodified substitutability of
pleasures. It seems innocent enough, and it is. The only problem, as Plato
clearly shows, is that it can't tolerate Ideas ("If it detects in the man any
desires or opinions which can be regarded as decent . . . it kills them off
or banishes them from its presence"). So that's where violence is: it's at
the place where the substitutability of desires and the commodified body
with its benevolence, with its protection, are confronted with something
like a different hypothesis. A different hypothesis about humanity, about
the fact that humanity ultimately cannot be content with the imperative
"Live without any Ideas." So when this other hypothesis takes hold,
there's intolerance and violence on the democratic side. Institutional,
state-based, constant, persistent intolerance, nonstop aggression, which,
once again, doesn't need to kill people. But, as Plato says, it's enough just

to kill the Ideas in them. There are lots of ways to kill Ideas in people without having to kill *them*. Banish them from their mind. But what do you get then? The subject falls prey to a foreign madness. For I think that, behind the consensual emblem of democracy, that is, behind the emblem of something we'd all consent to, there is a kind of a foreign madness. It's what I call endless violence. This foreign madness is a subjective disposition, a kind of violence against the subject as such, and the unnaturalness of this subjective figure stems from the fact that it imposes on the body a singular disposition that is not at all natural to it and therefore requires constant violence. I think it's important to note, or to try to realize, that we are living—obviously not just in the vast regions of the world that are subjected to imperial looting and where dead bodies are strewn all over the ground, but even here, in our own countries, in our dear democratic West, yes—that we are living in an utterly violent world, a pathological world, not a quiet, peaceful one at all. The only way we can think we're living in a quiet, peaceful world is if we assume that the only violence existing is the violence against bodies and that it's reserved for others, for the people over there, there where the West must kill in order to get rich and keep us happy. But such is not the case. There is violence other than violence against bodies, violence that is no less devastating and inhumane. It is the imperial-democratic system as a whole, here as elsewhere, in which, under its fine trappings, naked power is totally violent.

In light of this, what is the problem? It's a classic problem of contemporary philosophy: determining how this power will be interpreted, what its nature is, in what ways it is wielded, what its meaning is.

In current philosophy there are two hypotheses about this, concerning the true nature of the naked power hidden under the democratic emblem of contemporary states, two fundamental hypotheses that are not unrelated:

- The hypothesis that this power is a biopower
- The hypothesis that this power is basically the power of technology

Those are the two main, albeit equally false, hypotheses: biopower or technology, with some cross-linkages between them.

Let me give you some reference points.

"Biopower" is a term that was coined by Foucault. The canonical text is his 1976 lecture *Society Must Be Defended*. It was published in book form, and you can read it. It is entirely devoted to the category of power, in its genealogy from the eighteenth century on. Foucault uses the category of biopower as the classic figure of state power during the nineteenth century, and this enables him to provide an analysis of the nature of Nazi power and power in the socialist states. This is a theory of naked power as, in the final analysis, an apparatus for legitimizing killing. We'll come back to this category, which has since been taken up again and developed, in particular by Giorgio Agamben, especially in *Homo Sacer*, where the term "bare life," counterbalancing that of "naked power," can moreover be found. Foucault, as developed by Agamben, is a filiation that attempts to think through the singularity of contemporary power in terms of its relationship with the body, whence, as the name implies, "biopower." Power over the disposition or the life of bodies, as a combination of biological sovereignty and theory. As we'll see, in that context, particularly in Foucault's analysis, power is essentially racist. This is a strong theory, a theory according to which it is of the essence of this form of power to be racist. Foucault tries to use the adjective in a neutral way, "racist" being understood in a sense that's a little more general than its ordinary meaning.

The second set of hypotheses is that for which the meaning of modern forms of power is encapsulated in technological power, in technology as power. Here, it's basically the Heideggerian filiation. The interesting thing to understand about Heidegger, the most controversial point and the one that concerns us, is the correlation he attempts to establish between democracy and technology. It's important to see that Heidegger is someone who believed that National Socialism, far from being the technicizing pinnacle of power, was something that gauged the true extent of the technological takeover and was a match for technology. He was thus convinced that Nazism was the one form of power that was free from technology's control. That shows you the extent to which he suspected the democratic order, by contrast, of being in an essential connection with technology. Heidegger would maintain his positions, in a disguised and cautious way, up to the end, in particular his position on the relationship between democracy and technology. The essence of democracy is to not gauge the extent of technology, to let it be in its blind sovereignty. This is a thesis that merits consideration, and we don't need to be National Socialists for that.

We will examine both these issues. In a way, the thesis that naked power is biopower will raise the question of the categories used by that power, and in particular the question as to why racism, or racialism, is essential to it. That will prompt us to ask what the position of racialism is at the present time, in terms of its connection with the categories of power. The other aspect will be the relationship between democracy and technology, from a perspective that assumes the legacy of Heidegger.

What we'll see—I'm giving you a little glimpse of the trajectory—is that, ultimately, in all these hypotheses, just as with Guyotat, what is in fact left out is politics, because power is attributed to something other than itself, which is not, however, of the order of politics as thought. In the case of biopower, it is attributed to life and the body. It is ultimately the control over bodies, which, in Deleuze's work, results in the idea of the "society of control." In the technological hypothesis, it is attributed to science, technology, or the economy in the broad sense of the term. In all these cases, it is assumed that the violence of contemporary power can be identified on the basis of categories extrinsic to political sovereignty strictly speaking, either on the basis of life and bodies or on the basis of the economy and technology.

I, for my part, would like to examine the hypothesis that violence is still political in nature. My thesis is that naked power is political, but its political nature is disguised, and that by attributing it to something other than itself, we are not helping to expose it. We are leaving it shrouded in its political obscurity, as if external objectivities of whatever kind could somehow explain it. After that, we'll take up the hypothesis that there are political traces of a possible world in the nonworld. For the time being, I'll just stick with this brief look ahead, because it will have to be unpacked all at once.

Session 7

May 15, 2002

In this final session of the year, I'm going to cobble together a bit of what we've covered this year.

Let me just remind you that in order for bodies to be commodified bodies, as required by the democratic emblem, they must be separated from their capacity for Ideas, that is, placed under the imperative "Live without any Ideas." That's the sole meaning of the theme of the end of ideologies. It paves the way for bodies' submission to this imperative, to the separation of the body from its capacity for Ideas, its capacity for projects or for a general vision of the order of things.

We can define quite precisely the naked power that is ours, and that is no one's. It's an anonymous power that controls bodies. It's the very operation of separation, a way of treating singular bodies that separates them from their capacity for Ideas. This naked power is a separating operation that distances bodies from part of their own power. We will see that there is reason to believe that any real power is of this type. As a process of separation, it makes a cut between subjective singularities and what they're capable of. Power is far more concerned with possibilities than with actualities. It's an operation that restricts, limits, cuts, whittles away at, redefines, and formats possibilities.

We saw that, in terms of philosophy, this separating of bodies from Ideas was conceptualized in particular as biopower—the power exerted over bodies, the power of regulation and normativity with life as its object—but also as technology. These two contemporary interpretations are related to the precise nature of naked power: it is conceived of either as biopower (the regulation of living bodies) or as technology (the take-over of or control over the earth itself). I will simply indicate, with a few references, what these two perspectives are.

The specific source, the person who introduced the theory of power as biopower into the contemporary debate, is Foucault. The genealogy of this matter dates back to his lecture courses at the end of the 1970s and specifically to his March 17, 1976 lecture ("Society Must Be Defended"), a lecture that had a huge influence and has been abundantly discussed. Incidentally, I should point out that Foucault himself didn't really develop this conception. He moved on to other things. This phase of his work was quite unusual, provocative (Foucault said there were things resembling fascism), and against the grain, and it was analyzed and taken up by others but not used very much by Foucault himself.

What is, broadly summarized, Foucault's thesis? It boils down to saying that the essence of power and the essence of politics can be understood from war. If you want to arrive at a thinking of power, you have to approach things from the perspective of war. Reversing Clausewitz's aphorism ("War is the continuation of politics by other means"), Foucault, through an interpretation of the thinkers of the seventeenth and eighteenth centuries, proposed to examine the thesis that politics is the continuation of war. That's the gist of it. According to him, that was the nineteenth century's conception, in the twin form of politics as class war, the Marxist version, and politics as race war, the protofascist version. The singularity of political thought in the nineteenth century was to have conceived of politics as the continuation of war and to have claimed that the essence of a power can only be understood from the perspective of a fundamental war (once again, class war, the classic Marxist tradition, or race war, in a Gobineau-type logic, a protofascist logic, and also an expanded colonialist logic).

If the essence of power is war, if we can only understand power through war, then the system of legitimation of killing is crucial. Insofar as war is the destruction of the enemy, if power is rooted in war, its essence will be revealed in the legitimation of killing and, in particular, in the question of who can be killed as such, without necessarily having recourse to a judicial process. People who, either because they're of an inferior race or because they're class enemies, are exposed to being killed, must die. They are exposed, just by existing, to being killed. And that's how political singularity is defined.

The thinker who drew the most radical conclusions from this is Giorgio Agamben, in *Homo Sacer*. He cites Foucault and anchors in Foucault the idea that the essence of power is the determination of an absolutely expendable bare life. All power decides on the person or persons who, as pure existence, are expendable. The paradigm of the death camp underlies and is implicit in this demonstration. Basically, the thesis is that the camp is nothing other than the paradigm of politics, as biopower. It's the extreme or extremist form of it, but it is actually a revelation of its essence. The extreme and contemporary consequences connect biopower to the death camps and define all power as that which is able to determine bare life, expendable bare life. There was already something of this sort in the way the soldiers of World War I were sacrificed, something that treated them like expendable life material, not worthy of any particular consideration. There would thus be a tradition going back to the nineteenth century, which, in regarding power as the continuation of a biological war in the broad sense of the term, would lead to the determination of the expendable as the definition of naked power itself.

This isn't exactly Foucault's position. What *he's* interested in is redefining the state, the functions of the modern state, on the basis of a hygienicist and purificationist conception of the state. If the state is of a biopower type, then one of its essential functions becomes being responsible for public health, something that can be understood in many ways, in particular being responsible for the vital purity of the population. These will be the purificationist theses of generalized racialism. Among the Nazis, the hygienicist vocabulary was in absolutely constant use. The incessant comparisons of the Jews with vermin, the Jews with germs, and so on, clearly showed that power was implicitly bound up with medical (in the distorted sense of anything having to do with the health of bodies), hygienicist, and purificationist categories. I'm going to read you a passage from Foucault's lecture that's about racism as the exemplary figure of the state thus conceived and about ethnic, racial purification as the main determinant of power.

> At the end of the nineteenth century, we have then a new racism modeled on war. It was, I think, required by the fact that a biopower that wished to wage war had to articulate the will to destroy the adversary with the risk that it might kill those whose lives it had, by definition, to protect, manage and multiply. . . . I think that, broadly speaking, racism justifies the death-function in the economy of biopower by appealing to the principle that the death of others makes one biologically stronger insofar as one is a member of a race or a population, insofar as one is an element in a unitary, living plurality. . . . The specificity of modern racism, or what gives it its specificity, is not bound up with mentalities, ideologies, or the lies of power. It is bound up with the technique of power, with the technology of power. It is bound up with this, and that takes us as far away as possible from the race wars and the intelligibility of history. We are dealing with a mechanism that allows biopower to work. So racism is bound up with the workings of a state that is obliged to use race, the elimination of races and the purification of the race, to exercise its sovereign power. The juxtaposition of—or the way biopower functions through—the old sovereign power of life and death, implies the workings, the introduction and activation, of racism.[1]

Foucault thus attempts to conceptualize the racial determinants of power. He was to do the same for the class determinants, which work identically, not as ideologies, lies, or abstract concepts but as a technology of power. It's not because power is racist that it commits racist crimes. It's because it is exercised as sovereign that it needs racism in order to be exercised as biopower. So power is a disposition of bodies. It is that which takes care of bodies, that which must organize and control bodies, all bodies. And since it is a modern power that cares for everyone, it can't be a caste or a slavery power; in this sense, it is hygienicist. But then how can it kill? It's this paradox that is inevitably dealt with by dividing bodies into good ones and bad ones: there are some bodies whose nature is such that they are expendable for the good of other bodies. There can be no solution to the contradiction between the fact that the sovereign power's right to kill is maintained and the fact that, as a biopower, it must take care of life, other than by a racial division in the broad sense of the term, between the bodies that are taken care of and the bodies that are expendable in order to take care of the others. Hence the crucial significance of the principle that killing others is a way of making oneself biologically stronger. This is a clear sign that, for Foucault, the theory of biopower, as a theory of naked power, is ultimately dependent on a technological conception, on an explicit relationship between the means and the end.

So there aren't two completely different hypotheses about modern naked power, one that's racialist and biologizing and the other technological. Racialism, or exterminative racism, is *also* a technology, which aims to solve the following problem: if the state is defined by the care of bodies and if it wants to wage war, some provision or accommodation that will allow it to do so must be found. We can see that we're led back, via the question of the technologies of power, to an identity or a connection between the modern state and technology. Why is this so? Because sovereignty as the right to kill claims that it has nontranscendent legitimacy, that it wants to operate without transcendent legitimacy. We're no longer in the age of divine right, of the theological state. What authorizes you to kill, to kill en masse? Inasmuch as you are supposed to care about public health, there has to be a theory to the effect that killing others means caring for all bodies. There has to be a necessary connection between death and life in the sense of biopower. And that's a technological operation. It sheds some light on a feature that the film *Shoah*, among others, stressed a lot, and rightly so—I say this all the more readily since Lanzmann's issues aren't mine. The film clearly shows the extent to which the extermination of the European Jews was a technological process, triggering problems of trains, railroad switches, organization, organizational charts, and so on. Ultimately, the problem to be solved was an administratively and technically very complicated technological problem. There was a horrendous, chilling connection between the killing of millions of people in horrific conditions and the diligent bureaucrats, for whom the crux of the problem was to resolve complicated technical issues, such as, for example, whether there would be enough boxcars on a given track. The questions concerning the technology of power shed light on this singular connection between technicity and death, but with hypotheses other than the one that technology itself brings death. There is indeed a technology of deadly power, connected with death, not as technology but under the condition of a certain exercise, a certain arrangement, of sovereign power.

This brings us back to the other aspect of the hypothesis: the connection between technology and naked power, between technological apparatus and organization of power. Here, we're dealing with Heidegger's hypothesis. Very early on, Heidegger put forward the thesis that there was a sort of complicity between democracy and technology. Or, more precisely, democracy, for him, was that figure of politics that, being no match for the violence of technology, ultimately subordinated itself to it. His argument needs to be reconstructed, because, from a certain point on, he avoided being too explicit. It's not that democracy is deadly the way technology is. It's that, lacking any rational measure of technology, democracy remains subservient to technology. In the interview he gave *Der Spiegel*, which was published right after his death in 1976, he was grilled about this. The interview dates from 1966, but Heidegger prohibited its publication until after his death. He said:

> Meanwhile, in the past thirty years [*This is why I mentioned that the date was 1966, because "the past thirty years" refers to 1936, hence to 1933, more or less, and "meanwhile" essentially means Nazism, the Second World War, and the Cold War*], it should have become clearer that the global movement of modern technology is a force whose scope in determining history can scarcely be overestimated. A decisive question for me today is: how can a political system accommodate itself to the technological age, and which political system would this be? I have no answer to this question. I am not convinced that it is democracy.

The journalist presses him:

> "Democracy" is a catch-all word under which quite different ideas can be brought together. The question is whether a transformation of this political structure is still possible. After 1945 you addressed yourself to

the political aspirations of the Western world and then you spoke also of democracy, of the political expression of the Christian worldview, and even of the idea of a constitutional state—and you have labeled all these aspirations "half-measures."

Heidegger's answer is:

> First of all, would you please tell me where I spoke about democracy and all the other things you refer to? I would characterize them as half-measures because I do not see in them a genuine confrontation with the technological world, because behind them there is in my view a notion that technology is in its essence something over which man has control. In my opinion, that is not possible. Technology is in its essence something which man cannot master by himself.[2]

Let's summarize the thesis and align it with our question. Heidegger claims that, in reality, we are under the naked power of technology. Man is not a being who has control over technology; on the contrary, it's technology that controls *him*. This is a moment in the history of being. It's destinal. It's not intrinsically linked to a figure of politics or to a figure of power. It's more far-reaching. Technology's takeover of the earth is the ultimate form of the forgetting of being and of nihilism. This point is a diagnosis of thinking: we are under the naked power of technology. How does democracy come into the question? It is well-nigh defined by Heidegger as the political system that assumes that we are not under the power of technology but that, on the contrary, *we* are the ones who wield power over technology. It is the conviction, formulated in political terms, that technology is subservient to the generic figure of the human. And Heidegger's critique is that that's not true. One could argue that, in the end, for Heidegger, too, democracy is indeed an emblem, the emblem of politics' supposed domination over technology, a false emblem (since the opposite is true) but an emblem all the same. Those who believe in democracy, Heidegger tells us, believe that democracy is a political mastery of technology. They believe—I'm using Heidegger's own phrase—that technology is "something over which man has control."

The journalist asks him: What is a measure? For, as you know, Heidegger thought that Nazism—this is how he defined it in his period of National Socialist activism between 1933 and 1934—was a different political proposition that really took the measure of technology. Of course, he later ended up saying that this wasn't the case. But why would he have thought it was?

I think that, without this amounting to a judgment, the following can be said about this issue. Regardless of whether you assume the biopower hypothesis—you think naked power can be attributed to life, to the figures of the body as a living body, and to the technology of life (a provisional hypothesis)—or you assume the hypothesis of the unfettered supremacy of technology as unlimited power, the only way you can come up with a positive solution is by invoking something else, by attributing power to something other than life or technology. In other words, the question of power will have to be decentered. It's not a matter of representing this issue of power, as democratic capitalo-parliamentarianism purports to do. It has to be recentered, something else has to be invoked, power has to be attributed to other ends. Basically, what Heidegger thought at a particular moment is that, to wrest power away from its domination by technology, the idea of the nation could be invoked. The national idea, in this particular case, was for him the ontological destiny of the German nation. Because Heidegger's National Socialism was fundamentally nationalistic, no one has ever detected any overt racism in him, in the sense of race or biology being major concepts in his construction. He may have made a few anti-Semitic remarks here and there: he was a consummate reactionary, and German nationalism can be regarded, if you will, as a sort of ontological and language-based racialism (Being, after having first spoken Greek, speaks German—idiotic notions like that). What he firmly believed, which is already deplorable, is that the national idea as a German category had the capacity not to be subjected to technology, that it was capable of recovering, of regaining control over technology, something that democracy claims to do but is incapable of doing. For Heidegger, the abstract, anonymous supremacy of technology could only be countered by invoking a positive substantiality, in this case the German nation, that could itself be referred to a proper name, the name of the Führer. You can only offset the anonymity of technology with a proper name, since this proper name epitomizes the nation's spirit.

———— ∞ ————

To digress for a moment, we're all familiar with the temptation to invoke the national idea in the face of technology, the market, and globalization. And in a more tepid version than Heidegger's! It's the version of everyone who appeals to the good old French nation in the face of globalized Capital. It's sort of the farce version of what Heidegger expressed as an appalling tragedy. I'm not saying this to endorse the Heideggerian version: it went hand in hand with heinous crimes. It was what might be called a dark-epic logic (to conquer the earth, an insane scheme, which lent an eschatological figure to the national idea: the thousand-year Reich, etc.). Today, our sovereignists' proposals are more limited in scope! At any rate, I haven't seen what fundamental project they were urging on the nation, in its reaffirmation. But what's of interest to me is that every time power is controlled by some abstract force, there's a constant temptation to call for an alternative substantiality, and the national idea is what is most typically proposed. This operation was taken to its extreme by Nazism, but we need to look elsewhere. We won't do any better, if you'll pardon the expression, since "better" is the same as "worse" here. We won't perform that incredible apocalyptical tragedy again; we'll perform it again only as a farce, a potentially bloody one, as in the former Yugoslavia. What lesson can be learned from all this?

I think it's absolutely essential to attribute naked power to its political nature, not to attribute it to either biology or technology, or to the figure of the living body in general, or to the figure of the economy. I am convinced that the effective identification of the naked power behind the democratic emblem must involve working toward identifying it as political, not attributing it to entities unrelated to politics. We've gone over all of them: we've had Marxist-type economism, the racialist biologism of the fascisms, technocratism, and the financialism of the modern gurus. In a way, what needs to be restored is that, when all is said and done, we should approach the problem of power from within.

Immanently. I'm not saying this is easy, because we have a tradition of politics being understood in terms of something other than itself, as we saw when we ran through the hypotheses that define power in terms of something other than its political nature. No, we need to start with what is most fundamentally self-evident about it, namely that power, in subjectivity, consists in obtaining submission. Before defining it in objectivity, in its economic dimension, by the care of bodies, or technology, naked power is what disposes in a certain place. While it's true that the disposition of bodies in a place means the position of bodies vis-à-vis the market, this doesn't mean that the power of disposition of bodies shouldn't be conceived of as a political power. Just because bodies are controlled in the space of the market doesn't mean that the definition of power will reside in the economic sphere. They're two separate issues. We first have to ask how we can approach the question of power, of naked power, of what subjects bodies under a certain emblem, from a point of view that involves nothing but this operation itself. How are bodies separated from Ideas? Let's look at what the possible separation operations are and try to identify them for themselves.

The key certainly doesn't lie in the brute mechanisms of constraint. If we were to explain the structure of naked power strictly in terms of constraint, of the coercive operations themselves, we wouldn't understand why it can always give way, why it has no structural permanence per se. Something completely different from a mere coercive capacity, used only reluctantly, is involved. That's why we pride ourselves on being wonderfully civilized people (as compared with the places where we and others kill a lot more). The coercive capacity does exist: I'm not saying that there's no forcing of bodies, but it's not the essential definition of power. Power is what extorts consent. It's the mechanism of consent that's key, not coercion, which only exists to supplement the consent. All power relies heavily on consent. Coercion is secondary. We need to give an account of consent and submission. And lastly, since we're dealing with the present time, our question is: To what do we consent, and how? What is our own particular figure of submission?

We can see right away that our submission certainly has to do with the fact that we think we're exceptionally free, that we flaunt our freedoms, our autonomy. We're amazingly free, actually. It's in this kind of thinking that we need to seek our particular figure of consent, which appears in the discourse of freedom and not, like other kinds of submission, in slavery or servitude.

Nor does the key lie in the simple scheme of voluntary servitude, because it presents itself as servitude. Our situation isn't voluntary servitude; it's a submission, which is somehow in the form of an invisible consent, whose visibility, or whose appearance, is freedom. It's a consent whose specific form of representation is free being. I think that it's absolutely characteristic of our modernity to have invented this extraordinary thing, the consent to submission duplicated in the public figure of freedom.

We're always saying that everyone wants to assert their autonomy. This is a super-popular sociological topic: people no longer belong to large collectives, large organizations; they want to construct their individuality, etc. Yet it seems as though that individuality is highly serial: the autonomies in question are a lot alike; they're formally indistinguishable from one another. Everyone says and does pretty much the same thing. Saying "I" or saying "we" is more often than not the exact same thing. Of course, nobody tells you that you have to go here or there by order of the king. But, at the same time, how is it that the figure of autonomy adopts such powerful serial schemes? And who gave the order of vacation departure, which propels millions of [French] people onto the same roads, on the same day, at the same time? How can you explain, how can you account for, a power that produces sameness en masse, though in the subjective figure of difference? This enormous production of sameness in the subjective figure of difference is truly remarkable! Other systems of government have produced the figure of difference in the guise of sameness. This was true of the socialist states, if you look closely: their so-called totalitarian homogeneity was nothing but differences, disorder, irony, skepticism, and fragmentation. All such things are singular figures of power. So what is the nature of a power that produces consent in the guise of freedom, in the guise of disobedience? There are loads of people who think they're rebels, but the figures of rebellion are themselves standardized. This problem calls for a sophisticated analytic of power because it's not easy to explain. Indeed, you have to begin in a general way by distinguishing between two different types of submission, two levels of consent ("submission" may be an exaggeration). This is a very analytically important point.

There's a first level of consent that depends directly on the emblems or images. The images operate in such a way as to make me believe I'm acting in accordance with my own desire, through its relation to the image, but in reality I'm doing what is willed by the Other. This is alienated consent in the classic sense. There is semblance, and I can connect my desire to this semblance in the belief that it's my own desire, but since the semblance is controlled by an outside power, when I do so I'm actually doing what the power wants me to do. That's the first point, the emblematic operation properly speaking, the operation of semblance, which is closest to that described by Marxism under the name of "ideology." It's a figure of alienation: my own desire is alienated in emblems whose reality and purpose are other than what I believe they are. For example, if I'm deathly afraid of how well Le Pen might fare in the presidential election, so I take action, I demonstrate in the street, I vote against the abyss of fascism that, as I've been told and as I believe, has opened up before me, and actually I elect Chirac with 80 percent of the vote, is that the scenario we're in? Am I acting, as I believe I am, driven by my own desire to preserve my freedom, or am I actually doing what the parliamentary situation required in order to overcome a crisis whose nature I was unaware of? I'm not deciding this issue one way or another. I'm just mentioning it to give you an idea of the tenor of things. We might also think of the case in which some people, mobilizing under certain emblems, thought they were doing one thing but were actually being used politically for something else. The classic example is the Three Glorious Days of 1830. They were out in the street with their rifles fighting for the Republic, but they helped put Louis-Philippe on the throne instead. It's not just a matter of manipulation. Rather, it's because the idea under which the thing occurred was such that it could only be linked in real life to something other than the system of representations that corresponded to it. This is a fairly well-known mechanism, identifiable as a subversion of the Subject by the imaginary. The emblem says

"This is your desire," and then the real deployed on that basis ultimately has nothing to do with that desire.

The second level of consent is not consent, so to speak, to the emblems but to the need for emblems, to the fact that there have to be emblems, to the belief that I have to share in the emblematic figure. But consenting to the need for the emblematic figure is not the same thing as being alienated in the emblem. In the former case, I consent to the emblem, possibly being aware of its arbitrary nature but with the absolute conviction that I have no choice but to share in an emblematic figure. As, for example, when I'm convinced that I have no choice but to share in the democratic emblem. That's not the same as doing something, on its behalf and at any given time, that I believe is a defense or an illustration of democracy but is actually something else. *That* is how the emblem works, which must be distinguished from the need to consent to it. It is, in my view, on this level that real power is exercised. Naked power is not, strictly speaking, the power of emblems, which can be exercised to a greater or lesser degree depending on the circumstances and the subjectivities. Naked power is what creates the subjectively recognized necessity of the need for emblems. In other words, the essence of power isn't alienation, even though alienation is an absolutely fundamental operation. *The essence of naked power is ultimately the belief that alienation is necessary*, in one form or another. We have to be forced, not so much to go along with images as not to be able to claim that we can do without them. I want to emphasize that these are two subjectively very different levels. I contend that real power doesn't consist in deceiving but in making us consent to the fact that there is deception, however much we proclaim the contrary. Because proclaiming is only one side of the story. In actual fact, we are really subjected to what they want us to be subjected to, namely that we consent to the fact that there's deception, hence to the fact that there are emblems, and to the fact that therefore we can't do otherwise. In the contemporary world, this conviction took a negative form at first: it took the basic negative form whereby revolution was impossible. This needs to be said, calmly, because it's probably impossible and meaningless to assert the contrary today. Saying that revolution is possible is like saying nothing. If consent has taken this form, it's because revolution is the hypothesis that we can do without the emblems. That's why it presented itself as unalienation, as the affirmation of a real society, as the end of commodity fetishism (the end of one kind of emblem), as the hypothesis that we didn't have to consent to the need for emblems. The agreed consensus statement is that revolution is impossible or that it's not a recognizable ideality. There's a general consent to capitalism, and when someone says that "capitalism is no good," it's an innocuous statement, they're not committed to really destroying it. All it ultimately means is that they consent to the need for emblems, even if they don't necessarily buy into the actual alienation the emblem proposes.

⁓

This brings us back to one of our points of departure. This second level of consent—rather than consenting to be alienated in the dominant images, actually having consented to the inescapable need for their alienating presence—is precisely the subject of the revolutionaries' argument in *The Balcony*. The sixth scene of *The Balcony* is expressly devoted to the problem of whether the revolutionaries can do without emblems or not, and therefore to whether the revolutionaries can be asymmetrical or not in relation to power. This question of asymmetry is crucial. The question of naked power, considered from the standpoint of consent, is ultimately the question of whether or not there can be any asymmetry when it comes to power, or whether, in the final analysis, every form of power is the mirror image of another, i.e., the same in or under different emblems. This is a very relevant question, since, in the last presidential elections, everyone basically wanted there to be a second round pitting Chirac against Jospin, which would have been nicely symmetrical. That's, moreover, what was said afterwards: at least *they're* both democrats! In fact, people had gotten a glimpse, in the pathetic guise of Le Pen, of the horror of the asymmetrical, which no one was happy about, except perhaps those who had voted for him and had done so with a certain dread of the situation. You can see just how profound the issue of consent and asymmetry is. Indeed, naked power's main argument, the argument that makes people consent to the need for emblems, is the danger of asymmetry. Generally speaking, you can be sure that, beneath the horror of the hideous character we were shown—emerging from an old trunk like a grimacing puppet that astonishes everyone because they'd thought he was dead, and so there was something zombielike about him as well—lurked the secret horror of asymmetry. The understandable horror at the sight of that obscene resurrected vampire should be distinguished from the terrible fear aroused by asymmetry, which represents the prioritizing of the noncontinuation of things as they are. Suddenly the fact looms up that it's not certain that things will go on as they are, even though the deep desire is for them to go on. Conservatism is a fundamental passion. But what did conservatism consist of in this particular case? Well, of the fact that we consented to the need for emblems. That's the primordial consent.

Let me digress for a minute. A lot of people said: "We've reforged our republican compact." Some even said: "We've reestablished the social contract!" Rousseau would have been touched by this, and that's an understatement! What is the republican compact? We can finally see what it's all about. It's: "Whew, things will go on the way they were before!" That's what the republican compact is. "That was a close call." Which, truth be told, was never in any way a real possibility: there wasn't the slightest chance that the monster in question would get into power. But it was obviously a close call; we dodged a bullet. It's easier to go vote for Chirac than to have to confront the beast.

I'm saying this because we're very close to the issue of naked power here. That's what actually controls us, not the bogeymen of external constraint that we imagine, fantasize about, and project onto the distant countries that don't have the good fortune to be democracies. What do we consent to? I really think that the consent to what we call the republican compact is the consent to the fact that our current fundamental political misery is necessary. That's what we consent to. I don't know anyone who thinks our political situation is fantastic, except for a handful of journalists. If you ask people individually, no one says: "It's great, it's all good." You can take this on the level of opinions. That would be the first level. But the opinions are all more or less critical, and when public opinion is critical, it means people are not marching in lockstep with the emblems, they can only speak "critically" about the emblems. And as for the fact that it can't really be otherwise, that we can't do without this emblem system, there's a basic consent, namely, the presence in us of what I call the naked power of what's behind the emblematic disposition.

———✺———

Ultimately, this will lead to the final stage of this question of naked power, and Genet's characters' discussion in *The Balcony* is about this very subject. We need to find a way to reopen that discussion. If philosophy can help do so, so much the better. It's basically a discussion about the relationship in politics among consent, emblems, and action. That's the triangulation. What is the relationship between political action and a consent more fundamental than it, the problem of which is images and emblems? Let me read you an excerpt from scene 6, to show the way forward. Roger and Mark are two revolutionaries. Mark has just been appointed to the Central Committee.

ROGER (*to* MARK): What's to be done?

MARK: Give orders to design posters showing Chantal on the barricades and on the balcony of the Palace. See to it that they're pasted on every wall and billboard. (ROGER *makes a gesture.*) Do as I tell you. According to information, the Grand Chamberlain has gone to The Balcony, where the Chief of Police is said to be. They've gone there to work out the usual kind of operation. They know very well that as far as they're concerned the revolt must have only one purpose: to heighten their glory by putting down the insurrection. We're going to cramp their carnival by countering with our own.

ROGER: A carnival?

MARK (*forcefully*): We're going to use Chantal. Her job is to embody the revolution. The job of the mothers and widows is to mourn the dead. The job of the dead is to cry for revenge. The job of our heroes is to die with a smile . . . The Palace will be occupied this evening. From the balcony of the Palace Chantal will rouse the people, and sing. The time for reasoning is past; now's the time to get steamed up and fight like mad. Chantal embodies the struggle; the people are waiting for her to represent victory.[3]

This is the moment of the first decision made by the revolutionaries, who think they're victorious (which they won't be, because in the game of images they'll ultimately lose), the decision to showcase an emblem. We need emblems: Chantal has symbolized the struggle, and now she must represent victory. Victory mustn't be reduced to mere nonconsent to the existing political power; it must appear in the form of consent to the new, revamped emblems. It's carnival versus carnival, disposition of images versus disposition of images.

Roger represents the other alternative, especially since he's Chantal's lover, and he has the feeling that she's going to fade away like an illusion:

ROGER (*vehemently*): But I dragged you—dragged you!—from the grave! And you're already escaping me and mounting to the sky. . . . Your name's on the lips of people who've never seen or heard you. Before long, they'll think it's for you they're fighting. You're already a kind of saint. Women try to imitate you. . . . (*In a fury.*) I didn't carry you off, I didn't steal you, for you to become a unicorn or a two-headed eagle . . .

GEORGETTE (*contemptuously*): Don't you like unicorns?

CHANTAL (*to* ROGER): I'll come back, and everything will be the same. We love each other. . . .

ROGER: Nothing will be the same, and you know it. You'll be what you've always dreamt of being: an emblem forever escaping from her womanliness. (349)

So you see: the discussion will go on, and the revolution will ultimately fail. This discussion, transposed to today's context, would be the discussion about the media's role in the figure of power: Is it propaganda machine versus propaganda machine? Is it emblem versus emblem? Mark claims that that's the way it is. What Genet has his play say is that if that's really the way it is, if consent wins out over the revolution, if symmetry wins out over asymmetry, then you won't really have changed your subjectivity, your subjectivity of power, that is, the figure by which you contribute to power. If we say that power is consent, that power is us, that it's everyone, it can't be identified by separation. If we don't accept asymmetry, if we think we have to consent to emblems, then conservatism and symmetry will necessarily prevail—symmetry, insofar as symmetry is, in the final analysis, death. This is also what the play will say, for the great master of symmetry, the Chief of Police, is identical to death.

Incidentally, this is also true as regards esthetics. Just think about what Stravinsky said about Haydn: that he was the only one of the classical composers to have understood that to be perfectly symmetrical is to be perfectly dead.

We've got something similar here. If the subjectivity of power tolerates symmetry, and tolerates nothing but symmetry, then it is rooted in something equivalent to the conservative death of politics. We could say that the understanding of naked power, its real identification, requires us to accept real passages with no images. The best definition that could be given of what the revolutionary subjectivity was—provided it wasn't made symmetrical by the state, as was usually the case—is probably that it is a real passage, a real experience, with no images. That's the only thing that gives it the reality of nonconsent. Can there be a real experience with no images? I'm going to leave you in suspense till next year!

Year Two

The Logic of
Exceptions

Session 1

October 9, 2002

The question I asked last year about the present time, which I'd begun to deal with, can take the form of a question addressed to Hegel: Is he right when he claims that philosophy always comes after the fact, and therefore too late? It's his famous aphorism: "The owl of Minerva only takes flight at dusk." The owl of knowledge, the owl of wisdom, only takes flight when the day of History is done. What was to have taken place has already taken place by the time the owl takes its flight. The taking place of history is already over by the time philosophical wisdom produces its concept.

Hegel's thesis is that of an essentially recapitulative, or retroactive, dimension of philosophy, although, for Hegel, that doesn't prevent this retroaction from taking the form of the absolute Idea. By recovering becoming and raising it to a concept, it establishes the absoluteness of what it is the retroaction of. But the fact remains that it's a retroaction. Philosophy is not concerned, strictly speaking, with the pure present. So my question is: Is there really any possibility of a *contemporary* philosophy, in the radical sense of the word, i.e., a philosophy contemporary with its own time, a philosophy adequate to its own present? For Hegel, philosophy is always in the dimension of a future anterior. It is what understands the process when it's over. We might also say: Is there a philosophy of our time, of the present we share, that is not lagging behind this present time, that is not always and constitutively a kind of hindsight [*après-coup*]? There has been a lot of playing on the term *après-coup*, so let's play on it too: Can philosophy be "in the loop" [*dans le coup*] and not always "after the fact" [*après coup*]?[1] What about the way it infiltrates the present or approaches it otherwise than as a synthesis of the past?

The first consideration has to do with the present, with our present, with the presence of the present, with "what there is." Indeed, if you accept that philosophy can be a philosophy of the present, a contemporary philosophy, it implies that there's a present. Prior to the question we're asking, there is implicitly already the thesis that there's a present, that the present exists. Unlike its empirical appearance, however, this thesis is not self-evident. I touched on this point last year when I said that one of the features of the contemporary era might be that there was no world, or that a new world hadn't yet come, that we were in an in-between time where we weren't sure whether there was a world. More radically, we might wonder whether there's a present, a living present. But when would we be able to say that there's no present? What does such a hypothesis mean? To my mind, there are two reasons why there may be no present.

◦◦◦

The first hypothesis is that there's no present when what there is is too obviously or imperiously consumed by the past, when we're under the tyranny of the past, when we're living in what could be called "flat" times, times that are in fact times of continuation, of repetition. Or times with no projects. Times that are not engaged in the tension of their present but are convinced that they are stuck in the past. In the latter case, the subjectivity is a subjectivity of survival, "survival" to be understood in Debord's and the Situationists' sense. People aren't anxious about survival in the material sense of the term; rather, life itself is survival or continuation, life is the continuance of itself through the repetition of what it is based on. It is not engaged in the projective intensity of itself but only in the continuation of its being.

Let's say that a time of that sort has no present because it is consumed by the temporality of tradition. The first example of exhaustion of the present is therefore when life is lived out in the element of tradition. This is a world detemporalized by the sheer weight of the past.

But it's not only tradition that can create the effect of a negation of the present. In actual fact, a certain kind of nontraditional, or indeed antitraditional, modernity can also involve stagnation or negation of the present. A little later, I'll use some poems to try to help you grasp this in a tangible way. But it's important to understand that the restlessness of modernity can be perfectly compatible with the idea that there is nothing but the continuation of this restlessness itself.

So there are two types of subjection to the past or negation of the present through repetition. First, there's the traditional type, which is something like symbolic repetition. The system of customs, generations, religious phrases, and so on is repeated. But so is the system of novelty without innovation, without rupture, continual and constant novelty, where everything changes except for the nature of the novelty. Change can be just as repetitive as immobility. This is a very important point when it comes to contemporary debates over what is modern and what is old-fashioned. The old-fashioned are accused of being tradition bound. But there can also be no present because of change itself, which, on account of its own constant restlessness, can be an erasure of the present.

As metaphors of the two possible kinds of exhaustion of the present, I propose, first, as regards the poetic perception of a traditional world, an excerpt from book 4, section 2 of Saint-John Perse's "Winds." I'm using this poem because I enjoy rereading Saint-John Perse, who was the poet of my adolescence. "Winds," as its title implies, is explicitly a poem about change. It is about the westward movement, the conquest of America, the pioneers, the crossing of great distances. It's the poetic complement of the Western: lone riders in the vast wilderness, someone trekking onward toward an elusive ocean. Within this epic figure of change—which, in a sense, is a form of unchanging or predestined change—we come at a given moment upon a definitive image of what the world of tradition is. This world of tradition is revealed poetically when the expedition reaches the high plateaus and discovers, in a world of stone and the sacred, something that has been preserved and maintained. Although "Winds" is a poem about North America, it's a lot more reminiscent of the plateaus of the Andes and the Indian communities descended from the Incas.

I can say from personal experience that this is the case. I took a long trip to Bolivia in the 1960s, at the time when Régis Debray was a prisoner of the local military authorities. Along with my good friend, the Belgian lawyer Roger Lallemand, I was representing the *Ligue des Droits de l'Homme et du Citoyen* [the Human Rights League] on his behalf. When you reach the Quechua communities of the high plateaus of the Andes, you get the powerful feeling that they have held onto something that colonization, the Spaniards, and modernity haven't been able to destroy. At the time of the land occupation movements, in subsequent years, the Indians came down from the mountains and occupied the lands that they considered belonged to them traditionally, from before the Spanish occupation. They stopped at a precise boundary, which was incomprehensible to the landowners. They stopped and planted stakes: this was their land register, their concessions, a land register preserved down through the centuries by a sort of secret, unspoken memory. These tribes knew what their territory was, but that territory no longer had any sort of reality in the modern world. It is striking that Saint-John Perse, in search of a metaphor of tradition, of a present bound by the law of a vanished past, a past that is no longer even represented, chose this world of the high plateaus. Here is the excerpt:

> I remember the high nameless country, illumined with horror and void of all sense. No dues and no excise. There the wind claims its franchises; there the earth yields its birthright for a shepherd's pottage—earth more grave, under the gravitation of the women moving slowly, smelling of sheep. . . . And the Mountain is honoured by the perambulation of women and of men. And its worshippers offer up to it foetuses of llamas. Brew resinous plants before it. Fling to it the tripe of slaughtered animals. Excrements set apart for the treating of the hides.
>
> I remember the high stone land where, before the storm, the white earth pigsties shine at evening like the approaches to sacred towns. And very late in the low night, at the great salt-flats, light will come to the marshes bordered with wallows for the sows. And to little shelters for travellers, smoky with copal . . .
>
> —What would you go there to seek?[2]

This is a metaphor of what I'm trying to convey to you with this first figure of the subreption of the present, of the burying of the present beneath something far vaster than itself, a sort of ageless past embedded in the land itself, commensurate with the land itself.

And now, as for the present wiped out by the restlessness of modernity, I'll borrow its metaphor from a poem by Brecht entitled "Late Lamented Fame of the Giant City of New York." What Brecht is trying to say in this poem is that capitalist prosperity, the restlessness and self-assurance of Capital, are a sort of false present, a sort of intensity of presence that's actually false. It's a present of restlessness, but without the real life of the present. This poem is remarkable—you'd think it was contemporary. The second section was revised, because it takes place after the 1929 financial crisis: the false present had had some of the wind taken out of its sails! The description of the false present is very typical of things that could be said nowadays. Let me read you an excerpt from it:

We too perpetually smiled, as if before or after a good piece of business
Which is the proof of a well-ordered digestion.
We too liked to slap our companions (all of them future customers)
On arm and thigh and between the shoulder-blades
Testing how to get such fellows into our hands
By the same caressing or grabbing motions as for dogs.
So we imitated this renowned race of men who seemed destined
To rule the world by helping it to progress.

What confidence! What an inspiration!
Those machine rooms: the biggest in the world!
The car factories campaigned for an increase in the birthrate: they
        had started making cars (on hire purchase)
For the unborn. Whoever threw away
Practically unused clothing (but so
That it rotted at once, preferably in quicklime)
Was paid a bonus. Those bridges
Which linked flourishing land with flourishing land! Endless! The
        longest in the world! Those skyscrapers—

The men who piled their stones so high
That they towered over all, anxiously watched from their summits the
    new buildings
Springing up from the ground, soon to overtower
Their own mammoth size.

(Some were beginning to fear that the growth of such cities
Could no longer be stopped, that they would have to finish their days
With twenty storeys of other cities above them
And would be stacked in coffins which would be buried
One on top of the other.)
But apart from that: what confidence! Even the dead
Were made up and given a cosy smile
(These are characteristics I am setting down from memory; others
I have forgotten) for not even those who had got away
Were allowed to be without hope.[3]

It's not the high plateaus of the Indians anymore; it's the big skyscrapers of the moderns. Feeling anxious about the skyscrapers! But it's the same sort of thing that's said in both cases. What we have here, either in silent immobility or in absolute frenzied activity and self-confidence, is something like the exhaustion of the present.

⎯⎯∞⎯⎯

Our first case is therefore the one in which the figures of repetition—whether they are the traditional structures or the structures of change itself—block all access to the present. In the second case, there is no present either, because the future exhausts the present. The lack of project is clearly an exhaustion of the present, but a hyperbolic project is also an exhaustion of the present. In other words, if all the actualized meaning of what is is in the future, if the future is the absolute meaning of the present, then it might be said that the project devours the present itself. An example of this would be the radiant future of the construction of socialism: a lot of deaths in the present, but since the meaning of the present is in the future, it doesn't matter. Except that, if the whole meaning of the present is in the future, the present is exhausted. The present may thus be devoured by the past, but it may also be devoured by the future. The twentieth century was proof of this. And before it, there was something about the nineteenth century that was haunted, through the idea of progress or development, by something like a devouring of the present, such that the representation of the future, the chance for a future, constituted a sort of redemption for the suffering of the present.

This point can be found in a completely characteristic way in Victor Hugo. Hugo was the great poet of the ideology of progress; he gave it its form, because the natural poetic force of this tremendous poet lay in describing the world as mired in metaphysical suffering. Where he excels is in the image of terror. He's remarkable when it comes to this. There's an epic grandeur to Hugo because he confronts terror head on. Most of his great poems and the great moments in his novels are terrifying ones. It was really wrong to turn him into a prophet with a flowing white beard, a kindly, senile old grandfather! He is a poet of horror: his depiction of the Middle Ages, of poverty, of adversity, of the fate of revolutions, makes him a poet of blood and of night. However, apart from all that, there is a depiction of the future as the ultimate meaning of the present. Often the movement of a poem by Hugo is, first, an extraordinarily intense focus on nocturnal horror, and then a separate, redemptive mode comes in, which is like a sense of being able to diminish the horror-filled present. This present will be redeemed with a separate promise. I'll give you one example, but you can find others. Hugo is like Balzac: they're both superlative writers, and the more you read of them the better. You have to read thousands of lines of poetry. And there are some real nuggets in them. I'm going to read you an excerpt from "Ce que dit la bouche d'ombre" ["What the shadow-mouth said"], the last poem of the concluding book of *Les Contemplations*, which, characteristically, is called "On the Brink of the Infinite" [Au bord de l'infini]. On the brink of the infinite: that's right. First, there's a depiction of the real of the world as something terrifying, as a metaphysics of suffering, and then there's something else, namely, the ideology of progress in its separate form, the scientific promise of the Enlightenment. The first movement is enormously long, with hundreds of lines. I'm only going to read you the end, where all the bitterness of a metaphysics of suffering is expressed.

All these dark cells which are called flowers Quiver; . . .

Note that this is a mind-boggling idea! The flower, instead of being a blossoming, an opening up, is treated as something closed and mysterious.

. . . the rock begins to dissolve into tears.
Arms are raised out of the sleeping tomb;
The wind groans, the night complains, the water laments.
And, under the softened eye which looks on from above,
The whole abyss is nothing now but an immense sob.

That's the world. Then there's a white space in the text and a change of rhythm: instead of a regular series of oppressive alexandrine lines, there will be [in the French] an alternation of alexandrines and half-lines:

Hope! Hope! Hope, wretches!
No infinite mourning, no incurable ills,
No eternal hell!
Pains go to God, like arrows to the target.
Good deeds are the invisible hinges
Of the gate of Heaven.[4]

This is another way of saying that the present may be, or must be, erased. "Hope!": on the brink of the infinite there is the attribution of a finitude to the metaphysics of suffering and a virtual, unattributable, unrepresented infinity regarding what, perhaps, is to come. No eternal hell: suffering is limited to the finitude of the world, which is accompanied by an infinite hope that is nevertheless only a promise.

I call this vision of the world vision as projection. The alienation of the present by the past is the figure of repetition; the alienation of the present by the future is projection. The real present must be created, a path must be shown and explored, in a space that is neither the space of repetition nor that of projection. It is not enough to say that the world today is repetitive and lacking a project. Actually, there has also been an experience of metaphysical projection in this world. The question of the present is complex and is not exhausted by the opposition between vitality of the project and repetitiveness. The present, our present, requires the conflictual interaction of repetition and projection. I'm not saying that the present exists as soon as there's such an interaction, but in any case, it doesn't exist if that interaction isn't there. It is a condition for the present. There is only a present if there are experiences (we'll come back to this) in which a sort of mysterious copresence of repetition and projection occurs. There has to be an instance of the past, an element of repetition, and also, of course, a future, an element of projection. The present is both retention of the past and anticipation of the future (as Husserl might say).

This is precisely what Mallarmé says in a famous essay, "L'Action restreinte" ["Restricted action"], dating from 1895, an exceedingly deep, rich essay. I'm going to read you an excerpt from it because part of the seminar could ultimately be said to be an enormous commentary on it:

> There is no Present, no—a present does not exist. . . . For lack of the Crowd's declaring itself, lack—of everything. Ill-informed is anyone who would proclaim himself his own contemporary, deserting, usurping with equal impudence, when the past ceased and when a future is slow to come, or when the two mingle perplexingly to cover up the gap.[5]

This is a theory of the present, about which Mallarmé says a number of things that will be very important for us:

1.   The present must exist in order for us to be able to declare ourselves our own contemporaries. This is a simple but crucial remark: anyone who declares themself their own contemporary must first determine whether there is a present, whether the present exists. I regard this as an advance critique of the great contemporary hue and cry over modernity: people are always screeching that we have to be contemporary. . . . For Mallarmé, that's impudence, because you are not demonstrating that a present really exists. You can't declare yourself your own contemporary or proclaim that you're the individual of today unless you've first determined whether there's a present. And if the present doesn't exist—which was Mallarmé's thesis in 1895—then loudly declaring yourself to be a modern, a contemporary, is nothing but deceit, impudence, usurpation.

2. The lack of a present also means that there's no past or future: a past ceased, a future is slow to come. This brings us back to what I called the in-between structure, the time when the present disappears into the gap. The gap [*l'écart*] is a Mallarmé word, too. The present can be negated by the past, it can be negated by the future, and the present is problematic if it's not an overlapping of the two. If there's no past or future, and therefore no repetition or projection, then no construction of the present is possible. What Mallarmé means (this is his own opinion) is that the age of great revolutions, of great historical creations, is a thing of the past, and we don't know what will come in its place. The past is over, and the future is not yet here. We are in a time of historical flatness, an in-between time. A century later we can say something similar: the age of revolutions is past, and what is going to come hasn't taken shape yet. Mallarmé's conclusion is that a present is lacking. So we have a definition of the present in terms not of simplicity but of complexity. The present isn't simple presence. Subtle, complex conditions are required, namely that the past not be past and that the future already be here. Extraordinary conditions! There has to be a copresence of the past and the future. That's why we need to speak about a complexity of the present. When Mallarmé says that the present is lacking, he means that this complexity is lacking, and, as a result, the present isn't named, constructed, or articulated. But why is that so? And what will indicate that there is no present?

3. The fact that the Crowd doesn't declare itself. What constitutes the present is in the form of the declaration, in this case the historical or collective declaration. If the Crowd doesn't declare itself, then, in a way, everything is lacking; as regards the present, there's nothing. The Crowd is the subject of the declaration. It is what makes a declaration historically a declaration, what conveys the declaratory speech whereby a present exists. In this sense, the present is a collective creation. It's not a decision made somewhere apart, let alone a presumptuous—and repetitive!—self-assertion. We could call "a declaration" something that signifies a present. Now a declaration is when, at one point at least, repetition is indistinguishable from projection. Or, if you will, when repetition is blocked by projection. At one point, there's a retrospective overlay of the power of the past in the form of a projection. There's no

separate projection, as with Hugo. Instead, there's a projective capacity that is indexed to the repetitive power of the past and reorients it by attributing to the past as a whole a different meaning from the one given it by repetition. This is difficult but very important: the present contained in the declaration, in what the Crowd declares, is something that raises repetition to the level of projection. It's not the replacing of the one by the other. On the contrary, it is something that will absorb and give meaning to repetition in a world that is no longer the world of repetition but of the skewing of repetition. There's no white space, disjunction, or separation, as with Hugo. There's no device of a separate projection. What we see with Hugo and with all the theorists of separate projection is that there's a device of projection. The real nature of the projection is, in a way, that it leads to repetition itself. However, the only revolution is a revolution in traditions. The traditions themselves have to be completely changed. It's not just a matter of something happening that's separate from them, because in that case they'll inevitably come back. Experience has shown this: whenever you have the theory of an absolute beginning, you actually have the return of the old. But then what is the present, if it is a beginning? It's what Mallarmé is trying to say with the word "declaration," i.e., something in the declaration acknowledges the past and prevents the past from merely passing away. It's a use of the past other than the fact that it passes away, a use that projects the past onto the present and thereby creates a future. But the whole point is to determine what aspect of repetition is swept up in the projection. A disjunctive thesis is not sufficient. In other words—this was a strong intuition of Deleuze's—there is something about the present that is of course a disjunction, but a disjunction within synthesis. Deleuze called this a "disjunctive synthesis." His disjunctive synthesis is really what I'm trying to illustrate here. It's something that prevents there being a gap, a white space, a pure disjunction. If there were one, it would be a case of analytic, not synthetic, disjunction. Synthetic disjunction is when there's a present, when there's creation, because something of the past, of repetition, of tradition, has itself been subverted and swept up in the projection. So we need to return to the ambiguous meaning of the word "revolution." Revolution is something that makes an additional turn; it's not an absolute beginning but something swept up in the spiral of a new cycle. I think we need to imagine the present as the declaration of a sweeping up, of what is effectively swept up in projection. The declaration—to use Mallarmé's term, which is the perfect word—is the "swept up" coextension of repetition and projection.

And finally, if the present is the declaration, then the Crowd, in effect, must declare itself. The Crowd could be any number of things, which shows that the declaration is a dimension of historical creativity, of human creativity. A single person might constitute the Crowd, because the declaration constitutes the Crowd. It will be this on the basis of what Mallarmé calls a mingling or a perplexity ("mingle perplexingly to cover up the gap"), that on which the declaration will arise, attempting to sweep up the past and repetition into projection and creation.

That's an assessment of the twentieth century: it was the century of the hypothesis of the absolute beginning. That's its dimension of terror, which is related to the fact that projection was conceived of as separation from repetition. And, in the end, because there was this terror of projective separation, we've been advised to give up on the present and trust in the reign of what there is. It's true that it's a real challenge to come up with a nonunilaterally projective conception of the present, one that is not just separation from repetition. This means that revolutionary thinking must, in some way, assimilate or transmute, transfigure something of tradition.

Let's not be intimidated by modernity's criticism of archaism. That's just the restless way of denying the present by criticizing a different way of denying it, the repetitive or traditional way. That's not our problem. Our problem is to determine how repetition can be swept up, contained as it is in the declaration. That's why—and we saw this in a distorted, contorted way in the twentieth century—it is quite possible for there to be something seemingly more traditional in creative thinking than in modern conservative thinking. We needn't worry about it. In the attempt to seek a present, there is sometimes something that seems to absorb elements of tradition, unlike what happens with cynical modernity, which will readily say it has no past, no tradition, no law, no rule other than the law of the market. This is because there's a problem at its heart, the problem of the declaration: what is being declared? A true declaration always involves a skewing of tradition, not a pure separation from it. I think the word that best describes this is "torsion." It is a matter of putting tradition into torsion so as to connect it to projection, an occasionally violent torsion that's exerted on tradition but doesn't separate from it altogether. It's not a disjunction. It is this movement of torsion that will go through the heart of the situation, its perplexed, entangled, ambiguous, and complicated heart, to produce what will be called the complexity of the present.

To sum up regarding the complexity of the present, we could say that the complexity of the present is the declaration—that is, the overlapping of repetition and projection—the declaration insofar as it exerts a torsion on repetition in order to hook it up or connect it to projection. This is an electrification that is different from tradition: a different current will be made to flow. It's something other than destroying it for the sake of an absolute beginning, of a new world.

⸙

Last year I dealt primarily with the imagistic temporal ground, which I called "images of the present time." I dealt with the possible horizon of the present, with what the declaration can and must place the creation of the present on. I would now like to explain the general logic of the three years of this seminar.

The first year dealt with the operations by which the general context of the question of the present can be identified. It was a kind of putting-in-place [*mise en place*]. I presented a method, a method for placing the perplexity, as Mallarmé put it, or the entanglement.

This year will be devoted to the search for the exception, for what is declaratively an exception to pure and simple placement.

Next year we'll ask how we can base ourselves on both the placement and the exception to define what a true life is, a life that is faithful to the present. The situation, the exceptional conditions of the present, the fidelity to the present or the true life: these will be our topics. We'll return to the old problem of the true life, Rimbaud's problem: the true life is absent. But why may we still, perhaps, affirm its present?

So our starting point will be: What is an exception? What makes something like a declaration ultimately, locally, possible? To discuss this, I will have to give a brief summary of what was covered last year, since the declaration will stand out against the perplexity or the entanglement of the background, as constituted by the images of the present time.

I had proposed a four-step method for investigating contemporaneity, a general method, which I applied to the contemporary world:

1.   Identifying what I called the emblem, what acts as a spiritual community: What is shared? What constitutes the claim of a spiritual community to the present? What validates what there is? It's the emblem. What is the validation process? Or, to use a Lacanian-psychoanalytic vocabulary, what is the master signifier, the one that both unites and rallies? I suggested that democracy is the emblem of the present time.

I'd like to make a comment about this. There's a necessary distinction, which is not sufficiently made, between the question of democracy, in the sense we're talking about it here, and the question of freedoms. If you think about it, the word "democracy," as it operates today, is in coalescence with the question of freedom(s). But in what sense? Democracy is related to freedom in the sense that what is meant by democracy is that which does not prohibit or restrain, or not excessively. It's a negative characterization. Democracy is the political system of freedom, because such and such a thing isn't prohibited, restrained, or banned. Let's take a closer look at this. You can assemble and you won't get beaten up, you can write something in the press and you won't be apprehended, you can walk down the street and, provided you're not undocumented, you won't be instantly arrested, and so on. The correlation between the political regime—the form of government—known as democracy and the question of freedoms is wholly negative. A sort of liberalism with regard to prohibitions: that's what accounts for the undeniable success of these regimes. And it's true, to look at things from a positive angle, that there seem to be fewer and fewer things prohibited. It is even conceivable—because, as its proponents are constantly reminding us, democracy can always be improved—that someday nothing, or just about, will be prohibited anymore.

My position is that this negative correlation leaves the question of freedom unresolved. For "freedom" cannot be satisfied with a negative definition. Descartes already said as much: the freedom to do whatever one pleases, or indiscriminate freedom, is at best "the lowest degree of freedom." Thinking you're a free Subject just because whatever you want to do or say is not prohibited is sheer nonsense. We need to examine public freedoms (never mind metaphysics) and take a close look at what freedom reduced to the democratic-type negative correlation is.

Let's take a simple example. Suppose that anything at all can be said publicly, that nothing is really prohibited in public speech. Does that mean that something has been said, however? That something important, something that affects the public interest in a crucial way, has been publicly pronounced? Absolutely not. The formal authorization to say anything at all does not, by itself, create any particular speech. But if nothing is prohibited and yet nothing, properly speaking, has been said, freedom does not exist. The question of what is really said cannot be reduced to the fact that it is possible to say it. And, conversely, it is by no means certain that the fact that something hasn't been said is related to the fact that saying it is prohibited, because it is by no means certain that the real can be defined in terms of possibility. The expansion of possibility, of the possibility of speaking, for example, doesn't imply the expansion of real speech, because real speech is not the realization of a formal possibility. It's not because you're allowed to say a lot of things, or even everything, that it can be inferred from this that there's really a free ability to speak. That would be too easy, and it implies a specific, dubious ontological axiom, namely that freedom is ultimately directly connected with the formal, authorized space of possibilities. That implies a theory of freedom that could be called a weak theory. Because, once again, it may be that real speech, far from being conditioned by formal prohibitions on freedom of speech, only in fact exists at the point where the impossible-to-say is encountered.

We are forced to note that in extremely despotic periods, when, officially, very little could be said, as in the seventeenth century, much was in fact said. In that era, in principle you couldn't say very much: you couldn't speak ill, even moderately, of the Catholic religion, of the king, and so on. But does that mean there was less real speech? Was there less than there is today, for instance, when we can speak ill of anything we feel like? That's far from certain. We can see in an utterly naïve and ordinary way that, in terms of what is really said, hence in terms of freedom as freedom that effectively creates real speech, the relationship to the question of the expansion of prohibitions is a far more complicated one than a simple relationship of correlation. Does this mean that it's necessary to prohibit? No! There's no obvious correlation, either, between the fact that something is prohibited and the fact that it is really said. Especially since there are real prohibitions and fake ones. When you prohibit something that everyone does, it's a fake prohibition. It's as though you weren't prohibiting it at all. I'm saying all this because it is quite possible that democracy is the emblem of the present time not in real life in the sense of freedom, but only in the sense of the formal expansion of possibility. And this expansion of possibility might actually be meaningless from the standpoint of reality, because it is blocked for the most part by commodities. Ultimately, the expansion of possibility goes hand in hand with the expansion of commercial, including pornographic, possibility, and don't take that as a puritanical remark. If the expansion of possibility is the only internal content of what is presented as freedom under the emblem of democracy, then it may well be that, in reality, there is a blockage of that freedom by commodities, which provide a circulating body to what, without them, is nothing but the formal lack of possibility. Once again, real speech, really free speech, doesn't have to do with the expansion of possibility but with the *creation* of possibility. Freedom isn't the fulfillment of a possibility but the creation of a possibility that was previously impossible.

2.   Then, after we've determined what the emblem is, I said we had to analyze the type of naked power concealed by the consent to the emblem. What type of authority is concealed by the consent to the democratic emblem? I can sum up in one sentence what I said about this: fidelity to the democratic emblem comes at the cost of a constraint on the form of the subject, a constraint that involves the subject's having to confront commodities, because that, overall, is what defines it as a subject. The subject is the consumer, in the broadest and practically the most metaphysical sense of the term. The subject confronts the commercialized world as a consuming subjectivity. This is a constraint: the

subject isn't free to be elsewhere because it consents to the democratic emblem and won't enjoy the perks that go with the emblem unless it remains in that position.

3.   That being said, we need to see what the logic of exceptions is, i.e., what constitutes an exception to all the foregoing?

4.   Finally, once we've identified the exception, we'll have to conclude that there may be systemic vulnerabilities and that there may be a present, in the strongest sense of the term, a present such that a Crowd can declare itself. This is the issue of the systematic synthesis of the exceptions that would challenge both naked power and its emblem.

Last year we focused mainly on points 1 and 2. This year we'll be dealing with point 3. What is an exception to the emblem or to the naked power that the emblem sustains? Basically, we could say that this year will be devoted to declarations. What declares itself? What is declared or is declarable? It could be said that in the world as it is, declaration is the absolute opposite of communication. The antinomy is this: the identification of what constitutes a declaration is also effected by means of a break with what is merely circulation or communication. Indeed, a declaration does not circulate; it is addressed to everyone. It's not an object dependent on the type of circulation, whether commodity or otherwise. Nor is it a form of communication. It's a creation of the present.

As for point 4, the systemic vulnerability, we're going to see what it means to think and live in the present. What can we hope for? We're not going to say "Hope! Hope! Hope, wretches!" as Hugo does.

⸺⸙⸺

Let me give you the somewhat rough outline for next time.

We're going to attempt to find criteria for the exception, criteria answering the question "What makes a declaration possible?" We'll see that there are two main criteria, which are interrelated.

The first is obviously that, formally, a declaration must contain some element that is not reducible to commodity circulation. This, as I will show, must be absolutely distinguished from the question of whether the declaration is successful or not, which is an empirical question. There can be successful declarations—I'm in no way offering a defense of some secret thing that nobody knows about. But in any case, in a declaration there must be something heterogeneous to commodity circulation and communication. But if it's neither commodities nor communication, what is it? I suggest that we consider four possible types:

- Demonstration
- Contemplation
- Action (under certain conditions)
- Passion

The second criterion will have to do more specifically with what is not under the democratic emblem, in the sense we're using it here. This will be the tricky part! If we're not under the democratic emblem, we'll be totalitarian! Don't worry, we won't be. Far from any totality, I will present what I call "fivefold indifference," indifference to certain notions, which I'll list here for you:

- Indifference to number and therefore to the majority principle in all its forms, hence indifference to number as a criterion.
- Indifference to the established regime of the possible.
- Indifference to particularities, and especially to respect for particularities. I think every declaration is disrespectful in a fundamental way; it doesn't respect conventional ethics.
- Indifference to the supposed antinomy between authoritarian and tolerant: it will be neither authoritarian versus tolerant, nor authoritarian rather than tolerant, but an indifference to, a destitution of, this antinomy.
- Indifference to anything that separates repetition and projection.

This is what I call fivefold indifference, whereby something breaks free from the contemporary emblem and makes a present possible.

Session 2

November 20, 2002

This seminar is a place. An open place, which is less an integrated part of an institution than—in line with what I said last time—the unfolding of a potential declaration. This place, as you may have heard, has come under a number of threats. For the time being, the danger has been averted, and I want to thank everyone who spoke up or acted, anywhere at all, to ensure this. Our free place is still here.

What is a place? This happens to be one of the issues I wanted to talk to you about this year. What, in fact, is the construction, in a given world, of a heterogeneous place, a place that is not institutionally, or discursively, or in terms of the type of gathering it represents, wholly homogeneous with the prevailing situation? This question of place is important because every genuine innovation can probably be considered as being always also and at the same time the construction of a place.

"Place" denotes a topological category here: a place is something that inscribes a duration in space. Paradoxically, place is a concept of time. The place is what gives substance to the possibility of a duration, the duration of what I've called a declaration, the duration of the present (another paradox), the duration of what has declared a present.

The main problem of the contemporary world, in my view, is less the problem of what creates innovation than that of inscribing innovation in duration. We must impose the construction of a different time, a time internal to ordinary time. The place is what denotes, even if in a sporadic, transient, ephemeral way, the construction of a different time.

It is what reveals the possible novelty, the possibility of a new possibility, but reveals it as duration, through a sort of stability of its local foundation. The crystallization of the present as creation is also the problem of the place, of the establishment of a place. In a greater logic, my own particular one, it will be said to be the problem of the place of a truth. A truth is always something that constructs the place of its unfolding or the place of its consequences. This is because, at the outset, a truth is always located in a single point. Truth is not given as a totality. A truth is always in a single point at first. This point must be developed as its place, even if the place grows, expands, or branches out. Every truth is local, where "local" must be understood in its strongest sense as the requirement of a place. This obviously means that any protection of a truth is also the protection of a place. Places must be defended. It's very striking to note—this would be geopolitics—that the question of places, of the defense of places, of sovereignty over places, in a sense that is not at all territorial or nationalistic but is more radical, is the point where something begins and must be protected in its emergence, in its inception. The place is the place of the beginning and must be protected as such, because that is what will protect its duration.

—∞∞∞—

Now, after these few remarks about place, let's go back to that pressing question of the present, since—let me remind you—what I intend to do is test or assess whether something like a philosophical thinking of our present, of this present, is possible. Last time, using a number of texts—in particular a text by Mallarmé—I ultimately said (I'm summing this up very succinctly) that the present had to be conceived of as the nexus between a repetition and a projection, with no gap between them. The present should not be the gap between the repetition of the past and the projection of the future. There is only a present when there's no gap, no visible white space, between what persists from the past and what can be imagined or anticipated about the future. We saw that, in Hugo's poem, the dreadfulness of the present and the promise of the future were somehow separate. The present is when this disjunction doesn't exist, so it's when something of repetition itself is diverted or captured in a projection toward the future. In other words, the present isn't simply a cessation of repetition, something new that's absolutely separate from what persists. We're parting company here with the twentieth century, which almost always conceived of the present as an absolute beginning, the beginning of the "new man," the fraternal participant in a completely new world. I spoke at length about this in my seminar, for three years in a row.[1] And the conclusion from all of that was that the present needs to be conceived of otherwise than in the figure of a radical beginning. Something of projection has to absorb repetition and subject it to itself, of course, but also reorient and deploy it. In other words, the present must be an incorporation of the past into the future. Not of the whole past, but at least of something of the past. You'll note, moreover, that one of the features of the contemporary world in all its bad aspects often takes the form of contempt for the past. The future, the proposals about the future, have been deemed to be utopias and regarded as utopian nonsense. That's the "modern" critique of the future. But there's also a "modern" critique of the past, i.e., we have to be modern, not old-fashioned. The commodified present—let's call it that—is a present that sees itself as having no future and no past. It is the present of its own existence, and that's all. It has often been said that its symbol was really stock market activity, whose temporality, as you know, is quite short, often only a few seconds, a temporality that's also very nervous and tense. We live in a world where time is a time of the present dilated with a tiny sliver of the past and a tiny sliver of the future. So there's an entrenchment in a sort of subjective state that's neither project nor memory, or else when memory *is* evoked, it's for specific purposes, to support the need for this particular present and not some other one.

So we need to reconstruct the present. Mallarmé said, "A present is lacking." Today, this is even more the case: a present is lacking because that present, without project or memory, is a false present, inarticulable as a living present, as a true present. The present is the nexus between repetition and projection because projection reorients repetition without eradicating or eliminating it. That's why defending old-fashioned values may be progressive today. You'll be told: "You're defending public service—that's so old-fashioned." That isn't wrong, but there's something about the defense of the old-fashioned value that is more progressive than its elimination would be. It's not just a conflict between modernity and tradition. Today the conflict is about the very definition of the present. A common definition of the present is that it's the present of business. That's neither crazy nor stupid. It even has a very powerful reality, but it's a present that's disconnected from its major temporal articulations. The idea of proposing something different about the present means reincorporating into the vision and practice of the present temporal intervals that are on a different scale and that ultimately include a long memory and a strong project. Both are needed, because there's not just the lack of a project but the lack of fullness of the past as well. Our slogan can no longer be "Let's make a clean slate of the past," as is sung in "The Internationale," because making a clean slate of the past, as Marx stated in the *Communist Manifesto*, has been taken over to some extent by Capital, inasmuch as it has a vicious capacity for destroying the past. Capital's main argument is modernity; it is coextensive with an idea of modernity. Nor it is a question of taking refuge in the past, of becoming the nostalgic crusader for a particular figure of the past. What really matters is constructing a future that reincorporates the past, that reincorporates its fullness.

<hr>

Let me digress for a moment on this point. One of the basic advantages of philosophy is that it is the quintessential discipline of time on a vast scale. Only in philosophy can you claim without sounding ridiculous that the problems raised in the fourth century BCE are still highly relevant. Try to find that anywhere else! We're still dealing with Plato and Aristotle, from a certain point of view. Only the academic morons of analytic philosophy, chasing after the false democratic present of Capital, think that the only thing that matters in philosophy are the articles written in the past ten years. Our strength, on the contrary, is that we think on the scale of millennia. Philosophy is a teaching of time on a vast scale, of a past and a project on a vast scale, because it has always created impossible, far-reaching ideals. When Plato said that philosophy is a long detour, he was contrasting it with sophistry, whose aim is to reach a quick conclusion. Taking time and going slow are vital ideas today. The long detour isn't just the long discursive detour of considering questions; it's the creation of a unique temporality that is also the span of time in which a present exists. Ultimately, the real question has to do with the temporal span of the present itself. We need to have a conception of the present that affords a broad time span, encompassing the past as well as the future. It is of course a question of being under the emblem of the new. The project will subordinate repetition to itself, not the other way around. But such a subordination is not a negation. I want to stress the fact that it affords a possible vision of philosophy as a teaching of time, of the time of thinking, of the time of existence, because time is the main factor of oppression in today's world. There is, as has often been observed, a fundamental temporal dispossession at the heart of which lies wage labor and the purchase of time itself. Time is money. With the means it has at its disposal, which are partly theoretical but not nonexistent means, philosophy is a struggle against that dispossession, by way of a different proposition about time: time should be that of disinterested thought. Philosophy attempts to impose the subjective need for a broad time span. It does so as a proposition, because, as far as real-life solutions are concerned, it has no control over them. And, as I said, ultimately, this time that is different from commercial immediacy and wage labor can only be declared. Its mode of existence is a declaration. A different time must be declared, with its legitimacy, its construction, and its persistence. In other words, there is no objective advent of such a time. It does not inhabit the time of the false present as something that would simply have to be developed. No, it must necessarily be declared. That's why there are really three terms involved: repetition, projection, and declaration. Repetition denotes the persistence of the past. Projection denotes the possibility of the project or of what is possible. Declaration establishes the present that binds them together, that binds the past under the projective law of a future imagined as possible. It is thanks to declaration that there is no gap, because declaration is what comes where there would otherwise be an unbridgeable gap between tradition and project, unbridgeable because the false present has become lodged in that gap. And this false present will say: "The past is unnecessary and outmoded; the future is unrepresentable; and the project is an empty utopia whose realization is always criminal. So live in the present!"

The imperative of living in the present is one we'd gladly comply with, provided we were told what this present is. We agree that life is in the present, but the question is what the essence of this present is. If a gap is allowed to develop, then the injunction becomes that of the false present, the present of the market, of restlessness and communication. So the conjunction of repetition and projection must be declared. Otherwise, what takes hold is the false present of commodity circulation.

What we're interested in now in the investigation of our present is basically to determine what is declared today. As for what's communicated, we know all about that: we've got the media, which are the channels for general communication, for that. But when it comes to declaration, it's a different story! Declaring is situated in the nongap between repetition and projection, hence always in a position of exception in relation to the false present. Our problem now will be the logic of the exception, whereas last year we focused on the logic of the structure, of the "there is" (the emblems and naked power). Now we'll be looking for a logic of the exception, "exception" meaning what is declared as a novelty of the present.

We can begin with the formal criteria, i.e., the features by which a declaration, a contemporary creation, the fashioning of a new present, of whatever sort, can be identified. I said that there were two formal criteria. The first is that, with a genuine declaration, something does not circulate, is not reducible to commodity circulation, and therefore remains intractable in the contemporary false present. The second criterion is that there is something that's not directly homogeneous with the emblem, in the sense that the democratic emblem is the subjective organization of circulation. To sum up: an element of irreducibility to commodity circulation and an element of indifference to the common emblems. These are the two negative criteria that can be proposed and that we are now going to take a closer look at.

As regards the first criterion, we need to focus on what is heterogeneous, irreducible to pure and simple exchange, on what is not subject to a law of exchange or circulation. A declaration cannot be exchanged for another one. A declaration may respond to another one, but it is not exchangeable, not even a declaration of love, the paradigm of declaration. If you make a declaration of love, it's a risk, but you won't say: "I'll retract it if I'm not given one in return." You accept that there's something non-negotiable, and that's precisely why many people steer clear of it! If the person to whom you make your declaration makes one in return, there will be two declarations, not an exchange of declarations. Love is not an exchange; love doesn't exchange anything. Thinking of it as an exchange is really the commercial vision of love. I bargain, you bargain, I love you a little, how much is that worth? That's the vision of love in the false present, with no declaration. Regardless of whether it's a declaration of art, love, or anything else, a true declaration is not subject to the laws of exchange. It therefore takes the risk of making its proposal; it doesn't expect something equivalent in return. It is in this sense that it doesn't circulate, that it isn't exchangeable. It may not even be heard—that's a risk you have to take—as is perfectly the case with a declaration of love. But in no way does this mean that you have to retract it. On the contrary, it usually means you need to be persistent, to take the risk of being persistent! The declaration is persistent, and always with ever-increasing risk. If you're given the brush-off once, that's all right; twice, and it's a bit hard to take, so just imagine what five or six times is like! But this persistence is precisely persistence for a new present. It's the formal criterion of the heterogeneity to the terms of exchange.

What other examples can be given of a declaration situation exhibiting heterogeneity to the terms of exchange in this way, including in the contemporary world? The simplest example of something that's in a necessarily declaratory form is a demonstration. It's the oldest paradigm. A mathematical demonstration, for example. This is a declaratory form with no exchange whatsoever and with absolute authority. It is truly a case of "take it or leave it," in the strictest sense. If the demonstration is rigorous, either you accept its general principles or it is intractable, not negotiable. That's even what always inspires a certain subjective loathing for this sort of thing. You may understand a demonstration or not understand it, be interested in it or not, but in any case, it has nothing to do with the space of exchange. That's moreover why in the contemporary world—a world that, by the way, always claims to be scientific—mathematical demonstrations are frowned upon, ideologically frowned upon, as can be seen from educational curricula. In just a few decades, mathematics has gone from being presented as the epitome of rigor to being presented more like a bunch of recipes—which hasn't increased its popularity with students. It takes a lot of effort to learn dry and abstract, although comprehensible, stuff, but to have to learn it for no reason is, well, sheer torture. Philosophy has always highlighted the purely declaratory nature of mathematics, and that is indeed why it was originally connected to it. Because it saw that there was something in mathematics that, in terms of thinking, was of an intractable nature, of the nature of something that is not part of any circulation other than its own self-validation. A demonstration can be understood and transmitted, but that's all.

Now let's imagine that you stop in front of a beautiful statue in a park and you look at it. It's clear, in this case, too, that there's truly no circulation involved: you just stop in front of something. But this something stands motionless in its place and only offers you (if what captivates you is really just looking at it) what's known as contemplation, however long or short.

As is clear, contemplation is to art what a demonstration is to science, namely, a figure of subjective access—access to the theorem through the demonstration, access to the work of art simply by experiencing it— which, once again, does not open any particular circuit of exchange. Provided, of course, that you're not an art dealer calculating how much you might make from stealing the statue! If that's the case, then you're in a relationship with its abstract equivalent, the general equivalent, money. But in the sense I'm talking about it, the contemplation of a work of art is strictly nonnegotiable. It doesn't appear in any circuit of exchange and is its own end. It's very interesting that contemplation always occurs in the figure of stopping. It is the present's own stopping point, at the same time, of course, that it is the recapitulation of an enormously long past, because it's always the crystallization of a changeless duration. The statue is an immensely long, absent, unrepresented genealogy, but one that is present there in a single object. This, too, philosophers have emphasized from the outset, saying that there was something about contemplation that was ultimately, to use Plato's vocabulary, on the way to the Idea. You're all familiar with that passage in the *Symposium* where Plato says that the contemplation of beautiful bodies leads to the contemplation of the beautiful in itself. So to be a Platonist philosopher, you have to

love two things: demonstration and contemplation, or, in the final analysis, theorems and beautiful bodies! That's indeed something you can fill
a life with. This demonstration/contemplation pair shows that we are
by no means in abstract/concrete or concept/sensible types of registers.
That's not what's at work; a different logic is involved. At some point,
something that can't enter into the transactional structure of the false
present acts as a present, in a suspensive but intractable way, vis-à-vis
the false present.

My third example is taking part in a political protest. Or in an uprising
(let's dream!), or in a revolution (let's dream even bigger!). Here, too, you
are obviously subjectively taken over by the creative and violent intensity of a heterogeneous present, a present that in this case is a present of
action, but action in a sense that needs to be clarified. Action, not in the
sense of the orderly or rational management of our acts but in the sense
of action as an upsurge that creates its own present. But it can be much
more ordinary things. For example, at some point, even in just a meeting,
just a gathering, or even a discussion, there can suddenly be a moment
when something like this happens, something like action, like thought as
action, not just in the sense of how things are handled but in the sense
of something that's inscribed in active bodies, living bodies, and that,
once again, is absolutely intractable, exactly the way a genuine political
protest is intractable and can't be absorbed by repetition. There are failed
protests, which are not intractable and are completely controlled from
the very outset. They're like many other protests of the same sort, which
were organized bureaucratically by the unions, where people march along
gloomily and even carrying the banner is a real pain. We've all been there
to some extent. It's not insignificant, but it's absorbed into the false
present. Since the project fails to subordinate repetition to itself, repetition subordinates the project dimension to itself. I would contrast management with action here. Even a protest can be simply managed instead
of being active. There can be a management of protest that's not a form
of the intractable. But if there's action, there's also this collective, unpredictable, incalculable, really present linkage of something that reorients
the elements of the past.

Passion is also intractable, also involves self-consummation, as a
codeclaration inscribed in the temporal becoming of the pure present.

There is an ecstatic element about it, which makes the present emerge as absoluteness. This is what I suggest we call passion, but here, too, in a special sense. Passion not in the sense of the dreadful capture of one's subjectivity by an overwhelming sense of hopelessness, but in the sense of something that cannot be reduced to any calculation. In the sense of something that puts bodies in an unforeseeable state of ecstasy and matches them to each other, in such a way that utter indifference to everything else develops.

—∞—

The actions heterogeneous to circulation are thus demonstration, action, passion, and contemplation. There may occasionally be combinations among these creative adventures, but in every case, I must stress, a subjectivity of indifference to everything else is created. This aspect may seem terrible, but it has to be accepted. There can be no genuine present without there being a period of indifference to everything else, and this is what makes its expansion possible. We have to trust it. As the crystallization of an enormously long past and a projective future, it is in no way concerned about the rest but is ultimately in a provisional temporality of indifference to everything else.

If you take each of the different examples one by one, you'll experience this. When you're really trying to understand a proof, it's totally impossible for you to think about anything else. This explains why mathematicians are always somewhat strange people! Their days and nights are consumed in working on a problem that only they understand. This very strong aspect of indifference is the price that absolutely has to be paid for creativity. When you're engrossed in contemplating a work of art you can't focus on anything else, you're like a hunting dog, pointing. In the heat of the action of an uprising, you withdraw from everything else. And the same is true for ecstatic passion.

In more abstract terms, we could say: the construction of a genuine present is not, as one might think, a pure and simple cessation of repetition, of tradition. It is not a creation or a pure beginning. It is subjectively what I'd call an isolation structure—not in the sense of solitude but of isolation from ordinary temporality. In other words, the creation of the present means that one point and the whole world can be equivalent to each other, that in one point there is something like the whole world, not called forth, not classified, but present in one point, and thus absent anywhere other than in that point. Absent, undifferentiated, but concentrated, encapsulated in one point, a point that will in fact be the place of the present. For demonstrations, it could be a formal place, a place of the mind; for contemplation, a place of the senses; for action, a collective site on the move; for love, the absolutized amorous declaration. The whole world exists subjectively in one point.

Actually, there will be (and this excludes any and all circulation) a powerful concentration in one point, a period of indifference to anything other than this point, and then a period of expansion. There is a return to the world, but the return starts from this point, because a new perspective on the worldly totality emerges from it. That's precisely why it's a place. You may subsequently—and this is actually inevitable—be taken back over by some element of repetition. As I said, there's no such thing as a completely absolute beginning. It's more subtle. You'll start from the point in which your intractable world became concentrated at a given moment. And there will be a rearrangement, a readjustment to the ordinary world. But this reinhabiting of the ordinary world takes place on a different time scale, on the basis of a different present, a different conception of what the present is. We'll return to all these issues in greater detail. It's very important to measure this sort of rhythm—diastolic/systolic, like a beating heart—of concentration of the totality of the experience in one point and then of reinvestment of the experience based on the emergence of a new point, a new place, a new subjective foundation of the present. That's why it's a genuine creation and not just an exception. It's an exception that, as an exception, has to create something like at least the possibility of a new world, like the possibility that the world might be a different world from that of the false present. That's why we shouldn't get locked into an overly exceptional view of the exception. It's an experience. Only what is an exception, in existence, in life, has any value, of course. But that value is one that returns to the world, that's not simply kept apart as a separate exception. We'll come back to this, because it is the question of universality. In a certain sense, any exception, even the seemingly most exceptional exception, has universal value. For example, a moment of true love has value for humanity as a whole. Of that we can be sure. If all songs are ultimately love songs, it goes to show that, on the level of everyday life, what is uniquely exceptional has universal value, that it's a moment in the universal becoming of humanity, as are a great revolution, an extraordinary work of art, and the demonstration of a beautiful theorem. They are absolute singularities, but that is what has universal value. Since what is only average has no value, we need to begin with the present's construction as it is found in the exception, and then return and implement the universal possibility it contains. This is for reasons I've often mentioned here: what matters, in reality, is the creation of possibility. The big opposition is between those who think that becoming is the *realization* of possibility and those who think that becoming is the *creation* of possibility. When it comes to demonstration, contemplation, action, or passion, the problem isn't the success or the outcome; what matters is that possibilities that were previously unimaginable can be created. That's why it occurs in one point, and that point is a point of impossibility. Lacan's genius was to have said that the real is a point of impossibility: to touch the real is to touch a point of impossibility. But how do we do it? Not by having a cataclysmic vision of it (the experience of death, and so on) but by creating a possibility. Yet if it is *created*, it's because it didn't exist before; it was therefore lying dormant in the impossible. Formally, we could say that the intractable, that which doesn't enter into circulation, is the process whereby something is created that is not the realization of a possibility. As you know, it has often been said that politics is the art of the possible. But insofar as politics is the creation of something in the history of humanity, it is much more likely the art of the *impossible*, the art of the creation of an unnoticed, nonnegotiable possibility. This doesn't mean that the possible should not be realized. That's something else. The possible may occur in the false present, but it has no universality. It doesn't change the fate of humanity; it realizes it.

To conclude this section, it could be said that an exception to the regime of the false present is always of either the demonstration type or the contemplation type, either action or passion. Those are the main formal types of what can be classified as figures of creative exception. As regards our times, this means: what cannot be traded in the generalized exchange system, what cannot present itself as commodified. But now we must see what the exception is opposed to.

• Demonstration is the opposite of discussion, of debate—the debate over opinions, for example. This is why Plato loved mathematics, which is anything but a debate over opinions. When it comes to a theorem, your opinion is irrelevant: "I prefer that one!" "*I've* always preferred Pythagoras's theorem to Thales's theorem, and you prefer Thales? Well, to each his own . . ." Mathematics has nothing to do with opinion. It's even a remedy for the debate over opinions. Demonstration, owing to its rigor, is the opposite of the laxity of debate with no normative conclusion. Philosophical critique has to make a distinction between discussion, or debate, and dialogue. Plato clearly realized that, rather than involving a principle of truth, discussion or debate involves a principle of prestige. As there's no established argumentative criterion, a discussion or a debate ultimately amounts to a rhetorical contest, whatever the kind of rhetoric concerned. The philosopher wondered what point there was in a debate in that sense, in the ordinary sense, which ultimately links the theme of thought to that of rhetorical prestige. This is why an explicit opposition was set up between the demonstrative style, on the one hand, and the so-called discursive style, on the other. Discussion and debate would be set aside for the time being, even if they would be brought back in later on. They'd be set aside as the opposite of demonstration, on account of their linkage with a conception of the battle of words as a battle for prestige.

• Contemplation is directly opposed to judgment or to opinion. Contemplation is self-sufficient; it is disinterested. Judgment and evaluation are intended to circulate, to be the subject of discussion. I'm taking "contemplation" in a very radical sense here: the focus on something contemplated is sufficient unto itself and doesn't seek to take judgment into account. So artistic contemplation will be opposed to the play of opinions or judgments about works of art.

I'd just like to comment briefly on this. If there's one issue that's very difficult, it is that of subjectivity vis-à-vis the different types of artistic activity. Indeed, there's a strong tendency to think that the relationship to art is a relationship of judgment, that what realizes or completes the relationship to art is to be able to make a judgment, even if only a very basic one, of the sort: "Was it any good?" "Yeah, it was good, it was great." On that basis, there can be sophistical judgments, which consist simply in asserting the argument system appropriate to the fact that it's legitimate to say: "Yeah, it's good." It is telling that Kant placed the question of art in his third critique, entitled, as it happens, *Critique of Judgment*. In fact, contemplation, in the sense I mean it here, is not concerned with the subjectivity of judgment. The subjectivity of judgment is the way the relationship to art enters into circulation. This doesn't mean that there shouldn't be any judgments. Let's not be obscurantists. But we need to be precise. When contemplation develops as judgment, it is no longer heterogeneous to circulation. With respect to art, it is judgments that circulate, as though works of art were made for critics. Even someone who says "Yeah, it's good" is a critic, a rudimentary critic but a critic nonetheless. Contemplation refers to that moment of the artistic proposition, or the contemplative proposition, that is not realized in judgment, in the confrontation between judgments, but is self-sufficient, is satisfied with itself. It is this time that's involved in contemplation. This explains why contemplation will be opposed to opinion and judgment and, at the same time, be connected to them. Opinion and judgment are what use contemplation as a means of entering into circulation. This is the worldly moment in the broad sense of the term.

• Action is the opposite of management, i.e., of the rational practice of handling things or people. An action properly speaking, of any kind, is heteronomous to management. It cannot manage because, if it's a genuine action, it has no principle of management of what it is. At the time of the Third International, a time that now seems light-years away, there were manuals for revolution. I read one of them. But it's striking that, once such manuals existed, there was never again a single revolution! There were lots of other things: you had guerilla fighters, the protracted war in China, and so on. But there were no more revolutions, in the sense that the manuals meant it. Manuals provided a figure of management of revolution. There was moreover excellent advice in them, drawn from experience. Lessons were learned from why the

Commune had failed, why the 1917 revolution had, on the contrary, succeeded, why the Shanghai Commune had been crushed, and so on. Action, even on epoch-making days, is the opposite of management in that action creates a present, a collective present.

Naturally, it creates it by absorbing an entire past. I maintain the fact that there is an expansion of time. For example, Lenin very carefully analyzed why the Commune had failed. He was even obsessed with that. Why had there been such a failure? What should be done to ensure that the revolution wouldn't fail? The terrible bloodbaths of June 1848 and 1871 were on the minds of all the revolutionaries as uprisings drowned in blood and as examples of the impossibility of revolution. That past was incorporated through the Russian invention of revolution, but there can be no such incorporation with a management protocol. Once it has entered the sphere of management, a revolution is no longer of any use for creating a present. It will have become a pure space of repetition, with no separation, with no present. So action and management must be opposed to each other, even though management is unavoidable. Action is that aspect of human agency that can't be managed, for which there can in fact be no manual.

Just as an aside, it's the same for a night of love! If it follows a manual, well, forget about it. Our age does nothing but provide us with manuals on these kinds of issues. *How to Score Every Time! Have a 92 percent Chance of Success!* We'll come back to this feature of the present. It is what could be called true pornography, not just when it's applied to love and sex but in a much broader way. We could call "pornography" anything that subjects to a principle of management what cannot be subjected to it. It's the management of the unmanageable, the manual for what there can be no manual for. It's especially pornographic when it's a manual for good sex. That's a nightmare, and a ridiculous one. Our age is the age of manuals. There are manuals for everything. This is no accident. It's because the idea has become prevalent that there is no present other than the present of management. Manuals will be provided even for what obviously exists only as a singularity. You can't produce a manual for what exists only as a singularity. But our age tries to provide manuals for singularity itself, for learning how to be unique. *How to Be Fully Yourself*: now that could be the title of a best seller! If you follow the advice in such a book to the letter, it's a foregone conclusion: you'll end up being just like everyone else!

•   The opposite of passion is consumption. There might be some hesitation about this, if you remember what I said about the contemporary idea of nihilistic enjoyment. We could speak of enjoyment, but that would be treating enjoyment way too unfairly, even if in its nihilistic, commodified form it's the opposite of genuine passion. So let's say "consumption" instead. Consumption as a figure of what could be called enjoying without passion, that is, what is offered to desire in general, or to passion, in a figure devoid of any singularity. It's the idea that you can find the object of your passion on the market. That's the general principle. "You've got passions? Then come see us, we'll sell you just the thing for your passion!" This is in fact the means by which some element of the dynamic of passion and desire is connected or sutured to the general space of the consumer citizen's subjectivity. There's no passion that doesn't have its object. That's the theory of consumption. But I contend that passion is, strictly speaking, objectless, because the Other is not an object. Passion is a shared declaration. There is no object of passion. By contrast, the central thesis of the regime of consumption is that every passion has its object and that this object is on the market, or if it's not there, it should be put there as soon as possible. I'm not saying that we shouldn't consume, or that there aren't lots of appealing objects for sale on the market. We all have our toys, our fetishes, our ornaments, our pleasures. But you can clearly see what this is all about. It's about breaking away from the theory that the general regime of passion is the availability of the object. The propaganda about this—the structure of passion is correlated to an available object—is relentless. When it comes to all these points, we're at the heart of the phenomenon, of advertising, in all its forms, including its propagandist forms: politics is a form of advertising; the same people deal with both. Candidates hire publicists to make themselves into objects of political passion, to sell themselves the right way in the space of number. The space of advertising can be defined: it assumes a theory that every passion is bound to an object. We'll say no to that, and we'll oppose passion and consumption to each other by extolling objectless passion. Just as demonstration isn't up for debate, contemplation is not intended for judgment, and action is the unmanageable part of human agency, so, too, passion can't be taken over by any consumable object.

———❧———

So two sets can be defined, the first of which includes demonstration, action, passion, and contemplation, and the second, judgment, management, consumption, and opinion. This is really the way the present is divided up. There is an ordinary present, which is constructed out of the elements of the second set. It is empirically true that that's the ordinary present. As for the exceptional present, if we experience it at all, it is the present of the first set, and, in every instance, it is objectless, if what is understood by "object" is something that's available in circulation. Here we're touching on something really speculative or philosophical.

The real present, whose construction we would like (I would like!) to commit to, as subjects, is basically an anobjective present, in the sense that it is not bound to an object. And, ultimately, we could say, more philosophically, about the present of the ordinary world, our commodified world that we inhabit and live in today, that that world is subject to the law of objects. This means that it is subject to the law of objects in that it claims there is no anobjective subjectivity, no subjectivity that is not bound to an object. What I, for my part, claim is that, in the case of passion, action, contemplation, and demonstration, the Subject is not bound to an object.

That's the basic quarrel: does there exist something like an anobjective subjectivity, i.e., a subjectivity that is not definable in terms of the object it targets, wants, desires, loves? An anobjective subjectivity is something like a pure subjectivity that must be understood on its own terms and not in terms of the object that defines it. It's a subjectivity characterized by its disinterested self-assumption, a subjectivity that exists not in relation to the object but in terms of its self-affirmation, an affirmation with no guarantor, no reference, no definable objectivity. What this obviously means is that an anobjective subjectivity cannot circulate, cannot be subject to the law of exchange. By definition, what circulates is an object. Subjects can be made to circulate but only if they are subject to the law of objects. You can replace one consumer with another one: it makes no difference, provided the object is the same. This issue of the possibility of an anobjective subjectivity is the same as the possibility of a present that is not the present of commodified subjectivity, which, for its part, is based on the circulation of objects, whether tangible or intangible. Regardless of whether it's a credit card, a check, or the absolute intangibility of monetary flows, the fact is, they are all objects. The ultimate formal criterion that encapsulates this first aspect of things is anobjectivity, that is, the possibility that a subject may be constituted that doesn't depend on an object. Does this mean that it doesn't depend on anything, that it is therefore like a pure beginning, like an affirmation that has come out of nowhere? I will suggest that that's not the case: just because a subject doesn't depend on an object doesn't mean that it doesn't depend on anything at all. As we clearly see, there are conditions for anobjective subjectivity, conditions for demonstration, passion, action, and contemplation. In those spheres, we won't say that the anobjective subject emerges without conditions, as an unconditioned subject: it's just that these conditions aren't those of an object, in the sense of an object able or in a condition to circulate.

So our question, at which we'll stop for now, is: What can a condition for a subject be that is not in the form of an object? That sounds like a theoretical formulation, but it's not theoretical at all. If we look at our own lives, we realize that this anobjective condition is really what's involved. Modern freedom doesn't mean being an unconditioned subject, in the sense of Kant's categorical imperative, for example, but being a Subject for which a condition exists but isn't an object.

The contemporary democratic ethos urges us to be "ourselves," that is, anyone at all, vis-à-vis objects. Determination by objects is the key to the democratic emblem. The democratic axiom is that a subject only exists through the desire for an object. Our task is to anticipate the existence of Subjects whose condition of existence is anobjective. I will suggest calling this anticipated Subject "the post-democratic Subject."

Session 3

December 4, 2002

Well, let's begin this time with a simple maxim, taken from what I already said in the previous sessions. This maxim is opposed to the present of the contemporary world, a present consumed by the immediate and measured as the shortest possible time by the commodities cycle. The maxim states: Destroying the past is a way of destroying the present.

This is something we should pay close attention to. Especially when people on all sides are wondering who the "new reactionaries" are.[1] Here, in one of my previous seminars, I maintained that there were some innovations among the forces of reaction, too.[2] I even constructed the concept of the reactive subject as being precisely the subject that conveys reactionary innovations in the present. So I'm the first to be convinced that there are new reactionaries. The debate is about the people this label applies to. As such, it's a judgment-oriented debate, therefore not very interesting, a journalistic debate. Still, there's no denying that there's something going on in the reactionary camp. One of the possible reactionary innovations, always available, is, paradoxically, to falsify or erase whole stretches of the past. For instance, a basic figure of reactionary innovation consists in making the revolutionary subjectivities of the past, in particular of the recent past, unintelligible. It's not just about saying they were horrible and bloodthirsty but above all about making them unintelligible as subjectivities. Who were the people who were there, who did this or that? What was going through their minds? What was their subjective purpose? Those are the kinds of questions the new reactionaries will render pointless, obscure, and unanswerable. I used the label "Thermidorean" for this. A Thermidorean is someone whose job is to make the revolution unintelligible, incomprehensible, nonsensical. And it's always a job that has to be done over and over again! Coming up with new ways of making the creative past incomprehensible is always a reactionary innovation. It's this operation that is basically responsible for the idea taking hold that the world cannot be changed, that the world is the way it is, and that you just have to deal with it. It's a basic tool for instilling subjective resignation. The Ancients already knew that the great examples of subjects in the past were something important. *The Lives of Illustrious Men*, Plutarch, all that sort of thing, was the teaching of the great figures of the past as vibrant figures of human existence. You'll say: "We put Alexandre Dumas in the Pantheon, didn't we?!"[3] He's a minor figure in the glorification of the valiant subjectivities of the past, a rather conventional and bureaucratized figure. The Ancients already knew that there can be no nonresigned present, no inventive present, no creative present, without a certain incorporation of the creative splendor of the past. Erasing and obfuscating the past whenever it appeared as a creative past is a characteristic reactionary operation.

Incidentally, the widely held thesis that the world is changing at breakneck speed serves the same purpose. It's a major propaganda thesis. The world has always changed, and the idea that we're living in an age when it's changing at breakneck speed is the idea that it's changing so fast that we can no longer have access to the past. It's the same operation. The past is useless, and in fact inaccessible, because of the staggering changes of the present or the recent past. So it's very important to convince everyone that the race is so fast that you don't have time to look back. If you look back for even five seconds, you're already obsolete, you've become a pathetic old fossil.

I think all these operations can be lumped together under the idea that the deterioration of the present, its falsification, stems, in part, from the impossibility for this present to reconstruct the splendor of its own past. I am stressing this because you often hear the idea that the past is reactionary per se and that anyone who wants to return to the past is a reactionary. There are certainly reactionary nostalgias, but the most important thing is that the idea that what was creative about the past is obscure or incomprehensible is reactionary. Therefore, the idea of the almost immeasurable speed of the present time actually serves to destroy the present based on the unintelligibility of the past.

The radical critique of projection is also a key feature of reactionary apologetics. It's the good old critique of "utopias." It's the flip side: after the senselessness of the past, the insanity of the future! Anyone who imagines anything other than what there is is living in an idealistic, unfeasible, utopian, impossible, etc. dream. For the reactionary, anyone who isn't one is either archaic, hung up on a senseless past, or utopian, mesmerized by an impossible future. These are the pincers in which the reactionary destruction of the present is held. Thus, there is a polemical couple formed by utopianism and archaism, which reactionary innovation constantly repackages to fit the times. The real aim of this couple is the destruction of any true present, insofar as the present is the torsion of repetition by projection, the creative incorporation of the past into the projection of the future. That is what constitutes a true present, which the reactionary, who is only interested in protecting their own interests, most definitely does not want.

The general trend of the present time is clearly to dissolve the present in a general regime that is one of communication, of circulation. Circulation and communication are instantaneous exchanges, with no repetition and no projection. This creates the spectacle—Debord's term is right—of the false present. The basic aim of the propaganda is to convince people that there's no present. Why? Because anyone who thinks there's a present will prefer the present to commodities. That's my optimistic hypothesis about humanity! I'm making it, and I stand by it absolutely, because I think it can be proved. Anyone who is convinced that the present is possible will ultimately prefer that present to anything else. If humanity is resigned, it's because it has been robbed of the present. However, I intend to engage in counterpropaganda—which is a good definition of philosophy: Plato said that philosophy develops in opposition to opinion, meaning in opposition to the dominant propaganda. So it's a counterpropaganda, obviously rationalized, and therefore more subtle than propaganda. It will be absolutely essential to create or discover points of the present or irregularities on the surface of things that we can cling to in the subjective overlapping of a clarified past and a viable future.

—⊶⊷—

I'd attempted to make a list of the categories for identifying what is not in the regime of circulation or communication, in the regime of the false present, hence subjective points that are irreducible or that may become so. I'd identified four kinds: demonstration, contemplation, action, and passion. I will keep the word "passion," even though a few objections to it have been made to me. I like that old word, and I want to give back a positive meaning to it. I think passion is a great thing.

Demonstration, contemplation, action, and passion all have opposites. There are dialectical couples when it comes to this issue of potential indifference to propaganda images. Demonstration is the opposite of debate. It's the verdict of science, as opposed to idle chatter. Contemplation is the opposite of the haste, the circulation of judgment. It is the immediate shock of the work of art, as opposed to the rhetoric of esthetics. Action is the opposite of management. It is the intensity of the present, the intense torsion between repetition and projection, as opposed to a supposed technique for controlling time, to the false knowledge of an actual passage of time. Finally, passion is the opposite of consumption. It is consummation, as opposed to consumption.

We thus end up with two distinct subjective operational sets. On the one hand, there's the demonstration/contemplation/action/passion set, which defines the registers of noncirculation, the registers of heterogeneity to the false present, the subjective states of indifference to the dominant emblems. And then there's another set, namely, debate/judgment/management/consumption, which is the operational set that I propose to call "the democratic operational set." These are the operations of modern, contemporary democracy: not Greek democracy, not the democracy of the French revolutionaries, but democracy as today's nonworld.

At this point, I would like to place into evidence the two poems by Rimbaud that I handed out to you, which we'll now look at together. They are two famous poems from *Illuminations*. This is when we can relax our thinking a bit under the banner of poetry, because poetry has already done the work for us, so we may as well use it. It has done the work without knowing what it was doing, which allows us to say a little more than it does, and less, because it has said it in a timeless form.

DEMOCRACY
The flag goes with the foul landscape, and our jargon muffles the drum.
In the great centers we'll nurture the most cynical prostitution. We'll massacre logical revolts.
In spicy and drenched lands!—at the service of the most monstrous exploitations, industrial or military.
Farewell here, no matter where. Conscripts of good will, ours will be a ferocious philosophy:
ignorant as to science, rabid for comfort; and to hell with the world around us.
This is the real advance. Forward, march![4]

The first question is: Why this title, "Democracy"? This poem was probably written between 1873 and 1875. That's hardly today! But it nonetheless is, because it was democracy under colonial, imperial dictates, which is still our lot today. This was probably the time when Rimbaud, who did a lot of things in his life, joined the Dutch Foreign Legion and left for Java and Sumatra, which were colonies of the Netherlands at the time. This poem is a real fantasy, contrasting democracy's pretension, the democratic civilized person's pretension, with the concrete conditions of its exercise, with what actually happens on the ground of imperial reality, in the colonies. The underlying thesis, a thesis born of poetic intuition, is that we only really know what democracy is when we know the reality of empire. And that the proving ground of democracy's global pretension is there, in the colonial military reality—now more than ever, in the imperialist military reality—which Rimbaud will describe. And the poem will basically indicate what the subject of all this is, once it's approached from this angle. It's not a bad angle: we always have to end up there, sooner or later. The democrat has, by definition, a universal pretension, namely, good rules, he says, and good intentions.

But we need to see how he puts them into practice. What is the democrat where there's no democracy? What is the democrat without democracy, the exported, extraterritorialized, deterritorialized democrat, as Deleuze would have said? Rimbaud undertakes an analysis of this. It is in effect an illumination, an illumination of the democrat by the light of colonial lanterns. Here, we see him from a somewhat spectral point of view that Rimbaud takes, especially since what he is talking about, with extraordinary honesty, is himself, a virtual or real soldier of a colonial foreign legion. It is not a facile, external judgment. No, it's "we," Rimbaud is inside it: he's a democrat himself, a democrat in the guise of the legionnaire, who is the military arm of democracy and therefore its active, global essence. Today, it would be the GI and his various escort ships, or the humanitarian paratrooper, but it's the same idea.

A few comments now about this poem, which is a little enigmatic but ultimately remarkably limpid, striking, and focused.

First, there's the opposition between what will be done in the cities and what will be done out in the sticks. This has to do with territoriality: "great centers" and "spicy and drenched lands."

"In the great centers" is ambiguous. It can be interpreted either as "in the cities of the mainlands" or "the colonial city centers." But either way, the center is where there's a centrality. What does the democrat do? He does two things: he "nurtures the most cynical prostitution" and "massacres logical revolts." Let me remind you that a group that came out of May '68 founded a journal, *Logical Revolts*, which was run by Jacques Rancière. The title came from this poem of Rimbaud's. They were absolutely right to choose that title! It's a very fine phrase, an inspired choice that I like a lot.

"The most cynical prostitution": I've spoken here in this seminar about the democratic "prostitutional" in a very general sense. As regards Rimbaud's poem, we can be more specific. We know that prostitution, in its most brutal, commodified sense is, still today, and to an overwhelming extent, closely associated with imperial economic activity. It sometimes leads to the devastation of entire urban districts and involves young boys and very young girls in an imperial sexual consumption that we weakly protest against now and then. It's a fundamental commercial base. That's what "prostitution" connotes, but it means a lot more. "The most cynical prostitution" refers to the most cynical trafficking. "We" will establish the icy law of trafficking everywhere. Where there was once a custom-based, traditional society, delicate agricultural balances, little segmentary societies, there will be only the most cynical prostitution in every domain. This is the colonial version of what Marx was getting at when he spoke about the "icy water of egotistical calculation." Everything will be reduced to that icy water of egotistical calculation.

On the other hand, as regards the revolts rationally stirred up by this ruthless cynicism, those "logical revolts," well, these revolts are logic itself, the revolt that is logical humanity in its relationship to imperial democracy. And since it's consistent with a rational conception of human subjectivity and not with the most cynical prostitutions, well, we'll massacre these revolts, these rebels. Rimbaud is speaking here, with his usual sobriety, about repression, the terrible repression of anti-colonial revolts. The history of these repressions is an inconceivably bloody history, when considered from the time of the Spaniards in the sixteenth century up to today. It's something almost unimaginable in scope. Entire populations wiped out, demographic deficits that can still be seen today, mass deportations of populations, inconceivable forced labor, what happened in the Congo, what happened in the West Indies. Rimbaud knew all about that horror.

But in the background, there is also the idea that logic *tout court* will be massacred. The logical revolt is the massacre and destruction of a principle of minimal coherence of human existence. There is the idea, which can be found in a number of Rimbaud's texts, that to consign humanity to prostitutional cynicism, to the law of trafficking—which he knew intimately (he was part of it, he was involved in it: Rimbaud always experimented and put himself on the line)—the logic of existence must be eradicated. Something that is actually related to the logic of humanity, to the cohesion of humanity as such, must be eradicated. Indeed, the consignment of humanity to the law of trafficking is a disintegration. That doesn't mean that we can reverse it, that we need to dream of restoring the old bonds. Marx had already observed this, and Rimbaud repeats it: you can only force people to submit to the cynical law of trafficking by completely unraveling the unifying fabric, whatever it may be, of humanity. Marx said that capital dissolves the old bonds, the old customs, in the icy water of egotistical calculation. There's a process of dismemberment, of general atomization, of breakdown of basic solidarities, of constitution of the isolated individual facing global commodities, which is effectively not just the repression of the very logical revolts but also the destruction of logic itself.

As for the colonial countries as a whole, the productive rural territories, they are, says Rimbaud, "at the service of the most monstrous exploitations, industrial or military." The poem exhibits perfect lucidity; it is tantamount to a brutal, matter-of-fact assessment of imperial democracy. That is what is expressed by "the flag goes with the foul landscape," while "our jargon muffles the drum" means that our language of democratic civilized people attempts to destroy all the indigenous ways of thinking and speaking, all the traditional forms of expression. The drum is the symbol of the music of the people, of what can be heard of the indigenous populations, and "our jargon" is any one of the imperial languages, which, when compared with true humanity, become vile jargons. Rimbaud turns things on their head: what presents itself as the civilized people's language is a foul, oppressive jargon, incomprehensible to the populations who never asked anyone to come speak to them in that dialect.

The last paragraph clearly shows that, for imperial savagery, "here," a specific place, is "no matter where." The true spirit of the place in its deepest sense is disregarded. For people who live somewhere, the "here" is of vital importance. The imperial idea is to change the "here" into a "no matter where." This is like the eerie feeling you get when you're in an airport: of course you're in an airport, but you could just as easily be in Rio de Janeiro as in Paris or Singapore. Airports are the ultimate "no matter where." This transformation of the "here" into "no matter where" is an essential operation. I think it's amazing that Rimbaud had this concise intuition that imperial logic isn't the logic of the appropriation of a place but its inclusion in the law of the general equivalent.

Let's indulge for a change in a historical meditation, in the style of Montesquieu or Hegel. Is modern imperialism fundamentally different from Roman imperialism? In Roman imperialism, that ancient figure, however violent, fearsome, and bent on conquest it may have been, there was still the feeling that something of the "here" couldn't be totally changed. The idea of the colony in its original sense, its Roman sense, was the idea of a "here" that was certainly subject to a foreign law, certainly part of a greater whole, but that had an indomitable character that had to be preserved for the benefit of the empire itself, so that, in a way, the empire could pride itself on its diversity. This was a characteristic of ancient colonialism: the Romans could occupy Egypt, but Egypt was a nation, and the empire's glory didn't lie in Egypt's disappearing but in its being subject to Roman law, *as* Egypt. This was something the emperor himself could be proud of: he was the one who ruled over the world's diversity, a diversity that would in fact be regulated by the Empire, and in the most brutal way possible, but never destroyed, because destroying it would not be to the glory of Rome. Glory lay in subjugating nations, because they were these nations. Whereas the aim of modern imperialism is the widespread creation of a "no matter where," both internally and externally, through a gradual blurring of difference between the inside and the outside as the absolute anonymity of the place. Naturally, the place resists. Some places resist more than others. It's not something irreversible or final. But the essence of contemporary finance imperialism is the transformation of the "here" in its absolute singularity into a primitive "no matter where." Contemporary savagery, contemporary barbarism, is a barbarism that treats a place as if it weren't a place, that treats a place as if it were only a point in space. I would say that in this sense it's an inferior topology. The place is reduced to being a point, or a possible location in a space that's presumed to be homogeneous, or at any rate virtually homogeneous. Ultimately, all the points are the same. It's amazing that Rimbaud understood this.

The "conscript of good will" that the next sentence introduces is the soldier of democratic good will, the soldier of human rights, of civilization. "Good will" means the Kantian "good will." It is the good will of which the soldier is the conscript. The idea that one is a soldier of the categorical imperative is a very modern idea. "Conscripts of good will, ours will be a ferocious philosophy." That's fantastic! Rimbaud clearly sees that if good will appears in the guise of the conscript, then the philosophy of this good will has to be a ferocious philosophy. This is an absolutely brilliant prediction. This sentence blows me away. It is perfect, as if it had been written only last year, or a couple of years ago. It's a theorem: if good will—morality, civilization—appears in the guise of the conscript, of the soldier, of armed intervention, then that means that there's a sort of barbarization of the philosophy behind the operation.

It's a philosophy of aggression and of the lack of differentiation between places. Try to guess who, today, might be the slickest of ferocious philosophers behind humanitarian colonial aggression.

I'm very struck by the next two adjective phrases: "ignorant as to science, rabid for comfort." With extraordinary insight, Rimbaud understood that the constant promotion of science and technology in the advanced world is actually not genuine knowledge at all but a figure of brute ignorance. The subservience of science to global technological concerns turns it into ignorance. And any intellect in it is subordinated to self-interest, to comfort. Science is nothing but ignorance, but where intelligence does exist, it is corrupt and calculating, and focused only on comfort. This is a subjective disposition: you've got debased intelligence, on the one hand, and, on the other, intellect subordinated to the unbroken development of civilized, democratic Western comfort.

As for the world, the fate of the world, to hell with it! We couldn't care less about it. There are only two ways of caring about the world. The first is to have a genuine desire for knowledge, for learning, a desire for an intellectual understanding of the world with its diversity, its places, its particular "here's." Rimbaud says that in this kind of world, that doesn't exist. All people ever talk about is science, but its real is ignorance. The second alternative is to be politically dedicated to the world, to an internationalism that's committed to bringing about the emancipation, the liberation, of the world, of humanity as a whole. Rimbaud says that that doesn't exist either. We're only "rabid for comfort"; we're totally subservient to self-interest. In such circumstances, the relationship to the world is one of utter indifference: the world can go to hell. That's actually the maxim. It's very similar to the thesis that there's no world. The fate of the world is its going to hell.

Rimbaud concludes by enlisting us in "the real advance." This is what we're always being told: it's progress, the modern world, modernity. And this modernity is a combination of ignorance, ferocity, and self-interest. So it's an objective and subjective denial of the fate of the world, actually presented as the world's advance. It's a very intriguing dialectic: something that's actually the most profound indifference to the world is presented as the world's advance. This is a lesson we're often given: this identification of something pernicious and indifferent that spreads throughout the world but is actually the development of its anonymity and ultimately its nonexistence, is presented as its advance, its natural, essential, and fundamental advance. So we get *en avant, route* ["forward, march!"], which is a play on words on *en avant toute* ["full steam ahead"].[5] Forward, march, the road has been mapped out! The imperial road mapped out by ignorance and the brutality of cynical profit.

In conclusion, let's say that it was Rimbaud's genius to have seen very early on, when confronted with a real that was the modern imperial real, that, under the signifier "democracy," in other respects essential and admirable, including from the point of view of Rimbaud himself— Rimbaud had been a Communard, hence an exemplary democrat in his own way—that beneath this same word, with its glorious history, there lies an attitude of indifference to the world that would be articulated in several ways: the most cynical prostitution, the massacre of logical revolts, exploitation, the combination of philosophical ferocity, scientific ignorance, and the cunning of self-interest.

The poem "Democracy," as you can see, matches my analysis. It's like a poetic synthesis of it, a century in advance. The poets are there to anticipate our painful thoughts. That's what poetry is for.

<hr />

The second poem is counterposed, although not consciously so, to the first, because it shows how to support the possibility for there to be something other than this morass. Rimbaud entitled it "War." Here is the poem.

WAR

When a child, certain skies sharpened my vision: all their characters were reflected in my face. The Phenomena were moved.—At present, the eternal inflection of moments and the infinity of mathematics drive me through this world where I meet with every civil honor, respected by a strange childhood and prodigious affections.—I dream of a War of right or of might, of logic quite unforeseen.

It is as simple as a musical phrase.[6]

I'll begin with the end: "I dream of a War of right or of might, of logic quite unforeseen." Rimbaud tells us that, confronted with the world as it is, we need to dream of a War with a capital W, wage war against the world as it is. But, of course, "War" doesn't mean war, exactly. "War" denotes the heterogeneous subjective figure. We must construct the subjective figure that is heterogeneous to the world. It is not certain that might is necessary ("of right or of might.") It's not a war in the sense of obligatory violence or destruction. "Of right" simply indicates the opposite of might. It is not "right" or "law" in the sense of my thinking about bringing a lawsuit. War, the great War that constructs a subject, is not necessarily destructive violence. What is crucial, however, is that it establishes a heterogeneous logic: a logic quite unforeseen. No one can predict what this logic will be. The definition of the war Rimbaud is dreaming about is the invention of a different logic. It's the establishment of a heterogeneous logic—the logic of action, contemplation, demonstration, passion. It's a logic capable of producing an effect of surprise: the world must be surprised by an unforeseen logic. On the one hand, there's the massacre of logical revolts, and, on the other, the "I dream of a War [. . .] of logic quite unforeseen." For Rimbaud, the question of the world is essentially a logical question. Imperial democracy is the destruction of logic. And for the overtly resisting subjectivity, which must be invented, it is the creation of a logic. It's not the restoration of logic, it's not the logic that was massacred that has to be recovered: it's the invention of a *new* logic. The purpose of subjectivity is its ability to make the world logical in a new way. It's a different "Forward, march," a "Forward, march" for a new figure of the logic of the world. Between the world whose logic was destroyed by imperial democracy and the world that must be restored, the question of logic, of an invention of a logic, arises. What, now, prompts Rimbaud to say that he is dreaming of this war, of right or of might, of logic quite unforeseen? If we go back a few lines in the poem, we'll find a list of the sources of support that make this new logic possible.

Thus, we've got "When a child, certain skies sharpened my vision." So he sees clearly. This is the theme of clarity. Furthermore, in the world as it is, we need to have a discriminating eye; we can't take a broad view of things. If we take a broad view of things, we see nothing but what is given to be seen. We need to have a discriminating eye, sharpened vision. And as far as the child he once was is concerned, Rimbaud tells us, the colors of the skies served that purpose. Added to that, he goes on, was the fact that "all their characters were reflected in my face." So we need to have a subtly shaded subjectivity, a figure—the face is the figure of the subject—that's subtly shaded. We need to have the greatest possible subjective multiplicity, to cover the widest possible subjective spectrum, and to attend to the subtlest differences. We need to have a discriminating eye and attend to the subtlest subjective distinctions. We also need to have an attentive, sympathetic appreciation of things and empathize with the subtlest phenomena ("the Phenomena were moved").

Next come "the eternal inflection of moments and the infinity of mathematics," or, in other words, contemplation and demonstration. The eternal inflection of a moment is a moment's ability to be an eternity as a single moment, which is a perfect definition of contemplation, contemplation being a momentary stopping point in something that is given as eternal. As for the infinity of mathematics, it seems that at the time he wrote this poem Rimbaud was considering going for a doctorate in mathematics. In any case, it is the eternal inflection of moments and the infinity of mathematics that will drive the poet from this foul world and force him to invent a new logic.

Just as an aside, Rimbaud was a pretty amazing individual because he came up with all the hypotheses about himself. And then he discarded them. There's no way to pin him down at any point of his trajectory. He was someone who was constantly coming up with new hypotheses about himself, someone who would say in turn: I'm a hoodlum, a homosexual, a scientist, a seer, a demon lover, Christ, a worker—and he'd say it with the utmost seriousness. He applied to himself the maxim he formulated about the systematic derangement of all the senses, about this traversal of widely differing subjective hypotheses in the speed of the trajectory.

When Rimbaud speaks of the infinity of mathematics, it's important to understand that this is not just some abstract notion but something from the time when being a mathematician was of vital importance to him. But he didn't actually become one. He discarded that hypothesis and went on to something else. Nevertheless, at the time he came up with it, it was a pure existential hypothesis, not a game of abstract possibilities. That's why, for anyone who reads Rimbaud, there's something utterly timeless about him. With the first poem, for example, we had the feeling that it had been written only yesterday. There are a few, very rare writers, who we know wrote at a given point in time, but in the language and the thought conveyed by their language the existential hypothesis is so authentic that it relates not only to their own times. The same could be said of Pascal: there are things he says that could have been written only yesterday. In that regard, Rimbaud and Pascal are a lot alike. They're people whose regime of existence is a hypothesis about themselves, an absolute hypothesis and not just some hazy daydream. One morning you wake up and come up with the hypothesis that you have to be a mathematician and that everything else is irrelevant. Even if the next day the hypothesis is discarded as an absolute hypothesis, it remains inscribed as an absolute hypothesis. This is what is contained in Rimbaud's saying that he "noted dizzy spells." The noting of dizzy spells is the time when your identity is spinning wildly and you switch from one identity to another. It remains as an eternal inscription, because it is the inscription of an absolute subjective hypothesis. Rimbaud is someone who threw out all the absolute hypotheses of this sort. That's why he remains one of a kind. He discarded the hypotheses so quickly that at some point it was all over; there were no more hypotheses, except for the last one: being nobody, being a trader, a colonial trader. Since all the subjective hypotheses have been discarded, you adopt the null hypothesis, the zero hypothesis. The eternal inflection of moments and the infinity of mathematics are inscribed as absolute hypotheses, one as a *contemplative* hypothesis—the moment rises to the level of eternity—and the other, naturally, as a *demonstrative* hypothesis—the infinity of mathematics.

The next thing you come to is the phrase "respected by a strange childhood and prodigious affections" as conditions for the logical war. What's at stake here is the sphere of love, which, with Rimbaud, always has to do with childhood, as the evocation of an eternal childhood. And finally, there's the war of right or of might, and therefore action, the possibility of action.

Thus, with contemplation, demonstration, love, and action, you have in Rimbaud the basic agenda for what may make it possible to escape from what "democracy" designates in the first poem. What you do in the second poem makes it possible to escape from what is done in the first. The maxims in the second poem make it possible not to become the conscript of good will amid the horror of colonialism. How can you avoid being the conscript of good will? You'll have to think about a different war, not the imperialists' war but one that establishes a different logic in the world, a logic whose determinants are demonstration, contemplation, passion, and action.

The poem concludes with: "It is as simple as a musical phrase." That's the problem in a nutshell. Rimbaud's thesis is that we should be able to experience the simplicity of all this. The possibility of escaping from the world of good will, from the abject world of imperial democracy, isn't something complicated, fanciful, or theoretical but a figure of simplicity. This is obviously the subject of much debate. I personally think it's a poet's thesis. It's the mark of the poet. The poet would absolutely like, wants, desires all his acts to occur with a simplicity, an innocence, comparable to that of a musical phrase. In particular, he would like for all the acts to be combined in this simplicity, for passion, contemplation, action, and demonstration to merge in a simplicity that is the simplicity of poetry itself and the simplicity of life. That is the dream of poetry, and of certain poet-philosophers: that there should be this simple combination of basic acts whereby a subject can escape the fate of the false present. Unfortunately, it's not certain that it can be as simple as a musical phrase.

What we have here is something that's a little like Rimbaud's agenda. And I'm going to say something very conceited: when I read this text "War," this poem, I read it as though it were my own biography in a way! Certain skies sharpened my vision, all their characters were reflected in my face, the phenomena were moved, the infinity of mathematics, the honors, a strange childhood, a war of might, a logic quite unforeseen . . . most definitely. I'm familiar with all of that; parts of my own life could serve as an epigraph for the poem. But is it as simple as a musical phrase? Life's not a poem. Rimbaud ended up admitting that it wasn't, and so he stopped wishing for that war for an unforeseen logic. It was only of interest to him if it was as simple as a musical phrase. He didn't hear that musical phrase; he heard illuminations. But the illuminations remained scattered; they remained the dream of their unity, and he abandoned them to their fate. At the end of *A Season in Hell*, Rimbaud says that by holding the ground gained, we shall enter the splendid cities. Is it really certain that that's how you enter the splendid cities? Entering the splendid cities is as complicated as hearing all the subject's acts in their musical simplicity. In the end, the poet always fails at one point. Or else, shall we say, he proposes something that is to come but at the same time doesn't come, namely, that simplicity. In my own terminology, this is expressed as: there is a multiplicity of truth procedures. Truth is multiple. The world can only be saved bit by bit. There is no simple recollection that would allow us to have the ultimate melody, the ultimate musical phrase that would resonate with the world, that would be in harmony with the world, as harmony among the subject's acts, the phrase that would make mathematics harmonize with love, love with politics, and politics with art, all of them circulating in the simplicity of a new humanity. The poet is someone who at some point proposes that there be a new humanity characterized by its simplicity. As for me, what I'd take away from this desire for simplicity is not the desire itself, because it is the poem's fate to give up on it sooner or later (this was the case with Hölderlin, Rimbaud, and Trakl). The poets who are the most vitally committed to the promise of dawnlike simplicity are those who end up renouncing poetry. They saw the reduction that was necessary, they saw the multiplicity, but they couldn't resign themselves to that simplicity. There is a desire for the simple in the poet, an essential desire for the simple, for harmony or for harmonious transparency. But there is also bitter renunciation when the test of nonsimplicity comes.

This doesn't mean that there's nothing we can take away from the poem-idea that "it is as simple as a musical phrase." I, for one, would take away the idea of the invention of a calm, an idea that's present, after all, in the musical phrase. In other words, in order to invent a logic quite unforeseen, in order for there really to be a war (because it is really a war), a space must be created for protecting that logic. The birth of that logic must be able to be protected, and it can only be so

by the invention of a kind of calm, a calm that the world won't allow
to develop. The truth is, the world requires us *not* to be calm. That's the
secret relationship between commodities and hysteria, the fundamental hystericization of commodities. Calmness is something else. A different kind of hysteria, perhaps? Might the world's problem be how to
invent a different kind of hysteria from the one that has already been
identified and is ubiquitous? I don't know. But I'm sure that it will first
occur as a strange calm, the strangeness of a calm, not the strangeness
of an excitement.

How can this calm be obtained? How can it be invented? It is
necessarily invented through the possibility of being indifferent to a
number of things. This is what I presented under the heading of "the
fivefold indifference," the *five major types of indifference*. The five major
types of indifference are, in my opinion, the basic operators of the creation of a new kind of calm, of a calm in which any subject can protect
the birth of a new logic, of a logic quite unforeseen. Because the great
modern problem of creation is, in my opinion, the problem of protecting it. Basically, everyone says they want creation. I'm not saying
creation has to be opposed subversively to the world as it is. Where
creation is concerned, there's always a buyer and a seller, a taker. But
the problem is how to protect it from being instantly put into circulation, because that's the time when, however creative the act may be,
it is subjected to the law of the world. If the issue is really to protect
things from being circulated, that protection must be created; it's not
a given. Everything is offered up, everything is sellable, everything
is sold, and everything is bought. So it must be really protected. But
protected from what? From the fact that people like it. If no one likes
it, there's no more problem. But it must be protected *even though* people like it. It must be liked and yet kept out of circulation so that
this liking isn't immediately changed into selling. Otherwise, there
won't be any unforeseen logic. You'll end up with a new element of the
foreseen logic. It will be a little creation, which is no small feat, but
it won't be an unforeseen logic. There has to be a space of protection,
and constructing the space of protection is essential. There has to be a
subjectivity that arranges the space of creation in such a way that this
space acts as the protection or the birth of an unforeseen logic. This

surely means that there's something that makes success ambiguous. Not that there needs to be failure, which is only ever the mirror image of success. Failure may mean your product wasn't marketable. What is needed is to protect the unforeseen logic from the whole success/failure, circulation/noncirculation opposition.

How can we determine where the protection of the unforeseen logic lies? What I call the five types of indifference are precisely procedures for protecting the unforeseen. The word "indifference" means that you're dealing with a norm you don't care about. You're not indifferent to the thing in question, only to its normative aspect. In this particular case, you're indifferent to the different images of the world the dominant emblem affords you.

Let me now give you those five types of indifference again, which we'll start off from next time.

1. Indifference to the criterion of number
2. Indifference to the established regime of the possible
3. Indifference to particularities
4. Indifference to the presumed antinomy between authority and tolerance
5. Indifference to repetition and projection when they're separated from each other

All this will lead to the problem of the law: does this system of indifference (to number, to the regime of the possible, to particularities, to the opposition between tolerance and authority, to the separation between projection and repetition) mean that we're indifferent to all law? Must the regime of indifference, which I think is the real protection of creation, be itself characterized by indifference? Looking at the list, you might be tempted to sum it up that way: we're indifferent to the different aspects of what a law is. But this isn't exactly tantamount to indifference to the law. I had the opportunity to deal with this in regard to Saint Paul and the dispute with the law. It is actually a question of indifference to identities. This is what we'll be dealing with next time: the protection of creation sparks a debate on the question of the law and identity. I won't advocate the suspension of all law, which is always a barbaric figure. To be indifferent doesn't mean to be barbaric. Indeed, indifference to particularities can also be barbarism, i.e., I'm indifferent to other people's lives. There is an extremist version of indifference that is barbaric—indifference pushed to the extreme of barbarism, as we saw with Guyotat. And there is a compromise with the law, something that maintains a horizon of the law but with the acceptance of a certain nullification of identity, the acceptance of a subjective anonymity, in the face of everything that weighs the subject down with a preformed identity. Next time, this will be an important discussion.

Session 4

February 26, 2003

I intend to speak to you about the war today, because it's a topic everyone's interested in. So I'll be speaking about it out of shameful opportunism! But the truth is, the connection is obvious, because we are here, as you well know, in search of knowledge about what the present is. What is the present of the world? What are the images of the present? How should the present be thought? Our investigation is based on the assumption that there is no present, that the present, or the world, is lacking, in part. So the question arises as to how we confront a present, especially a historical present. What is the presence of the historical present? What is the subjectivity of thought when it is really in the present? We wondered whether, contrary to Hegel's thesis that philosophy is always retrospective, always coming after the fact, philosophy could be in the present. Our question is that of the present, and we are focusing on the idea that, at least in the world as it is, the present is in the figure of an exception. This means that the present may not be the present in the greater scheme of things but that there is some present, or some fragmentary present, in the regime of points of truth, points of contemplation, points of genuine action, which are like little stars standing out against a background that is one of incorporation of the present itself.

We can begin with the fact that, for a very long time, war was a figure of the historical present. It was even one of the most important names of the present, sometimes its terrible name, its negative name, the name of the bad present, but in any case, a name of the present. And this was so on a large scale, for reasons having to do with the fact that war has always been a point of reference in the very construction of the scansions of history. It's as though some aspect of historicity moved from one war to another, or was located in the interval between wars, wars being periods of transformation or reorganization capable of constituting new presents. The three reasons for this connection between war and present will serve as a starting point for us.

1.   The simplest phrases express the fact that war has long been something with a before and an after: we're either in a prewar era or a postwar era. Even the time of the twentieth century was popularly, commonly, structured this way. The temporal, sequential description constitutes war as a scansion, as the basis on which it makes sense to speak of a before and an after, which is ultimately the function of the present. War is in a way regarded as an exception in time, an exception considered as a temporal scansion.

2.   War is the demand for a decision. It is the occasion for a kind of decision, including in possibly deceptive and dubious figures. The figure of decision isn't always a politically innocent notion, far from it—just think of its function in Carl Schmitt's work. But the philosophy of decision often has to do with war, which represents the moment when something will be decided or settled over the course of history, the moment we are no longer in the element of continuation or conservation. This naturally extends to the figures of the war decision properly speaking, as Clausewitz analyzes them in *On War*. Clausewitz attaches great importance to the commander's decision-making ability. Making a decision is, in his eyes, the commander's most difficult task, and it makes him vulnerable. Clausewitz clearly shows how the whole problem is actually the battle to constitute the present, the need to decide in the present. There is a pure present of the battle—it will be either won or lost—and that lends the decision a sort of cutting edge of pure presentation.

3.   The third reason is that war is an exceptional experience. It's an experience of the sharing of the exception, an experience that uproots men and sends them elsewhere, settles them elsewhere. And in this elsewhere there develops a spatial exception, a temporal exception, as well as a new kind of community, a unique kind of sharing, which is a sharing of the present. In war, you no longer share marital stability, professional continuity, family continuity. You share the present of war, including the utter tedium of this present or its violence. This explains the extraordinary literary and cinematic success of the military community in combat. In peacetime, it's usually a farcical subject. But in wartime it's really the community in the present, the sharing of the present. Not many figures of the sharing of the present are on a scale comparable with the figure of war, as a figure of the shared exception, of the subsequent formation of a group or a community sharing danger. To share danger, to share the risk of death, is obviously to share the intensity of the present itself at every moment.

What I'd like to argue is that, for complicated reasons, the war or wars in question today cannot constitute a present. I say "wars" because, as we'll see, they've been telling us for a long time that we're in a war on terror—that's the first war—within which there's the Iraq war, a potential stepping-stone to a war against Iran. We should note in this connection that there are three sequences, as it were, in the current situation. There's the sequence of military preparations, of preparation for war; there's the sequence of mass, popular opposition to the war; and there's the sequence of the UN, which is in an awkward position between the other two. It's the interrelationship of these three sequences that makes me say that they can't constitute a present, that they may even represent the end of the war as the constitution of the present. This is good news, but only if there's a different constitution of the present. It's in fact from the outcome of the opposition to the war that the eventual development of a new present will result, under certain conditions that I'd like to try to explain to you. So we'd have a figure that, in the final analysis, and provided that a present develops in this forsaken world, would not be the sharing of war, of the figure of war, but instead, by a singular reversal, would be the development or the consequences of the structuring internal to the figure that opposes war or attempts to oppose it. That would be the basic hypothesis.

As for the present time, it could be called the post-postwar era. It's important to see that we are currently living at the end of the postwar era. We're in the postwar era of World War II. But why is this so? What was this postwar era, which actually lasted a long time? Let me mention a few of its features.

It was characterized first of all by the existence of two superpowers, in a balance of terror. As a result, the world—I'm not saying it was a good world, or that we should be nostalgic for it—was structured by a fundamental interstate conflict, in the context of which all the developments occurred, more or less openly. But there are no longer two superpowers. Thus, the collapse of the USSR as a potentially hegemonic power meant, among other things, that the postwar era was over. The division of Germany was another characteristic and distinctive feature of the postwar era. But that division no longer exists. Additionally, the postwar era represented a figure of global isolation of China. During that period, China was of course an important power, but an inward-looking one. It was separate and distinct, especially after the Korean War ended in defeat or a tie. After the Korean War, China could be seen as an immobile reserve, removed from the global political game. However, China's isolation from the rest of the world came to an end. China has become and will increasingly become a, if not *the*, great alternative world power. All these constitutive features of the postwar era have now become obsolete.

To this must be added the fact that, in the postwar period, and in the context of the central conflict that structured the world, there was still an intrinsic definition of revolution. The idea of revolution was relevant, relevant in a subjective sense, which meant it was generally accepted as a politically defensible idea. The endless quarrels over what revolution was and how to make it did not alter the fact that there was an intrinsic definition of revolution. Consequently, there was a dialectic of war and revolution, which Mao summed up in this way: either war will give rise to revolution or revolution will prevent war. There was a subjective contradiction between the idea of colonial wars, imperialist wars, on the one hand, and, on the other, the system of revolutions. One of the major subjective features of the post-postwar era is thus that there is no longer any intrinsic definition of revolution, no longer any living, subjectively accepted dialectic between war and revolution. The terms for all these things have become unclear. So the postwar era is really over.

When exactly did it end? That's debatable. Let's say, empirically, around 1989–90, for sure. Maybe before, subjectively speaking. But in terms of its full effects, only later, probably now. Whether it's a matter of the war that is currently brewing or the string of wars touched off by the first Gulf War, a sequence that began in 1991, these wars are wars of the post-postwar era. They would be inconceivable in the postwar order. They are truly wars of the post-postwar era.

So the postwar era is over, and yet this end, as an end, doesn't constitute a present. It's not a new present, which put an end to the postwar era, as a revolution might have done. In particular, there was no revolution in the USSR: it collapsed all by itself, on itself, not through the dynamic creation of a new present. There was no subjective development, strictly speaking, of a present. There was the crystallization of an uncertainty and what I have called an in-between world, full of potential. A world suspended between the old figure and what was to come, or could claim to be coming but had not yet come. It's a bit like the feeling of a false present but a false present that is trying to develop its future.

How can the problem of war be described from this point of view? Well, in this false present, in this uncertainty, in this in-between world, in this post-postwar world, there is a very important feature, which, I believe, is a significant obfuscation of the category of war itself, and this will make it impossible for it to represent the present.

First of all, the distinction between war and peace is blurry today. Is the world at war or at peace? You might say: the world is at peace. But that depends on where you are! This question made sense when war meant war between the USSR and the United States. But what does it mean today, that there's no war? What war? Here are two striking examples.

The Bush administration has characterized the period as a period of war, in other words, that we're in a war on terror. Bush didn't say "We're at peace" but "We're at war (on terror)." Moreover, military operations against Iraq have never stopped. Iraq is a country that has been enduring war for ten years now; the bombing has never stopped, nor have the armed incursions.

Another highly significant characteristic is the complete disappearance of the concept of the declaration of war. I'm especially struck by this because no one ever talks about it. War used to be something that was declared. The declaration of war is the protocol whereby a virtually performative statement distinguished the period of war from the period of nonwar. Nowadays nothing is distinguished anymore, you just bomb. This is clearly a blurring of the distinction between war and peace. You carry out policing operations, humanitarian interventions, you disarm someone, you go in and overthrow a dictator. It's done with bombs and paratroopers. Is it war or not war? Either way, it's not declared.

Finally, the question of the protagonists of war is increasingly ambiguous: who are the subjects of war? Traditionally, the protagonists were states, wars between blocs, states, alliances, hence state configurations. Or else there were qualitatively asymmetrical wars, popular wars, wars of liberation or of resistance. So you had two scenarios: traditional wars, wars between states, "interimperialist wars" as they're called in the modern age, or the wars by which a people liberated itself from colonial oppression, such as in Vietnam or Algeria. The protagonists were clearly identified. From the formal point of view, there were symmetrical state wars and asymmetrical wars between a state, on the one hand, and a people, on the other. (I'm oversimplifying.) Nowadays we have nonqualitative asymmetrical wars, i.e., wars with no true asymmetry. We have extremely powerful states against very weak states, without our being able to say, strictly speaking, that it's an intervention against peoples. It's an interstate war with maximal asymmetry. Or else there are wars with elusive, slippery enemies, such as the war on terror, with states on one side and, on the other, something with no definable identity, whose support representable as a subject is undefinable.

 In summary: the distinction between war and peace has become blurred, the declaration of war has disappeared, the protagonists are hard to pin down, and the symmetries nowhere to be found.

So the very concept of war is an absolutely unclear concept today. In terms of neither its subjects, nor its process, nor its political characteristics does it connote anything that can be stabilized for thought, apart, of course, from the empirical fact of the use of violence. But that's not enough to expose something like war to thought and to political characterization.

⁕

So, as a first step, we could say that what we call war, which is actually a multiplicity of violent interventions, organized for about the past ten years in different asymmetries, is a completely different situation of violence from what used to be meant by war, whether in the Classical Age or in the postwar era. Neither popular wars of liberation nor interimperialist wars properly speaking, these are nonqualitatively asymmetrical wars and, precisely because of this, extremely difficult to distinguish from what is otherwise called peace. I think it would be right, for the time being, to call them "military interventions." "War" is ambiguous. They're military interventions on a variable scale, among which must be included, to begin with, the first Gulf War (1991)—it's not a question of justifying Saddam Hussein's invasion of Kuwait—which was the kickoff, and I should point out that it occurred almost immediately after the collapse of the Soviet Union (1989). The sequence began there, and it includes, with a variety of forms and many different alleged sponsors, the intervention in Serbia, the intervention in Afghanistan, and now the intervention in Iraq. These interventions of Western forces are organized by the United States in weak asymmetries with many different pretexts. It is not at all certain that it is useful to call this "war." Besides, there's very little war: there's bombardment but very little war. There are preferably zero deaths (on the intervening forces' side). So as little war as possible! Pulverizing yes, but war no.

A first conclusion that can be drawn from this is that the slogan "No to war!" is very weak. It has a specific weakness, which is not just the generic weakness of pacifism. Criticizing the slogan by saying that you're criticizing pacifism at the same time is as weak as the slogan itself. Pacifism dates from the time when war had a specific, politically precise meaning. You could be for or against it, you could be right or wrong, but it had a meaning. Now that war has become much hazier, more confused, internal to peace, the slogan "No to war" doesn't just have the weakness of pacifism, it's intrinsically weak, but not for the usual reasons that could be mentioned. As, for example, when Chirac said that France wasn't a pacifist country.[1] What a strange statement! What is clear is that France is certainly a capitulationist country, but that's not the same thing! It's not a question of pacifism, because saying no to war is either too much or too little today. Too much, because we haven't developed the political system that would make it possible to be opposed to the general scheme of interventions of this type, which are something other than wars. And too little, because we can't just settle for saying no to what is going on there. It's not adequate. This has nothing to do with an ideological critique of pacifism; it's a different problem. The identification of the situation isn't attained through the "no to war," which I otherwise respect. I admit I'm extremely happy that millions of people are against the war. But the internal content of this is weak and won't suffice when there is war. It won't be enough for the inner logic of war. For reasons that are not ideological ones or reasons of weakness but reasons having to do with the current situation, with the characterization of the situation, I think that that slogan is weak. The idea that this war would be fine if it had international legitimacy is also very weak. It's the idea that's still fairly common, in political circles in particular, that if the UN gave its blessing to the war, it would be a lot better. This point deserves to be examined on its own, because it has a whole history behind it, the history of the concept of "the international community," a concept that emerged after the fall of the USSR. Before that, there was no international community, by definition. You had a divided totality, whose strategic objectives, whether real or imaginary, were fundamentally different from one another. "The international community" is the name of the vague ideal of the post-postwar world situation. The UN is the parliament of the international community. It's clear that a host of people and governments, who experienced this at the time of the first Gulf War, at the time of the war in Serbia, at the time of the war in Afghanistan, wonder whether it wouldn't be better for the war to have the international community as its subject. The problem is that we've long known that the real essence of the international community is the American military, so in this case it's pretty obvious. It's hard to cover up or disguise. This time around, it's difficult to make the war—with its massive American backbone—look as though its subject is the international community, combined with the idea that the international community is working toward democracy and the liberation of peoples, and so it's very good for everyone, quite apart from the descriptions that could be given of Saddam Hussein's regime. Our President Chirac has taken on the role of the opponent. In Parliament and in the world situation, he's the opponent of the decision of power made by those who claim to be the majority, the government, the powers that be, etc. But opposition is always a complicated game: does it really work toward stopping the war or just toward making it not seem entirely like the war of those who are really waging it? In effect, one traditional function of opposition, among others, is to invent the new conditions for consensus. You have a plan, the opposition debates it heatedly, you make concessions, or you don't make any, but in the end you tailor things in such a way that the opposition won't turn it into a case of civil war. So it will eventually go along, in the sense that you will have proved to them that the plan isn't grossly out of line with the general conditions, which are those of parliamentarianism itself.

In the case that concerns us here, it's similar: they are desperately seeking the minimal conditions under which this war, which has in a sense already been decided on, might nevertheless be the international community's war, owing to the fact that it will have been debated and discussed within the framework of an established opposition. This is also very typical of the current period, possibly with the precedent of the League of Nations debate about Italy's invasion of Ethiopia, a distant colonial precedent. Whatever the case may be, we've got a very interesting figure of the precise relationship between a radical decision (to wage war, even with the total ambiguity of the word "war," to engage in a military intervention) and the complicated game of voting in a supposedly representative forum (here, representative of the international community, its divisions, its contradictions, its various countries, its geography, and its history). Is it possible, within such a framework, to maintain to the bitter end the opposition to the decision that was made? Does that framework make it possible to do so? The truth is, if such were the case at that level, we'd be dealing with something more than simple opposition.

That's why, little by little, enormous tensions are crystallizing around this majority/minority, opposition/veto issue. It could be argued: if Chirac is against the war, he'll vote against it. But that's not how it works: Chirac is not exactly against the war; he is the opponent of the war. I make a distinction between the two. In the popular antiwar movement, there is certainly something against the war, but in the diplomatic game being played by the French government, it's different. The French government has never said it was really against the war. It has simply said that war should be the last resort, that time was needed, that the inspectors should go on with their work . . . It agrees that Iraq should be disarmed. Incidentally, why should Iraq be disarmed? That's an act of banditry. Iraq is an utterly shattered country, and the people are dying on account of the embargo. Of course, Saddam Hussein is a loathsome character. That's not the point. But his missiles aren't a threat to the United States. I've just come back from the United States, and a lot of people there think Saddam Hussein was behind 9/11 and that he poses a nuclear threat to the United States! It takes a lot of propaganda to get people to swallow such a thing! The consensus around the war's objective already shows that it's not exactly a fundamental opposition. What is really involved, in the diplomatic sphere? It's about deciding what the new rules will be for the constitution of the international community. In accordance with the new rules of the post-postwar era, now that the ideological and geopolitical balances of the postwar era have disappeared, what will the rules be for the internal constitution of what's called "the international community," in the context of American hegemony, of course? The opposition is creative: it is creating new rules for the constitution of this community. I'm not saying that Chirac and the French government aren't doing anything. They *are* doing something, but what? Personally, my hypothesis is that, as opponents, they are making up new rules for decision making, which can't be the same rules as when there were two superpowers. Previously, the veto was either American or Soviet. There was never any other real veto. Now, France's veto is a different story! A lot of people say: "They're a bit small for that!" It's true, the veto wasn't created for that. The veto was created for the two blocs, to get around majority rule. That was its purpose. As there were two blocs, the two leaders of these blocs, like bandit chiefs, had to agree on the line that couldn't be crossed, and then there were the secondary vetoes, just to keep the former great powers happy. But it's unsuitable now. And so, whereas previous military interventions were decided on the basis of consensus, the question raised by this one, which is actually coming up for the first time, is the very important question specific to the post-postwar era. What can the UN's parliamentary rules be in the post-postwar period, given that they can't be either majority rule, which the United States won't comply with, or the current rules of the Security Council, with its anarchic, unsuitable veto? France's opposition is helping shape this new configuration. The game with the UN is at the heart of the dialectic of representation and power, of representation and force. Given that, for the time being, there's one dominant, semi-hegemonic power, what can the decision-making, parliamentary-type shaping represent? Hence the importance of the UN issue. Even for the Americans, it's not so easy to ignore (though it's not for lack of trying), because behind it is the issue of the new diplomatic rules of the post-postwar era.

In this parliamentary dialectic, in which France, as the opposition, has some room to maneuver, the other term must now be discussed: the term "power," or "force," by which I mean the nature of American power today. What basic observations about the nature of this power can be made on the basis of the past ten years? What is American power now that it has been freed from the confrontation with the Soviet Union and is no longer controlled by that binary system? I am in no way nostalgic for the Soviet Union, but the fact is, the United States used to be enmeshed in that binary control system, and that's no longer the case. This makes American power seem somewhat out of control. That's only natural: there used to be an implicit rule, for which the UN served as the official cover, but when you're no longer controlled by a rule, you're consequently out of control.

What strikes me first and foremost today is the way the U.S. military has become grossly out of proportion with the rest of the world. America's military budget is higher than the combined budgets of France, Germany, Russia, and China! That's a staggering figure. It's especially striking in that this hasn't happened in the context of a conflict with another superpower. One might have imagined that the demise of the USSR would lead to a *Pax americana*, so to speak, with a significant decrease in military expenditures. That seemed logical. It would have been as though the new sequence were the continuation of the previous one. But the opposite happened. Never has the United States worked so hard and systematically to develop new military technologies, new concentrations of force, new destructive capabilities, as in the current period, when its hegemony is seemingly total. Indeed, American hegemony is not limited to the economic sphere: it's as though there were a relative independence of politico-military factors. These factors are growing on their own, out of all proportion, and have consequences of their own. For example, when you read certain documents, it really seems as if the American military is very tempted to use tactical nuclear weapons in the war with Iraq—which would be a disaster and an outrageous, incredibly violent step—partly just to test them! Maybe they ultimately won't do so. Maybe the only favor Tony Blair could do for humanity as a whole would be to dissuade the Americans from doing so. This state of affairs is typical of the relative independence of the military factor, but, even more importantly, of the fact that it's accepted all over the world today as something that's sort of inevitable, except ultimately, perhaps, by China. In particular, it's altogether outrageous that Europe stands by and watches this stupendous buildup of a qualitatively and not just quantitatively unrivaled military apparatus, which some even say is impossible to catch up with. This is incidentally the logic of the American military experts: they require American military might to be built up in such a way that it will be impossible for anyone to compete with it, i.e., that the degree of qualitative lag in weapons development be so great that no other industry will be competitive enough to catch up with them. That such a thing could be accepted is truly mind-boggling, and its practical consequences are enormous. For example, it is striking that, even just to carry out a paltry expedition against Serbia (let's leave aside whether it was justified or not), the Europeans needed American air support. When you think about it in terms of previous wars, it amounts to saying that France + Germany + Great Britain are incapable of waging war against Serbia! It's unimaginable. It is subjectively accepted that military intervention today means American intervention, even when it occurs in the heart of Europe. At most, you can be backup troops, participants, with the British in the role of the good pupil in the class and the French in the role of the bad one, but it's still the same class. This point should be given serious consideration. There's an element of independent military supremacy in American power that seems to be accepted, particularly by the Europeans, as irreversible.

The second point I'm struck by is American self-centeredness. What I mean by this is the fact that American power is of course a global power, but it's a global power that is strictly in line with its own interests and its fundamental introversion. The world is regarded by the United States as the repository of, the arena for, its interests. It's not exactly an empire. A genuine empire is something that offers to take care of the foreign populations, educate them, instruct them, organize them, and so forth. The word "empire" is ambiguous. I'm well aware that in Negri's work it means something different from the United States, but as such it is ambiguous. Indeed, there is something about the dominant political conception in the United States that is not imperial as such, that doesn't reach out to the foreign populations with a sense of its organizational superiority. Rather, it's a sort of general construction of the world arena as an arena for the protection of its interests, and that's different from the imperial dynamic. The well-known anecdotal aspect of this tendency is Americans' unbelievable ignorance about the rest of the world: only 10 percent of Americans have a passport, and 90 percent of them have never considered going abroad! Going abroad is unnecessary. They don't even know where Iraq is. It's not a question of subjective psychological features or of ignorance. It's just that the world is merely the mediation of their conception of themselves. This is completely unlike the way the great nineteenth-century empires were constructed

The third point, which hinges on the second, is that American power relates to the world through what I'd call "zoning." There are no countries, strictly speaking, only zones. Zones of interest or indifference. It's a zoning that varies according to strategic or opportunistic considerations. Thus, to the extent that the United States relates to the world, it does so through a vision that includes zones to which it can remain indifferent for decades and other zones that are instead vitally important for a certain amount of time. The question is how to be a player in the zone, how to transform it, but it's never a question of what organic relationship it has with what is going on there. The Middle East zone is a problem, so they are calmly planning to reshape it. They're going to reshape the Middle East . . . These are shocking statements! We've stopped being surprised by them, but we're wrong to. What is this power that says it's going to reshape the Middle East? What is this vision of the world as a system of zones of intervention, or of nonintervention, depending on the case? This is really why tension has mounted between the international community's parliamentarianism and American power. If someone says they're going to reshape the Middle East, all you can do is say you're going to try to grab a few crumbs (that's Spain's tactic). Zoning and military supremacy can't be shared with any kind of international community.

The three empirical features of American power are therefore the disproportionality of its military, its systematic self-centeredness, and its relation to the world as to zones of intervention. In this sense, it's a new type of power that cannot be directly interpreted using the standard model of empire—domination—hegemony. We need to stop talking about imperialism in the traditional sense. The same goes for hegemony, because hegemony is domination in a whole that is nevertheless equal, a whole that's hegemonic in relation to other ones that could eventually be hegemonic. I think the old political categories don't allow us to fully grasp what this new type of power is, probably because it presents itself as a figure of limitlessness. There are really no limits to its power. This is necessarily related to the post-postwar era: like it or not, back in the days of the Soviet Union there was a limit, and since there was one, there were others as well. What we're dealing with now is a figure of limitlessness— I'm putting this in quasi-philosophical terms. In this connection, I remember one of Chomsky's analyses, which dates from the Nixon years and was popular in American government circles.[2] Its subject was the politics of the madman: you had to convince the enemy that you were capable of anything. Strategic victory could only be achieved if the enemy was convinced that you were capable of anything, of a response out of all proportion to the issue at stake, absolutely exceeding the issue at stake. The politics of the madman consists in convincing the enemy that you are capable of reacting like a madman: he says hello to you, and you punch him in the face. And if you manage to convince the whole world, well, then you can breathe easy. This was an explicit subject in the intellectual circles that were close to the far right. I see in this a kind of metaphor of limitlessness. Even just to consider using nuclear weapons against Saddam Hussein, you have to have an unlimited conception of your ability to act, especially since you're simultaneously saying that anyone who has nuclear weapons has to be disarmed. You're going to nuke a country to rid it of nuclear weapons! This is an accepted figure, the direct aim of which is clearly not to disarm Saddam Hussein but to convince humanity as a whole that your power knows no limits. It's a quasi-metaphysical aim. If you look closely at the ideas about imperial power, at the height of the British empire in the nineteenth century, for example, you immediately see that it was never really about limitlessness. It was about arrogance and power . . . but there was also an idea about the necessary limit, an idea about partitioning. Don't forget that the great age of colonialism was all about partitioning the world. The ideology of partitioning was dominant; partitioning was the name of the game. Africa was going to be carved up into pieces! It was messy: it was like dividing up the loot after a robbery! It was completely different from a politics of the limitless: every imperium was an imperium in the element of partitioning. By contrast, American power's current conception of itself is such that there are no limits anymore. So there you have it! The impending war is a test of limitlessness. This is why I think that, apart from its being a war, with all its attendant horrors, this war is truly catastrophic; it's catastrophic in a speculative, philosophical way. Because if it takes place, it will take place in the context of a demonstration of limitlessness. Furthermore, by the way, it's the proof of the limitlessness of *what*? Only of American comfort. It's not a limitlessness that creates anything; it's not a spiritual infinity. Next to this, Muslim fundamentalist limitlessness is in a way a lofty spirituality. We have to face facts. Muslim fundamentalist limitlessness is terroristic and thuggish, it even borders on fascism, but in terms of its explicit motivation, it at least involves the sublimity of transcendence. Whereas American limitlessness is about material comfort through the mediation of the whole world at its service. Bush claims to be the Good. But, ever since Plato, a few justifications of the Good and the idea of the Good still need to be given. It's no small thing to present yourself as the Good. The content is self-righteousness, nothing else: it's the Good because it is limitless in the order of power. It's limitless inasmuch as it's the protection and safeguarding of the Americans' own comfort and wealth. It's the Good because they're sitting on their pile of gold, that's all; no need to justify it any other way. If it were rooted in or connected to some figure of thought or intellectuality, we could still say that it was the infinity of the idea, the limitlessness of thought. We would then criticize it the same way we did the late USSR. We'd denounce the sublime of the idea as a criminal sublime. The Americans promise us a wonderful Good, but in actual fact they beat the crap out of everyone. You should see the people who propound this idea. Next to them, even Chirac is a towering intellect! Ultimately, we old Europeans are like the Greeks vis-à-vis those Roman yokels! I'm saying all this to highlight the extremely violent nature of this limitlessness. What is involved in the impending empiric adventure, in this military intervention, is not just a simple incident; it's really a sort of philosophical situation. If the power is a new figure, a figure of power with its linkage to limitlessness, then this is the beginning of the figure of the disaster of that limitlessness. Provided, of course, that nothing opposes it, but we already know that something is opposing it. It's just that we need to appreciate the scale of what's involved. It is really a radical opposition to the figure of limitlessness as absence of the idea. We need to stand up and say no to this intervention.

I'll conclude with this: What is not only the practical but the philosophical task? Obviously, demonstrating, protesting, is what we've got to do, but, strategically, when you're dealing with a pretension to limitlessness, you've got to produce something that is separate and distinct from that pretension. It's not enough to stay on the sidelines of limitlessness. I fear that Chirac will only ever be on the sidelines of limitlessness. That's of course better than being inside it or being its lackey, but it's not likely to stop the spread of the limitlessness of the absence of the idea. It's absolutely imperative to produce some separation. I hope some is beginning to be produced. The debate is not at all about pro-Americanism versus anti-Americanism. We shouldn't be taken in by that argument. We know what American creators have contributed to the world, and it's a great deal: the American novel is extraordinary, American cinema is extraordinary, etc. Here, we're opposed to a state politics, which is something completely different. In relation to this figure of limitlessness, we must produce separation.

Just as an aside, the post-postwar era can be defined as follows: pre-separation is no longer an available option. The USSR represented ready-made separation. You might not have liked it, but it was nonetheless objectified separation. You might be opposed to Soviet bureaucratism, but every situation was part of a situation in which this separation existed. Separation as such existed objectively. Now there's no longer any pre-separation, be it subjective or objective. We absolutely must produce separation; that's the contemporary problem. We must produce separation without imagining that we can rely, even in the form of protest, on any pre-separation. We must produce separation and produce separation from limitlessness. This is the question of how we can separate from infinity. It can also be expressed as: how can we be atheists? This is a good opportunity to separate from infinity, because it's not a good infinity, it's a bad one, a military infinity in the service of the preservation of wealth.

There are always two aspects to producing separation. As regards subjectivity, things are progressing, but we need to find the right words. Producing separation from the limitlessness of contemporary power isn't exactly the same thing as being anti-imperialist, against war, or anticapitalist. I think we need to find different words. But words aren't produced by force of will. Political words are created from experience, in movements. New words will emerge to designate this production of collective, political separation that the current situation requires of us.

In terms of power, which is the other aspect, the production of separation cannot be solely a subjective declaration; it must deal with the consequences with its own power. What is needed is a disjunctive production, a production of separation, connected to or capable of giving rise to a regime of power that, for its part, is distinct from limitlessness but still asserts itself through a real restriction of limitlessness. This is a problem of collective organization, or something like that, a problem of discipline, but in the sense of a party form. There can be no power without discipline. When you produce separation, you also need to have the discipline of that production, to a sufficient extent to ensure that the separation has power. So discipline has to be reinvented in new terms. We can't get around this. And the problem is going to come up very soon. The question as to what the real targets of the action against this military intervention are going to be is very complex. It's a lot harder than just saying no to the war. Once the war has begun, it's a different kettle of fish, a different situation.

Session 5

March 12, 2003

Today we are going to examine the role, situation, and capacities of theater in connection with the production, capture, or interpolation of the images of the present time. I'd just like to say a little about our guest. François Regnault is unique in standing alone at the intersection of three ways, of which he is the guardian, in a manner of speaking. First, the way of philosophy: he's actually a great, more or less secret, Hegelian. Second, the way of psychoanalysis: he epitomizes the great figure of the independent Lacanians. And third, the way of theater. He thus stands at the unique crossroads of psychoanalysis, theater, and philosophy. François Regnault is a man of the theater, not just a theorist of theater. He works with directors, and in particular with Brigitte Jaques-Wajeman, whom I want to thank for being here with us this evening. He works in philosophy, he writes, and he thinks. And his perspective is based on psychoanalysis and Lacanian concepts. This is obviously why he is ideally suited to being here, so that we can ask him about the status of theater as an indicator of the present time, or as symptomatic of the present time.

I'll begin with a very general, almost emblematic question, which is to ask him whether, from his point of view, and therefore from the theater's, the phrase "images of the present time" means anything to him or raises questions about anything for him.

Francois Regnault: The term "present time" is opposed in a way to the terms "modernity" and "contemporaneity."

I'm not talking only about theater as it's read, or as it's performed, but also about theater as it's *staged*. My experiences are actually always connected with stage productions and directors: Patrice Chéreau, Brigitte Jaques-Wajeman, and Emmanuel Demarcy-Mota, to name the three main directors I have worked with or am currently working with. They have taught me, and are still teaching me, that a play can't be separated from its performance. I learned this, assuming that I didn't know it right away, from Bernard Dort, who, at the invitation of Louis Althusser, came to the rue d'Ulm [the École Normale Supérieure] to introduce us to Brecht. He explained that the concept of *representation* was useful for speaking about theater.[1] This posed problems for some of my fellow philosophers, who understood "representation" in a strictly philosophical sense (*Vorstellung*). By "theatrical representation" Dort simply meant, I think, what happens between the time the curtain goes up and the time the curtain comes down. When there's no curtain, you just do the best you can: the audience can usually figure it out. Unless they're in the same situation as Chateaubriand was, who tells how, when he was very young, he was taken to the theater and saw people speaking to each other for a couple of hours on the stage. He kept waiting for the play to begin, and when the curtain came down at the end, he realized that *that* was what theater was. He hadn't understood: "Such was the first impression I obtained of the art of Sophocles and Molière," he says.[2]

So the play can't be separated from its performance on a stage. No one, be it Aeschylus, Sophocles, Euripides, Shakespeare, or Molière, would have imagined that a play was written to be published: you published it later, but first you performed it. You wrote it, albeit sometimes it wasn't written (as in the Commedia dell'arte). In the seventeenth century, in France, for example, a play was kept from being published as long as possible because, once published, it went into the public domain, and then anyone could get their hands on it. Shakespeare, too, must have saved his plays for the companies that performed them, and Molière, as we know, originally didn't want his plays to be published. (*Les Précieuses ridicules* was first published without his permission.) So it's lucky for us that his *Dom Juan* was copied, or surreptitiously pilfered, by someone, because, as it had been banned in Paris, we have a so-called Amsterdam edition that provides us with a more complete version, notably including the blasphemous scene of the Poor Man. That scene was banned after the second performance of the play, and we would otherwise not have it.

The deep experience of theater is therefore, as I think you'll agree, a play that is performed, not a play that is studied in class.

The other experience is that stagecraft is an art that emerged in the twentieth century, one of the great arts of that century, and can be dated by a number of texts, by André Antoine and Firmin Gémier in particular.[3] It can be dated from the time when it became clear that not only did you have to write a play and then perform it, but you also had to *stage* it and not just be satisfied with the actors finding some way to perform it, even under the direction of a troupe leader, and that there could be a conception of the play provided by the *director*, who thereby became an artist in his own right.

From then on, it is clear that the concept of present time becomes complicated: the question of whether the play is recent, absolutely contemporary, by a living author, or about current events is less of an issue than whether it can be *made present*. In other words, I've always adopted the following viewpoint, and, I believe, the directors I've worked with have adopted the same one (I could paradoxically mention Ossip Mandelstam's line here: "I am no one's contemporary"): no matter what play you're producing, be it by Aeschylus or by the latest young man to show you the tragedy he wrote at home, or even a play written collectively, the question is how to *make it present* today, how to ensure that it is *heard*. This means you have to aim, almost in terms of projective geometry, at *a point at infinity* where any play of the past and any play of the present would meet. The conservative, museographic point of view would be to say, for example, that ever since the death of Genet, Claudel, Koltès, and Beckett there are no more playwrights, so let's only produce the masterpieces of the past. That's not my view, nor is it that of the directors I work with. Nor is it my view that only recent plays from this year or the past ten years should be produced—which is the aim of a number of theaters. When you manage a theater, as I have done, I think the right question to ask, theatrically and philosophically speaking, is: what is the right combination, the right blend, the right mix, of the great masterpieces of the past and the masterpieces (you don't know whether they really are or not, but it doesn't matter) of the present? I think the present time can be defined as the *meeting point* of a great play of the past and a play of the present. It is there that the staging reaches its full potential: the director will ask himself how a play by Aeschylus can have resonance today, how it can be interpreted, how it can be heard, without having to be tampered with or altered, although it can also be, if not tampered with, at least altered.

Conversely, how can a play that has just been written be produced, not in such a way that it will be inscribed in eternity but in such a way that it can resonate within itself, like a figured bass in music, in such a way that we can hear, through thoroughly modern speech, the present time, with all its sparkle, *but also because it contains a past*, like an iceberg whose submerged part suddenly emerges, even though the visible part of it seems so slight, so frail, so fragile?

So what I mean by staging is *that point of view*. Psychoanalysis could help situate this point, where the individual must place himself so as to make this infinite meeting point of the past and the present heard, if need be by bringing it back to the essential and not just turning it into what is called a *reading*. (Brigitte Jaques-Wajeman often complains about the remarks that are made about the staging, of the sort: "He directed *Tartuffe*, and what an interesting *reading* he did of it: through *Tartuffe* he was actually talking about Islam," and so on.) Yet theater critics love that attitude: they're bored, either by definition or by profession, by a Shakespeare or an Aeschylus play, so they have to come up with some hook for it on the evening news. They thus force the work to *bear witness*. Rather than a "reading," in which all the play's different aspects would be made to correspond one-to-one with aspects of the contemporary world or current events, a far more mysterious art or method, which can't be decided on before the play is produced, should be aimed for. Here, Louis Jouvet's practice was impressive, because he would tell the actor who was to perform: "Put all your preconceptions aside." And he'd recommend the same thing to the eventual director. There's nothing more dangerous than a director who says: "I've decided to produce one of Aeschylus's plays, or Molière's *Tartuffe*, or *The Merchant of Venice* in order to talk about such and such a problem facing our society." You can be sure that such a voluntaristic approach is bound to fail. Gradually, as he directs a play that interests him for subjective reasons, out of some private desire, the director will need to find something—if he's a man of the present time (being of the present time is an art)—that will allow him, through his execution of the staging, to make heard what the play contains of the present time, which was unknown to him at the beginning, regardless of the hunches he may have had about it. This dialecticizes the concept of the present time in terms of both the written play and the performed play.

—✺—

Alain Badiou: I'd like to pick up on what you said, from a speculative point of view, as a follow-up to what was said earlier in the seminar. So I'm naturally going to incorporate your remarks a bit into my own—I know you'll forgive me.

I'm struck by two things you ascribe to theater that I think are absolutely right, or even essential.

First, you point out that the question of the present time is a question of construction and/or decision, not of reception or passivity. To be of the present time is a whole art, you said. It's certainly an art in the theater, but it can be taken, more generally, as the conviction that knowing whether there's a present and whether one is contemporary with what will be known as a present constitutes an extraordinary production. It's an extraordinary production, not just something cut up that's shuffled around like a succession of instants. I, for one, think—you can tell me what *you* think—that, in this sense, the theater has a specific function of revealing the present, because, among other things, it has to decide to construct that present. You mentioned this in connection with plays of the past: the problem isn't to provide an interpretation, a reading, a hermeneutics, of them in the present but to *present* them in the present, to give the feeling, in the performance itself, of the actuality, the presentness, of the play.

So I'd like to nudge you further in that direction. With regard to this question of the production or the actualization of the present, does the theater, in your opinion, hold a unique place among the arts?

Second of all, here in this seminar I developed, albeit in a conceptual language different from your own, the idea that the present is always the figure of a certain possibility of the past. I had put it like this: the present is a dialectic between repetition and projection. In the construction of the present there is an element of repetition or of capture of what has happened, at the same time as there is a version of what has happened that's projected toward something that's open, i.e., that can't be calculated before it has been produced. So it's neither a continuation nor a clear-cut break that would leave the present indifferent to the past. What you said about the theater is that the present is a point of contact or a meeting point between a selection made in the past and something projective. That prompts me to ask you what exactly the past of the theater is. You said the play exists in the performance, but it doesn't exist in the past as performance. The past of the play is its writing, its inscription; it is in a certain sense its deposition. So what is the exact nature, in terms of theater's components, of the relationship between what is inscribed or deposited and what is active and performed? I agree with the general figure you describe, namely that the present is always a presentification of the density of a past, but in the theater there's the special issue of the mode of presence of the past not being exactly the thing itself. This is different from the past of painting: the past of painting gives us the painting and we inscribe it in our present frame of reference. We see the painting in the present, but there is something in the painting that is the thing itself. What is the thing itself in the case of a tragedy by Aeschylus? It's a real problem.

François Regnault: I'm not absolutely sure you're right about painting, even if a painting is *the thing itself.* I'm not sure that the Renaissance princes who commissioned paintings from painters for their palaces or the Popes who commissioned them for their churches would understand the attitude we have today when we look at paintings in museums. They'd say: "What an odd attitude you have toward works of art! That Raphael was made to go in my bedroom, not to be put on display for everyone." Likewise, the Popes would say: "You see the Sistine Chapel frescoes?

They were made for here, and here they'll stay. They're not going to make the rounds of the Emirates." I think that the notion of painting for a museum would have been foreign to the Renaissance painters. They painted for a palace or a hall, but the idea of a museum that would keep them forever away from what they were intended for wasn't something they entertained.

<hr />

Alain Badiou: Still, they understood that a painting was something that could be bought, and sold! Which isn't the case for plays.

<hr />

François Regnault: As far as the theater is concerned, it's very true that the thing exists independently of the performance, if it's regarded as a written masterpiece. But that's a modern attitude, too. Take the classical French theater of the seventeenth century: back then, it never occurred to anyone to perform *a play of the past*. In that sense, they were moderns. They always sided with the moderns, and they all regarded themselves as moderns (even in spite of the famous Quarrel of the Ancients and the Moderns, which didn't really have to do with that). When they sought out models from Antiquity, they *incorporated* the ancient model and *eliminated* it at the same time. Nobody at that time would have dreamed of re-creating an ancient tragedy. When Racine wrote *Phèdre*, it was, so to speak, to prevent Euripides' *Hyppolitus* or Seneca's *Phaedra*, which he was nevertheless the first to admire, from being performed. But in a way, his *Phèdre* did away with the *Phaedras* of the past. Molière's *Amphitryon* was written so that there would be no need to perform the one by Plautus. Likewise, Shakespeare took models from the past in order to write present-day plays that replaced and enhanced them. The problem of the status of a play didn't arise until the modern age.

Even in Romantic theater, which, God knows, is focused on the past and adores the Middle Ages, nobody would have thought of putting on "classics" first, and if Racine and Corneille were still performed, it was because, as Voltaire showed in his *Century of Louis XIV*, he considered that they were still close to them, and because the Comédie-Française presented them as a recent tradition. Victor Hugo himself could still regard himself as a rival, rather than as an heir, of Corneille and Racine.

It was in the twentieth century that people began to question the performance of plays of the past. It was precisely when contemporary staging appeared that it raised the question of the past and that the play in a way became a "masterpiece," a treasure that glowed in the dark and could be brought back out into the light.

When Giraudoux wrote his *Amphitryon 38*, he naturally thought that Molière's masterpiece would always be greater than his, so he would only offer an *Amphitryon* in the style of 1938. This meant that, for him, the play of the past was somehow threatening him a bit and looking down disdainfully on him, which wasn't Molière's attitude toward Plautus, from whom he borrowed *his* play.

Starting in the twentieth century, when a specific art of staging emerged, it could be said, oddly enough, that the plays of the past *became things from the past*, treasures, and that the question then arose of how to make them heard again as if they were modern plays, and how to give them whatever resonance they might have. I think there's an attitude toward the density of history that changed with the emergence of staging. Nobody would dream of getting rid of the plays of the past today, unless you're talking about deliberate barbarism. Rather, the problem is not to be intimidated by them. It's because Brecht knew that the classics now existed "forever" that he attacked "intimidation by the classics"!

———❧———

Alain Badiou: Let me ask you a general question. You said: once staging emerged, the relationship to the theatrical past changed, since the question arose as to what performing a play of the past meant. And you clearly say that there are two possible approaches: a hermeneutic approach, if you will, which consists in proposing a new interpretation of the play of the past, and an interpretation, which I'd call literal, in the present, which consists in taking the play at face value and performing it as though it were a contemporary play. I understand that distinction perfectly. But we might still hypothesize that it's not since staging emerged that the relationship to the past has changed but, rather, it's since the relationship to the past changed that staging has emerged. We might imagine that, for reasons more fundamental than the theater, the historical construction of the past, and therefore that of the present, has changed, and that the relationship to the theater of the past changed at the same time. Here, too, I come back to my question: as regards this issue, is the theater an exception or an indicator? The issue of staging is an extremely interesting one. I would like to say a word about it myself.

There is no question that in the late nineteenth century, there emerged a new artist figure, the figure of the stage director. Up until then, the theater consisted of the playwright and the actors. Then along came someone who, as we know, is difficult to define exactly: the director. It's understandable that the director should be hard to define since there are conflicting definitions of him. On the one hand, he's regarded as a hermeneut, a reader, an interpreter, and, on the other, he's regarded as an agent of the present, a man of the present time. So the question then arises as to whether staging is completely thinkable in the history of theater, if that's where it should first be intelligible, or whether it has a broader significance. It was also at that time, or slightly before, that the position of orchestra conductor in music first emerged, and this gradually inscribed the question of musical masterpieces in a somewhat different temporal perspective. We might wonder whether, ultimately, the emergence of the director in theater, which is clearly related to theater's own history, to its transformations, isn't also symptomatic of an overall change in the conditions of construction of the present in its relationship to the past. You mentioned that when it comes to painting, museography is also a new dimension, that it's a special relationship to the pictorial art of the past, the creation of a special relationship between the present and the past. Is contemporary theatricality—heavily influenced by the singular history of this new type of theater artist, the director—exhausted by the internal transformations in the history of theater, or is the whole of it dominated by a very important problem, that of a long crisis of the present? What I call "crisis of the present" is the need to find other operators of its existence or its construction, in the sense that, in the theater, the construction of the present now has a special connection to the figure of the past.

Let me give another twist to my question now. As we both know, Mallarmé wrote somewhere that the problem is that a present is lacking and also that what he wished for, what he longed for, was a new figure of theatrical representation, a new kind of collective theater. There was really this connection, where he was concerned, between the question of the present and the question of theater, theoretically at least, since he never completed the project. So let me submit the following hypothesis to you, which I'm sure you'll quickly deconstruct or reconstruct: the emergence of stagecraft and its history are indicative of theater's unique role in the general regime of the arts. This has to do with the question of how, in modern times—since the early twentieth century, say—the problem of the construction of time appeared. Specifically, how, in the realm of art, the question of the relationship between present and past, the relationship between art and art history, between a given art and the history of that art, between the pure present of that art and its genealogy, appeared, with the clear understanding that comparable phenomena (the emergence of the conductor in music, the emergence of museography in painting) can be found in the other arts. But theater is unique in that it is itself, in its existence, absolutely in the present. This is a thesis contained in the fact that, between the text and its performance, there is no real distinction, and that the theatrical act truly epitomizes the figure of this relationship between present and past.

Let me rephrase the complete hypothesis in a more articulate and intelligible way. Among all the arts, theater has a special function when it comes to the problem of the construction of the present, because, like all the others, it is subjected to a new type of relationship between present and past, which could be called a necessary relationship of historicity: it's impossible to construct the present of the art without reassessing and taking a stand, in a way, on its past. However, in the case of theater, there's an additional level to this operation, which is simply the construction of a special present, the present of performance [représentation]. The present of performance is different from the museum of performance. It is situated in a temporal intensity of a different kind.

François Regnault: I completely agree with what you just said. I'm going to do what they do in Plato's dialogues and say "Oh, yes, for sure, absolutely, of course, etc.!" The example of the orchestra conductor is an excellent one. In a sense, you could say: conductors came on the scene when there were too many musicians in the orchestra and such difficult symphonies, with such subtle counterpoints and contrasting time schemes, that someone was needed to bring some order to them. The dissemination of the works of the past emerged at the same time as the modern orchestra conductor. Mendelssohn, it was said, "re-created" Bach's *Saint Matthew Passion*. As for Wagner, he had a vision of himself as a conductor with all that implied in terms of control, state and phallocratic power, and so on. When, as a young child, he looked out his window and saw Weber going by, Weber was the very image for him of what he wanted to be later on: a conductor! You may just want to become a musician because, like the young Johann Sebastian Bach, you've seen some sublime scribblings on a score, but you may also want to become one in order to conduct great symphonies. Wagner is moreover situated in a historical perspective: he conducted Beethoven's symphonies, Mozart's operas, and so on, the music of a recent past. So he is situated, for that very reason, at a time when the meaning of the past itself was changing. And what's more, he is also regarded—though this is the same issue—as *the inventor of modern stagecraft*, and he is often mentioned as such in theater histories.

Coming back now to the uniqueness of theater, there is a uniqueness of the theater that's a sign of change, of a new conceptualization, of new approaches, of the new attitude that can be had toward the idea of time itself, and I like the phrase you used, "crisis of the present," too much not to adopt it myself. This means that "director" is the very name of this crisis of the present and the solution that's been found for it within theater. But we need to be careful: the directors don't necessarily see it as a crisis of the present. Stagecraft emerged in France around 1900, at the time when famous historical plays were being produced. Directors wanted to mount great Shakespeare plays, with lots of extras, as did André Antoine, the founder of the Théâtre Libre in 1887, for example, or Firmin Gémier, the founder of the Théâtre National Populaire in 1920 (a name Jean Vilar would use again in 1951), who also put on mass spectacles at the Cirque d'Hiver. For productions like that, a director was definitely needed. You couldn't get by solely with actors arranging things among themselves. What Alain's and my friend Antoine Vitez, the great man of theater, called "a cathedral of signs" needed to be constructed. This may be a legacy of a certain nineteenth-century megalomania, but it shows that a crisis of the present can be addressed similarly when it comes to a certain way of treating the past. What's more, I can't help but think that the same is also true for museography in painting and for the conductor in music.

I would just add two observations, which are not objections to this redefinition of the present, as well as a controversial remark about a certain contemporary theater.

1.   We shouldn't forget that the situation at the turn of the twentieth century was contemporaneous with the birth of *cinema*, and that cinema's function was not to revisit the past. When cinema does revisit the past, it may be in theatrical form. When cinema came into being, its aim was not to deal with the past of its art, which was non-existent. When it became an art in its own right, we might wonder whether it didn't then borrow its way of situating the present from painting or from theater, etc. When Eisenstein drew on opera, theater, and painting in his films, you can't help but think that he was forcing cinema to undergo experiences that cinema could not necessarily know about, let alone treat, and which it could do without when it created its own masterpieces. Yet, at the same time as he was drawing on the other arts in his films, he was inventing a kind of editing that existed nowhere else . . . apart from in cinema!

2.   I'd also like to mention something I've thought about repeatedly, without being able to really solve the problem: the birth of *psychoanalysis*, namely, the birth of kinds of interpretation (in the Freudian and Lacanian sense) that have nothing to do with traditional (hermeneutic, exegetical, paraphrastic) interpretations, if analytic interpretation is understood as a way of making something heard that no one had heard before. I think that, first of all, it probably emerged at a time when the past needed to be resituated, the past of the subject itself in analysis as well. And, second of all, it's perhaps no coincidence that stagecraft came into being at the same time. So, cinema and psychoanalysis?

Finally, my controversial remark: you and I thereby do away, I think, with any conception of or position on theater that would say it should only be about the present. Thinking that we have to deal with what's going on today, here and now, in a realistic, "concrete" way, as they say, well, it's killing the theater! It's possible that masterpieces may be written about the "here and now," but as soon as theater focuses exclusively on that, it dies out.

I'll just take one strange but eloquent example. During the 1917 Revolution or shortly thereafter, at a very tense moment of the war and the revolution, the great Russian Soviet director Meyerhold directed *Les Aubes* (*The Dawn*), by the Belgian poet Émile Verhaeren, a symbolist play disconnected from current events. In order not to be cut off from "the real," however, Meyerhold had news reports, direct from the front, read during intermission. So if you're dead set on making theater current, just have the news from the newsreel read "between the acts," to borrow one of Virginia Woolf's titles! That would be more honest, and it's a solution I'd consider elegant.

Meyerhold also said: Sometimes the play is more interesting than the staging, but at other times the staging might be more interesting than the play!

Alain Badiou: We're making progress. We can make a first point, which would be to finally give the art of theater credit for having proposed, from within its artistic activity and the history of that activity, a specific treatment of this huge problem of modern times, which is essentially that the construction of the present cannot do without the past. And the name of this solution is directing, the director. This is a significant change because it's the name of a new type, a new possibility, of relationship between the present and the past, and therefore of the construction of the present.

I'm now going to begin a new assessment cycle, still closely related to this problem of the present. It has to do with how to interpret this need—indicated by the staging from within the present—for a certain contact, a certain relationship between, a certain combination of, the present and the past, how to interpret it in terms of the intensity, so to speak, of the present itself. Couldn't it be claimed that at the time when the theater felt itself to be capable of eliminating its past—as you very aptly said, that's the right way of putting it as regards the classical theater: a *Phèdre* is written that, however much it refers to antiquity, is still the theatrical elimination of it—couldn't it be claimed that this attests to an inherent vitality or intensity of the theatrical present, which our historicized culturalism dilutes or weakens? I'm playing devil's advocate here: I may not really think so. But I'm saying this to shed some light on the point of view of those who say that only contemporary plays should be performed, that they should only deal with the present time, that theater has become an elitist and effete art because it's crushed by the cultural weight of the past, because all its masterpieces are behind it. This discourse can base its argument on one point at least, which is that the construction of the present, whose name is stagecraft, is something that makes the past one (but not the only one) of the requisite mediations of the present. But a present that needs such a mediation is in a sense a weaker or less intense present than one that doesn't need it. Does the arrogant audacity of those who do away with the masterpieces of the past and replace them with their contemporary productions bespeak a greater vitality or intensity as compared with those who need a suppression, a mediation, or a recovery of the whole of the past?

I'm saying this because if we're getting into a debate about contemporary theater, a debate that's actually a very heated one, what is it all about? The debate is about the recovery of the actor's spontaneity, the immediacy of the body, the misuse of stereotypes and contemporary vulgarities, and so on, a topic whose basic argument is that, under the name of staging, a museographic spirit has taken root in theater itself. The comparison with the museum is often made to show that there's something of the deathly power of the past about this, and that this is why only contemporary plays should be performed, they should only deal with the contemporary world, and so on. François Regnault, I should mention in passing, has recently written two books, *Équinoxes* and *Solstices* (*Écrits sur le théâtre*, volumes 1 and 2), which I highly recommend if you want a wide and varied panorama of contemporary theater. I'll take almost at random page 265, on Claudel: "*La Ville* [*The City*] happens to be one of the only

French plays that deals with communism. Even Brecht rarely addresses the question of communism per se, let alone the Party."[4] One might say: that's a real shame! If twentieth-century theater so rarely addresses the questions of communism and the Party, this is clear evidence that, unlike seventeenth-century theater, for which the question of the monarchy's power was central, it has moved away from the major historical currents of the century and remains at a distance from the political present. As a result of performing the masterpieces of the past, it has lost the vitality of the present. Ultimately, under the name of staging, and in the theatrical history of staging, isn't there reflected a position on the construction of the present, a more distanced, less immediate, and ultimately milder, less intense position than in earlier periods, which you said even included romanticism? In those periods, they had the brazen capacity to simply eradicate the past, a bit like the way people in the seventeenth century considered Gothic cathedrals to be monstrosities. Isn't a real present always in a slightly iconoclastic position vis-à-vis the past? If it's too slavishly reverential toward the past, isn't it because the fact that a present is lacking, as Mallarmé says, secretly persists beneath?

<hr />

François Regnault: When it comes to theater, I always have two kinds of responses, which I realize may contradict each other. The first kind are contingent and the second, necessary; the first kind are about theater as actuality and presentification, and the second about theater as eternity. By playing one kind off against the other, I can get away with it.

You're right to think there's a crisis of the theater, *if* we assume that there's been this change in the relationship to the past, leading to a certain disappointment on the part of theater people with regard to theater itself, which isn't giving them what the theater of Shakespeare's or Corneille's time gave *them*. I would say it's the same with painting. There's a line of Francis Bacon's that struck me: "It's great," he said, more or less, "we're rid of the religious agenda and we don't have to paint annunciations, crucifixions, and so on anymore." (This is in his *Interviews with David Sylvester*.) "But then again," he added, "the trouble is, we don't know what to paint anymore." Some may say he got around it by painting crucifixions of sorts! His comment should be taken in all its force. The same force with which Picasso used to visit museums to see whether his paintings held their own against the great masters' paintings. That was clearly not the attitude of the Renaissance. Raphael might have wondered whether his paintings held their own against Perugino's, but he more likely thought he could outdo his master.

There's a similar situation in the cinema. Serge Daney once remarked to me that when we used to go see Jean-Luc Godard's films in the 1950s and '60s, they were in a way contemporaneous for us with Griffith, Eisenstein, et al.[5] One film might be better or worse than another, but the context was the same. Now, young people who see films think that these films have nothing to do with the history of cinema. They're willing to admire Eisenstein, but, for them, he's the history, the past, of cinema, whereas X's or Y's latest film is contemporary cinema. A friend of mine told me that when he was talking to his son about a film, his son exclaimed "But that's an old film!" when the film in question was only from the year before!

How can theater cope with this? It can cope, first of all, by means of theater people's recurrent *despair*, a frequent despair and an interesting one. Sometimes you've got to prefer those who have a grudge against theater because of what it lacks or what's disappointing about it to those who piously revere it because it's *Theeeater* with a capital T![6]

When these theater people lose faith in theater because cinema would do a better job of it, would better reflect the present, when they think that the visual arts achieve a greater modernity, or when they lose faith in theater as compared with music, which, in their opinion, is capable of more contemporary, more abstract, better structured, more formal conceptions than some pathetic play in which there are only ever the actors' bodies, and so on, these complaints should be turned around in favor of theater's greatness. For two reasons. The first is that the form of the present specific to theater, and specific to concerts and dance, too, is still and always a form of *performance*. This means that human beings (or simply *people*) are gathered together in a place and that they are alive and present in it (even if theater is also for the dead, as Jean Genet thought: the dead are in attendance, but they hardly bother us). And the other reason is that people are there for their pleasure, or because they get a certain feeling, or they experience a certain *catharsis*. Something like psychoanalysis really needs to be brought in to explain this being-together, which Aristotle was no doubt the first to conceptualize under the name of "catharsis," of the purging of the passions. This is a capacity within the purview of theater. Whether one criticizes it, castigates it, mocks it, wants no more of it, or wants a lot more of it, it makes no difference: the performance always occurs with this purview, this capacity, in mind, to condemn it or to glorify it.

Even though it is of a superior essence,[7] the theater is nevertheless often reduced to being presented merely as "the performing arts," to use the Ministry of Culture's terminology. But when you want to return to this essence of the theater, it's obviously *the present moment of the performance* that you highlight. What then comes to light is that the present moment is the moment when the theater confronts all the density of its past in order to free itself from it all at once, thanks to a director who has discovered the art of eliminating it in his own way (staging as an art of the past and of its elimination). In other words, the director must be able to do with Racine's play what Racine did with Euripides's play. If he succeeds, he benefits from a thesis that must be held simultaneously with that of the present moment and which is none other than *the eternal nature* of theater: the fact that the present moment is at the same time an eternal moment.

Indeed, something like repetition occurs in the theater, something that Lacan applies even to the spectator, when he declares that the spectator has always been the same: "From a certain point of view, the audience must always have been at the same level. *Sub specie aeternitatis*, everything is equal, everything is always there, although it isn't always in the same place."[8] This has been the case for only a relatively short time, actually, since it's only 2500 years old, which is nothing on the scale of the human species.

People's ability to *tell a story to you*, for you, facing you, whatever story it may be, is a human experience we come back to when everything is lacking, an experience that resolves the crisis or at least tries to introduce itself by saying: "Yes, I know, I can't do much, but I can at least do this, which is something you won't find in either painting or literature but you *will* find in poetry when it's recited, in music when it's played, and in dance when it's performed before you, hence in the performing arts, in a specific time and place, and inevitably with a beginning, middle, and end."

———∞———

Alain Badiou: You end up saying what I was suggesting, namely that the specific figure by means of which the theater treats the contemporary construction of the present, with the need for incorporating a certain past, is related to the second meaning of the present, which is that theater is an art of the present, a construction of the present, of the present of the performance. We might provisionally claim that, when all is said and done, what is meant by staging or contemporary theater is a special form of the problem of the treatment of the present, because the weight of the past is negated, lightened, or even done away with, as you suggested, in the time of the performance, which is itself a present. That would mean that there's something in theater that's like the relationship between two presents. There would thus be a splitting of the word "present," and this is very important to me because I'm absolutely convinced that the contemporary construction of the present involves both the incorporation of the past and a present figuration of the present. This indeed implies that there are two meanings of the word "present," that there's a kind of presentification in the present, namely the performance, which is the time of the quasi-empirical, fragile, given present. The performance is involved in or meant to capture a construction of the present in a broader sense, which encompasses a position or a localization with respect to the past. I remember how Vitez used to say that the theater was a device for localizing time and that it helped us understand where we were in history. There's the question: "Where in time are we?" The theater's purpose is to tell us.

As for the question of cinema, the comparison always eventually comes up. It can't be helped! I'd say that cinema happens to be a wonderful index of the present, and that's why some theater artists are envious of that capacity, a capacity for producing a very fine crystallization of the present. But in my opinion cinema doesn't have the localizing function I mentioned; it doesn't tell us where the present is in the present.

It shows the present, it reveals it more quickly or with a greater degree of crystallization than theater does. But it doesn't localize it in the same way. It doesn't indicate the parameterizations or the localizations of the present. That's why I would affirm the ultimate superiority of theater for the philosopher. Theater is "of a superior essence" (Mallarmé) because the process of construction of the present is shown at the same time as the present. In the cinema, what the director does is different: he does everything; he makes the film, he directs it. In the theater, the director has a much more complicated relationship with what is given. Why? Because he is really dealing with a process of construction of the present, which is visible or legible in the present of the performance. The fragility of the present of the performance recapitulates the construction of the present. We might provisionally conclude that there is something in cinema that's the capacity for donation of the present, while in theater there is a capacity for construction of the present. Construction reveals its localizations while donation may or may not do so; it's not something intrinsic.

Ultimately, as regards the original question—the position of theater in the general idea of a crisis of the present—what's important to note is that we're looking for the theatrical solution to the problem of the crisis of the present in the essence of theater, in what you called its eternity. It's really quite striking that, with all the other arts, it's not the case that the means for dealing with the current crisis, or the current state of the problem of the present, needs to be sought in their eternity or their essence. With other arts, on the contrary, it's often said that their ability to overcome the crisis can be found in the radical renunciation of their essence, in their eradication even, in their outright elimination. Just look at how pictorial activities are being replaced by semi-theatrical activities, as with performance art, or semi-playful activities as in the case of situation creations. I'd ask you whether you'd then agree—to open up a third sequence of investigation into theater's relationship with the present—that there's a uniqueness of theater as regards the preservation of its own essence, and whether, in the case of theater's construction of the present, the resource, the force, isn't to be found in the essence of theater, which is not the usual case. This would mean that theater is the presentation of a construction of the present, that it's the present of that construction, and that this is something that is related to its essence. We might therefore conclude that it's because theater ultimately has its own essence as a resource in the present that there has only been one great philosophical treatise on theater, namely Aristotle's *Poetics*. This is a question we were discussing before coming here: could a definitive treatise on theater be written again today, under totally different circumstances? And we agreed that it hardly seemed possible. If even Brecht never went beyond collections, essays, or experiments, it's for one essential reason: despite the theses on the non-Aristotelian theater, on the actor's corporeality, on the need for an absolutely contemporary theater, there might be something about the life of theater, about its very actuality, that is more closely related to the presentation of its essence than is the case with the other arts. Would you agree that this explains why Mallarmé regarded theater as being of a superior essence?

⌘

François Regnault: I do agree. Let me give two examples that are symptomatic.

It's possible to write about painting without discussing fine art. Gérard Wajcman wrote a wonderful book, *L'Objet du siècle* [The object of the century], in which he discusses Duchamp, who exhibited a readymade object, not a sculpture, and Malevitch's square, which has little to do with Raphael's paintings. At a certain moment, for a seemingly interminable period of painting, you may wonder "What is a painting?" (Lacan's question), but you may also ask yourself what the modernity of a painting is that has done away with frame composition, perspective, color, and so on. You then realize that painting may well have morphed into dance, performance, or performance art, as is the case with action painting and so on.

But let's take a different example for theater: the cubist ballet *Parade*, by Erik Satie, with a scenario by Jean Cocteau and sets, costumes, and stage curtain by Picasso. Satie composed honky-tonk music, which was intended to break with beautiful high-toned music: a typewriter combined with the orchestra instruments, sirens, car horns, etc. There were stiff, sharp-edged, machinelike costumes that were impossible to feel comfortable in. I saw *Parade*, or at least a re-creation of it. It was pretty bizarre, a little weird, but—I'm going to be harsh—it was very boring and dull. You get the sense of *a dead-end* (which might have pleased Satie). This experiment was no threat to Picasso, or Cocteau, or even cubism, and hardly to Satie himself (who can be regarded as a minor composer, or maybe as a major noncomposer!). The issue raised by *Parade* was that the human body is always something you can do a great deal with, but not everything. The human body's resistance to geometrization, to mechanization, to being lengthened or shortened, to suffering, rape, crime, sexuality, secrets, or what have you, is such that even if you try to do everything with a body, such as breaking it, slicing it up, scarifying it, making holes in it, or making it perform sadistic, masochistic, sexual, etc. acts (the extreme being death, obviously), there's a moment when you really have the feeling of shattering "the superior essence of theater"—"Serves it right!" you'll say, except that *the theater withdraws*. I think that there's a limit, which is simultaneously a kind of greatness, even if we don't know what a body can do, to borrow Spinoza's enigmatic phrase, and whether this body is malleable and flexible, albeit only up to a point.

Or, to approach things from a different angle, let me take the two terms Plato uses about theater (in Book 3 of the *Republic*), *voice* and *gestures* (the bearing, the demeanor—the acting, in short). Let's assume you regard them as two fundamental concepts through which theatricality, in its essence, is conveyed. It might then be objected that you can separate the voice from the rest of the body (as in Beckett's very successful *Krapp's Last Tape*), that you can cut up the body into as many pieces as possible, that you can do a whole play without anything being heard, without a text, with only purely physical actions (Peter Handke wrote a whole play—a very good one—without a single word), or with just a head emerging from the ground or just a mouth speaking (Beckett again). Well, it's clear, in my opinion, that these outstanding successes are limit cases, which, as in geometry, consist in corroborating the main theorem. All this rambling around the essence of theater amounts, perhaps fortunately for the spectator although unfortunately for the philosopher—or the other way around!—to reaffirming more than ever the essence (or the main attribute) of theater. To the point where it may sometimes be better just to place yourself respectfully at the heart of the theater's essence in order to try to change it from within, or at least to renew it, like Parsifal taking up the cult of the Grail again in his own way! Richard Wagner definitely confronted this issue in the most daring way!

Antoine Vitez said: "When I direct a play, there comes a moment when I have to be *against* the play." So we need to be wary of directors who are in love with the play from start to finish. At some point, the director has to say to himself: "I don't have a clue, it's so old-hat, it's not working, this play is terrible, it has nothing to do with the present," and so on. There's a big chance that it will be an outright disaster, but there's also the chance that that splitting of the present you were talking about might be treated, in the analytic sense of the term, not evacuated, and might really produce something new.

***

Alain Badiou: I'd like to take things in a slightly different direction. You have put forward in what I think is a practically irrefutable way some ideas about the essence of theater drawn from the question we've been addressing, namely, the staging's construction of the relationship to the present and the past. It's possible to take another approach, which you actually suggested right at the start of this conversation, i.e., that staging was first introduced because plays were being produced in which the organization of the complexity made staging necessary, just as the orchestra conductor was first introduced when the conditions of the public performance, with the enormous postromantic symphony orchestra or the great operas after Mozart, had become so unwieldy that someone was needed to manage it all. So we can approach things from the standpoint of multiplicity. Indeed, the present moment of the theatrical performance results from the arrangement of extremely diverse and heterogeneous elements, with absolutely no predetermined harmony among them. This is also a feature of modernity, and I think that one of the imperatives, a difficult one, of the construction of the present today is that it cannot be achieved by a simple accumulation of traditional elements. There is always a kind of heterogeneous, disjunctive whole, a disjunctive synthesis, Deleuze would say, that must be achieved. Staging also involves this ability to achieve a disjunctive synthesis. If it were harmonious or predetermined, there would be no need for a director, or so it was formerly believed: the actors and the text would come together in a simplifiable process . . . But the theater is a heterogeneous multiplicity. There are bodies, but insofar as they are voiced; there are men and women, young and old people, but also sets; there are costumes (with nudity itself being one costume among others); there's a text or the lack of a text, but the lack of a text is an extreme form of text, and so on and so forth. It's really an assortment of components, and the question of producing a present of the performance (I'm not saying a unity) out of this multiplicity is a problem peculiar to the theater. In cinematic creation, synthesizing all of this is a very different thing; it is a sleight of hand, if only because the elements are so extremely mysterious, secret, and incomplete, and what will be seen is a finished product. Theater is very different. It is obliged to show the process of construction of its present. It will show the way its complex components construct the present. This is also what staging involves. I was just thinking that, in a way, this complexity, too, is an originary or fundamental element. Even Greek theater was already very complicated. It had music, costumes, cothurni, masks, a chorus, several different performance spaces, and so on. I'm not saying that a director was needed, but there was in any case, right from the beginning, a construction of the present implying a disjunctive synthesis between elements with no predetermined harmony, which had to be channeled through the story and its performance. I was thinking that many of the experiments in theatrical modernism are strange in that they consist in reducing this complexity rather than in treating it. It's very striking. For example, it will be said that theater, in essence, is the actor's body, or that it's a particular kind of imagery or an electronics of image representations, and so on. So it could be said—but you'll have to let us know what *you* think about this—that the real resource of theater as an indicator of the present lies in its accepting its basic multiplicity and the disjunctive synthesis of this multiplicity, not in reducing or simplifying it. In my view, this is a major contemporary debate: ultimately, is the price that must be paid for there to be a present a price of simplification, or is it a price that consists in having, accepting, and holding onto the heterogeneous complexity? You can see why I say this. Behind it, there is the modern theme of specialized singularity. There's that, and at the same time there's the opposite theme of the blending of everything and of universal interdisciplinarity. Theater, however, has something particular to say about this. On the one hand, it says that it is the result of a distinctive heterogeneous complexity, and, on the other, that this complexity is unique to it, that it's *not* the mixture of everything, nor is it, Wagner's claims to the contrary notwithstanding, total art, absolute art, or the recapitulation of all the arts. It's neither one nor the other. Basically, I would argue that theater is the proposition of the construction of a singularity in the present, but of a singularity as complexity, a complexity that also includes a significant element of chance, contingency, and control as well, but remaining poised above it, in a position that, when all is said and done, makes the construction visible. I wanted to ask you: What would you think of the idea that theater's superior essence, as an ever-available resource for treating the question of the construction of the present, despite the weight of the past and so on, is ultimately a certain relationship, which is utterly unique to it, between synthesis and multiplicity, between the homogeneous and the heterogeneous, between complexity and unity, between repetition and the present, and that there's an operator of construction of the present in it that makes that complexity visible? From the point of view, this time, of the spectator that I am, I've always found theater to be a unique experience, because it's exhausting and exhilarating all at once. I've always wondered why. I think it's exhilarating and exhausting because, when it's working, it's a complexity made miraculously present, it's the transparent present of a heterogeneous complexity. It's also an utterly fascinating combination of contingency and necessity. There's an element of absolute contingency (the actors' bodies, etc.) and, miraculously, this contingency results in the representation in the present of something like a necessity. To perceive it, to take it in, to accept it, requires a stillness, a concentration, a response that's utterly unique. This is something like a philosophical essence of theater, which is the fact that what's proposed in the pure present of the performance is the possibility that's always open to humanity, to all of us, that the complexity, the heterogeneous multiplicity, all the messiness of the world, doesn't prevent our attaining something like an essential simplicity. What about you? What do you yourself think about the theater, ultimately?

—∞∞—

François Regnault: I often say to myself: "When it comes right down to it, the only thing you like about theater is the whole theater and nothing but the theater, and whenever it's less than that you get bored, or you disapprove." Jacques Copeau said that he wanted "a bare stage": you get rid of the sets, the costumes, and so on. There's nothing but the actor and the text. Actually, Copeau wanted to include *the whole of theater* in this bare minimum. As for Strehler, he made use of the best lighting, the best costumes; he had the best sets, and sublime actors, in keeping with the idea of an absolute unity of the production, harmonious and sublime . . . You and I both saw Goldoni's *Harlequin: Servant of Two Masters*, directed by Strehler at the Grand Théâtre in Reims, and we were enthralled by an incredibly harmonious production, which he later staged again and constantly revised, no doubt one of the finest productions of the latter half of the twentieth century. So we're always wondering—let's speak in Cartesian or Spinozist terms—what is the substance of theater, what are its essential attributes? Is the body attribute of the actor the attribute of substance, or is it only a secondary attribute? Is the text attribute an essential attribute or a secondary one, or is it only a mode? Essential attributes, secondary attributes, modes: that's a pretty classical ontology, but it seems to me that we're always dealing with some variation of this ontology. So when the spectator, whose ontology is basically spontaneous, suddenly encounters, if not attributes, at least modes or elements that are entirely contingent (let's say video, etc.), what happens is that, if he's a conservative, he rejects it, or if he's a modernist, he says: "As far as I'm concerned, video is the future of theater." And if video lasts, the artist will try to recover the theatricality of video, to reintegrate video into theater, to ask himself the kind of questions that music asked itself about electronic machines, as Boulez did with the 4X machine in *Répons*, and so on. All the special components can be used this way. For example, God knows how huge a thing stage lighting was in the history of theater: we no longer see productions the same way as before (here, too, Wagner led the way with gas lighting in Bayreuth). Or even more simply, are costumes necessary? Why don't we just have nudity? Or identical tunics for everyone, and so on? But it's always based on thinking that there's an essential core, a core that may be indefinable but without which we'd be giving up on theatricality itself. In that respect, you're right to think that theater is constantly inviting you or unfailingly referring you back to its "superior essence." And I don't think this questioning occurs in the same way in the other arts, or at least not to this extent. You can always be part of a new modernity of painting, or of sculpture, as with *Fontaine*, Duchamp's urinal, as I said a moment ago: Duchamp's urinal was accepted into the museum (even if on occasion a visitor might take the liberty of peeing in it), and people reflected on the object, or on what a museum is. Of course, there's something about theater that we want to see remain, but what? I'm not saying that its essence is pure, but what you call its multiplicity is indeed complex, versatile, diverse, variable. I don't have a norm of theater or a normative idea of theater. I accept seeing only images, hearing only a voice in the dark or watching an actor who's shut up in a room with only a couple of spectators and speaks to them, or a Greek tragedy performed in the middle of an amphitheater with thirty thousand people, but my gut feeling (Aristotle had sensed this and probably imagined, aspired to, an ontology, a metaphysics of poetics, referring at least to his science of being or of first principles) is that the theater is a *thing* in which *something* is always being *repeated*, something that makes us repeat (ourselves) constantly, in the theater.[9] Repetition in the theater is not necessarily love punished, as Jean Anouilh said (*The Rehearsal: Or Love Punished*). There's always repetition in theater; it's a present of repetition. *Theater—I'm falling back on an age-old cliché—is the art that's between repetition and representation.*

<hr />

Alain Badiou: That might serve as the last word on the subject. Seeing the present as a pure break or as an isolated epiphany is a fantasy: the present is always constructed in the form of some repeating series or other. And, in effect, "repetition" is a key word in theater. It is doubly so: repetition in the sense of the rehearsal of the play but also repetition in the sense that the play itself is repeated. So we can conclude, for all the reasons that François Regnault's friendship and knowledge have enabled us to set forth today, that there is really a unique, absolutely irreducible relationship between theater and the problem and construction of the present. Ultimately, it is likely that when the theater is in trouble, that trouble must eventually be interpreted as a telltale sign of a crisis of the present. The theater always demands our cooperation and our assistance, because, like it or not, its trouble is our own. Its troubles and its triumphs are our own. Therefore, contrary to Plato, or at any rate contrary to what Plato thought he had to do, or contrary to what we think he thought he had to do, we'll focus philosophy on an unconditional defense of theater. Thank you, thank you so much, dear François.

Session 6

March 26, 2003

Today I'd like to return once more to the war, but in a way that is more closely related to our subject. First, I'll discuss the war in terms of images, in terms of the relationship between the war and images, in terms of its transmission or presentation through images. As regards the present, I'll return to the question of what is presented to us therein as a present, and I'll ask what the temporal figure occasioned by the war, or, more precisely, by the current military intervention, is, since I told you the reasons why the designation "war" should be considered suspect. In what follows, I'll use the word "war" for short. But please understand that it carries with it the suspicion attaching to it, and each time it's used you should understand "the imperialist military intervention in Iraq."

⁂

It's clear that the general relationship to the war today also concerns the debate, or the deliberation, about what is shown of it, and therefore about what constitutes an image. This is a long tradition. The question of what constitutes an image based on or about war, of what is shown or not shown, and ultimately of what is said and not said about war, has always been a special question, for the very simple and banal reason that it's part of war. There's an active function of showing or not showing, and the problem is even more acute today in that we live in a world with an endless array of images, and since the current "war" is not really a war, the propaganda has to configure it in such a way that the exact nature of what's going on is left in doubt.

That said, the question has always arisen as to how what was said or shown about war fit into the intentions of war. I'm pointing this out because we sometimes have the impression that propaganda was invented only today. Yet it's actually a very old story. There's a long history of doctored accounts of war incidents and of fake images displayed, because that's part of each side's propaganda and of intelligence and disinformation. So let's just keep in mind the principle that the special role of images in wartime is that, in a way, they are far more a *part* of war than they are the knowledge or truth of it. It is, moreover, a unique relationship in that we're not dealing only, or even mainly, with philosophico-metaphysical questions of representation. Everything is immediately bound up with problems of strategy, or, as we'd say today, "communication strategy." Philosophy also exists, as I never stop saying, to properly assess the ideology of novelty. It is an authority critical of the new, which it suspects of being the old in disguise. Well, this is especially true when it comes to these questions of strategy.

<hr/>

With this in mind, it is clear why images are hardly a reliable guide for entering into the understanding of the situation. In a war situation, images are an entryway that's not absolutely impossible to get through but difficult nonetheless, and I'll explain what I mean by this. First of all, three types of image representations of war can be identified, types that might also apply to what is said about it. We'll confine ourselves, however, to images, based on the question of their presence or absence, of their being shown or not being shown.

1. First there are the images shown by both sides. In other words, what could be called openly available images, the ones that circulate and will establish emblems for the current war—I'm not saying neutral ones, but ones that are seemingly not subject to a particular, restricted, or divided principle of circulation.

2. Second, there are the images that are shown only by one of the sides, which are therefore not openly available and are more or less censored or withheld by the other side.

3. Finally, there are the images that neither side shows: if they exist, they will not be shown intentionally by anyone. They'll be seen only by chance, or thanks to a third party, but their being shown doesn't inscribe them in one of the sides involved.

How can the images of the invasion of Iraq be assessed on the basis of this typology?

As regards the first type, the ubiquitous image of the first bombing of Baghdad is worth noting. The function of this image is to announce that the war had begun. But this, as everyone knows and can see, has no particular dynamic function. This image, as such, has no dynamics of its own. It an image that's static with respect to the situation. It marks the beginning, the beginning of a phase: that of the bombings.

Note that also falling into this category is an image that might be shown in a general way, i.e., by both sides, not because it's static or neutral but because it's open to two conflicting interpretations. Some images of casualties can, for example, be displayed by one of the sides to signify that the enemy has been hit hard, but they can also be used by the other side to show that there are casualties, atrocities, terrible things. Actually, images are amphibological: you can show something as a form of propaganda about the horror of the situation, and you can show the same thing to indicate that you've struck hard and are victorious. The same is true of images of prisoners. "It's outrageous! Look how they treat them! They're barbarians!" or: "We have taken prisoners and we're showing them to you. Look how strong we are, and look how merciful we are, even: they're not dead!" Basically, you could say that these images circulate as a form of disjunctive complicity. Their ambiguous meaning allows them to be shown by both sides. So the first image, the one of the first airstrikes, is an image with no particular dynamics, a static image as regards the situation, appropriable by everyone, while the second operates as disjunctive complicity since it can circulate everywhere while leaving open the interpretation attached to it. You'll nevertheless note that in both cases something makes the meaning elusive. The image is difficult for thought to grasp. It doesn't fit easily into a real under-standing of the situation, either because it's overly static or because it's overly ambiguous. The meaning slips away, either because it's too weak or is well-nigh absent, or because the ambiguity is such that the meaning isn't really established. This covers a wide array of the war images we've been seeing for a number of days now.

Type 2 includes the images that can be shown by one side but not by the other. For example, an image will be of this type because it has obviously been contrived to be shown by one of the sides. It was selected by one of the opposing sides for the express purpose of being shown. The truth is, if such were not the case, the image wouldn't signify anything. It's only because it's been contrived, staged, inscribed in what one of the sides says, that it becomes meaningful. Take the image of the ruins of an apartment building in Baghdad. As such, the image will be shown by the Iraqi side, not by the other side, which claims there aren't any civilian ruins, that their "surgical" strikes only destroy military or government objectives. Meanwhile, the image has been contrived for just such a pur-pose; it is an integral part of its display by one of the sides. Actually, it does show something about the destruction—if indeed it is a real image (you'd have to verify)—but it is an integral part of its propagandistic protocol of display.

By contrast, an image may be selected negatively, and therefore not be shown, precisely because it is considered to be displayable or usable only by the other side. The typical image is that of the American pris-oners. It was not shown by the American side because that side felt it had no possible protocol for displaying it within the framework of its propaganda. It acknowledged that the only possible protocol of display of this image belonged to the other side. Here, too, we could easily show that there is, whether positively or negatively, a set of images of this type, either because the protocol of display is an integral part of the image, or because suppressing or eliminating the image signals its nondisplay-ability by one of the sides. This type of image also makes it difficult to gain access to the situation through thought, since more important than the image is its protocol of display. The assignment of methods of contrivance is more important than the image itself, and this protocol is actually partly detached from the image. It is not directly shown by the image itself. There will always be something about the image that is lacking in meaning, because, in order for it to be filled with meaning, its protocol of display must absolutely be attached to it, and that protocol belongs to one of the sides. In the case of this type of image, Type 2, it is hard to separate what the image itself is, so to speak, from the propaganda in which it's embedded (I mean propaganda in its neutral sense here: the necessary subjectivity of one of the sides).

With Type 1 images, the problem is that either there's a weakness in the original meaning, a statics of meaning, or there's an excessive ambiguity, while with Type 2 images, there's the fact that the image, attached to a protocol of display that is itself unilateral, is necessarily ascribed to the propaganda of one of the sides, and it's this that fills it and gives it meaning.

That leaves Type 3 images, which it seems paradoxical to speak about since they're the ones no one sees, no one shows. In fact, when you do see them, it's strictly by chance. You may come across them, encounter them, or else you'll see them later on. They're assumed to exist. The question is why no one shows them. They have no protocol of display on either of the sides, which means that, in this case, we're dealing with a conjunctive, not a disjunctive, complicity. A disjunctive complicity is when both sides agree to show the image because they have two opposite interpretations of it. A conjunctive complicity is when neither side has an adequate interpretation. This probably concerns images or potential images, many important possibilities of images, which don't fit in with the potential rhetoric of the war from either side's point of view. What sorts of images are they? Images that, in one way or another, have to do with what I'd call the shared real of war, the real that is not really split between the two sides. There are real aspects of war that are shared; they have the same meaning for both sides, and the image registers this in such a way that it's basically impossible to say what the image might mean for the rhetoric of one of the sides. It has to do with that aspect of the real of war, an essential aspect, which is shared, even if the war is asymmetrical.

It will be objected that it's likely that in the current war the asymmetry is such that what has to do with the real of war as a shared real is nonexistent. In actual fact, this aspect of the real always exists. It's very striking that the images of World War I—some were eventually seen afterwards: those that were seen during the war were practically all fake and fabricated—are overwhelmingly Type 3 images. Trench warfare, whether seen from the German or the French point of view, was the same: the situation of the infantryman in the trench was shared. They are horrifying, terrifying images, and it makes no difference whether it was the French or the German side. As a result, neither side showed them. They're images of the third type, which are so closely related to the real of the war that it can't be ideologized. It's not a real that can be directly captured in the imaginary or the rhetoric of either side, or even in the ambiguity of two opposing interpretations. Ultimately, there were images such as those of the exhausted or distraught soldiers on both sides, images of shared atrocities, even fleeting images of fraternization, in which the soldiers on both sides were captured on film at a moment when they became aware of the aspect of sameness between them. It depends on the symmetry or the asymmetry. I'm not saying there aren't different situations, from one war to another. But such images always exist, and they express the war at that level, which is different from its politico-strategic level. Of course, these kinds of images are probably able to capture something of the situation that could be better grasped by independent thinking than many others, but as a rule we don't see them, or we see them only too late.

My point is that the situation with regard to images is never great. None of the three types provides really good access to war situations because, once again, images are part of war. If they're part of it in a shared or a complicit way, they're propaganda images, and if they're part of it in a real way, they're withheld images.

Consequently, we must start out courageously from the idea that, in reality, we don't see anything. I say "courageously" because we'd prefer to see something, and we're tempted to think that we have. We see, but with the suspicious enjoyment of someone who has seen something they weren't supposed to see. To some extent we're always voyeurs of a war, myself included. I usually don't believe anyone who flatly denies being a voyeur of war. But for the analytical reasons I've just given, we must assume the axiom that we don't see anything. We see Type 1 or 2 images, or even Type 3 images by chance. But, in most cases, we don't see anything. So if we don't see anything, we inevitably have to think and judge without seeing, since it's impossible not to think or judge. But that's better than thinking and judging by seeing. What you see is invariably precoded, predetermined, and drags you into one of the available propagandas.

Yet from time to time we might see something. What does "see something" mean? It means seeing a Type 3 image that has escaped concealment, escaped the complicity of the two sides in the war as regards their own real. Because a war situation is a situation in which each side always has a complicit interest, at some point, in concealing its own real. It is telling that, during the first Gulf War, there was no information provided, from the Iraqi side, about their casualties. It's understandable that the Coalition should have concealed the fact that there were thousands and thousands of casualties: after all, they had indisputable just, humanitarian intentions, didn't they? But the Iraqis didn't say any more about it than they did. Everyone maintained a complicit silence about the real of the situation.

Typically, the two sides in a war are constantly engaged in concealing the image of their own real. We'll only get something if the concealment fails. We'll get the real image instead of the propaganda image when the image has been caught by surprise, when something has happened that has escaped the control of the powers involved.

Such an escape can be of two kinds. There's the obvious kind of escape: an image that wasn't supposed to be seen and to circulate is seen and circulates. This is a surprise effect: something escaped the complicity to conceal the real. Then there's the second case: with a Type 1 or 2 image, which is not, strictly speaking, concealed, a sort of immanent excess of the image over its own function occurs. There's an inner sign, a trait of the real, so to speak, internal to the image, because it is excessive in relation to its own intention. I'll give two examples of this, one for each side. When it comes to these questions, let's not immediately be propagandistic!

Take an image that has been seen everywhere: the American flag planted over the Iraqi port. This is unquestionably a Type 2 image, which was contrived and partly doctored by the American side with a view to disseminating it. It has two features that make it totally excessive in relation to its protocol of display. First, it's an image that was intended to signify the capture of the port, even though the port hadn't been captured yet. It showed a victory that hadn't yet occurred (the port was captured a few days later). So it was a preemptive image, which purposely conveyed a piece of false information. That's its first feature, which came to light only later. But it was also, politically speaking, an aberrant image, because it showed that this was actually a war of occupation and conquest. The idea that the Americans were working for the emancipation of the people there was at odds with the liberating troops' eagerness to plant their flag on the conquered territory, a gesture that's always been the symbol of conquest and territorial occupation. That image was real because it showed something about the political intention, which, under the circumstances, shouldn't have been revealed, but *was* revealed in this image in excess over the propaganda protocol. So it's possible to catch an image off guard from within itself. Those who disseminated it had good intentions, namely, to show that things had got off to a flying start and the Yanks were hard at work. But they ascribed to it a real in excess over the propaganda. An image may thus be useful when something in it exceeds its protocol of display.

The second image, which is of a different type, amounted to the same, in my opinion. It was the wide broadcast of Saddam Hussein's first televised address. In this case, there is no doubt that the image clearly showed the figure of a worn-out, fearful regime. It has since recovered somewhat. But its protocol of display, as well as the explicit content of the text that was read, was supposed to be a call to resistance. Nevertheless, the image of the figure of Saddam Hussein also revealed something about a certain relationship of the Iraqi leadership to the situation (I'm not saying the whole relationship but a certain one), namely, the fact that there was something about this regime that was characterized by undeniable fear and attrition. The image showed that at that precise moment, at the time of that image, it seemed impossible for the leaders to embody a genuine patriotic subjectivity. The image could be said to be ineffective because of a lack rather than an excess. Something was lacking in it, as a result of which it, too, wasn't adequate to its protocol of display. It was intended to show the regime's strength, dedication, and resolve, but something about its shakiness, its configuration, even its materiality, was lacking in terms of how it was represented.

These two examples show that we shouldn't conclude that images are completely useless, even though, broadly speaking, the three types of images make it very difficult to attain an understanding of the situation from them. What we need to do is clarify the protocol for reading images. Images must be interpreted not just by the interplay of presence and absence, or of what is shown by one of the sides and not by the other. Rather, what should guide our reading of images are the internal principles of excess and lack, when they're visible, i.e., anything that detaches the image, either by excess or by lack, from its protocol of display. You have a kernel of the real, where the image is either cut into or hollowed out by a visible lack, or, on the contrary, by an obvious excess, in excessive tension in relation to its circulation. The paradoxical result is that a fabricated image may be more real than a real image. So we should beware of the idea that the value of an image, in these kinds of situations, is its representative value, i.e., the fact that it really shows something. It would be better to assume the axiom that we aren't seeing anything, that nothing is really being represented. It's not the question of the honesty or authenticity of the image that matters. It is in itself that the image can convey a kernel of the real, even if it's a fabricated, staged image and is therefore unable to claim to have a genuine capacity of representation. A completely fabricated, artificial, propaganda image may convey the kernel of the real that a highly realistic image won't convey in the least.

This prompts us to ask ourselves the following question: *What does it mean to look at images when we assume the axiom that we aren't seeing anything?* We should bear in mind that when we look at images, how realistic or artificial they are is a secondary criterion. This is even truer given that, in the case of war, there may be a draconian control over the images, and there are a great many fabricated images. It doesn't matter anyway: images, after all, aren't very interesting, and there's no reason to be outraged that they contribute to the general misery and corruption of the contemporary world. However, what we need to pay attention to is the protocol for reading them. So that's what I wanted to say about images.

Now, what about the interpretation of time? Where do we stand with regard to these images and, beyond them, to the question of time, the present time? What does what's going on tell us about the interpretation of the present time? In an earlier session of this seminar, I proposed a three-point characterization of the American leadership that decided to launch this military intervention. It didn't involve secret decisions but blatant, openly avowed, politically declared characteristics. Let me go back over them briefly.

1. Where the United States is concerned, we are dealing with a power that aims to create an absolute military disproportion and to be militarily—let's use the mathematicians' technical word—incommensurable with everyone else. I'm stressing this: it's more radical than a desire for superiority. Superiority is what the United States sought to constantly maintain back in the days of the face-off with the Soviet Union. The policy of deterrence sought to establish a balance of terror, with, if at all possible, a little more than just a balance. Reagan even undertook to create a "more" that would wear the USSR down. Today, they're no longer after superiority but incommensurability.

2. The policy is one of global zoning. It is transversal to the old question of states and alliances. The relevant categories aren't states and alliances but zones that are strategic, or less strategic, or of no interest. It's a question of opportunity. It's about deciding on the zoning by taking into account a number of specific factors and destroying the states that attempt to oppose it.

3. Everything is subordinated to a sort of fundamental self-centeredness. The relationship to self is in fact the measure of the whole.

Accordingly, I'd like to suggest that there is no real contradiction between the two great trends of American diplomacy: isolationism and interventionism. Since the late nineteenth century there's been a tendency to view U.S. foreign policy as a confrontation between two sides. In the isolationists' view, America should fall back on its own defenses, expanded, if need be, to the whole American continent (this was the Monroe Doctrine). It should fall back on its "continentality." And, on the other hand, there's been an interventionist tendency, which holds that the United States should get involved in world affairs—its involvement in World Wars I and II and now its involvement all over the place. What should be kept in mind is that isolationism is internal to interventionism. It's an apparent contradiction that does not preclude the fact that even the interventionists are isolationists in a certain sense and ultimately only relate intervention to the conditions of isolation, to the comfort of isolation. In this sense, the United States is really a lone power, especially since it no longer has a worthy opposite number. This is why, as I've already mentioned, the idea that it's able to create an empire should be challenged: with an empire, there has to be a prudent incorporation of the Other. But the United States couldn't care less about that. This is also the reason why its relationship to situations is so readily abstractly violent. It's violent not with a thematized, theorized, systematic violence but with a mechanical violence. Bombing the Other is not problematic. It should always be remembered that the Americans were the ones who dropped an atomic bomb on Hiroshima. That was the inaugural event. In a certain sense, that's what they do and are continuing to do. The idea of destroying the Other under the onslaught of unparalleled new technology remains their fundamental vision of what a war is. War, in this vision, has nothing chivalric about it anymore, even residually. It's not a strategically definable confrontation; it's truly the moment when incommensurability is brought to bear. Today, that incommensurability is radically thematized, but the atomic bomb was the same thing. The point was to inflict the figure of an absolute destructive incommensurability on the Japanese. That's why the pathetic Saddam Hussein isn't the one we need to worry about having weapons of mass destruction but the people in power in the United States! It's to them that Sri Lankan or Swiss inspectors should be sent, to see where the silos, weapons, and so on are located. Up till now, the United States is the only country to have used them. It has them, and it publicly declares that it has more of them than anyone else. And what guarantee do we have of anything? Only that the Americans say they're the champions of the Good! That's our only guarantee! But when put to the test, that's a somewhat scary guarantee, inasmuch as the United States also reserves the right to define the meaning of "good" . . .

Returning now to the three points (which are facts)—military incommensurability, global zoning, the self-centeredness of a lone power—we can conclude, as I did, that we're dealing with a tendentially unlimited figure of power, power whose universal value content is virtually zero. There's an enormous disproportion between the incommensurability of the power and the emptiness of the content this power offers humanity as a whole.

My first comment is that when the Americans declare that they are the Good (under a variety of different names, such as democracy, freedom, or power), a declaration that should be taken seriously since it's their ultimate source of legitimacy, I think that "the Good" denotes the void. The Good is the name of the lack of universality of which this otherwise unlimited power is the repository. And Evil is basically just the nonrecognition of the Good. The evil powers are those who refuse to recognize that America is the Good. That's the only definition. I don't see any other. The evil powers are those that don't publicly, diplomatically, militarily, politically acknowledge that the United States is the Good. So "the Good" is the name of the void, while Evil is the name of the opposition to that name. It's a rhetoric in the space of which power unlimits itself. But here's where things become complicated. For if a power is unlimited, or represents itself as such, and if, in addition, it is under the sign of the transcendence of the Good, the slightest obstacle will profoundly undermine that self-representation. The problem with a power's limitlessness is that the power must no longer encounter any limits. The slightest limit, the slightest obstacle, constitutes an extreme breakdown of its self-representation. That's what we've been seeing lately. You might say that if it takes a month for the Americans to defeat Iraq it won't be a problem, since this unlimited power knows no limits. But, as a result, the slightest resistance, the slightest bump in the road, any resister, any soldier who kills an American will spell disaster for its self-representation. Naturally not a military disaster in the ordinary sense of the word.

Everyone understands that. Just because five Americans were killed doesn't mean the United States is headed for a military disaster, but we still have the feeling—the commentators are saying as much—that things aren't going the way they thought they would. This has nothing to do with military tactics, because, when all is said and done, the Americans will most likely win the war and achieve their objectives, the tactical ones at least, one way or another. So where does this feeling come from? In my opinion, it's directly related to the doctrine of unlimited power. A variant of that doctrine of unlimited power was the zero-casualties theory. One casualty is serious, since there's no comparison between zero and one. If you hold the theory of military superiority, you win the war with more casualties or fewer casualties. But zero casualties—which the doctrine of incommensurability involves—means there are no casualties on your side and all the casualties on the other side. Therefore, regardless of whether there are one, five, or twenty casualties, it really contradicts the system of representation. In this case, where the validity of the representativeness of unlimited power is at stake, the slightest obstacle is a problem. This is something that, to my mind, is a sign that the professions of unlimited power will run into serious problems, which will unfortunately lead to further displays of power. You have to constantly prove the limitlessness of power again, prove again that all the obstacles can be overcome, and so on. We can't rule out the possibility that we're entering a cycle of wars, although not necessarily an intentional or deliberate one, because the immanent logic of unlimited power cannot tolerate obstacles. And there are bound to be ones. This is a sort of a paradoxical matrix whereby you somehow assert the infinite, in the form of military incommensurability, but this infinite is never absolutely infinite, nor can it ever be. There are American casualties, there are people who resist, and it is well known that the weaker side, the less well armed side, or even the more disorganized side, is nevertheless capable of inflicting damage on the imperial power facing it.

This can be put another way, and my second comment will be more dialectical. We could say that the problem with the unlimited is that any exteriority is conceived of as a real limit. The unlimited is that which does not accept the evidence of anything exterior to it. Because if there is an exterior, an exteriority, that means the unlimited has a limit. As

Spinoza put it, what is finite, the finite, is the reason there is something else that is of the same order, the reason it is not the exhaustion of its category or of its order. In the case at hand, the order is the military order, and the unlimited properly speaking is that which has no exteriority. In a certain sense, the Iraqis should not have existed militarily at all. Even if only three of them fire a shot from behind a sand dune, that's already too many. And the commentators are astonished that they exist! Everyone's convinced that the mere fact that they exist imposes a limit on unlimited power. This is paradoxical only because the unlimited's claim is precisely not to have any limits, or even any exteriority. So there's something about the dominant American self-representation or about the American government—let's not say the Americans in general: large numbers of Americans, may I remind you, have staunchly and nobly opposed this war. Let's not let anyone pull the "kneejerk anti-Americanism" number on us, which is the number always pulled by those who shelter their hateful thoughts under the Yankee nuclear umbrella, the people so obtuse that, to overcome their deepest fears, they need the certainty that an unlimited imperial power exists to protect them. So, as I was saying, there's something about the American leaders that is partly hostage to their own system of representation, which connects the Good and the unlimited. A system of representation is never entirely imposed from without. It is never entirely propagandistic. There's always a subjectivity behind it. This subjectivity is the belief that the Iraqis did not exist as such; there was only an amorphous mass waiting to be liberated. That was the idea the Americans had of the Iraqis, to such an extent that when they saw that the Iraqis weren't all out in the streets to greet them with bouquets of flowers, it came as a shock to them all. It was mind-boggling! God knows, I don't think Saddam Hussein's regime was popular. Everyone knows how cruel and oppressive it was, and how opportunistic the war against Iran was, and so on. But still, very few Iraqis thought the Americans' bombing of Baghdad, however surgical a strike it might have been, was really great.

We should note that one of Saddam Hussein's greatest vices was that he was for a long time the lackey of the French and the Americans against Iran. Basically, the Americans are always cultivating friends who bite the hand that feeds them. Then they want to strangle them. And, to that end, they rely in a way on a predicate of nonexistence. This is extremely interesting from a philosophical point of view. Hegel would have been interested in it because it's not a master-slave dialectic. For Hegel, there's a struggle within which the issue is who's afraid of dying, who surrenders out of fear of death. The one who surrenders becomes the slave, and the one who has overcome the fear of death in himself becomes the master. It is the figure of the struggle for recognition. The slave will recognize the master's superiority; he recognizes the fact that the master wasn't afraid of death. He recognizes Spirit, because Spirit is that which does not shrink from death. The slave is therefore someone who recognizes the vitality of Spirit in the master. In the case at hand, the unlimited power relates to the Other under a predicate of nonexistence. This is a special dialectic. The enemy is demonized: it is Evil, and, as we know ever since classical theology, Evil has no being. Evil is nothingness. If we take this metaphoric seriously, Evil doesn't exist. Here you have a paradoxical figure, which presents the at once terrible and perplexing ideological spectacle of the destruction of nothingness. It doesn't exist, and yet it must be destroyed, bombed. But what is bombed, ultimately? I was struck by the fact that the Americans started the war saying: "We're going to take out Saddam Hussein with a missile, and the problem will be solved." But it's not so simple! They'd already tried to kill Gaddafi a few years ago. He was in his tent having tea, but the missile missed him. The idea is that a war can be replaced by an assassination, that, with an assassination, a war can be avoided. But this idea is based wholly on the assumption that you're only up against Saddam Hussein, that is, nothing at all. Saddam Hussein, as a mere body, isn't an established, national, organized enemy. I think that, with this technique of targeted assassinations, so popular today, there's always the belief that what one is dealing with doesn't really exist. I think we're entering into a whole new dialectic, which is no longer the master-slave dialectic but the dialectic of the imaginary and very naturally criminal relationship between the limitlessness of the power (of the Good) and the nothingness of its enemy (Evil). But to everyone's shock, the enemy turns out to exist, even if it's not very strong! And from the standpoint of the formal and general matrix, it's even conceivable that, since what doesn't exist must be dealt with violently, you might actually be helping it exist. Not only does it exist, but this existence develops, and, as presumed nonexistence, it calls for violence, because nothingness must be destroyed. The phenomenon is perfectly obvious: Saddam Hussein exists much more today than ever before. It'll last as long as it lasts. His nonexistence has been a magnet for so much violence that it's turning into an ultra-existence. His existence in the Arab world has led to sudden prudence on the part of all the Arab countries' leaders, who had remained neutral, expecting him to be . . . taken down. It's a fascinating dialectic because it has the form of what Plato would have treated as the relationship between the idea of the One and the idea of the Other. The United States is the One, the One that has no Other, the One everyone rallies around because it's the only One. And, on the other side, apart from the One, there is the Other, which is nonexistent or is supposed to be nonexistent. This is a very peculiar dialectic, in which the nonexistent exists and the One breaks up, in which it has to divide when faced with the fact that the nonexistent exists. This is why there's a certain upside to this horrible situation, an upside that's related to the development, whatever it may be, not just now but in the longer term, of this peculiar dialectic of unlimited power in the desirable direction of its demise.

My third comment has to do with the subjectivity at work in all this. I note that a spectacular turnaround has occurred. Let's not forget that at the time of the September 11 attacks, a broad coalition formed around the United States. There was high public emotion, declarations being made on all sides, and that truly extraordinary event: the UN unanimously passed a resolution authorizing the United States to exercise the right of self-defense anywhere in the world. It's striking that, today, this has all turned into a sort of global dissent against the same United States. I don't know what will become of it. There are people demonstrating all over the globe against this war, people from very disparate worlds: the Americas, Europe, Bangladesh, and even Bahrein. This situation is a complete reversal of what happened in connection with September 11. I find this especially striking given that, in the case of September 11, it was really a murderous attack carried out by an anonymous closed group, which didn't identify itself. And there was an enormous, outspoken public protest. But this widespread sympathy has now been followed by a dissent involving millions of people.

At first, public opinion passively approved the invasion of Afghanistan. Was there really much more reason for invading Afghanistan than for invading Iraq? It's debatable. Some people say that Saddam Hussein was worse than the Afghans and Milosevic. The fact remains, however, that the turnaround in public opinion has been absolutely spectacular. I think there's a deep reason (aside from the political reasons) for this, a reason that, for us philosophers, is subjectively interesting. If the U.S. government, perfectly complacent about its aggression, thinks it can rally a part of domestic and foreign public opinion around it, it's because it believes it is entitled to revenge, since, subjectively, this war is a war of revenge. It was virtually decided on right from September 11. At the time, there were internal tensions within the U.S. government, and not everyone was in agreement. However, one whole group had decided to wage this war right from September 11 and thought it possible on the basis of revenge, on the basis of the right of self-defense that the UN had approved, which the Americans took as permission to strike wherever they pleased.

I think, however, that the question of revenge is a point of subjectivity, even an unconscious one, which explains the global anti-American dissent. Indeed, fundamentally, the idea of war as pure revenge repulses any number of people, and the repulsion they feel is greater than any that Saddam Hussein may inspire.

Historically, the United Sates has always nurtured a culture of revenge. It's an inherent trait of American history and has long been identified as such. In American historicity, there is a unique dialectic between the Law and revenge. The Law itself is a vengeful law. This is, moreover, one of the reasons behind the steadfast maintenance of the death penalty in the United States and the unbelievable proliferation of prisons there. The death penalty has been abolished in the other so-called advanced countries, including all the countries of the European Union, but in the United States it hasn't been and is not about to be. This calls for an explanation. The idea that upholding the law requires real, corporal, murderous revenge to be exacted, that unique dialectic of the intertwining of the law and revenge, is a fundamental historical feature in the United States, and the Western is one of the great formal testaments to it. The whole problem in Westerns is how the law accommodates revenge, or how revenge accommodates the law. That's the main subject of every Western. Revenge is legitimate, but it must not be completely detached from the horizon of the law. Countless Westerns are about how the legitimate avenger has to deal, or not deal, with various figures of the law. This is a major feature, and its formalization in the Western is telling. Note that there are two tendencies when it comes to this issue in the Western. The first tendency is for revenge ultimately to be subordinated to the law. The film will be about how someone who's been the victim of heinous crimes committed by horrible outlaws, who represent Evil, will take revenge, and how, although blinded by the spirit of revenge, he will nevertheless have to defer his revenge and return to the fold of the law. There's also the plot in which the avenger remedies the shortcomings of the law. The lone vigilante avenges crimes where the law was powerless to do so. Hence the recurring figure of the lone vigilante, who is ultimately almost as much a killer as the killer himself. Human life is not often spared, on either side. So there is a basic ambiguity about the figure of the Law. When conservatives talk about law and order, they introduce this ambiguity about the law into the figure of what they call "order." In the end, the law is subordinated to a vision of order that, in its turn, legitimizes revenge and the restoration of balances though violence. This formalization is not peculiar to the Western; there are also major literary formalizations. I'll just mention three works, three masterpieces.

1. In Melville's *Billy Budd*, the young hero, who is the victim of an injustice, is executed but hails his own execution as an obligatory figure of the restoration of order.

2. One feature of Faulkner's "The Bear" illustrates how America is completely organized around the original sin that defines it, and how it is ultimately always marked by it. The dialectic of the law and revenge can be explained by an original, unfillable debt, which may be the slaughter of animals, the elimination of the Indians, or Black slavery.

3. Finally, there's Russell Banks's great book *Cloudsplitter*. I'd like to pay tribute to Russell Banks here because he was one of the sponsors of the remarkable American petition that, in very forceful and beautiful language, took a stand against the war

and the overall policy that made it possible. The book is a work of fiction whose main character is John Brown, the man who rose up almost alone against Black slavery in the nineteenth century and, after waging a war against it on his own, with a small band of people, ended up on the gallows. Russell Banks constructs his novel by showing that there, too, even in the subjectivity of John Brown, that figure of liberation and solidarity with Black people, the relationship between revenge and the law, between violence and its rationalization, remains problematic.

In the final analysis, I think it must be said that the relationship between revenge and the law as the key problem of the American sense of justice is unstable, because it is controlled by an indestructible Manichean paradigm that produces an invincible opposition between good and evil. That's why, rather than take Bush's declarations lightly or make fun of them, we should take them seriously: it is a profound, American, historical conviction that he is repeating, with the stupidity typical of tradition. His statement—America is leading the struggle of Good versus Evil—is characterized by the very powerful stupidity of tradition. That said, the good-versus-evil paradigm is in actual fact more profound than the dialectic of the law, which it constantly destabilizes. That's why there are so many American TV series, stories, novels, and films explaining how the champion of the good had to settle his score with evil outside the law. And behind the figure of the lone vigilante who kills off the agents of evil, there always lurks the idea that the law is corrupt and that you're going to have to settle your score with evil with only the self-guarantee of the good. This is a basic plot, which is the opposite of the one that was established in Greece from the time of Aeschylus's *Oresteia*. There's something non-Greek about the American world. One is sometimes tempted to say it's because the Americans are so like the Romans! The *Oresteia* reminds us how the cycle of vengeance, the cycle of the struggle between good and evil, must be stopped by the rationally motivated decision of a judge. It tells how the cycle of primitive vengeance, of the vendetta (you killed my mother, so I'm going to kill your daughter, and so on), the bloodletting, must be ended by a law, by the sovereignty of a law organized in the figure of a democratic court of law. What is absolutely essential in the *Oresteia* is that the court ruling on the metaphysics of good and evil cannot be disputed. The case will be judged, and once it is judged, it will be judged once and for all. The opposition between good and evil is less important than the matter judged. The world of collective justice cannot be allowed to be destabilized by a Manichean metaphysics of good and evil. Yet this is precisely what happens in the American tradition: the calm world of rational lawfulness is destabilized by the figure of good and evil in the ultimately lawless and savage figure of the vigilante. That is why the history of the war without the UN's backing is significant. If there had been war with the UN's backing, we wouldn't have been much better off, we might even have been less so. But there wouldn't have been the clear conscience of the American vigilante, confirming once again the corruption of the law, in this case the corruption of what five minutes earlier had been called "the international community." Since the UN didn't approve the extermination of Saddam Hussein, well, the vigilante would just have to take care of it by itself since the law was corrupt. There *was* a tribunal that was supposed to judge the situation, but it was corrupted by the French (the Frenchman played the role of the corrupt judge) and didn't want to hang the bad guy. So the Americans decided they'd go over there and take him out all by themselves. At a deep level, this is the very important idea that the metaphysics of good and evil can't eliminate American sinfulness, America's original sinfulness. This metaphysics destabilizes both the basic prudence of justice and its real becoming. It's an old story that really has a historicity, and therefore a strength; it's not just some crazy idea of a moron named Bush. What's more, being a moron is an additional strength in this type of affair: you have to be a little stupid to be the avenger of the Good. The characters in Westerns are monomaniacal. All they think about is killing the bad guy, even if they first have to kill fifteen or twenty other people, just like Bush has to kill lots of people before he can kill Saddam Hussein, or maybe even thousands or hundreds of thousands: that's the law of the genre.

That was the second point I wanted to highlight: the historical, and I daresay spiritual, dimension of this issue. The central paradigm, the one that leads to the dialectic of the One and the nonexistent (which was my first point), is the Manichean destabilization of the basic system of justice, a system corrupted or corroded by the fact that an outlaw personification of the Good is needed: the man of revenge. The man of revenge must be available.

I'll conclude now with something that, as a result, has to do with the different ways of being against the current war, namely, by developing an analytics of the different ways of being against this war. Taking into account what I've said up to now, I think it's possible to identify four different ways of being against this war, four kinds of opposition to the war.

1.   First, you can be against the war precisely because you're against war, against all wars, against war as such. This is the so-called pacifist position. It needs to be clarified: you're against this war because you're against all wars, as when your slogan is "War is bullshit!" [*Quelle connerie la guerre!*].[1] Unfortunately, it's the slogan that's bullshit. Because there's not one war but many different kinds of war, and war can be an absolutely necessary rational demand. It's not true in general that war is bullshit: it's horrible, and everyone wants to put an end to it, but there are circumstances in which, on the contrary, it is the capacity for waging war that represents strength and intelligence, and opposition to war that represents surrender, Pétainism, and so on. Pacifism nonetheless has a particular dignity, which is its potential universalism.

2.   You can be against the American war because you're for the other side, through solidarity with the Arab world, for example, in the belief that Saddam Hussein is a defender of the Palestinian cause. In the current situation, the weakness of that position stems from the fact that it doesn't lead to a universal principle; it is confined to a local, religious representation of the world and therefore remains rooted in particularism. Nor, what's more, does it lead to a dialectical principle. The other side, in my opinion, is not really constituted as a side in the figure of this war. It's a symbolic side, but it's not a real side. I don't think there can be a dialectical development of that position, of a protracted war type.

3.   You're against this war insofar as it testifies to the unlimited nature of the power that presents itself with unparalleled destructive arrogance in the war situation. That's an appropriate position. But the

problem is then to oppose another type of power to that power, and that's quite a complicated political issue. You may possibly think of a different state power, but you can clearly see the limits of that, which are really, as far as I'm concerned, the limits of Chirac's position. It comes down in a way to asking, once the war begins, what we can do. Hoping that the war will be short is a pretty flimsy position. Yet that was the argument Villepin [the French foreign minister] gave for authorizing British planes to fly over France: it would be better if the war were short and the planes could get to Baghdad sooner . . .

4.   The fourth position is that of being against this war precisely because it is being fought on the basis of revenge, not just in the figure of unlimited power but in that of the lawless vigilante, insofar as it is outside the law. "Outside the law" should be understood in the American sense, that of the legitimacy of the vigilante against the corrupt law. This position evokes the contemporary problem of international law. Is there any figure of international law today that is not worthless? I'll conclude with this issue. One of the reasons for the current situation is that, in the previous historical sequence, the very principle of international law was severely undermined. The Americans aren't wrong to say that international law is corrupt, but *they* are its chief corrupters: it's corrupt on account of them, even as they pose as vigilantes. International law was destroyed for all sorts of reasons. First, there was a conflation of the law and Western norms of power. This principle of corruption appeared early on. Second, there was a conflation of laws and interests. The Western norm was reduced to a norm for interests. Last but not least, these interests were conflated with the interests of the United States. International law amounted to Western domination, Western domination purported to be normative but was corrupted by interests, and those interests, which claimed to be universal, were in reality the interests of the United States. A false subject known as "the international community" was thus created. There is no such thing as the international community; it doesn't exist—even if we never stop talking about it. Since the war began, it has been silent: its specious nature has become glaringly obvious. "The international community" ultimately meant the people close to the United States. For the time being, it's in shambles. But it will come back together once the reconstruction of Iraq begins. It's a

community of crooks, and France, which is a member of it, is getting ready to say: "I wasn't involved in the heist, but I want my share." That's when France's very respectable position could turn into a perfectly disgraceful one: first you oppose the war, and then you line up to reap the rewards. If that's the case, it would be better to do as the British are doing and just go to war. A false historical subject was created, which claimed, moreover, to be a moral subject. By way of this triple conflation (law and Western norm, norm and Western interests, Western interests and American interests), a false subject, which is also a subject that presumes to lay down the law, emerged.

Last but not least, the positivity of the situation, a negative positivity, is very important. The worldwide dissent against the American war marks the beginning of the end of this false subject. We are putting this false subject and its ideological system, its claim to lay down the law, to the test. The idea will dawn that the law is laid down elsewhere. Where? Maybe among those who are demonstrating. We'll see. It's important to recognize that the law is laid down elsewhere. The situation is that of a shift in the center of gravity of justice, or in the center of gravity of the law, or in the locus of the law, in relation to the false subject of the previous sequence. Last time, I said that the aim is to produce separation, a different subjectivity. It is already significant that a deconstruction of the false subject is occurring. Such a deconstruction enables or facilitates the construction of a different subjectivity.

So much for the "war." I hope I won't have to talk about it again, or at any rate that I'll be able to talk about it in different terms, next time, that is to say, in May.

Session 7

May 14, 2003

I 'll begin with a quick comment on the first point on the handout
you have before you, which concerns the announcement of Pierre
Macherey's lecture on "Philosophy and History of Philosophy."

It's interesting to note that this lecture is part of a series entitled
"Philosophy and Its Outsides." What's interesting about this lecture
series is that it considers the history of philosophy as one possible
"outside" of philosophy. This is consistent with the fact that Macherey
has long thought that philosophy is not just in its history. There is
philosophy elsewhere than in the history of philosophy. There is, for
example, as Pierre Macherey brilliantly argues, something of philosophical thinking that is immanent in works of literature. I'm extremely
interested in all this because I have often wondered whether the history
of philosophy might not be one of the conditions of philosophy. Or
more than a condition.

Very broadly speaking, there are three major positions in the history
of philosophy:

1. The one that makes it the site of the unfolding of truth itself.
   The history of philosophy is, in a way, the history of being
   itself. There is a self-exposure of being-in-truth, of which
   philosophy is the record. This is a position that holds that
   the history of philosophy isn't the history of a discipline, of
   a branch of knowledge. It is the expressive history of being

itself. This is the great eschatological vision, Hegel's as well as Heidegger's.

2. At the other extreme: the history of philosophy is a contingent material; it's the history of a multifaceted creation, which is used for new discoveries, both within and outside of philosophy. This would be Deleuze's position.

3. The third position is the one that holds that the history of philosophy is the history of a particular figure of knowledge. This is the academic position.

Let's get back to our own subject now.

For quite some time now, we've been in a period characterized by a complex, saturated historico-political context, including September 11, the March 20–21 airstrikes, the second Gulf War, the social movements. It's clear that history's agenda is filling up, but we don't really know with what events. This is a time when we may be conscripted unexpectedly: we don't know how history will interpellate us when, like a wild animal, it lets out a few roars. There's a confused and complex historicity that is coming to life in different ways and is experiencing a new form of (subjective and objective) power. I think we need to be vigilant in these times, because we may possibly be conscripted. This is why I came to the conclusion that we needed to go back to our speculative core, the question of the present time, so as to maintain the distance required by this rampant, unclear, intricate, and confused historicity. In other words, it's unlikely, though not impossible, that something like a present may be developing. And a present is always surprising: it is never, by definition, a clear consequence of the past, even if it's the projective torsion of the past, as I've argued here. So we're going to return to the question: What can we expect from philosophy regarding the construction of a real present? That is, a real present of the truths we're capable of. What is philosophy's specific contribution in this regard?

The answer I'd like to suggest today will emerge through a comparison, an overlapping, with Heidegger's views, since that avowed Nazi's key question is, in a nutshell: What are the tasks of thinking in an identifiable moment in time? In the destiny of the age? It is on the basis of this question that he interrogates philosophy. And one very interesting answer of Heidegger's is that philosophy, strictly speaking, is now incapable of accomplishing the tasks our age assigns to thinking. This, of course, means philosophy as metaphysics, but for Heidegger there was no other. For a number of years, Heidegger believed that National Socialism and its Führer were capable of accomplishing them, that they were coming to grips with the historial destiny. But then that turned out to be criminally false.

We're going to try to focus a bit on this answer, this statement. You can refer for support to two absolutely canonical, fundamental essays.

a. "The End of Philosophy and the Task of Thinking" (in *Basic Writings*). The first version dates from 1964 and appeared [in French] for the first time in 1966, in Jean Beaufret's translation.

b. "The Turn" (in *Bremen and Freiburg Lectures: Insight Into That Which Is and Basic Principles of Thinking*). The original, more precise title was "Technology and the Turn." This was one of the lectures he gave in 1949–50.

Why did I choose these two texts? Because they are crucial for the question we're dealing with today (let me remind you): "Is philosophy capable of accomplishing the tasks our age assigns to thinking?", which I'd translate as: "Is philosophy capable of contributing to the construction of the present?" I will proceed in the following way. I'll extract from these two texts four points, four theses, or rather four questions, and in each case, I'll indicate what I think is valid and what I reject.

1. Philosophy refers to something more fundamental than itself.
2. The philosophical concept of truth is incapable of what thinking demands of us today.
3. How can the contemporary obstacle be identified?
4. How can we meet the demands of the tasks of thinking?

To really grasp Heidegger's thesis, it's important to understand that, throughout its history, philosophy has been assigned to a condition of possibility more fundamental, more originary, than itself, a sort of more original disclosure, because it is only possible on the basis of the existence of thinking as a dimension of being. Thinking must be a dimension of the "there is" as such in order for something like philosophy to come about. Thinking must be given permission to be a dimension of being. It is this issue that Heidegger actually calls "the open." That's the most frequent name for it in both essays.

Let me just digress for a moment about point 5 on the sheet that was handed out to you. On the "Philosophy and Mathematics" study day, there will be three talks on the concept of the open, without there having been any prior consultation about this. As you know, a book by Agamben entitled *The Open* came out not long ago. And as you also know, the open/closed opposition is at the heart of Bergson's philosophy and thus resonates strongly in Deleuze's philosophy. It might almost be said that contemporary philosophical reflection has focused largely on the open, over the whole spectrum opened up, so to speak, by this word. If I had to define contemporary philosophy, and French philosophy in particular, I would say that it is a reflection on the relationship between multiplicity and the open. It's clear, moreover, that the question of the Other is that of the open. This is obvious in the case of Levinas, for example, who investigates the availability in openness to something that is not oneself. This amounts to a questioning of the identity of the self as closure. A metaphysics of the open is essential in all of this.

What Heidegger will say is that there is something about the open that is necessarily prior to philosophy itself. Philosophy as possibility lies in the event through which being itself opens up. Being, in this sense, is the same as thinking. Heidegger's interpretation ultimately reprises Parmenides's axiom, "Being and thinking are the Same" but relieved of its closing by the One. Being is in the dimension of the open because, if it were closed, it wouldn't make any sense, for Heidegger, to say that it is identical to thinking. Heidegger will designate this with the famous phrase "the clearing of the open." The clearing of the open is the original site of philosophy itself, its primary ontological condition. If there were no clearing, philosophy wouldn't be established under the jurisdiction of thinking as identical to being.

The theme of the open naturally runs though many philosophies other than Heidegger's. But his own particular enterprise was to make the open a destiny; the open is essentially destinal. It is not, for him, in opposition with the closed, nor does it have the ethical meaning of an openness to the Other, nor is its basic meaning that of a theory of freedom. It's not Bergson, Levinas, or Sartre. The clearing of the open is a site, an originary site. It's a state of being that destines and has destined thinking to philosophy. Thus, philosophy is a figure of the destiny of being as openness. But what Heidegger will tell us—and this means that this philosophizing destiny of being is also a loss—is that philosophy, as the destinal unfolding of being, *is in reality the erasure of the open*. Philosophy is made possible by the open, even as it obstructs it. Being in the open without knowing it, inducing, under the influence of the One, a forgetting of the open, philosophy restrains thinking more than it contains it, by producing closure, separateness, which removes thinking from the clearing of the open.

Let me mention a formal issue here. Every theorist of the open shows us how the closed is a way of realizing the possibility of the open. You find this in Deleuze also. The closed is that which is realized on the basis of the open. The closed can only be understood in terms of the open. Conversely, it's impossible to understand the open, and therefore the closed as well, on the basis of closure. The closed is always that on the basis of which the closed itself is misunderstood. It is the misunderstanding of closure. This is quite interesting because it shows that what is closed is unable to produce any understanding of itself. The closed as closed can only be understood from the standpoint of the open, since only the open is the creation of possibility.

Ultimately, we'll get the following situation: philosophy is under condition of the open, but it realizes this condition in the form of a closure that it misinterprets. The history of philosophy is the history of this misinterpretation, Platonism essentially being the beginning of it. Let's take a look at "The End of Philosophy and the Task of Thinking":

All philosophical thinking that explicitly or inexplicitly follows the call "to the matter itself" is in its movement and with its method already admitted to the free space of the clearing. But philosophy knows nothing of the clearing.

What is realized is blind to what realizes it:

Philosophy does speak about the light of reason, but does not heed the clearing of Being.[1]

This whole setup requires a conception of philosophy as being under the historial condition of something more originary than itself, namely, the radical possibility that being comes about as thinking, that thinking emerges on the ground of the open. So the fundamental question on the basis of which one determines where one stands vis-à-vis Heidegger is clearly as follows: Is philosophy really under the condition of something more originary than itself?

My own answer, my own proposition, will be given in four points, so it will be a bit fragmented. First, I will say yes, philosophy is under condition. It is not such that we can say it is self-sufficient, or that it is entirely its own self-foundation. I don't believe it is. So there are one or more conditions of philosophy, and Heidegger is right to say that if we want to know whether philosophy is able to meet the challenges our age imposes on thinking, we'll have to step aside and look not only at the empirical character of the philosophical discourse but at what makes philosophy possible. It's important to understand that philosophy, however it is defined, cannot be examined strictly from the perspective of itself; it needs to be examined under condition. So we can say that, formally, the Heideggerian diagnosis is correct.

Second, I will say, on the contrary, that I don't think it's possible to go all the way back to an originary condition. Philosophy's conditions are always singular, i.e., bound up with a regime of singularity that does not combine them into a destiny. This is an everyday debate: If I'm conditioned by something, does that mean it's a destiny? Everyday life may have all sorts of conditions without that constituting a destinal sending. This is a heated debate when it comes to the theory of heredity, social determinisms, early childhood and its psychoanalytic conditions, and even when it comes to tastes.

The precise relationship between condition and conditioned, of course, allows for an interpretation in the form of a destiny. This is the case with Heidegger, for whom philosophy, as the blind unfolding of the "clearing of being" as its originary condition, is a destiny, and ultimately a tragic one. I, for my part, will say that there are conditions, but these conditions aren't destinal ones. I will therefore attempt to separate the idea of condition from the idea of destiny.

What constitutes the unity of philosophy for Heidegger is precisely the fact that there is a destiny of being. If we accept that the task of thinking today is to construct the present, to put an end to the lack of a present, we could say that there are conditions for this. Even before the conceptual undertaking, there are things we need to rely on in order to remain untouched by the imperatives of opinion. I mentioned four of them: demonstration, contemplation, action, and love. I'm saying "love" now because some people just couldn't accept the word "passion," so, since I'm accommodating by nature, I substituted "love" for it, though I'm not entirely sure that it's quite the same thing. Be that as it may, demonstration, contemplation, action, and love/passion are the four counterpoints to contemporary nihilism. They are real things, not just speculative topics. For example, demonstration isn't just anything, it's something that, in contemporary mathematics, produces new modes of relationship between the finite and the infinite, the infinite as non-all. It's this aspect of contemporary mathematics that enacts a critique of finitude. Contemplation refers to the figures of contemporary art inso-far as it manages to be something other than criticism, insofar as it is a stage or a new possibility of affirmation. Action refers to the different politics of rupture: what is a political rupture that, in actuality, in its own particular thinking, is heterogeneous to capitalo-parliamentarian-ism? And finally, love/passion is what is involved in the reinvention of love. For "love must be reinvented, that much we know"—I'm quoting Rimbaud—because there's been a total upheaval of everything that used to make up superego figures of the sexual (we can't just speak of censorship) as well as very significant changes in the family. We need to reinvent a figure of love that's heterogeneous to family values and gender-based role distribution. But none of this is a destiny. These are conditions of philosophy, as real conditions. It cannot be assumed either that there are no conditions or that the conditions are destinal, because, in reality, this system of conditions doesn't constitute a totality. This could be demonstrated.

Moreover, I wouldn't say that this system of conditions is exactly in the figure of the open; rather, it's in the figure of disconnection. The difference between "openness" and "disconnection" might seem a bit technical, but it's very useful. The figure of disconnection is not so much the figure of the reopening of a possibility as such; it's above all a figure that brings the inconsistency of being to the surface. Here, too, we're dealing with being, but as inconsistent multiplicity.

There's a big contemporary debate about whether the figure of the conditions of thought is of the order of the open or of inconsistency, of disconnection. Deleuze, for example, merges the two in the idea of chaos, which is indeed the originary site of all thinking and is both inconsistency and the open. My own hypothesis is explicitly on the side of disconnection. There is no clearing of the open; there is the absoluteness of inconsistent multiplicity.

So much for the first point. I'll sum it up by saying that philosophy is under condition, that philosophy's contribution to the construction of the present requires conditions, but I would add that it's a question of an inconsistent multiplicity with an absolute value, not a destiny.

The second point concerns the question of truth. The question of truth is a central concept inasmuch as philosophy is often regarded as the search for truth. The question now is whether this is a destining concept or whether it is at all relevant when it comes to meeting the challenges of the present. Heidegger's thesis about this is that the philosophical concept of truth, because of its originary dependence on Platonism, because of its subordination to knowledge, is inadequate for meeting the challenges of thinking, since it is itself a sort of erasure of the open and induces the forgetting of the clearing as originary site. You might say that, for Heidegger, the history of philosophy is the capture of truth by knowledge, the knowledge of the being that is actually a blocking, a philosophical or speculative obfuscation, of the truth of being. Truth in its originary sense is not a norm of knowledge for him but a state of thought. It's in a way the state that consists in being in the openness of the open. That's what must be called truth. And so it's the same thing as freedom. The essence of truth is freedom. You can't understand the essence of freedom and truth if you don't understand that truth as originary, when it's not captured by knowledge, is neither a judgment, nor an adequation, nor a criterion. It's not a norm; it's a state of thought. This means that thought is in its site, that it doesn't withdraw from its site, whereas when it's captured by knowledge, it will be withdrawn, as it were, from the very thing that originally conditions it.

In these late texts, Heidegger proposes to translate the Greek word ἀλήθεια, which means "truth," as what the French translation renders as "*l'ouvert sans retrait*" ["the open without withdrawal"]. I am sympathetic to this idea, which the great philosophies have always maintained, namely that "truth" is not really a category of knowledge. Heidegger is right about this. But if truth is not a criterion of knowledge, a model of knowledge, of truth or falsity, then it is of a different order than judgment or the essence of knowledge. Philosophical truth, for Heidegger, is the openness of the open, the withdrawal of the open as such, since the open is destined, precisely as open, to the withdrawal of the open. The interesting related idea is that of a courage of truth. Truth is what has a hold on you, what compels you to remain steadfastly in a certain place. As you know, I call this "fidelity," and I do in fact think that the only truth is a faithful truth, and that this fidelity requires a certain amount of courage. Opinion, "my" opinion, "that's *my* opinion,"—all that goes only so far, subjectively. Besides, "subjectively" is an exaggeration. Opinion has to do with the self, the individual, not the Subject that one may become. We could say the following, which is not as far from Heidegger as you might think: A truth is always something shared between pure theoretical reason and pure practical reason, to use Kant's vocabulary. And if "truth" in its most basic sense is a rule, a standard of conduct, a courage, that means that it's a figure of the subject, not of the individual or the self. Indeed, I would say that it's this figure that the contemporary world attempts to destroy. Make no mistake about it: the contemporary world is driven by a hatred of truth. A hatred of truth not in the sense that truth is opposed to lying or falsehood—to say as much is to lapse back into the idea that truth is a form of knowledge—but the hatred of something much more fundamental, which arises from the fact that there is a sort of standard of conduct, of fidelity, in truth, which is always related to a radical figure of the subject in every domain. Thus, there are truths of demonstration, contemplation, action, and passion. But our age, as I said, pits opinion against demonstration, judgment against contemplation, administration against action, and contentment against passion. So our age is alien to the subjectivity of truth.

How does Heidegger set out his position? Take a look at page 447 in *Basic Writings*:

> The talk about the "truth of Being" has a justified meaning in Hegel's *Science of Logic* because here truth means the certainty of absolute knowledge.

But Hegel, adds Heidegger, isn't at all concerned—any more than Husserl is—about being qua being, about how there can be presence as such, immediate presence, other than in the clearing of the open, about that aptly named *aletheia*, and he concludes:

> The natural concept of truth does not mean unconcealment, not in the philosophy of the Greeks either.[2]

Not in Plato either. Conversely, if you take "truth" in its absolutely original sense, in the pre-Socratics, it is indeed unconcealment in the clearing of the open that is at issue. But it's instantly forgotten or foreclosed in the earliest historical inception of philosophy.

We could say that, for Heidegger, the history of philosophy is the history of the perversion of truth by knowledges. The philosophical history of the category of truth is the history of the "capture of being by the One," since the One is always the power resource of a knowledge [*un savoir*]. He sometimes says that it's the "capture of being by logic." Consequently, the task of thinking is to reseparate truth and knowledges.

So our second question will be: Should a new gesture of separation between truth and knowledges be considered? This can also be put as: Should we accept Heidegger's diagnosis that truth is concealed and erased by the disposition of knowledges? Here, too, my answer is split. I think that truth has effectively become the "correctness of representations and statements" (447). And if that's what is meant by "truth," it is tantamount to making it a standard of judgment, and if it's made a standard of judgment, something of the fundamental meaning of truth is lost. I think that much should be granted Heidegger. Truth does, I believe, touch the openness of that of which there is truth.

I myself think that this touching of truth occurs in a triple form. First, there is truth only when there is nonfoundation, when there is something nonfounded, unfounded, something that is not its own self-guarantee, that has no guarantee. It is only where the foundation and the guarantee waver that truth can emerge. There has to be something that touches the precariousness of the unfounded. That's why we should always seek out a truth in the utter fragility of what is given, in obscure, maligned, fragile areas, where something is declared not to be. Knowledge, on the other hand, is closed. It is classification or judgment. It can then be said that there is truth only relative to the void of a situation, relative to what in the situation is not its fullness but its emptiness. Finally, it's not where the intensities are stable that truth discloses itself. On the contrary, it's where there's a difference of potential, a sudden variation in intensity. Nothing becomes everything. What didn't exist is now synonymous with potential. All this is consistent with Heidegger's idea that it is of the order of the open. We couldn't be further from "the correctness of representations and statements." You've got something that emerges in a previously unknown regime of enunciation. Truth emerges at your own risk where the nonrepresented appears. All you can do is say that truth is there. With no guarantee. This clearly shows that it is of the order of the open.

Here's an example. Where is there a possibility of a political truth? It's when something happens that has no legitimacy, is unfounded, with respect to the existing order. This is necessarily found in a situation of dispossession (void of the situation, manifestation) or in the context of an infinite variation in intensity (shift from nonexistence to existence). The usual order of things, on the other hand, is always founded, legitimate, with moderate variations in intensity. If you want any truth, you need to be closer to the open. The experience of love might also be used as an example. It is different from marriage, which has very moderate variations in intensity precisely when love isn't involved. We have to accept that there is something constantly unstable about love. There's no mutual agreement, it's closer to the void: it's the void of the Two, of the in-between, of that which is subject to maximum variation in intensity. It's not exposed to knowledge.

For all these reasons I agree with Heidegger that a potentially violent gesture of separating truth from knowledges is needed again today. The unfounded, the void, and the variation in intensity are needed. These are local, topological criteria that indicate a truth. So we must philosophically restore the operation of the unfounded. Philosophical work must focus on the unfounded as such, that is, on the illegitimate. For decades there has been considerable "legitimist" (let's use that old political vocabulary) pressure. It's the idea that only legitimacy can be validated. Legitimacy is whatever receives its seal of approval in a given society and is therefore knowable in a given society, as is the case with knowledge. But if you only accept what is legitimate, you exclude what is true, which cannot emerge otherwise than as a hole in legitimacy. Even in the case of a passionate love affair, that's how it happens. There's an imbalance in legitimacy.

In terms of philosophy, we need to stay as close as possible to what has not received the seal of foundation in a given society. We need to stay close to the void and be alert to any variation in intensity. This, at any rate, is the attitude that would allow philosophy to be open to the present, open to constructing a present under this system of conditions. And I'm willing to say, if you will, that this is a gesture of separation that is tantamount to staying in the open, in its very withdrawal.

For Heidegger, though, truth, in its original sense, is the protocol of questioning, the advent of a questioning regime of thought. We must adopt this questioning disposition—he sometimes says "determination"— as regards the open. Once the "classical" philosophical notion of truth has been deconstructed, once the diagnosis has been made, the problem is that of an active orientation of thought. Yet Heidegger remains in the disposition of questioning and waiting. I, for my part, think that, once proximity to the unfounded has been achieved, truth is a procedure, not a questioning. It is therefore a discipline. So I would oppose to the questioning of the open the discipline of the consequences. Hence my disagreement with him about the tasks of thinking. To appreciate this difference, let's turn to the final passage of "The End of Philosophy and the Tasks of Thinking":

Does the title for the task of thinking then read, instead of "Being and Time" [*Sein und Zeit*]: Clearing and Presence? (449)

So the name of the task of thinking would change.

> But where does the clearing come from and how is it given? What
> speaks in the "There is / It gives"? The task of thinking would then be
> the surrender of previous thinking to the determination of the matter
> for thinking. (449)

I would disagree with this statement, which seems still insufficiently
dialectical to me. What it ultimately says is that the task of thinking is the
surrender of the previous regimes of thinking to the questioning of the
new figure of thinking. But if there is really a situation of the open, you
can't just say that the previous figure of thinking must be "surrendered
to" something; you must immediately accept discipline, the discipline
of demonstration, contemplation, and so on. Ultimately, if there's no
immediacy of a conversion,[3] you are necessarily dealing with a questioning figure of a prophetic nature. You're dealing with the "not yet." But I
don't think the "not yet" dimension is applicable when it comes to truth.
You're either in the dimension of the consequences or nothing at all.
The regime of questioning and of the "not yet" is ultimately the regime
of prophecy. This is the crux of our disagreement: it is of the essence of
truth not to be prophesied. There can only be consequences of truth, no
prophecy. This is a deep, personal disagreement I have with Heidegger,
but perhaps an even earlier one with Nietzsche. I've always been struck
by the fact that Zarathustra says: "I am my own precursor." He is someone who prophesies his own coming, you might say, someone who speaks
of the coming of a new truth, insofar as he anticipates its coming because
truth is, in part, nothing other than the life of its prophet. *I* think there's
no such precursor. "Precursor" is a category of knowledge, not of truths.
You *experience* the unfounded, the void, the variation in intensity; no
one prophesies them to you. There's no mediation in the realm of truth.
There's no Annunciation, no angel of truth. The proper essence of a truth
is that "it happened."

My position is radically nonmessianic. I feel that, with Heidegger and
all his disciples, messianism is a very important part of their thinking.
But the basic question is how truth is given, since it is not given through
knowledge, since we reenact the gesture of separating out truth as the

foundation or creation of what matters, of what is really important, of what makes life something other than a constant and hostile animality. *Truth is the coming of what matters.* So the question of whether it is foretold or not foretold, whether it is in the form of an angel or not, whether there's a prophecy of it, whether there's a disposition of it, is an important question, because it dictates the form of fidelity, the form of becoming-subject of anyone who incorporates themself into the consequences that constitute the body of truth. I think that one of the breaks that has to be made with traditional Marxism, historicist Marxism, the Marxism that predicted the revolution, that predicted its inevitability—it had to come—is actually a break with what it still entailed in terms of messianism. A secularized, historicized messianism, to be sure, scientific but messianic just the same. That break is, in my view, a key, fundamental break. We must absolutely adopt a nonmessianic regime of truth. We must accept that truth is encountered in an experience that is unique every time, and when it is encountered, well, it's only after the fact that we know it has been encountered. We're already dealing with its consequences. That's why, in my philosophy, the key concept is fidelity. It connotes the fact that you have no relationship to a truth other than dealing with the system of consequences of having encountered it. I've always thought, in this regard, that love was one of the most illuminating paradigms. There's this paradox—which everyone has experienced—that there's an encounter, and that at the moment you know it's love, it's because it already exists. You can always say to yourself, "Someday my prince will come," but it's only in fairy tales that the prince arrives like that. Just because you say that someone will come doesn't mean they'll come, of course. They'll come because they've already come. This is a basic matrix, a matrix of every figure of truth. There's no angel saying: "Your soulmate is coming tomorrow. Be there, don't miss the date!" That's not how it happens. Nothing happens like that in the way we're captured, seized by, or caught up in a political truth, or in the way we experience a crucial artistic contemplation, or we finally understand a scientific theory, etc.

I completely agree with Heidegger about the fact that "truth" should be separated from "knowledge," about the fact that truths are captured or concealed by knowledges. Whether the primary responsibility for this is philosophy's is another question, but I agree at any rate that such a separation should be reinstated. I would even agree that the basic attributes of truth are related to the open, in the dimension I mentioned. However, I refuse to adopt a position of messianism, even a highly sophisticated one, with regard to all this. To be sure, Heidegger's messianism is not crudely religious, but it's a messianism all the same. We must accept to always be in the material, disciplined context of the procedure, of the consequences. To the extent that we constitute ourselves as subjects of a truth, we do so in the context of the ordering of the consequences. I don't agree that the task of thinking is "the determination of the matter for thinking," because to say that means being involved in a process whereby you end up saying you'll never get there. This is just what Heidegger says over and over in countless texts, and the Heideggerians go him one better: we need to wait, we're not there yet, it's much too complicated, we're not yet equal to the task, and besides, if a God doesn't help us out, we'll never get there. These are just rhetorical protocols. I have a disagreement with Heidegger about truth, about whether truth can be prophesied or not. I absolutely maintain that it cannot. And, to return to the issue at hand, namely, how philosophy can contribute to the construction of the present, I will argue that there is no regime of prophecy. We need to show what purpose constitutive fidelities can serve, in terms of philosophy, in the construction of the present. So we need to describe the symptoms of the present itself and of the system of consequences they entail. But it's impossible to say: "I can predict that things will be such and such a way and that they will be better tomorrow." The ways of the present are already indicated in what *I* regard, retrospectively, as constituting its possibility, as constituting a constellation of truth. We are responsible for an immanent constellation formed by the consequences of truth in the sky of the present, but there is no figure of prophecy for us.

So much for the second point. Let me remind you that my first point had to do with philosophy and its conditions, and the second, with the category of truth and its separation from knowledges. The third point, which I'll only indicate for now, has to do with determining the basic operations that result from all this. Indeed, if it's true that philosophy has conditions, including present conditions, and if it's true that the category of truth needs to be reconstructed, reformulated, then it's clear that the tasks of thinking are twofold. We should begin by putting philosophy back under the open jurisdiction of its condition(s). Then we should formulate a doctrine of truth, a thinking of truth, free from the influence of contemporary knowledges, hence restore the separation between them. This agenda, even if it's not formulated in the same language, can be said to be Heidegger's agenda too.

Heidegger refers to these two operations by two different terms, "the turn" and "questioning." He calls putting philosophy back under the open jurisdiction of its conditions "the turn." A "turn," almost in the sense of a turn that takes us back, or restores us, to the originary site of the open, is needed. Philosophy, which was destined by the open but has closed off this destination, must make a fundamental—nonphilosophical, or postphilosophical—turn so as to put itself back under the protection of the open. I myself would say: philosophy must be put back under the complex system of its conditions. And Heidegger calls the reformulation of the doctrine of truth "questioning." His aim is to restore the questioning dimension of thought.

Where Heidegger says "turn," I would instead say "placement." Indeed, for me it doesn't have to do with anything originary; it's simply a matter of placing philosophy within the system of its conditions. This is already a pretty complicated operation, and I'm surprised to see the extent to which many contemporary philosophical orientations seem removed, or even shielded, from, i.e., unexposed to, the intensity of their natural conditions. What I mean by this is that a good deal of contemporary philosophy, far more than opening itself up to contemporary mathematics, takes cover from it. What's more, entire sectors of contemporary philosophy are also completely shielded from the intensity of contemporary art. And most are barricaded against contemporary politics. So placement is quite a complex operation, since, as a rule, many philosophical orientations put up significant barriers to the natural conditions of philosophy. If it's a question now of reformulating the doctrine of truth, I would speak of creation, in the Deleuzian sense of concept creation. A new concept of truth needs to be created that is adequate to truth's separation from contemporary knowledges. The turn and questioning (Heidegger) versus placement and creation: the words certainly imply differences that will become clearer later on.

My fourth point will be to determine what we're dealing with when it comes to these operations. What makes placement (or the turn) so difficult, creation or questioning so rare? What impedes these two constitutive operations in the present—re-placing philosophy in the context of its conditions and reformulating the doctrine of truths—which are operations needed for philosophy to be equal to the tasks of the age? Next time, we'll begin again with this very point.

Session 8

June 4, 2003

Before I conclude this year's seminar today, there's one point I'd like to come back to. I've spoken twice here about the "war" in Iraq. So it's fair to ask the following question: What should we think about the protests against this military intervention, which were massive at the outset throughout the world? Admittedly, this movement suffered from a glaring political weakness, as it couldn't bear, so to speak, that what it was protesting against should become a reality. Everyone shouted "Down with the war!" but when the Anglo-American troops' invasion of Iraq began in earnest, they went home and kept quiet, or at least most of the protesters did. The protests were a prewar action, an attempt to stop the invasion from beginning, but the war itself dissipated the inner strength of the demonstrations.

No doubt the time of mass popular events, the time of triumphant, historically significant demonstrations, has not yet come, if it is to come at all . . . Is there nothing, then? No, there are some actions that are polycentric, as it were, which, in a way, increases their subjective determination locally. When small, determined groups proliferate and network with each other, it's clear that the figure—still prepolitical, of course—of what is going on is more serious, more significant. We have an active, developing awareness regarding the issue of schools, whose intrinsic theme is not just the state form of their organization but the historical destiny of education. Another issue is being given serious thought, that of retirement pensions, which is a seemingly technical issue, concerning how they're calculated, the qualification standards, and the amount of the payments. To my mind, however, it actually has to do with a very important issue in society today: in what regard is work, and particularly the hard and poorly paid work of so many people in every country, held? The issue of pensions seems to be about postwork life, but, even if that's an important aspect of it, public outrage about what's being planned is not fundamentally focused on the technical aspects of retirement. More importantly, it is focused on the concern—already expressed in other ways at the time of the big 1995 movement, and in that sense there's a certain continuity— that, increasingly, work doesn't matter.[1] One government after another has failed to acknowledge the fact that having a lifetime of work is a constituent element of the respect in which the people who make up a country should be held. And the more such work is actually hard, grueling, and necessary, the more worthless it is considered.

Does all this amount to a whole? Especially if you add to it the presidential election situation of April–May last year, the 1995 movement, which I just mentioned, the Jospin government, and so on.[2] It is actually a whole temporal arc, and I'm naturally not going to go into the details of this analysis. There is, however, one point I'd like to emphasize. Ultimately, both internationally, under U.S. hegemony, and domestically, under the leadership of successive governments, in different variations and with different points of application, the policy that's developing seems to me to have one inherent characteristic, namely, destruction. It's a policy one of whose constituent elements, an element of identity, is its negative characterization: its aim is to destroy a wide variety of things. Internationally, this means the destruction of figures of popular state consistency, figures of international law, figures of peace, and so on. And domestically, as everyone can see, figures of public service are being targeted, particularly schools as regards their functions of knowledge transmission and transfer between generations, but also hospitals, public transport, energy distribution, local governments, etc. Destruction is a negative and unifying component of the current situation, operating as "liberalism," "modernity," or "reforms." The fact is, today, whenever governments start talking about reforms, we should immediately be very concerned . . . If the idea of reform emerges intact from all this confusion, it will be very lucky indeed! "Reform" basically means that the meager benefits available to you in the form of any particular public good are outmoded and are going to be destroyed.

This is not a separate problem from what I was talking about before. Indeed, it's the problem, in politics, of one of the forms of contemporary nihilism. And ultimately nihilism means treating situations in such a way that only a disorganized multitude remains in them. That's the overall objective. The point is to be able to deal with as formless and ignorant a multitude as possible, whose figures of solidarity, of respect for the relationship to work, internal organizations, political projects, and so on have been completely dismantled, wrecked, demolished, and scattered to the winds, so as to arrive at what I have contended here is the fundamental contemporary subjectivity: an atomized individual, whether a winner or a loser (and if they're a loser, too bad for them) vis-à-vis the global market. That's why issues such as contributory retirement plans or funded retirement plans are important, even if they're very technical. It's moreover very clear that, behind the general idea of funded retirement plans, there's the intention, even when labor and workers are involved, to take into account only the consumer/saver, i.e., someone who can be identified by their financial provisions, by what they are prepared to purchase and prepared to sock away in the bank.

Ultimately, retirement, like everything else, will become a commodity; you'll have to buy it, if you can. That's really the strategic goal: on the one hand, there are only commodities, and, on the other, only disorganized masses. And then, of course, given that all this is a very dangerous mix, there are a number of coercive forces on hand, like the police and the courts, which, on the contrary, maintain their organizing principle and their discipline in the service of repression. At the very top of the instruments of power designed to work toward this destruction of any idea of the public interest, and to defend it, crowning the whole process, there is ultimately the incommensurable power of the U.S. military. That is really the way things stand in the world today.

How can the destruction be stopped? My conviction, at any rate, is that destruction can be stopped only with innovative affirmations. You can't stop it simply by remaining on the defensive, yelling "Down with destruction," or by being nostalgic for the restoration of something that's obviously already largely destroyed.

If we transform this philosophically, if we project it philosophically, we could say that what we need to work toward is a general antinihilist, therefore fundamentally affirmative, revolt. Over and above the very legitimate concerns about the future, material life, pensions (will I only get a measly amount? will I be penniless twenty years from now? etc.), this is what will create the shared conviction that we are not willing to become assimilated into contemporary nihilism, to sacrifice ourselves on that altar. This is what will create the positive form of the refusal to become that atomized individual who, whether powerful or poor, is summoned to appear before a world made up exclusively of tradable commodities.

All this fully conforms with a Marxist conception of the structures of the contemporary world. The Marxist critique of political economy claims that labor power itself is a commodity, that it becomes a commodity in the cycle of the expanded reproduction of capital. We might say that the final stage of this development occurs when, through a variety of measures, it's implied that there is effectively nothing but commodities, and that, even beyond the labor force, life itself, existence, is a commodity, that institutions are commodities, providers of products.

This future of destruction through commodification is alarming, and it's a problem of considerable scope, whose metaphysics, as things currently stand, is stronger than its politics. Maybe that's the problem. The political categories are probably not entirely equal to what I call, albeit in terms that are still very abstract, the metaphysical dimension of the attempt to oppose destruction, its immediate subjective dimension. And that's something that has been developing since 1995. At the time of the December 1995 movement, I'd been very struck by the fact that the one and only slogan was: "Together." But what does "together" mean? It could be given a narrow meaning: "Together, all together, in the movement, we will win, etc." But it could also be given a much stronger meaning, one that, I think, was evident, namely that the ability to be together is precisely the ability not to be that disorganized multitude summoned to the marketplace. Whatever this "together" may be, it is a multiplicity affirming itself as such, as Deleuze might have said. And indeed, in 1995, the self-affirmation of the multiplicities was expressed as "together." The system of unconditional demands was dominated, encapsulated by all that. This is what I'd call the metaphysics of the movement. It's not exactly a politics because a politics has to do with much more circumstantial, specific issues—the government, the political parties, ultimatums, slogans—and because a politics is a thought practice implemented in order to really change the overall situation. But, in this type of period, there is also a historical metaphysics of the movement, which was expressed in 1995 in that "together" and is being expressed today in the way multifaceted communities of interest are being organized, in the belief that something exceeding the usual categories of opinion is at stake. Something is creating a link, transversally to the individual categories, along with the quite striking empirical fact that a central role is being played by a few active groups of educators. In a sense, the educators are to 2003 what the railroad workers were to what took place in 1995.[3] It would seem that there is always a need for a kind of driving force, around or with regard to which the protest as a whole is organized, as if the protest or the revolt against nihilism always had to have a backbone. It's only natural, after all: lacking that backbone, it would itself be scattered, because its metaphysics is a lot weaker than its politics.

Those were the two points I wanted to speak about, because they're directly connected to both our concern about what we can do to combat contemporary nihilism and the essentially destructive nature of the politics being pursued, which is known as liberalism, despite the fact that the Socialists are capable of pursuing it vigorously. It is increasingly clear that liberalism is destruction, hence the sociopolitical operator of contemporary nihilism. And obviously, as opposed to that, the figures of collective cohesion, of the self-affirmation of the multiplicity as such, the figures of the determination to have work be taken into consideration, the fact of not wanting to be dissolved in the formless masses—well, these are the forces at work today, in an admittedly weak metaphysical chaos, but before you can be strong you have to be weak.

Therefore, as we used to say back in the day, the situation is excellent, isn't it?[4] This simply means that we can clearly see in what way it's bad. An excellent situation is one in which the revolt against its hatefulness results in an eye that observes it, a true eye, a clear eye that observes it and acts within it, that changes and transforms it. This could all be summed up by saying: is the development of a political singularity beginning to appear amid the current confusion? Well, I hope so.

From the possibility of a politics let's return now to the question: What is philosophy capable of? Or more to the point: Can philosophy be considered capable of measuring up, in its own field, to what our age demands? Can philosophy provide an answer to the epochal questions that are asked of it or condition it in its own immanence? I'd proposed that this could be expressed as: Does our own time have a capacity for truths? Is there a chance that some new truth procedures might emerge in our own time? And I'd begun to compare this with Heidegger's thesis. The latter, as you'll recall, is that philosophy as metaphysics, philosophy defined as metaphysics, is not really equal to the challenges of thinking imposed by the times. According to Heidegger, if we define philosophy as the long period of the history of being that can be regarded as metaphysics—and, according to him, that's all we can do—then philosophy is exhausted. As a result, it's not from within philosophy, as a form of thought, that we can hope to answer or even ask the questions of our times. Heidegger's position is one of waiting for the coming of something beyond philosophy, the coming of a "thinking thought," as he says, that will transcend the philosophical disposition, that is to say, the metaphysical disposition. In the Heideggerian construction, there is both a definition of philosophy as metaphysics and a provision of the answer to our question: in its historially metaphysical form, philosophy is not capable of meeting the challenges of the times.

I then proceeded in several stages, each time indicating my area of agreement with Heidegger's diagnosis and my protocol of disagreement. Let me give you a very brief summary.

First, Heidegger—and this is very important—shows that philosophy is in a way conditioned by something more fundamental than itself. Indeed, philosophy was originally destined or sent by a disposition of thought, which is also a disposition of being, more originary and fundamental than itself, namely, the clearing of being or the clearing of the open. That is why the destiny of philosophy, or its capability, must always be measured against this original sending, that is to say, this condition that is more important and decisive than philosophy itself can be.

I won't go back over the details, but I did make two comments.

First, I agree that philosophy is under condition. But I don't regard this condition, or precondition, as destinal, originary. For me, philosophy's conditions, which are themselves multifaceted, constitute the significance of an epoch, of course, but it's not a sort of general historiality that would cause there to be a univocal identity of philosophy. Thus, it's true that philosophy's capabilities are under condition, but this condition should itself be considered as constituting distinct philosophical epochs, not one single, homogenous history in which philosophy is intrinsically metaphysical.

My second point was that, for Heidegger, a feature of the age is the discovery (by Heidegger, in fact . . .) that the primordial clearing in which truth is supposed to originate is occluded or obscure due to its being buried in the figure of knowledges. Therefore, if we want to rely on the clearing of being again, we need to find a new, nonmetaphysical way of separating truth and knowledges. Basically, Heidegger says that a new gesture is necessary. If philosophy is powerless or exhausted, it's because our age requires a new gesture, a gesture of separation. I agree with Heidegger that our age does require a new figure of separation between truth and knowledges [savoirs], or between truth and cognition [connaissance], and that we therefore need a new concept of truth that will draw a dividing line with the pure and simple givenness of knowledges, in particular technico-scientific knowledges. But, for me, this is a properly philosophical task, which doesn't in the least require going beyond philosophy, or deconstructing metaphysics, or anything of the sort. It's a matter of constructing a new concept of what truths are. For his beyond-metaphysics, Heidegger introduces a rhetoric of "questioning," of the questioning disposition of thought, which endeavors to return to its erased or forgotten origins. As against this rhetoric and its extensions (the "deconstruction of metaphysics" is one of these extensions), I'll argue that the problem is that of a new rational discipline of the consequences of what constitutes an event in a given age. These would be the two options: the questioning method, on the one hand, and on the other, the creation of a new philosophical practice of the consequences, and therefore of a new way of submitting to the epochal conditions of philosophy, of a new discipline of speculative thought.

The new impetus of philosophy is not the claim that a new "fundamental questioning" overrides its whole history. What needs to be remedied concerns the discipline of thought, what has actually long been called reason or rationality. This was the traditional name, the metaphysical name—as Heidegger would say—of the discipline of thought, of what made it suitable for argument, logic, etc. So it could also be said that the problem is that of a new figure of rationality. What is rationality in what would be its figure of discipline today and wouldn't be simply traditional or classical argumentative rationality? Just as classical rationality was what made it possible to establish the demarcation between truth and opinion, the contemporary metaphysical duty, the new rationality, which, in Heidegger's wake, can be called dialectical, is to find the forms of demarcation between truth and knowledge.

After these debates with Heidegger over the relative essence of philosophy, we arrived at the conclusion that, in the current situation of philosophy, there are two basic operations. First, putting philosophy back into the open space of its conditions, which is a gesture of re-placing. And second, reformulating a doctrine of truth free from the influence of knowledges, from the relativism of knowledges. Even though, with Heidegger, they are decentered with regard to philosophy as a metaphysical destiny, these two operations do have names in his work. The first is *the turn*: a fundamental turn, a turning around, is needed to achieve a new disposition of thought in relation to its original condition. The second is *questioning*, i.e., replacing the rationalist agenda of truth with the thinking agenda of questioning, the questioning openness identifying a thinking that is on the way to its own salvation.

You can see that where Heidegger says "turn," I suggested saying "placement," and where Heidegger says "questioning," I say "constructing," constructing a new concept of truth and therefore a new figure of the discipline of thought.

The last point in this comparison, which I had only barely mentioned, consisted in asking what the obstacles were when it came to these operations. That is, what are the basic obstacles that our age imposes, or inflicts, on us and that have to be surmounted in order for thinking to be up to the challenge of the age?

Heidegger calls the main obstacle, which also happens to be the name of our epochal situation, *Ge-stell*, a term that many critics don't translate because the sacralization of the German language, after the

Greek language, as "the language of thinking thought" is such that, ultimately, if they translate it, they will be traitors. When they do translate it, it's translated [in English] as "enframing," or "positionality" [as a
more recent translation of "The Turn" has it].[5] This positionality is the
essence in thought of technology, i.e., our epochal situation as a situation in which being emerges as technology, where being itself appears
as the positionality, so to speak, of itself. Positionality is the making
available of the totality of the being, reduced to a standing reserve.
It is the moment in the history of being when being is realized as self-
exposure in an open-ended availability that is open only to conscription, to positionality, by the will to domination, which is ultimately
also the technological will. This is at once our situation and the obstacle to
the operations I mentioned above. Indeed, once being unfolds as wholly
available to a general will that positions and reduces it, it becomes naturally as impossible to resituate thinking in its sending or in its originary
clearing—because that clearing is eliminated by technological availability—
as it is to really engage in questioning, thinking as questioning. Thinking
is obscured as will and is itself positioned and positioning, is itself captured in this relationship to being that makes of it a pure and simple
exposure for its technological subjection or its deliberate destruction.
Ever since Descartes, the subjectivity that corresponds to this positionality of the being in totality has been none other than the metaphysical
figure of the subject as the subject that wills, the subject of the will as
will, which is essentially the will to power, realized as a will positioning
being itself in its exposure. Which is what Descartes said, without any
jargon, in the well-known maxim to the effect that man is now master
and owner of nature.

Here's another definition of our age, proposed by Heidegger: The *Ge-
stell* is being itself "in the self-endangering truth of its essence" (64). It is
being itself that absolutely exposes itself to the danger of the truth of its
own essence, the danger of being no more than an availability for a will,
a will to power. That is why our age can be characterized as nihilistic,
because, in it, being itself endangers the truth of its essence. It is a nihilism in the strictest sense, i.e., a figure in which being exposes itself to its
own annihilation, in which being presents itself as available for its own
destruction. In that sense, naturally, nihilism is not at all an ideology, a

worldview, an extrinsic occurrence, or a belief. On the contrary, it is a figure of the history of being itself, of that moment when being cannot present itself otherwise than as being entirely available for a will. Consequently, it exposes the danger of its own essence.

As usual with Heidegger, it must be added that what is most dangerous about this danger is its concealment, its not entirely visible nature. The exposure of being as availability to its own positionality appears in disguise, especially because technology, which is the tangible essence of the positionality of being, is represented as a means. In other words, the availability of the being in totality appears as if it were the means to ends that are more important, or better. But technology isn't a means. Technology, in the form of being's exposure to its own destruction, is the situation of being itself. In no way does man himself, so long as he continues to exist, entertain a relationship with technology in which it could be a means. In other words, technology is man's situation, not his means. As a result—and this is why we are dealing with genuine nihilism—there is no end other than destruction itself. This is consistent with things I said a little while ago but approached from a totally different angle. Heidegger wrote, for example, to choose from among a thousand possible passages, that "the essence of the human is now ordered to give a hand to the essence of technology" (64). The statement is clear: man, who would like to think he is that to which technology is related as a means for ends of emancipation, domination, control, is in reality ordered to give a hand to the very essence of technology, thus to the essence of being as exposure to positionality, and ultimately to destruction.

Let me read you a very important summary passage from "The Turn":

> Yet since beyng has sent itself as the essence of technology in positionality, and since the human *essence* belongs to the essence of beyng insofar as the essence of beyng needs the human essence, in accordance with its own essence, in order to remain guarded in the midst of beings as being, and thus needs it in order to essence as beyng, then for this reason the essence of technology cannot be led to a transformation of its destiny without the assistance of the human essence. Thereby technology is not humanly overcome. (65)

Technology is not humanly overcome. There's no way, for example, to oppose an antitechnological humanism to technology. Such an attempt would be absolutely illusory and futile, in Heidegger's eyes, because the humanity of humanism is itself contained within the destiny of technology. Much to the contrary, "the essence of technology is converted into its still concealed truth" (65). The way that is open is not to oppose man's humanity to technology but rather for man, as cobelonging to the destiny of technology, to take the measure of technology itself. Taking the measure of technology itself means bringing forth its truth, which is still obscure. As we saw, what is most dangerous about the danger is the fact that it is concealed. So we need to begin by bringing the essence of technology to light so that, in a certain way, we can be relieved of it. Let's remember what Heidegger says:

> This conversion [liberté] is similar to what occurs when, in the human realm, a pain is converted. (65; trans. slightly modified)[6]

The freedom [liberté] achieved by man's bringing the essence of technology to light determines technology in its essence, and therefore nihilism as nihilism. As a result, this freedom is similar to that of someone who overcomes their pain, in the sense that, far from getting rid of it and forgetting about it, they inhabit it. So we can say that Heidegger's aim with respect to the tasks of the age is to ask if we are capable of inhabiting the Ge-stell. It is in no way a matter of overcoming technology by an abstract figure of man, who imagines that it must be a means . . . All of that is absolutely foreclosed. Nor is it a matter of going back to a time before technology, which is meaningless. What we need to do is effect the turning by means of which technology can be thought and understood as the destiny of being. And that turning enables technology to be reconnected with the original openness, in that we think, we see, we decipher in it a destiny of being as the presentation of the being in totality to its positionality.

You'll note that this is the crux of what I'd call Heidegger's messianism, the figure of which is as follows: one can only free oneself from a destiny by inhabiting it, by becoming an inhabitant of that destiny. There is no question of being the plaything of one's destiny or of claiming to be exempt from it. Rather, we must partake in it with perfect lucidity of thought, with the force of thought. To inhabit one's destiny as a destiny, with the immanent understanding that it is a destiny. Another possibility then opens up. We're unable to realize this possibility completely—maybe a God is needed for that. But we are able to open it up by being the true inhabitants of this site or this moment of being that is the *Ge-stell* itself. The basic maxim is taken from Hölderlin: "But where danger grows, so does that which saves." That is what I call the absolute crux of Heideggerian messianism. The possibility of salvation opens up precisely where one is in the gravest danger, precisely where one makes intelligible what is most dangerous about the danger. Because to make intelligible what is most dangerous about the danger is to show that it is masked, to unmask it. If this isn't salvation itself, it's at least the possibility of it that opens up or opens up again.

What shall we say about all the foregoing? It is quite appealing, and it accords with a widely shared view of ecology, according to which unbridled technology threatens the very essence of the human habitat. All of this, as messianism (the end of the world is nigh . . .), is still pretty religious in terms of both its destinal theme and the at once catastrophist and preachy subjectivity that goes with it. But even so, I think we have to agree with Heidegger that the figure of the contemporary world is nihilism. It's true that something is placing the worldliness of the world in the process of its own destruction. There's a very real clarity about all this, which I think is related far more to the contemporary figures of power than to the theme, in my opinion neutral in itself, of technology. The real, contemporary figures of power are not figures of order: the Americans, who are always talking about order, won't create a new world order, which, incidentally, they couldn't care less about. On the contrary, what they're after is an affirmation of power, which, in a way, is the immanent and definitive creation of disorder—of disorder, destruction, deterioration, the formless multitude, colossal inequalities, mass deaths amid total indifference, etc. And, what's more, of the wanton destruction—I'll go that far—of tradition, of repetition. This sounds like a reactionary screed! But I've explained what's meant by this over the past year. Let me repeat that, in order for there to be a present, there has to be the possibility for a real incorporation of the past. Thus,

the notion of all-out modernization at any cost, with its attendant con-
demnation of the obsolescence of anything remaining from before, etc.,
is a notion that I insist leads to the destruction of the present, in the
interests of a single sacred cow: free enterprise, the market, or, in a
nutshell, capitalism, which has reached the age of its complete hegemony over the world. While pretending to be devoted to eradicating
the outmoded things of the past, it makes it impossible to inhabit the
present and proposes, in terms of the future, nothing but the endless
flight toward destruction.

I agree with Heidegger that the question is how to inhabit the present. The fact that a present exists or, as Mallarmé says, is not lacking, is
indeed incompatible with the exercise of unlimited power, which disre-
gards what exists in its heritage of existence and destroys the figures of
consistency that are not homogeneous with the market or with financial and military hegemony. I think that what Heidegger calls the withdrawal of unconcealment [le retrait du sans retrait], is the disappearance
of thought's real confrontation, of the possibility for thought to take
the time to come face to face with what it is thinking, the possibility
for really confronting what it is thinking. This destruction, attempted
by liberal ideology, of any real possibility for thought is effectively a
process of negation of the world as a habitat for subjects. The catastrophic image is this: before the disorganized masses, commodities
are displayed one after another. Thus, there are two series: on the one
hand, disorganized masses reduced to the atomic individuality of the
viewing of commodities and, on the other, the succession of these commodities with their endless substitutability. That's really what nihilism
is, this instance of destruction that makes the present uninhabitable,
"uninhabitable" meaning not affording enough time to be habitable,
not creating a dwelling place, where "dwelling" means the possibility
of confronting something. You could say, using Heidegger's lingo, that
there is a withdrawal of unconcealment, a dissolution of the present.
This dissolution is also the destruction of the incorporation of the past,
not of its memory or history but at any rate of its present vitality. You
know how important the possibility of making present what is precious
about the past is, in politics, for example. The destruction of the great
predecessors of the past has always resulted in a significant erosion of

the real present of politics, which draws and has always drawn on the figures of the past. It draws on them, but not randomly: the luminaries of the past are those who enable us to face difficult circumstances or to create the present's intensity.

Ultimately, can it be said that this nihilism is something like inhabiting pain, since that is how Heidegger puts it? It's true that there is pain associated with the lack of a present. Even in today's sparse movements—against the war, for education, and even for pensions—pain is being expressed, the pain caused by the fact that the present is being destroyed. The present with its intensity, therefore the true present, is always the disruption of a repetition and the possibility of a projection. This present is a whole period of time, and it's this that is being destroyed. That's something that causes pain. Pain should be distinguished from complaining, dissatisfaction, or grievance. It's deeper, more radical than that. In my opinion, there's a metaphysics of the movement, which is also an effect of what is happening.

However, I can't agree with Heidegger that the absolute crux of the problem is technology. I don't think it is. Nor do I think that the issue is the coming into availability of historial being. I think the crux of the problem is really the fact that every singularity is summoned to appear before the circulation of commodities, before the market, and therefore before something that is not reducible to technology. Nothing about technology per se, let alone about its underlying scientific availability, condemns it to being organized around the endless substitutability of commodities. It is a sui generis singularity, the singularity of capitalism. Let's call it by its old name, after all! It's actually this singularity that Heidegger doesn't want to really name. He envelops it in something vaster, more nebulous, something that actually harks back to old reactionary antitechnologism, to the old provincial hostility to industry, which is perfectly evident in his work. There's a side to Heidegger that is all about "Long live the Black Forest peasant! Down with technology, industry, positionality, man's control over nature, etc., etc.!" But that's not the point. I won't dispute the fact that the impact of the universal appearance before the abstraction of the market leads to widespread aberrations, but the relationship should not be reversed: it is the control over technology, and more seriously over science itself, of this appearance before the abstraction of the market that creates the site of nihilism. We dealt with this at length, and I'm not going to go back over it. A unique subjectivity is created, whereby the idea is that we basically don't need to think in order to live, because commodities do it for us. That is the great contemporary imperative. I have often said as much: the great idea dreamed up by the commodified contemporary world is really the imperative, the commandment, "Live without any ideas." It's clear that you can only live without ideas because commodities compensate for them, provided, of course, that you're lucky enough to have access to them. If you're not, you should at least have other ideas for surviving, other ways, other paths. The crux of it all, what desingularizes any present, is the imperative "Live without any ideas!"

And to my mind that's what pain is. When all is said and done, there is only pain where there is no thinking. You might say: "What unshakeable optimism!" Sure, but it's absolutely justified. It doesn't mean there's no pain. It just means that, where thinking can occur, pain can disappear. It's a well-known fact. Thinking, in its fullest definition, of course. It's obviously not the idea that if you think a little bit, you'll feel better! It's more complicated than that. But it's also the maxim that where there was pain, thinking can come into play. Conversely, I think it could be shown that all pain—I'm not talking about complaining or resentment—originates in a separation of the body from the capacity for thought. A body with no access to the thinkable is a body of pain. Such a separation can be obtained by various means. By torture, for instance. But on a more general level, it will be obtained if you can manage to make the body stake its fate on commodities. That's the gentlest way of separating the body from its capacity for thought. And yet, however gentle it may be, it is still pain. So we have to say that *the consumer suffers*. That's my thesis: the consumer suffers, as such. This doesn't mean that they derive no enjoyment from consumer goods. But as such, i.e., as someone reduced to having to appear before the system of commodities as substitutes for any thinking, they suffer. We know very well the forms this can take in the contemporary world, in particular in the suffering of adolescents, a suffering to which the problem of schools is very relevant. And today's teachers are the ones who overwhelmingly deal with this suffering. People say that teachers have to deal with violence. But first we need to talk about suffering and anxiety; all the rest is just a bunch of socialized projections. Teachers deal directly with this suffering, which is the suffering of those who are encouraged to sacrifice themselves to commodities. The fact is, the problem of schools, an extremely complex problem, is, among other things, the problem of this suffering. And the schools are being asked to deal with it! But it's not very easy. Because addressing this suffering means bringing in thinking where it needs to be brought in, which ultimately amounts to creating it as a possibility of bodies, as something available through bodies. That's not easy to do, and, what's more, it's outrageous to ask the schools to do it by themselves. It can only lead to destruction and absurd disciplinary procedures. I think that this is the true figure of contemporary nihilism.

To address the situation, as far as philosophy's humble task is concerned, I think the right way forward is of course to put philosophy back under the system of its conditions. But above all I would say that we need to aggravate the conditions of thought, make them more stringent, emphasize their rigor as such. Heidegger says somewhere in his *Introduction to Metaphysics* that the essence of philosophy is to aggravate the problems. To aggravate them rather than to solve them. Personally, I still like a few problems to be solved now and then! Constantly aggravating them or promising that they'll become increasingly serious is touchingly appealing. However, there is also something true about this idea of "aggravation." Taken in its etymological sense, it means weightier, heavier, of a more solid consistency. Just that, because we're dealing with circulation, or with communication (they're the same thing). It's true that the only hope is to weigh down the things that circulate to such an extent that we'll be able to bring them to at least a temporary standstill.

----- ❦ -----

Let me give you a few examples. I said that there were four procedures for distancing ourselves from the dominant images and emblems: demonstration, contemplation, rupture (political protests, action), and love or passion. It is on them that what we're capable of today ultimately hinges. I think that one of philosophy's tasks is to be concerned with these procedures in a dimension of relative aggravation.

It is very important today to vigorously separate what pertains to demonstration from what pertains to technology or usage. We need to reassert science's radical independence from technology. The crux of the issue is mathematics, because the initiation of this separation is achieved through mathematics inasmuch as mathematics works against the idea of usefulness. Mathematics shows us that science is essentially useless, useless in the sense of the general system of commodity circulation being regulated by usefulness. It's well-nigh impossible to read a report in the press about a scientific discovery, even a mathematical one, without being told right from the second line what it will be used for and when it will be marketed. Failing that, the journalist will be totally thrown for a loop and won't know what to say! They won't know how to present something to the reader that, it will have to be admitted, is totally useless, at least as far as commodity circulation is concerned. So they'll get around it by saying "It's still only basic research, but it will have a use someday! There are plenty of bizarre things that only had a use a hundred years later!" This is an odd, unconvincing argument, and the journalist would be better off defending the discovery's uselessness. In any case, this is a good possible example of "aggravation," in which philosophy has a role to play. Heidegger is right to say, in his always somewhat pompous language, that technology needs man to safeguard its destiny of being. The sciences certainly need philosophy to safeguard their destiny of thinking from subservience of every kind, from every quarter. I think there's something about philosophy that safeguards science itself, not in terms of its development and its actual methods but in terms of its own quality of being separated or separable from usefulness in the sense given that word by the dominance of Capital.

Likewise, the affirmative function of art will have to be safeguarded. What is art if not an instrument of combat against the imperative "Live without any ideas"? Because art, if it exists at all, is always the fictionalization of what a life under the Idea is. Every artform, every artistic proposition, fictionalizes the hypothesis that we can live under the Idea, that life can be exposed to the Idea. Art also depicts fictionally what life without ideas is like, how impoverished and worthless it is. That's art's critical function. But it does so on the basis of the possibility of life under the Idea. Even if art deals with pain, if it induces pain, and if pain is one of its materials, it remains—unless it's a subservient art, a decadent art—the fictional operator of a world that deals with what a world without pain might be like. Even when it seems completely pessimistic, art always remains, when all is said and done, a fiction of bliss. Art's radiance as such, what elevates art from within its process, is a proposition concerning the fiction of life under the Idea. There is no art, however bleak its appearance and virulent its critical impact, except of joy. That's why everyone loves art. When you read an utterly depressing story that makes you cry your eyes out, what is the art in the protocol of narration? It's not realism or the imitation of pain; it's the fact that pain itself is illuminated or elevated from within, in the figure—attested by the power of art itself—of the possibility of joy. Art is truly the radiance of joy as such, whatever its narrative subject may be. Philosophy must make itself the humble guardian of this vocation of art, protecting it from what would be an overly critical view of art, the view that art is just the critical dismantling of the contemporary world.

The fact is, we don't need criticism today. Everyone is able to criticize today's world, apart from the subsidized propagandists whose job is to celebrate it. Anybody on the street knows that the present is awful and can tell you why. Since that's the case, a critique of criticism ought to be written, and I'm grateful to Marx and Engels for having done so, in *The Holy Family, or The Critique of Critical Criticism*. "Critical criticism" simply adapts to dissolution in a different way. No, it's not criticism we need, but affirmation. Criticism has been around for a long time now and is worn out; its power is gone. The critique of political economy dates from the nineteenth century, and the critique of the contemporary world had already been accomplished by the early twentieth century. I myself constantly engage in criticism, but please note and keep in mind that my use of criticism here extends to self-criticism. You know what I mean. The question Heidegger calls the question of the turn is not that of criticism or negativity. It's the question of whether there is a heterogeneous affirmation, whether there is still a capacity for heterogeneous affirmation. Let me go back to the 1995 protests: even that minimal slogan, "Together," wasn't criticism. It meant that when we're together, we can at least say that much; we can say it together. It was already something that self-affirmed the multiplicity, and that's the real problem, of which art is a privileged witness. There's an inner struggle in art as to

whether its contemporary objective or purpose is criticism, the deconstruction of representation, or ultimately rather the germ of a capacity
for affirmation, heterogeneous to the world of the market, because it
maintains that life is only bearable under the Idea, and that art should at
least afford us a fiction of the Idea.

Where politics is concerned, the question is that of breaking away from
the conventional models, the prescribed models. No doubt also that of
breaking away from the representative or expressive view of politics, that
bland idea that freedom means when everyone can "express themselves."
The political question today is rather: What is the affirmative discipline
that does not think in terms of self-expression, let alone in terms of life
management, but thinks beyond self-expression and management, thinks
in terms of action as the transformation of the Subject?

As regards the question of passion or love, I think it's a matter of
"aggravating" the thinking of the dialectical power of the Two. To do
so, we need to draw on the different kinds of amorous discord. Amorous discord doesn't mean creating Oneness separate from the whole.
Passionate love affirms the Two as sovereign power, affirms the play of
difference, its creative and innovative capacity, at great risk to the individual himself, at great risk to the One.

In these different spheres, we thus have a variety of factors aggravating the contentious issues that are exceptions to commodification.
And this leads to the question of the tasks of thinking.

I'm only going to speak very briefly about this, because the question
of the tasks of thinking, of its orientation, will be our starting point
next year. As regards Heidegger again, I would say he sees very clearly
that the task of thinking is a task that concerns the present. He tackles
the subject vigorously, even though his present, as I said, is shaped from
within by a messianic figure. He sees clearly that it can't be a calculation
or a promise. He sees clearly that to calculate the future, to promise that
things will be fine, that "we'll get through this"—that all that is precisely
the dissolution of the present. His question is indeed that of the present,
and I think we've got to go along with him on that.

The metaphor Heidegger suggests is that of insight. It is the creation
or assumption of a new way of seeing, of an insight, as he says, "into
that which is." I'm going to read you a short excerpt, once again at

292 The Logic of Exceptions

the end of "The Turn." In it, he describes, negatively, what real insight would be:

> Insight does not name our inspection of the being, insight as flashing entry is the appropriative event of the constellation of the turn in the essence of beyng itself in the epoch of positionality. (70–71)

As you can see, the question of the possibility of the turn is the question of the possibility of an insight into that which is. I accept this metaphor. If there's a possibility of an insight into that which is, then, yes, philosophy can be in the service of that possibility. For Heidegger, naturally, it's an insight "into," in the sense that what is caught sight of, namely, the vitality of the present, is that insight itself. So there is a present when the new insight is also what there is to catch sight of. And in effect, when something happens, we are well aware that we can also say that what is happening is the creation of a new way of seeing things. But what does "things" mean? Well, it means precisely the fact that there's this new insight. When something happens, there's a new sort of blurring between the insight and what is caught sight of. There's a new insight, and there is something new that this new insight catches sight of, because there's this insight that's absolutely new. That sounds very abstruse, but it really isn't. It's a direct experience you have when something happens in either collective or individual life. You have the feeling, as the common phrase goes, of "seeing things differently." And that "differently" is precisely the fact that you see them differently. This is a very important point. Everyone has that experience, in the amorous encounter, or in the joy of a proof, or at the beginning of a strike, or a revolt, and so on. You see things differently, and you know that what you are seeing differently is precisely the fact that there is this "differently" which is making you see differently.

In innovation, there is an interplay between insight and what is caught sight of. Basically, what can be called an "event" is broadly this phenomenon. An event is also the fact that, in innovation, an indiscernibility develops between insight and what is caught sight of. Except that Heidegger claims that this indiscernibility between insight and what is caught sight of was previously lost—i.e., the clearing of the open—and hasn't yet returned. It's no longer here, and it's not yet here. That's why everything is a question, everything is adrift in the question of whether, when, and how what is not yet here will come. At the end of his essay, everything disappears into the question. Heidegger ends up writing: "Does the insight into that which is take place?" (72), without the slightest possibility of an answer to the question. What's very striking is that this question is indistinguishable, in Heidegger's eyes, from the question of the advent of the God. Ultimately, the metaphor of insight as what is caught sight of is the metaphor of salvation and is also the metaphor of the God. Right before this, Heidegger indeed wonders "whether the God lives or remains dead" (72). And the latter question is only a completely messianic version of the question "Does the insight into that which is take place?" Those two questions are the same: the question of the advent of the turn. And this gives rise to another question:

> Do we dwell at home in nearness such that we inceptually belong in the fourfold of sky and earth, mortals and divinities? (73)

This is still and always the same question. The advent of insight that is the same thing as what is caught sight of; the question of whether Nietzsche's dead God can be alive; the question of whether we belong in the fourfold of sky and earth, mortals and divinities. Heidegger's analytic concludes with these three versions of the same question. I can only be opposed to such a conclusion. While I can allow—this is my theory of the becoming-subject of individuals—that the eventual figure of the construction of the present involves the interdependence of insight and what is caught sight of, I can nonetheless not agree that the question of this new insight is the question of its coming. The question of its coming is an open question. Will it happen? Won't it happen? It doesn't matter: we have to deal with what happens. What happens, happens. And in a certain sense, something always happens. So the problem isn't to get bogged down in the question of the coming, in the question of whether the God is here or is dead. Just as something always happens, so too we know, irremediably, that the God is dead. And, as a result, the only question is: Are we capable of accepting the new discipline imposed by what happens? Are we capable of abiding by the consequences, the logical newness of the consequences, of what happens? In other words, what are we faithful to in the realm of demonstration, contemplation, action, and love? For fidelity isn't some empty spirituality; it's the discipline of the consequences. What new subject, which is constructed through this discipline, do we accept to be part of? And to do so not in some elsewhere that has finally been found, nor under the sway of a dead God, but right here where we are, and yet also at a distance, a few steps away, in an immanent flight from this familiar place.

This, after all, is a question Hölderlin also asked.

Let's divvy up Hölderlin! Let's not leave him to Heidegger! Let me remind you of the line Heidegger thinks he can take inspiration from: "But where danger grows, so does that which saves." I'd like to oppose to it my own Hölderlin, which splits Heidegger's up.

Thus, in the fifth stanza of "Homecoming":

Yes, it's still the same. It thrives and ripens.
For nothing that lives and loves relinquishes loyalty.[7]

Or these two lines from "The Traveler" (a title that has also been translated as "The Wanderer"):

Loyal you were, and loyal remain to the fugitive even,
Kindly as ever you were, heaven of home, take me back.[8]

For me, that's a maxim: we can be sure that, in the place he left, many people will remain faithful, and grateful, to the person who embodies departure, the person who does not in fact want to just stick around where danger grows but is able to change location, to take off and wander (as Mao did during the Long March), knowing that this departure is only undertaken with a view to a homecoming whose welcome will be all the more faithful to the one who left in that he will bring back with him the means for a higher loyalty, for a fidelity that incorporates the separation. To leave so as to better experience that, upon his return, the fidelity of the people who have remained behind will go not to the one who stays in place, not to the one plagued by danger, but to the one who seeks out the elsewhere, the Other, yet who, in returning to the Same, bestows a superior identity upon it.

In "To Landauer":

But the heart finds rest in all of life's effort,
Makes from it holy remembrance.[9]

"Holy remembrance" is not a static meditation; it is the fidelity to what has truth value. And if you interpret fidelity as the ability of thought to abide by the consequences of what happens, you can see that, here, it's also: What counteracts pain? What counteracts suffering? Finally, in the form of a definite imperative, the imperative of the consequences, in the poem "Mnemosyne," which should be analyzed word for word:

... And always
There is a yearning that seeks the unbound. But much
Must be retained. And loyalty is needed.
Forward, however, and back we will
Not look. Be lulled and rocked as
On a swaying skiff of the sea.[10]

"A yearning that seeks the unbound"—that's already magnificent, isn't it? It's not the yearning, the desire, for what is firmly rooted, consistent, to return. Here, too, it's a desire for what does not yet hold together, for what has not yet found what binds it together. There is therefore much to be preserved, hence the need to be faithful. And the maxim of the present is to look neither forward nor backward, because the present is the movement of torsion by which the before is immanent in the after. Being faithful, in this case, doesn't mean calculating the future or the past. It means that we accept, in a disciplined way, to work for the power of the consequences. As Hegel said, we "surrender to the life of the object," like a skiff on the sea.[11] (That last bit is not Hegel's!) Such a surrender is a discipline. Such a surrender must find or discover its discipline as a life discipline.

So this Hölderlin, the Hölderlin of the maxim of the fidelity that can be counted on by the person who has taken off in the direction of a new thinking and returns, like Plato's escaped prisoner returning to the cave—well, this is the Hölderlin I would separate from Heidegger's prophetic Hölderlin. It's for good reason that one of the most important imperatives today is to be faithful, to those African workers, for example, who left their country in order to support it, and to whom we owe the existence of the nomadic global proletariat that carries the hope for any new politics, and hopes to carry it within themselves in such a way that when they return home, they'll be greeted as the true resourceful offspring of their country, those who make such a country deserving of being returned to.

Hölderlin is the brother of those workers, rather than a prophet of the return to the forgotten "clearing." And it is to that Hölderlin that we can be faithful, as to a skiff on the sea of circumstances.

We're going to say good-bye to each other for this year. We'll pick up again next year and conclude this long series of lectures on the present with the question that has obviously been raised by everything I've been discussing, which, I remind you, is: What does it mean to live?

Good-bye, everyone.

Year Three

flourish

What Does It Mean
to Live?

Session 1

October 22, 2003

W hat does it mean to live? One might wonder why this question, which can be regarded as at once exorbitant and timeworn, should be asked. It's exorbitant because who can presume to answer a question like this, a classic question, associated with speculative, or even theological or metaphysical, pretensions? And it's timeworn because from time immemorial it has been the question asked by philosophies, wisdoms, and religions. So we really need to begin with some reflections on the current context. Namely, why is the question "What does it mean to live?" one that can be asked today, and in what sufficiently new terms can it be asked so that it will be more than just the repetition of an exorbitant, timeworn question?

A first, still too empirical, answer is that this question is significant for three reasons today:

1. The first is the renewed importance assumed by the category of life in the contemporary philosophical and ideological context. We may need to go back to Nietzsche to see it reappear in all its force, and then to its insistence in Bergson. It can be found today in Deleuze, obviously, and in Foucault, Negri, and Agamben, as well as in the theorists of biopolitics, of biopower. It's clear that the concept itself of life as a central or organizing concept of thought is topical right now. Furthermore, the distinctive feature of this category of "life" is that it's simultaneously ontological and normative, that is to say, it connotes

both the essence of what is grasped in the figure of its actual becoming, or of its immanence, and a norm on the basis of which important (or at least apparently important) questions are asked, such as: What does it mean to live in accordance with the immanence of life? What does it mean to "reclaim one's life"? Or how can we "invent new forms of life"? "Life" is no longer just the term that refers to the intrinsic force of becoming(s) but also refers to the form of what is sought in life itself. Because of this essential feature—being both ontological and normative—the question "What does it really mean to live?" or "What is an authentic, or true, life?" can be answered by saying that a true life is a life that affirms life, a life that is based on the affirmative element of life itself. We will see how this issue is absolutely central and how it's this type of thinking that we will try to rid ourselves of.

2. The second reason is that, from a more directly "ethical" point of view, as it is fashionable to say today when someone wants to lecture us, we're living in an age of affirmation of the rights of life, of the rights of the living. It is blatantly obvious that even so-called human rights are actually, on closer inspection, subsumed by the rights of the living, the rights of life, the rights of living beings qua living. Hence the current extension, which is gaining ground, of human rights to animal rights, by way of children's rights, since man, just like the child, is a slightly more advanced animal (if that!). Here we find the element of division and internal unity of the question of life, both empirical and normative, in the following form: basically, the rights of the living means the right to live, the right to affirm their own lives. There is always this close juxtaposition of an element of ontological immediacy (living beings are those who live, those whose existence can rightly be called a life) and the fact of having, from within life itself, an unalienable right to live. As a result, contemporary ethics tends to be an ethics of the living, as evidenced by the fact that social debates revolve around what is called bioethics. Indeed, bioethics very precisely raises the question of the rights and laws applicable to the living.

3. The third reason is that, at least in our societies, a tacit denial of the horizon of death has been gradually emerging, as if the horizon of life were somehow life itself. This is an undeniable change from the periods in which life was essentially measurable by death. And in our societies,

which are societies of the maintenance of life, death hasn't been eliminated but rather relegated to insignificance. For death to mean something, it has to be minimally sensational. There have to at least be throats
cuts or serial killers to make death a spectacle. When that isn't the case,
death is utterly insignificant and is gradually relegated to the margins of
the world of social representations. Either it's a spectacle or it's a mere
line of nonsense. Which, retroactively, so to speak, makes it incumbent
upon life to be itself the horizon of life. So once again we find that sort
of immanent split that makes life simultaneously affirmative power and
the horizon of that power, since the being of what there is is the norm of
this being.

———— ✺ ————

This system of empirical reasons, situations, conjunctures, prompts us to
ask what this circulating¹and essential category is that life has become,
in both its most sophisticated elaborations—such as Deleuze's speculative elaborations—and the most highly publicized debates—such as the
debate about euthanasia, the right "to die with dignity," which means
the right to die alive.

I'd like to begin by expanding the system of these reasons, by creating
a category that would represent today's common, ordinary metaphysics.
"Ordinary" meaning a metaphysics everyone shares. A metaphysics that
is a system of general conceptions, which includes theses about what
there is, about what is, about what is becoming, but at the same time sets
out a worldview. I propose to call this common or ordinary metaphysics,
which is ubiquitous and shared by everyone, including by all of us, *democratic materialism*. What are the constitutive theses of what I am naming "democratic materialism"? And what will I oppose to it? I'm getting
ahead of myself here. I'm not going to oppose an aristocratic idealism to
it. That would be a bit simplistic. Nor am I going to venture to oppose
an aristocratic materialism to it. What I'm going to oppose to it is a
ghost, a specter, namely, dialectical materialism, which is making quite
a comeback; it's truly coming back from the dead. I'm going to resurrect
dialectical materialism. Naturally, it may not be quite recognizable, but

all the same, at least where its name is concerned, it will have ceased to be living only in limbo.

But, while waiting for this spectacular resurrection of good old "dia-mat," let's go back to democratic materialism.[2] The basic thesis of democratic materialism is that there are only bodies and languages. That's why it's really a metaphysics, because it's a thesis about what there is. So there are bodies, on the one hand, and languages, on the other, and, consequently, bodies seized to varying degrees by languages, it being understood that the question of what is meant by a body being seized by a language is the crux of the problem of democratic materialism, what it defines as its question. There are countless variants of this: the influence of images, the diversity of cultures, the question of whether there's such a thing as "women's writing" [écriture féminine], or whatever you like . . . Ultimately, it all boils down to this: what it means for bodies—what there is—to be seized by languages, languages in the plural, I must stress, and taken in a broad sense, therefore including all possible semiotics. So that's the basic thesis of democratic materialism. It also happens to be what we all actually think. There's some level of ourselves that can't help thinking that way. That's why I spoke of a common metaphysics, shared by everyone. There is necessarily some level of our immediate representation of things that thinks there are only bodies and languages. Whenever we start thinking that there are minds, for example, that there are souls, that there are Subjects, irreducible to speaking bodies, it always feels like a bit of a stretch. Whereas, from a spontaneous point of view, when we're simply contemporaries of ourselves, democratic materialism ("there are, and there are only, bodies and languages") is necessarily what we think. So our whole effort will be to think otherwise. But I wanted to point out that, as usual, we'll be starting from an initial figure that we all share.

The first negative thesis that can be deduced from this "there are only" is that there are no categories. This is a metaphysics without categories, unlike Aristotle's metaphysics, which is based, as you know, on categories. There are no categories that can formalize any kind of universality. "There are only bodies and languages" means that there are no categories of logical universalism transversal to bodies or to languages. And this is commonly expressed as: there is a plurality of cultures; there are cultural universes, which should be understood as meaning that there are bodies seized by different languages but no transversal categories by which this dissemination can be understood. Democratic materialism is therefore a metaphysics without categories, and that is indeed what it claims for itself. It is democratic not to have categories: a category is totalitarian because it purports to subsume all the different bodies and languages. It is absolutely imperative that there not be any categories.

Second, there is no truth, strictly speaking, either. From the formal or logical point of view, there are no categories, and, from the point of view of procedures or contents, there is no category of truth. "Truth," moreover, is the name of a category and, as such, it must also fade away. What I mean is that there is basically a relativism. You can move around among the many different bodies and languages, but you can't extract anything like a truth from them. At best, there are relevancies. What I call a relevancy is a certain type of temporary seizing of bodies by languages. Normatively, they are correspondences, consonances. Thus, there are points of consonance between certain bodies and certain languages. There are relevancies but not truth. Truth is not a relevancy precisely because truth isn't a correspondence between the proposition and the thing, an adequation of the intellect and the thing. As critical theory shows, truth is something completely different from a relevancy. In a way, in the democratic world, there are only relevancies. And so there is always the law of relevancies. It's a world that is essentially legalistic. Legalistic in a sense that is not necessarily that of the courts but legalistic because, if you don't ensure that a universal norm is recognized, you necessarily end up with the law of relevancies. It can be the law of communities, activities, or associations, but ultimately, it's always the law of a certain type of relevancy. That's the second negative feature.

Third, there is no eternity. You'll say, because you, like me and everyone else, are living under democratic materialism, "What a strange consideration! Eternity? What's that?" But it's actually a very important consideration, and we'll have occasion to come back to it. There is no eternity, meaning there is only time. There is only the time of relevancies. Relevancies create different temporalities that overlap, intertwine, multiply, and so on. So there's an overall system of temporalities, of relevancies, but there is no eternity, which means no separable forms. Indeed, the idea of eternity was given concrete expression and introduced by

Plato in the figure of the separability of the forms. And "eternity," to the extent that it means anything at all, always more or less means the separability of the forms. If the forms aren't separable, if they're inseparable, they remain the prisoners of relevancies, of bodies, since they are trapped in the temporalities specific to relevancies. If you want eternity, there has to be a minimum separability of the forms. That was Plato's basic intuition, and he was right. This doesn't mean that there's an intelligible world or whatever, but if it's eternity you're after, then there has to be a minimum separability of the forms. You can, of course, get along without it, and, ultimately, democratic materialism gets along very well without it. For democratic materialism, there's the relevancy of the forms; there is neither any separability of them nor any eternity.

Incidentally, once you dispense with eternity, you end up only taking the present day into account. It's important to understand that eternity is a structure of time itself and not the Other of time. The immortality of the soul, perhaps, is the Other of time. Eternity, as such, is not the Other of time. It's a certain vision of time, specifically the one that combines the existence of time with a minimum separability of the forms. The introduction to the theory of eternity is when a certain separability of the forms is created within time itself. To represent this separability, there's something like the concept of eternity or what Descartes called "the eternal truths." What's meant by the eternal truths isn't the mystique of the afterlife of the soul or God's perfect goodness. Rather, what it means is that there's an infinite number of prime numbers, for example. That's an eternal truth. And, naturally, it appeared in time, i.e., when the Greek mathematicians proved it. Something like a separability of the forms was created, since this axiom was in no way related to the relevancy in which it was constituted. It was, to be sure, Greek mathematicians, in a specific historical context, who produced, with specific words and in the Greek language, the proof of this. So it was clearly connected to a relevancy, but it was, to some extent, separable from it. That's what eternity means. And you can clearly see that if you don't have that at all, then time will gradually contract, because eternity is what keeps it open. A time that is not open is a succession, a time in which the moments are successive. What makes us contemporaries of the Greeks and makes the long time separating us from them internal to our own time is the fact that we can relate to eternity and that our rational relationship to the Greeks is actually based on what is eternal. A Greek conceived and proved the idea that the series of prime numbers was infinite. We can conceive it in the exact same way he did. We can reproduce his proof because we understand it thoroughly. There's no shortage of examples. If we understand something about the democratic nature of the Greeks' politics or about a tragedy by Aeschylus, it's for the same reason. Ultimately, it's always because there is a certain separability of the forms that we have access to a time vaster than our own. Without a separability of the forms, everything tends to converge toward the pure "now." Last year, I already showed that there is only a real present if there is a temporal arc that crystallizes in that present. If all you have is the present, you have a pure "now" that is, in the final analysis, a dissolution of time itself. The denial of eternity is therefore the real basis of what we are witnessing, namely that people today tend to live for the enjoyment of the moment. Contemporary hedonism is commonplace: "If I have a great weekend, that's already pretty good!" Sure, why not?! Ultimately, that's part of democratic materialism. But my thesis is that there is eternity, and a separability of the forms. And that, without that, time can no longer be kept in its true space. It's as though the rubber band stretching it out had snapped: it will fold back up, like an accordion fading away on the note it's playing. Eternity is time's rubber band.

So those are the three basic features of democratic materialism. Once you accept that there are only bodies and languages, there are no categories; you're dealing with relativism, and there are no truths; and since there are only relevancies, there is no eternity, which, to my mind, means there's no time either.

You'll say, "But what does life have to do with it? What does it mean to live?" I'm getting to that.

My first comment is: "There are only bodies" actually means that there are bodies of enjoyment and suffering bodies. There are only two essential types of states, bodies of enjoyment, on the one hand, and suffering bodies, on the other. That's the whole basis of what's called ethics, which amounts to saying that a body of enjoyment is better than a suffering body. And suffering bodies are a nuisance; the fewer there are, the better. Why not, after all? . . . But it may not be true.

There tend to be only two kinds of languages, too: authoritarian language and contractual language. So you've got a rather elementary combinatorics: on the one hand, bodies of enjoyment and suffering bodies, with the intermediate degrees between them, including the neutral body that's neither one nor the other, and, on the other hand, tyrannical, prescriptive, authoritarian languages and contractual languages, the languages of negotiation. So you combine all of this, and you see that an authoritarian language produces a suffering body and that only contractual language is appropriate for the body of enjoyment. I'll let you put this contemporary confection together yourselves; it's one that we put together every day anyway and find in the press. But the point that interests me about this is how this multiplicity of bodies and languages gains access to thought. We'll allow, at least for the time being, that democratic materialism is a form of thought. But if that's so, how do we gain access to bodies and languages otherwise than because that's what there is? Here's where the question becomes interesting and complex: bodies can only be grasped as becoming, and the same goes for languages. Why? Because if bodies and languages could be grasped otherwise than through their actual becoming, it would mean that there are categories and not just relevancies. Indeed, if there's a possibility of a formal theory of bodies or of what a body can do, as Spinoza would say (you know that Spinoza once said, "We don't even know what a body can do," and our contemporaries adore that sentence, just as they adore anything resembling one of the typical passions of democratic materialism, ignorance), so if there are only bodies, that means there are things we don't know. Yet if we knew what a body could do, if we had a comprehensive formal thinking of what a body is, then, rather than democratic materialism, there would be a restoration of certain categories. For example, there would be categories adequate to the complete thinking of what a body is. As a result, we would not be dealing with democratic materialism but with a metaphysics of bodies. You can maintain the "there are only bodies" in the context of the absence of categories only if you link the body to its relevancy, if it is grasped in its unique temporality. Or, as we'd put it today, if it is apprehended immanently. And from this you can see that there is actually only the becoming of bodies. Becoming, reparation, and so on. The thinking of "there are bodies" is the thinking of temporal becoming, the thinking of bodily singularities, not the thinking of the category of bodies. But what is a body conceived of as becoming? It's a living body. That's ultimately why the experience of the singular life of bodies, rather than a rational knowledge of bodies, can be directly inferred from "there are only bodies."

The exact same thing will be true of languages—languages, cultures, images, or what have you. Languages can't be subsumed by formal, linguistic, semiotic, or metaphysical categories. They must always be grasped in immanence, in the singularity of their effectuation. This means that, here too, properly speaking, languages are life, and this is generally called their genealogy. But when it comes to cultural formations, languages, ideological dispositions, the fact that you can only approach them genealogically (as was demonstrated and affirmed by Nietzsche and Foucault) means that, as regards languages, too, access to thought is through the figure of becomings.

It follows that, in thought—that is, ultimately as genuine philosophy—the thesis that there are only bodies and languages becomes: there are life and genealogy, something Nietzsche immediately understood. For him, languages were morality, and he developed a genealogy of morality as the relevance of languages. And if you're dealing with the ontology of the forms of existence, it's a question of life. That's what we're dealing with. In the final analysis, democratic materialism is necessarily realized as the genealogical philosophy of life, meaning the philosophy of the becoming of bodies marked by languages. So it's perfectly logical to say that if you accept the "there are only bodies and languages," you also have to accept that the figure of philosophy or of thought will ultimately revolve around the question of life, of which the question of genealogy is but one variant. As Nietzsche perfectly established, and as Foucault further developed it, genealogical thought, or genealogical philosophy, is what could be called vitalist historicism. Understanding bodies and languages in terms of their evolution and history amounts to a history that is ultimately the history of life. Vitalist historicism is actually the philosophy adequate to democratic materialism, i.e., to the belief that the best we can hope for is a body of enjoyment adequate to contractual languages. That's the current ideal. And to uphold this ideal, the speculative investigation, the metaphysics, will be a genealogical metaphysics of life.

So we can understand why democratic materialism (which includes Foucault and a good deal of Deleuze) can only answer the question "What does it mean to live?" by affirming a philosophy of life that—as I remarked last year—is simultaneously ontological and normative. To live will therefore mean to affirm the creative power of life, that is, to develop what a body can do, and to develop what a body can do requires that the languages marking this body not be hindrances to what it can do. Thus, "What does it mean to live?" will come down to affirming life under conditions of language adequate to such an affirmation. We situate ourselves in a context of creation, of change, in which we will always find the norm, i.e., a body of enjoyment (if we call "a body of enjoyment" a body adequate to what it can do, using everything it can) compatible with a language, which cannot, must not, be an authoritarian crushing of what a body can do. So we'll be dealing with a contractual language, which gives the body permission to explore what it can do. This is, moreover, what we all ask of languages: to be such that they allow us to explore what we can do. Otherwise, we cry censorship. That's what's called freedom. In short, the philosophy of life could be said to be a philosophy of the free life. But "freedom" here takes on a very precise, new meaning: freedom is a question of relationship of bodies to languages. You can see that this is a standard, dominant answer, which we all more or less share, to the question "What does it mean to live?," namely, the answer: To live one's life, languages must not interfere with the exploration of bodies' possibilities.

That said, I am of course going to give you a few elements of strategy for this year's seminar, for what I'm going to attempt to argue or try out before you. I won't just argue, as a critical philosopher would, that it's not true that there are only bodies and languages. If I were to take that approach, I'd be done in no time, and you'd be left unsatisfied. Therefore, I will also argue the affirmative counterpart of the negative theses, namely that there are categories, truths, and eternity. All three. I will argue this in the form of a conflict between democratic materialism and the ghost come back from the dead that I mentioned a moment ago, dialectical materialism, which I'll rename "the materialist dialectic," to give it a new vibe. A seemingly very simple definition of the materialist dialectic can be given—there is the Three—whereas when I say that there are bodies and languages, we're still dealing with the Two. So what's involved is a dialectical endeavor insofar as I will attempt to argue that there is the Three.

By the way, I'd like to point out a historical, genealogical element (we should also use our own genealogies to combat the opposing genealogies). At the beginning of Descartes's treatise *The Passions of the Soul*, there's an absolutely remarkable passage that seemed enigmatic to me for quite a while, until democratic materialism, as it happens, cleared it up. In this passage, he says that there are three things. This is very striking because Descartes in exemplary fashion is known as a dualist. Yet he says that there's the soul, there's the body, and there are truths. He of course doesn't go into detail about this, but the three things are there. So we vaguely understand that truths are not, strictly speaking, either of the body or of the soul. What's more, when Spinoza took up this issue again, he had to say, in maintaining that thought and extension are parallel orders, that a truth is of both the body and the soul, because an adequate Idea applies to both. Descartes couldn't be a parallelist, but, as a result, truth could involve the body without being *of* the body; it could be a spiritual reality without being of the soul, strictly speaking. So, in post-Cartesian fashion, I'd say something like this: it's true that there are bodies and languages—that's contemporary materialism—but there's also something else. Something else that could perhaps be called "truth," "subject," or some such thing. Later on, we'll see the problem of names, which can't be resolved prematurely. But at any rate, I'll maintain that there can be something else, that we aren't condemned to the Two even though the Two—I'll admit as much—in a way represents the current state of affairs. After all, the statement "there are only bodies and languages" is, in a sense, obvious for modern materialist thought: it's the current state of affairs. I'll attempt to show that we're not condemned to the current state of affairs, that there may be something other than the way things are.

Today, I'd just like to introduce the way we're going to approach this counterposition to democratic materialism, or this reinstatement of dialectical materialism. My remarks will obviously be guided by the question "What does it mean to live?" because you can see that if there is the Three, the question can't be answered in the same way as if there were only the Two. In the latter case, the question could be answered simply by saying that we are really living when the two are working together. Broadly speaking, the true life is when the languages are more or less adequate to what a body can do and don't impede, hamper, harm, or cripple the creative capacity of bodies, which is to invent forms of life. In other words, when that capacity is not severely impaired by the languages. When there's the Two, we're always dealing with a norm of compatibility, and the languages are asked to be contractual, meaning compatible with the possibility of a body of enjoyment. But when there's the Three, the norm can no longer be one of harmony. And yet the contemporary world talks about nothing but harmony, as, for example: "Let's get in tune with ourselves, let's feel good about ourselves," and so on. And everything should be OK, our bodies should be well nourished, entertained, not too bothered by what's going on in the world outside, etc. And so, with a more or less contractual language and bodies that are more or less free to enjoy as they please, things can be fine. However, it's obvious that if we're dealing with three terms, if there might be something other than the law of things, which consists in effect of bodies and languages, the norm can't be the same. The answer to our question can't be the same. So there will be a complex interplay among the precise formulation of the question, the answer to the question, and ultimately the determination of what it means to live. Owing to the variability of the question, the question of living itself will be altered and modified.

⸙

I'm going to give you a quick, thematic introduction, using a number of somewhat scattered references. They'll allow us to examine all aspects of the problem of the move from the Two to the Three, of the transformation of the question "What does it mean to live?"

The first reference, as regards life, is what I believe is a real conflict between two of Aristotle's statements. When it comes to life, Aristotle is right there: he's the big philosophical ghost who claims to speak about life. He's nothing like Plato, for whom, as we'll see in a moment, life is not really a problem. But Aristotle is extremely interested in living forms, life forms, in what an animal is. And so there are two statements by Aristotle that are very well known but that, as is immediately clear, are problematic in terms of the question we are dealing with. The first statement is: "Man is a political animal." It's ζωον πολιτικον, that is, strictly speaking, man is a political being. Man as an animal, as a ζωον, that is, as a living organism, in his singular life, is political. Here we could say: this conveys an answer to our question. A very Greek answer. To live is to engage in politics, in the Greek sense, which is to say, to participate constructively in civic affairs. To live is to find one's true harmony in the most important context, which is the *polis*. This doesn't just mean that man is a being who engages in politics. It means that the essence of his singular life, and what actually distinguishes him from the other animals, is precisely the fact that he engages in politics, that he is involved in politics, that he lives in the *polis*. You might think this answer is consistent with democratic materialism because it's a pragmatic answer: what life really is, is the capacity to be involved in a harmonious way in civic affairs. But for that to happen, civic affairs have to allow it. That is, allow one to have an appropriate language. And Aristotle's *Politics* is precisely the search for an appropriate language, adequate to the political essence of the human animal. What the human body can do is politics, and what is needed is for the language of politics to be adequate to that purpose.

In another, completely different statement, however, Aristotle says that we must, as far as possible, live as immortals.[3] This strikes a different note: here, man is no longer a political animal. Because if there's one thing the immortals couldn't care less about, it's politics. To live as immortals essentially means to live under a certain regime of essential immobility. As you know, Aristotle's God is the primary unmoved mover. He moves all things, but he moves them in the dimension of his essential immobility. To live as immortals is to acquire this divine power of immobility, while to be concerned with civic affairs is to be involved in business, it's not at all to be immobile. It is, on the contrary, to worry constantly about the business running smoothly. The immortals are certainly not democratic; they are in the figure of their essential ontological immobility and their self-normativity. Ultimately, for Aristotle, to live as immortals is to attain, so far as possible, attributes of life that are not, in fact, those of life, because immortality isn't an attribute of life, of animal life, of biological life, and, according to Aristotle's categories, life properly speaking is generation and corruption. To live as immortals therefore means to live in an element that is more than life. As you can see, there's a very significant conflict between the two maxims. The first one is the democratic maxim, "Let's dutifully take care of business and civic affairs; let's keep things running smoothly," whereas the second one is in a much greater state of tension. In the first one, there is an underlying duality, the duality of animality, on the one hand, and the conventions of politics, on the other. So you can clearly recognize in the first maxim what I was just talking about, namely the ζωον, the reference to life—when you separate it, it becomes βίος—there's the living-being aspect and the language aspect. Whereas in the second maxim there's a third term, covered here by the concept of "immortal." The immortal is neither a living being nor a language. What is it? That's the whole problem. Aristotle says it's a principle. So to live as an immortal could be expressed as: to live as a principle. As a prince . . . This is not democratic materialism at all; it's something else.

It might be said that this is the origin of the question, its genealogy, namely that we realize right from Aristotle that the answer to the question "What does it mean to live?" is not easy. Because you first have to decide whether there are two terms or three. In the first answer, there are two, life and language, and in the second, without it being really clarified, there are three: the first two are still there, but there is the paradigm of the immortal, i.e., the principle. And no principle—this is what Aristotle's statement means—can be reduced to a combination of life and language. That's the basic thesis. And ultimately, I'm not going to say much more about it. Broadly speaking, if there is something like principles, then something is not reducible to a combination of life and language. Conversely, if everything is reducible to a combination of life and language, well, there's no principle then. I'd say that this is clearly the contemporary maxim: there are no principles. The great imperative is "Live without any principles, as far as possible," or, in other words,

"As far as possible, *don't live as an immortal.*" You can see how interesting this first reference is. Indeed, it's very clear that, already in Aristotle, who, on closer inspection, is actually a devious, complex character, there are two fundamentally different approaches to the question, because the ontological assumptions aren't the same. Just as Descartes says there is a soul, there are bodies, and then there are truths, without going into detail about it, so, too, Aristotle tells us there is life, there are social conventions, and then there are principles, or maybe *the* principle.

My second reference, which is of necessity a complement to the first, is a reference to Plato, a Platonic origin of the question. However, as I told you, the category of life is not one of Plato's immediate categories. Plato is not a biologist or a physiologist, shall we say, as Aristotle obviously is. He's not primarily interested in the animal dimension of man. Yet two significantly different guiding principles or maxims can also be found in Plato's work. First, the question of life is so unimportant to Plato that, for him, the essence of life is to prepare oneself for death. That's what you find in *The Apology of Socrates*, the *Phaedo*, and the *Phaedrus*. Plato will not hesitate to compare life, in the sense of immediate life, to a tomb, while he'll present death as true liberation. You know the tremendous success of that way of thinking. So we could say that Plato's philosophy is first and foremost the opposite of a philosophy of life, since the principle, the idea, assumes that we free ourselves from life itself. Plato is a thinker of the separability of the forms, and, as such, he may say: "The sooner they're separated the better. Let's get to the separability and stop engaging in that kind of trapping of the form in the immediacy of life, which means that, in a certain way, the form is imprisoned in life." It's very important to understand that Plato has a conception of life that is in no way a creative one: life itself is an alienation of the form. There's something like a desire to reach the moment of separability of the form, ultimately in death, which frees the form from the constraints of both the body and language. We're dealing here with an anti-vitalist and anti-historicist position. By contrast, if you take the *Timaeus* and its cosmology of the theory of the world, you'll find something very different: a tribute to the world's vitality as such, a tribute to what Plato will call "the visible living being," i.e., the cosmos, the world in its singularity, hence life as genuine life, as cosmic life, as the life of the world's materiality. And far from saying that it's a prison or alienation, at the end of the *Timaeus*—reread that beautiful, enigmatic ending—Plato offers a lavish, almost lyrical, tribute to the beauty of the world, precisely because the world is a living being. His tribute is delivered in honor of the life of the world because, as Plato will tell us, the world is a visible living being created in the image of the intelligible living being, and the fact that it is a visible living being contributes to its majesty and splendor. So here, too, there is a big conflict with respect to the question of life. On the one hand, life is how the alienation of the form, the nonseparation of the form, is accomplished, and, in this sense, speculative emancipation is death itself. But, on the other hand, life is also the reason why the world is worthy of the intelligible, inasmuch as the visible living being is a true copy, a noble and ultimately glorious copy, of the intelligible. And, last but not least, life is that which, in the real world this time, testifies to the power of the forms. This is really a major divergence.

All of the foregoing will provide two answers to the question "What does it mean to live?," two answers that have met with great success throughout history. As far as the first one is concerned, and it's an answer that's ubiquitous in our culture, to live is to die, that is to say, the moment of truth of life is death. The moment when what life is capable of is revealed is beyond life itself, in death. Indeed, dying isn't enough: to live is above all to die *well*, to die properly, that is, in such a way that this death expresses the truth of the life. The death of Socrates is the paradigm of what it means to die well. Dying well is the moment when a truth of the life, of a separation of the form, is distilled, regardless of whether the form is called the "soul" or is given other names. As for the second of Plato's answers, to live is ultimately to be adequate to the world, to be adequate to the power of life in the world, that is, to be a meaningful part of the living cosmos. This answer, too, has met with tremendous success. Being in the right place, playing the right role in the scheme of the living cosmos—that's what will make us worthy of the intelligible power of our cosmos.

Incidentally, this is what has always put the churches in an awkward position. What do the churches tell us? First, that we must prepare ourselves for death. That's their stock-in-trade: the true life only comes afterward. But at the same time, they have constantly said that to live well is also to remain in one's proper place in the world, to occupy in a faithful, uncomplaining, and dignified manner the place assigned to you in the cosmos, which is willed by God, after all. The idea of having created the world is very odd, but if we go along with it, we're obliged to think that God had his reasons, and so he also has his reasons for putting us in the place we're in. Accordingly, we must not only prepare ourselves for death but also stay in our place. The churches have always combined both of Plato's answers. They've made a spiritual specialty of preparing for death and a temporal specialty, so to speak, of occupying in a faithful, dignified manner the place you were put in: be a good citizen, a good father, and so on. What that has to do with preparing for death, as the truth of the separability of the forms, is not clear. It's true that Plato says both things. He says both, and that already gives us a glimpse of the extreme complexity of the concept of life, because "life" is always taken in two senses.

Aristotle and Plato are, in this respect, the founders of this duality. In a first sense, "life" is just sensible effectivity, what there is insofar as it becomes, and it's hard to see how that's compatible with the separability of the forms. But in a second sense, life is the intelligible power of what there is. The fact that it's a living being is how what there is asserts itself as something other than its pure "there is," as more than what it is, as a power that's beyond the simple effectivity of being there. In Plato's eyes, the fact that the cosmos is a living being and that, even though sensible, it is worthy of the intelligible, is what constitutes its life, what makes it a power rather than a lifeless machine. So life will always be simultaneously a state and a power. And the philosophies combine, in varying proportions, the dimension of life as creation, as power—which is basically how it affirms the form—and life as blind becoming, the continuation of what there is, the stubborn determination to go on living—by which it unsettles the stability of the form.

We'll come back to this, but we could see the same thing if we compared Hegel and Nietzsche regarding this question of life. Let me just briefly say a few words about this. Hegel says that the true life is not the life that shrinks from death but rather the life that maintains itself even in death. He calls this "the life of Spirit." It doesn't shrink in terror from death but faces up to it. The key question of life for him is ultimately the confrontation with death, and the entry point into the question of the true life is the question of death. Not that death is emancipation from life, as in a certain Platonism, but because life is only attested if it faces up to death. It is the concept of life itself only if it faces death rather than shrinking from it. Hegel would surely have thought that *we* are not living the true life because we don't face death. We think life is the purpose of life, that life can face itself, that it can deal with itself alone. Hegel would probably answer the question "What does it mean to live?" by saying that to live, in the final analysis, is to face death, but to face it truly, not just as the outside or the negation of life. No, to face it as that in which the power of life maintains itself even in this confrontation.

Take Nietzsche now. As I said a little while ago, Nietzsche is the prophet of all this. He made the question "What does it mean to live?" a central question of his whole philosophy. There's an absolutely fundamental statement of Nietzsche's to the effect that "the value of life cannot be assessed."[4] Nietzsche's key point is that life creates values, but, considered in itself, its value is unassessable. Therefore, life is not what has value. Life is the measure of all value but cannot be the measure of itself. Something that creates values has no value of its own. And so to our question, the only thing you can answer is: to live is to create. It's impossible to answer: to live is to live, or to live is to go on living, because that is tantamount to acting as if life's value were assessable, as if life had value in itself. But life has no value in itself; it creates all value. So to live is to create values, or (and this is the same thing) to destroy existing values, to go beyond existing values, to transvaluate values, and so on. And you can see that here, too, the question is extremely complex. For one thing, life is inextricably bound up with the question of values since it is the basis on which we understand that there are values. Why there's good and evil, why we can go beyond good and evil, why we can transvaluate values: it's life that enables us to understand all this. Values are not transcendent to life. That's a Nietzschean, anti-Christian, and basic anti-philosophical theme. No value surpasses life, with the result that life is the space of creation of all values. This is the first aspect of things, but the second aspect is that life itself cannot be assessed and that affirmative life is the creation of something other than life. So in Nietzsche's system, there will be a certain ambiguity about the word "life." In one way, it is wholly connected to the question of values, since life's creative capacity can only be measured by the values it creates. But life is also utterly indifferent to the question of values because life itself cannot be assessed. So you see how there's this problematic amphibology. In a certain sense, there's a complete connection between life and values, but in another sense, there's a complete disconnection between them. In the end, it's clear that, just as in Hegel, the true life is connected to death, but only if it faces it head-on, if it traverses it, if it is not reducible to it, so, too, in Nietzsche's case, life is at once connected to values and indifferent to any and all values. It is, if you will, the absolute neutral of values, at the same time as it is the space of creation of all values.

Let's sum all this up. These will all be entry points, or possible variations, or answers to the question "What does it mean to live?"

For Aristotle, the problem is practices. What are the practices through which ideas like "political animal," "creative animal," or, on the contrary, "immortal" can be formulated?

For Plato, the problem is transcendence. Is it possible to answer the question without in any way introducing an element of transcendence?

For Hegel, the problem is death. Is it really possible to conceive of the value of life without expressly introducing the figure of death?

For Nietzsche, the problem is values. Is it possible to answer the question without regarding life as the space of creation of values or assessments?

I'd now like to turn to the poets. Why the poets? Because the question of life is fundamental to poetry. I would say that poetry, in its own intensity, is always a proposition concerning the question "What does it mean to live?" It's a proposition in language concerning this question. That's why poetry matters to us, not because it's pretty or it sounds nice. It matters to us because what is called the beauty of the poem actually stems from the fact that it displaces a question in language, that it arranges it differently. This question can't be approached from a strictly speculative point of view for the reasons I mentioned at the beginning, namely because the category of life itself is a category of the immediate, of experience. And so the displacement of the question in language is of vital interest to us. It's particularly striking in poetry. Poetry wouldn't exist, and this is the case right from its beginnings, if it weren't the vector, in language, of a displacement of the question "What does it mean to live?" and of the propositions or answers to this question.

As far as this question is concerned, I will take a trio of poets from the end of the nineteenth century—Rimbaud, Mallarmé, and Valéry—because, as we'll see, they have a very interesting feature in common. As regards Rimbaud, you know the phrase—it's been repeated many times over—"the true life is absent." Just note in passing that he doesn't say "life is absent," which would be practically meaningless. Our question "What does it mean to live?" becomes, in his formulation, "What does it mean to live a true life?" But how can the true life be absent? What would such an eventuality mean? Well, it implies that there's a life that is *not* true, that the life that's present isn't the true life. So there's the idea that a life that isn't true takes the place of the true life. If there weren't a false life, a fake life, that takes the place of the true one, we wouldn't know, we couldn't know, that the true life is absent. And so the very complicated, and very intrinsically poetic, idea is that there's a place of life, that life is not just a matter of living. When Rimbaud speaks of the true life, he means something that has a place. Now, if something doesn't have a place, you can't know whether it's absent or present. Linguistically speaking, in order for something to be absent or present it has to have a place on the basis of which you can say that it's either absent or present. To say "the true life is absent" suggests that life has a place and that, rather than a true life, there's a false life in that place. This is the question of the location of life. The question "What does it mean to live?" also brings with it a certain thesis about the place of life, about the place of living. Only if we ask where life is can we say whether it's absent or present. And we'll see that this is a very important question. Indeed, life isn't something vague and unlocalized. It's not a hazy category. It has places, places of life . . .

This question runs through the other two references that I chose to consider. Take the second quatrain of Mallarmé's poem about the swan:

A swan of old remembers it is he
superb but strives to break free woebegone
for having left unsung the territory
to live when sterile winter's tedium shone.[5]

So it's the same thing here. There is "a territory to live"; you don't live just anywhere. And the swan's sin, its guilt, which may be a complicated metaphor for the poet, is not to have sung the territory to live. He was unable to identify the place to live.

And now for my last citation, a very well known line of Valéry's from the end of "Le Cimetière marin": "The wind is rising! We must try to live."[6] Earlier in the poem, Valéry had said: "Life is vast, being drunk on absence."[7] He had Rimbaud in mind, of course. As you can see, through these two lines we find, in poetic form, that constitutive ambiguity of the word "life," because the first life in question is in a way an immobile life, a life without a place, the life that is in fact absent, whose essence is absence. So there's a first meaning of the word "life," which is actually the being of what is, with its absence of meaning, movement, and purpose. It is life, blind life, life as blind becoming, absence of significance. And the rising wind is obviously the true life, the one we must try to live. The poem will serve as the connection between two meanings of the word "life." Life is first what continues to be in absence, but it is also the opposite: what we can "try," which is a possibility. Once you think about life as a place, once you think it has a location, you create a life as possibility, a life that can be tried or tried out. And this may be poetry's most profound lesson: life as true possibility, life as something worth trying, means that we have identified its place, that we know where living is located, and that, as opposed to the swan, we are able to sing "the territory to live."

The question "What does it mean to live?" imposes a twofold task on us. We need to begin by wresting life away from its absence, from its status of indifference, from its blindness, from its absence of place. "Life is vast," of course, but the life that is vast is the life that is "drunk

320 What Does It Mean to Live?

on absence." It is from that absence, from that blind becoming, from the tremendous power of inorganic life, as Deleuze used to say, that we must wrest life away so as to answer the question "What does it mean to live truly?" We must assign a place, a location, to life, where its intensity can be measured. The first step, the first task, is to locate life. Once life has been located, you'll be able to know what its presence is; you'll be able to try it. That will be the second step. As is clear, the question "What does it mean to live?" is engaged in a double struggle. A struggle with absence in general, or, in other words, with life in the sense of its impersonal blindness. That's the first conflict, the one that has to do with the question of the creation of a place, because life is not everywhere. When you think life is everywhere—and that's to some extent what democratic materialism thinks—all you find is a life drunk on absence. Once the place has been created, the second step will be to establish life as possibility, not as impersonal possibility but as possibility in its place.

Using these two steps and their interrelationship, I'll attempt to shed some light this year on the only really important question in philosophy: the question of the true life.

Thank you.

Session 2

November 27, 2003

I had begun to consider the question "What does it mean to live?", and I was trying to find an approach to this question. Of course, it may be the oldest question in philosophy, one that used to be called "the wisdom question." But it's also a question that constantly returns as a question in the present, a question that must construct its own present. That's why it has persisted. It has the ability to traverse the various figures of the present to ask once again, in the intensity of this very present, "What does it mean to live?" and "What is a true life?"

Let me give you two very brief summaries of what I started to say last time.

First of all, as regards the general framework, or, to use an old term, the ideological framework, we'll situate the inquiry in the opposition I proposed to set up between democratic materialism, considered as the dominant disposition of our present, and what I suggested we rename (because it's really a semantic resurrection) "dialectical materialism," or rather "the materialist dialectic." In the context of democratic materialism, there is a precise answer to the question "What does it mean to live?," namely, to live a good life is to ensure that the enjoyment of bodies isn't hampered by authoritarian languages. Our aim is to consider whether a different answer can be formulated and is feasible. We're in a situation that's very typical for philosophers: there's an answer to their question in prevailing opinion, and they attempt a sort of breakthrough or access to a different type of answer, which would fit into a different framework, into a different figure of materialism, for example, which I've called "dialectical materialism."

Note, incidentally, that I'm situating the question not, as is usually done, between materialism and idealism but between two possible figures of materialism itself. I'm saying this because, here, in the Dussane Auditorium of the École Normale Supérieure, Louis Althusser often argued that the materialism/idealism opposition was the fundamental invariant of the history of philosophy. In Althusser's view, the history of philosophy, as regards the successive issues imposed by the circumstances, is always in the final analysis an organic struggle between idealism and materialism. There are naturally a few difficulties, but there's this basic idea. I'd just like to point out that, for me, it's not a question of the opposition between materialism and idealism. At any rate, those terms don't seem appropriate to me. I think that the split within materialism itself is more important today than the opposition between materialism and idealism.

Let me remind you very briefly that the opposition between democratic materialism and dialectical materialism is expressed in two propositions. The key proposition of democratic materialism is that there are only bodies and languages. That will be its basic principle, whereas the basic principle of dialectical materialism will be that there are only bodies and languages, except that there are truths. We'll gradually see what the exact meaning of this is, once we're able to answer a number of difficult questions about the opposition between these two axioms. But you can see that, all in all, when reduced to its bare bones, it's a struggle pitting the Two (bodies and languages) against the Three (bodies and languages, except that there are also truths), it being understood that everything then depends on what is meant by this third term, this "except that," placed in exception. This placement in exception is crucial. Truths are not simply added to bodies and languages; there's the recognition, as a supplement, of an exception.

But what does the question of life have to do with this? Well, the point that we'll gradually see is that the meaning of life literally changes—or more precisely, that the meaning of the word "life," in the general system of its connotations, changes—when you move from democratic materialism to the materialist dialectic. To put it simply, democratic materialism regards life from the standpoint of the finitude of bodies prey to languages. Thus, life unfolds, with its various meanings, as though seized by languages, or by one language, as the case may be. "What does it mean to live?" becomes the question of how this vital unfolding of the finitude of bodies prey to languages can be regulated, that is, under what conditions we can recognize that this unfolding is acceptable, or unacceptable, inauthentic, and so on. By contrast, in the context of dialectical materialism, it is under the proposition "there are only bodies and languages, except that there are truths" that life unfolds as a subject's infinite capacity, a capacity developed in the field of consequences of an event. We're no longer dealing with the finitude of the activity of sensory bodies as marked or instrumentalized by languages but with the shift to an infinite capacity made possible by an event.

Clearly, the basic dispute will be about the problem of bodies. And our most difficult task will probably be to show that what pits the two maxims against each other is ultimately the problem of the body itself: "body" cannot have the same meaning under the first maxim as it does under the second. So we'll have to get into what can be called a physics, in the speculative sense of the term, with the question "What is a body?" For it is really from the difference between the answers to this question that the difference between the answers to the question "What does it mean to live?" ultimately results or develops. This is easy to understand, given that if the answer to the question "What is a body?" is itself heterogeneous, the answer to the question "What does to live mean for this body, or these bodies?" will also undergo a very significant change.

So that was a summary of the general framework. Now I'm going to propose a new approach to the question "What does it mean to live?" by listing seven problems, which also happen to be seven categories that I implicitly touched on last time in an unsystematic way and that I'll now sum up in list form. They are seven possibilities contained in the question "What does it mean to live?"

1. Practices, or, if you will, "forms of life," a phrase that's very popular today
2. Immanence and/or transcendence: this is ultimately about the immanent nature of the power of life as such

3. The body
4. Death
5. Art or values
6. What might be called givenness
7. Affirmation, or, in other words, what allows us to give a completely affirmative answer to the question "What does it mean to live?"

I'll explain these seven possibilities—all of which we'll examine—with a few quick references. I already provided the references for some of them last time.

1. As regards practices or forms of life, I mentioned the opposition between two of Aristotle's statements. Let me remind you of these two statements, both of which are very famous, although located in very difference places in his work. The first is "Man is a political being [or animal]." And the second is "We must try to live as immortals." Naturally, I immediately pointed out the conflict between these two statements regarding the question of life. It had to do with the form of life, with the practice. Is man, in order to live, destined for civic affairs, as a political animal or being? Or should he aim, beyond civic affairs, at the status of a soul, which is a status similar to that of an immobile god, because to live as an immortal is to live in the blissful immobility of the gods?

2. As regards immanence and transcendence, I used the example of the opposition between two of Plato's statements. First: "The body is a tomb." In Greek, this is a play on words between σωμα ("body") and σημα ("tomb"). This statement leads to all the well-known reflections on the fact that to live well is to prepare oneself for death, on the true life that is beyond life, etc., and therefore on something that immediately evokes a transcendence, a meaning of life situated beyond the immediacy of life and beyond the body in particular. The second statement is: "The cosmos, the universe, is a perfection." And indeed a living perfection. So it is anything but a material prison that needs to be escaped from. On the contrary, it is the epitome of the possible perfection of the visible world, and, as Plato tells us, this perfection is a living one. Here, too, we're at

a crossroads, as it were, since one of the answers to the question "What does it mean to live?" is that to live is to prepare oneself for the hereafter, while the other is that to live is to become, as far as possible, part of the living perfection of the cosmos.

3.   As regards the body, Saint Paul's distinction between the way of the flesh and the way of the spirit could be mentioned. This answer gives two meanings to the body. In my opinion, it's a misinterpretation to think that the opposition proposed by Saint Paul is the opposition between the body and the soul, as if the way of the flesh were the body and the way of the spirit, the soul. That's a neo-Platonic, dualistic interpretation. It's not at all what Saint Paul means: for him, life itself, i.e., the living body, which is called to become an immortal body, lies at the intersection of the two ways. The body itself is traversed, created, by the conflict between what's called the way of the flesh and what's called the way of the spirit. It could ultimately be said that the body is the intersection of two possible answers to the question "What does it mean to live?" This is expressly what Saint Paul is attempting to convey to us. Actually, if you try to think of what the living body is, what human life as real, material life is, you can see that it is the linkage of two contradictory answers. Here, too, as in all the examples, we find, with regard to living, a sort of conflict between seemingly incompatible predicates.

4.   As regards death, I mentioned the famous statement in the introduction to *Phenomenology of Spirit*, where Hegel says that the true life is the life that does not fear death, the life that maintains itself even in death. Hegel's thesis is not that the true life is beyond death but that it is what endures death, what is capable of facing death. There's also the idea in Hegel that, when it comes to death, there are two stances of life. There is the life that gives in to death, the life that doesn't face death directly, and there is the life that staunchly endures the existence of death and maintains its permanence in it. In neither case does this have anything to do with the question of survival. It's not the survival of some spiritual part of the subject after its bodily death. It's a basic subjective disposition of life in its relationship with death. And there are two possibilities: Does life face up to death and maintain its own infinity in this confrontation? Or is it under the sway of death, dreading its inevitability and thus succumbing to finitude?

5.   As regards value, it's of course to Nietzsche that we must turn. Let me remind you of Nietzsche's two basic theses on the relationship between life and values. First, it is our vital power that creates values, and so values are assessed from the standpoint of the creative capacity of life; value is effectively subordinated to the creative power of life. Second, however, the value of life cannot be assessed; life itself is exempt from assessment. There is what I called a dual relationship of life to values, a relationship of creation and a relationship of exemption. Here, too, there's a conflict between life and values. And as a result of this conflict, there's a sort of basic neutrality about life, an unassessable neutrality.

6.   As for givenness, I explained it with references to poetry. The starting point was Rimbaud's ultra-famous line "The true life is absent." This is clearly the problem of what, in terms of life, is there, is given us, is present. And I showed that the tricky problem in this business was the problem of a place of life. If the true life is absent, it means that where it should be, it is lacking. So a dialectic of localization of life opened up: Once we experience that life is possibly absent, then where is it? Where should we look for it? Where can we find it? We saw that the same problem came up in different ways in both Mallarmé and Valéry. In Mallarmé, it took the form of the swan that was not able to sing "the territory to live," which clearly indicated that there is a territory, a location, a place of life. Then there was Valéry's line: "We must try to live," meaning that we must try to locate ourselves in the place where we're swept up in life. In all three cases, there's the possibility that life may be at a remove from its own place. As a result, this leads to what I call givenness, that is, to the question of how life is given to us. Is it given to us in a location, in a place? And how do we receive this localization? How do we accept or refuse such a gift? We could mention the phrase "to give life" here, which, even though it's very common, is nonetheless absolutely enigmatic. How can life be given? What exactly is given? Where and how life is ultimately given us is a real question. It obviously means that life is something other here, too, than the survival of the body and that something other than mere biological persistence is meant by "life." Otherwise, the question wouldn't make any sense.

7.   The seventh approach has to do with the question of affirmation. How can life be affirmative? What are its affirmative attributes? In other

words, can life be understood otherwise than negatively? This is crucial, since life can be approached from the perspective of death, from
the perspective of finitude, of brevity, of fragility, or of human misery,
as Pascal would have said. There's a whole great tradition that involves
approaching life through negative categories, which immediately connote its precariousness, its fleeting and transient nature, and so on. So
the whole problem is whether there exists a possible approach to the
question of life that is *not* life as limitation, finitude, or the precariousness of existence in general. With regard to the attributes of affirmative
life, I thought of a poem by Saint-John Perse. We'll often talk about
poetry because there are natural links, as I've already told you, between
the question "What does it mean to live?" and poetry. You might even
say that poetry is nothing but a repeated attempt to say something about
this question. At the end of the collection *Éloges* [Praises], there's a poem
entitled "Song of the Heir Presumptive." This song has three stanzas,
each of which begins with "I honour the living." So it will be said three
times that poetry can and must honor life. We are therefore dealing
with the question of affirmative life: "I honour the living" means that I
immediately bestow on them the affirmative blessing of the poem, which
reads as follows:

I honour the living, among you I have face.
And a man speaks at my right in the noise of his soul
and another is riding the boats,
the Horseman leans on his lance to drink.
(Draw into the shade, on his threshold, the old man's painted chair.)

I honour the living, among you I find grace.
Say to the women they should nourish,
should nourish on the earth that thin thread of smoke . . .
And man walks through dreams and takes his way toward the sea
And the smoke rises at the end of the headlands.

I honour the living, among you I make haste.
Dogs, ho! my dogs, we're whistling for you . . .

And the house heavy with honors and the year yellow among the
     leaves
Are as nothing to man's heart when he thinks:
All the paths of the world eat out of our hand![1]

Note in particular the three phrases that the stanzas begin with. In
the first, it's "among you I have face." In the second, it's no longer "I have
face" but "I find grace." And this grace is the transience of the smokes
of the world. Finally, in the third stanza, it's "among you I make haste."
What I simply wanted to point out is that there's a triple characterization of affirmative life here: face, grace, haste. I think it's a pretty good
description because the "among you I have face" corresponds to a life
that declares its own presence, that is direct and asserts that it's facing
the whole world, facing everyone else. It's not an arrogant or domineer-
ing proposition; it's a proposition that establishes affirmative life as the
certainty of presence, amid the multiplicity of what there is. However,
even though there's the multiplicity of what there is, Perse won't conclude that we're next to nothing, mere atoms, that we are going to disappear into the immensity of being, as Pascal, for example, would do,
with his two infinites. On the contrary, Perse will conclude from this
that among the infinite multiplicity of what exists, life asserts its own
"facing." Next comes grace. This is the idea that life, when it is really
there, the true life, is a kind of magical receiving, which is to say that
it is always something the gift of which is incalculable. In the mere fact
of being able to face things, there's an underlying grace, which is that
something has been given absolutely. This is related to the question of
givenness, for grace is precisely a free gift. Life has been given freely. The
poem doesn't comment on givenness but on its effects. If life has been
given absolutely, then it is always livable. Third and last, affirmative life
always involves, is always distinguished by, a certain urgency. On the one
hand, there's this way of facing all that is, on the other, the fragile and
absolute receiving of a grace, and there's also a haste inherent in life, a
rush to live. When it is really guided by norms of affirmative life, every
life shares in the urgency of life.

With these seven points, these seven approaches, what emerges as a question, following on from our original question, is: What are the conditions of affirmative life, or of a life that has been given, once a body from which life can spring is assumed? And this condition of the possibility of affirmative life, under the assumption that a body has been given us, won't be expressed in the same way under democratic materialism as under dialectical materialism.

Let me say it one more time: for democratic materialism, that is, for all of us, actually, when it comes to what we all think spontaneously, the condition for life is that the languages to which the body is prey must allow the body to develop its virtualities. That's probably the most authentic and basic definition that can be given of democratic materialism, and even of democracy, because democracy is ultimately always a relationship between languages and bodies—the way languages seize bodies—and there are only languages and bodies under its rule. Therefore, the problem of affirmative life will be for the languages that seize bodies to be such that they allow the bodies to develop their virtualities as much as possible. You can easily see that all democratic imperatives stem from this, namely that bodies must not be injured, tortured, mutilated, etc. Above all, the languages must not require the bodies to be abused, subjugated, controlled, veiled, and so on. Human rights, minority rights, women's rights, etc., can all be considered as the complex system of consequences of affirmative life in a space where there are essentially only bodies and languages. In that space, we might say—and this is quite reasonable—that the conditions required for affirmative life are that the languages be such that the bodies can affirm their virtualities. This is, moreover, why something about sexuality is paradigmatic, because sexuality is a particularly explicit site of the seizure of bodies by languages: just think of all the prohibitions and permissions related to the sexual interaction of bodies. This is a guiding thread that could easily be followed. There's something about the democratic norm of affirmative life that's oriented or attracted by the successive figures of what has been called—quite incorrectly, moreover—"sexual liberation." Quite incorrectly because it's actually a matter of new adjustments between languages and bodies, in such a way that the forms of control do not unduly restrict affirmative life, that is, the virtuality of bodies. So it's very natural and, in my opinion, quite likely, that, when all is said and done, this issue of the adjustment of sexual virtualities to the system of existing languages will function as a sort of filter through which are analyzed, for a given location, the degrees of possibility of affirmative life, and, conversely, the degrees of oppression or submission that alienate bodies from their own capacities, that is to say, from their possibilities of affirmative life.

It is understandable that, from that point of view, "freedom" should be the ultimate norm. Freedom is a complicated issue, because it is also a metaphysical and normative issue. But it has a relatively materialist meaning at the same time. Freedom can be constructed from the relationship between language and body, from the types of control languages have over bodies, ultimately judged in terms of the possibility for affirmative life, which enables us to approach the question of life through affirmative categories rather than through solely negative, restrictive, crippling categories. So "freedom" in this sense, that is, from a materialist perspective, should be understood as the freedom of bodies relative to that other figure of the material existent, the system of languages. And here we have an answer that we all more or less share, namely that what makes a decent, normal life possible is the fact that bodies aren't seized by languages to such an extent that they are irremediably alienated from what they're capable of.

The condition will be formulated differently by dialectical materialism, which doesn't mean that it doesn't assume, at least in part, the democratic perspective. It assumes it, but it displaces it, transfers it to a different context, which it does for one very basic reason. In dialectical materialism, the condition for affirmative life necessarily includes the emergence of new bodies. It's not just a matter of a different adjustment of the relationship between languages and bodies, because, as a result of the shift from the Two to the Three, things that are exceptions will emerge. I'd put it this way: there is the real possibility of an affirmative life only when an evental rupture makes a new body possible, such that this body can be the support for a subject-form. In democratic materialism the question "What does it mean to live?"—if the question of the possibility of new forms of life is included in it, i.e., the question of living differently from the way we currently live—is dependent on the successive adjustments of the control of languages over bodies. In dialectical materialism, on the other hand, the possibility of affirmative life depends on the creation, on the emergence, of new bodies, under conditions that we'll come back to later. In any case, the absolute condition for affirmative life is that there must be an emergence of new, unfamiliar bodies. And, as we'll see, of bodies that are partly unrecognizable as bodies, which is to say bodies that don't conform to the usual norm of what a body is. "Glorious" bodies, as Christians used to say back when they really believed in affirmative life, which, I think, no Christians any longer do.

The first universe, that of democratic materialism, is basically the universe of an adjustment, even though this adjustment might be quite innovative—new rules, or perhaps, as Wittgenstein would say, new games—in terms of the relationship between languages and bodies. Whereas in the second scenario (even assuming that the first one is possible), there is a possibility of affirmative life only under more drastic conditions that allow us to speak of new bodies. To use a metaphor, it's basically something like a materialist conception of conversion, as opposed to a materialist conception of adjustment. Through the emergence of new bodies, the body is converted into something different from itself; the material given makes something different from itself appear. So there is really a conversion, not a spiritual but a material one. There's something new about the bodies, and we will see how this novelty affects them. In the first scenario, there are bodies, and there is what might be called their emancipation, meaning that the degrees of possible freedom attributed to these bodies are variable and that new freedoms of the bodies can be created. But in dialectical materialism, a new type of body, something of an exception to any adjustment of the bodies/languages dichotomy, is created by a rupture, under the influence of an event.

All this of course leads to the question: "What is a body?" Insofar as we maintain that the body is the possible object of either an adjustment or a conversion, this is the obvious question. And it's not a simple question. We're up against the wall; we've got to find the method. Because, ultimately, what we need to do is a physics. In philosophy, however, physics is always the most difficult thing. Metaphysics is easy, but physics is very hard. The fact is, we're used to physics being separate from philosophy. But physics was a basic component of Aristotle's philosophy, for example. Since then, physics has become a science . . . But it's clear that, here, we're forced to return to what is essentially a question of physics, a question that was, still for Spinoza, a philosophical question. "We do not know what a body can do," said Spinoza, and he attempted to find out through philosophy. But, for us, it's a question that has become difficult because it seems to have to do with physics in the scientific sense of the word. So how can we deal with a question of physics with means that are clearly not those of physics? I could talk about quantum physics here, but that's not what I intend to do. I intend to go back to the great tradition in which the question "What is a body?" can *also* be dealt with philosophically, which doesn't mean that there aren't some necessary elements of formalization.

—⚭—

We're going to use several different methods. The first will be to go line by line through a poem that's been mentioned several times before, Valéry's "Le Cimetière marin." Keep in mind that we are reading and interpreting this poem for the sole purpose of answering for ourselves the question "What is a body?," even if that might seem a little strange to you. So right off the bat, let's ask why I chose this poem. Actually, it's pretty simple. What are the space and functioning of this poem? Well, at one end of the poem, the beginning, it will describe a sort of complete disappearance of the subject, of the consciousness, into the immutability of being and will describe how, in the test of a specific place, this possible disappearance is experienced. Thus, what nonlife might mean, or, more precisely, what a life as a nonlife, or, if you will, the reduction of existence to being, might mean. That's the first test. And at the end of the poem, we'll get the destruction of this figure of the subject's annihilation in the immutability of being in favor of the imperative of life, in the form of "We must try to live," or "Let's run at the waves and be hurled back to living."[2] The poem describes the shift from one to the other, a shift that is not a shift but a rupture. The question is how this rupture can be thought. As you can see, this is crucial for our own question, because if access to affirmative life truly requires a rupture and not just a different kind of adjustment, then we need to know what type of discontinuity it is. And if affirmative life is ultimately a discontinuity and not a givenness, then discontinuity needs to be thought as such. But how can life be thought as discontinuity, or in terms of discontinuity? On the face of it, life is precisely the principle of continuity. We live, and it is in the element of this life continuity that we do this or that, that we meet people, and so on. You can see what the problem is. And if, as the poem contends, affirmative life is really under condition of a discontinuity, how should we consider the relationship between living and the continuity/discontinuity dialectic? What is this paradoxical relationship that is established there between the power of life and something like a radical discontinuity, since the stanzas that will deal with life begin with "No, no! Arise! The future years unfold. / Shatter, O body, meditation's mould!" In these two lines, there is at once the absolute negation and the acceptance of the body. For it is clearly asserted that the power of life demands an absolutely new conscription of the body. "Meditation's mould" [*la forme pensive*] is what there was before; it's the element into which the subjectivity dissolved to attain the immutability or greatness of being, and appealing to the body to shatter that mold really means that affirmative life's only weapon, its only resource, is the body.

This is what justifies our close reading of this poem, which deals precisely with our question. "What does it mean to live?" Well, it means to constitute life as discontinuity, in relation to being itself, since life is actually a rupture with being, in the form of a new affirmation. We'll reflect on the issue that, fundamentally, the idea contained here, which I think is the key to the answer to our question, is the idea of an *affirmative discontinuity*, rather than a negative or critical one. Affirmative rupture is a topic I'm very fond of, as you know, and you may think that I keep coming back to it like a dog to a bone. But the fact is, here, faced with the question "What does it mean to live?," this dialectical shift is inescapable; it's crucial. In the context of dialectical materialism, if the question of life has any meaning at all, it means that the affirmation of life is something other than the negation of what there is. The essence of affirmative life does not lie in the negation of what there is. In particular, if we branch out to politics, we could say that the vital essence of a politics isn't revolt, because revolt is negativity, and in negativity there is not yet the affirmative discontinuity of life. We tend to automatically think that the key to affirmative life is in fact negation and that we should reject anything that oppresses or cripples, that the body should free itself from the languages oppressing it. But if that's what we think, then what we actually believe is that there might be other kinds of adjustments, more conducive to life, between languages and bodies, and as a result we're in the element of the continuation of democratic materialism.

Valéry—poor Valéry, who will be subjected to an unexpected ordeal here—puts forward an extremely complex thesis, namely that the access to affirmative life is clearly a rupture but that a true rupture is never something negative. It is, on the contrary, the emergence of a different affirmation, which isn't mediated by negativity. We could say that, ultimately, the possibility of the true life is an axiomatic possibility, that it's the emergence of an axiom. But if we're materialists, we have to say that it's actually the emergence of a new body. We can't expect this new body to develop in the element of negativity. This is a thesis whose political, artistic, amorous, etc. implications are extremely important: negation does not create new bodies. Whereas the opposite, constantly propounded thesis holds that new bodies, new groups, new movements, new works of art, and so on, are created through the critique of what exists. While waiting for the answer to the question "What does it mean to live?," I'll attempt to show that that's not the case, that negation is not able to create new bodies by itself. To be sure, it always creates new relationships between existing bodies and languages, yes, that it does, and the big pitfall is to think that these new relationships are like new bodies. But that's not so: when it comes to the possibility of affirmative life, they are hindered by their worldly disposition. This is really a contemporary debate, a debate about the issue of at what price affirmative life can be established. Do active negations possess a sufficient capacity for generation and renewal or not? My thesis, which I'll try to elucidate through the reading and explication of the poem, is that it's possible to attribute real affirmative possibilities to bodies only on condition that they're new bodies, totally novel bodily recompositions. The poem expresses this in its own way, and I'm going to derive new categories from the way it expresses it in order to rethink our whole problem, which is "What is a new life?" or "What is an affirmative life?"

So, a few comments are in order. What exactly are we going to see in the poem? I'm trying to find something that will help prepare you for hearing it. First, we'll see the general conditions of this question of affirmative life. As I've already mentioned, the question has no abstract, general status. It's always relative to a specific world or place. The first basic thesis, which is moreover common to all materialisms, is: When you ask the question "What does it mean to live?," you are always asking it in relation to what you say is a world; you are not asking it apart from the world. As a result, the place—the world—where the question will emerge and operate has to have been set out sufficiently clearly. Thus, we'll find in the poem—this is the first feature of general significance—the establishment of a unique place where the question of the emergence of life will operate. This question of the place, or of the world (I could elaborate on it technically, but I won't do so now, I may do so later) could be called the question of the transcendental, transcendental singularity. But for the time being, "place" or "world" will be perfectly sufficient for our purposes.

Second, there must necessarily be the figure of discontinuity. So there will have to be an event, but an event that can be understood in terms of its connection to the world. That's the problem. Naturally, there will be a symbol of the rupture, but this symbol (which can be called "an event") has to manifest its material connection to the world itself or to the place where this event occurs. Otherwise, it would be a case of miraculous transcendence. The elements of the world themselves must therefore, at some point, become intelligible in a completely discontinuous way in relation to their own being. There has to be an uprising, as it were, of the world itself, an uprising internal to the world, which causes an upheaval within it or transforms one or another of its components. We will see that this is the role assigned to the sea in the poem. At a certain point, the status of the sea changes completely and becomes what will technically be called an evental site, whereas, in itself, it was something else, since it was trapped in the immutability of being, an immutability symbolized by the sun.

Third, there will be the birth of a body, the emergence, the genesis, of a new body. This birth consists, for the poem, in naming the components of the world that form the new body. That's a point I must stress: we are still materialists. The appearance of a new body doesn't mean an emergence ex nihilo. It means that something that wasn't a body becomes one, that a scattered multiplicity comes together as a body. Perhaps the most banal metaphor for the birth of a new body is a political demonstration: people who didn't know each other at all come together, and all of a sudden they form a body. It's an ephemeral body that will break up, but for the time that it exists, it's a body. If this body existed beforehand, it would mean that the demonstration wasn't great: it was mainly the usual suspects who showed up. But if it's a true demonstration, it's an absolutely new body. That's in fact what's surprising about it. This metaphor, I believe, says it all. In the poem, the new bodily assemblage involves the sea and the wind, "the wind is rising." It's like a demonstration: people rise up, the whole thing rises up, and in this uprising, there will be something that's not just an uprising but the creation of an internal coherence—a body's got to hold together. So there will be a coherent uprising as the emergence of a new body and consequently a new way of thinking about the question of living.

We have three things now: the place (the world), the event (the rupture, the break), and the birth of a body. There's still a fourth one, perhaps the most important and complicated of them all, the question of this body's ability to treat real points in the world, its ability to confront them affirmatively. And this obviously requires knowing what a point in the world is. Let me give you a provisional definition of a point right away, so that it won't remain a mystery. A point is the moment when you summon the world to appear in the yes or no of a decision. We'll call "point of a world" the possibility that, at a given moment, something of the totality of the world might be decided in the figure of the yes or no. It's the appearance of the world in the figure of a decision, or, if you will, it's the appearance of an infinity in the figure of the Two, the sudden filtering of infinity through the Two, the moment when the world appears in such a way that you're forced to say either yes or no. Consequently, a pure decision is required of you, even though what's summoned to appear in this decision is by no means reduced to only two things. That's what I call a point, and it's a really big deal, isn't it? We're not always treating points, thank goodness! It sometimes happens in life that we have to summon the world to appear in the form of a decision, but we really don't want that to be happening all the time. It's terribly demanding, this imperative necessity that your whole life, the whole world, should suddenly be forced through the needle's eye of a yes or a no. Should I accept, or should I refuse? That's what a point is.

Regarding this problem of points (though in a different language), there's a whole tradition—from which it's imperative to take our distance— that, I think, can lead us to a possible definition of "metaphysics" in a negative sense. Let me remind you in passing that the destiny of metaphysics is not negative, as far as I'm concerned, even if I do acknowledge the existence of a negative dimension of a certain metaphysics. So my definition of metaphysics based on the notion of points cannot be quite the same definition as that of Heidegger or Derrida, who instead think that "metaphysics" connotes a bygone age of thought. But it's nevertheless similar to theirs, since Heidegger and Derrida sometimes define metaphysics by the systematic use of massive conceptual dualities, such as substance and accident, being and nothingness, essence and existence, and so on. However, what I want to call "metaphysics" here has to do with the idea that if there's a point, if you're confronted with a point, it's because there is already a real, objective duality in the world where this point is located. In this view, you have to choose between entities in the world that predivide it in half. As a result, the point is not just subjective, i.e., in the form of a decision, but supported, shall we say, by the consideration of an objective duality. Perhaps the most classic example would be a certain use of Marxist class analysis, in which the political decision is ultimately supposed to refer to more or less objective entities (the proletariat and the bourgeoisie, for example), which means that there is always a preconstitution of sides. In the end, there are two sides, and any decision is in a way informed by an at least semiobjective horizon of duality. This is also the case when it comes to the love between a man and a woman. Sure, you can always say "I'm going to decide," but the truth is, you decide on the basis of the fact that, all things considered, women and men have different types of decision making. The decision is always considered as the articulation of something that refers to or is filtered through an objective duality. In short, there is a whole "metaphysical" tradition that, when confronted with the analytics of decision making, that is, of points, ultimately attempts to base it on objective dualities, i.e., on divisions in the world itself.

But I must stress that a point by no means suggests that there's a division in the world. A point summons the world to appear before a *principle* of division, which is not the same thing. And there is nothing to suggest that your choice, whatever it may be, might be based on an actual duality. It's just that when you have to treat a point, well, that's the way it is, you're in the situation of having to make the entire world appear before a division.

A whole mathematical construction can also be built on this, but I'll let you off the hook. I'm mentioning it, though, to show you that the problem of points lends itself to a wholly rational treatment. It's not a metaphor. There's a thoroughly established possibility of giving a rigorous formal definition of a point as the appearance of a systematic infinity before a duality that is not immanent to it, that doesn't share it as such.

So we'll call "metaphysics"—I think that's one of the possible definitions of this curious intellectual entity—the idea that the Two of the decision, the yes or no, always has an objective counterpart in the world, that it is firmly based on a duality in being itself.

Depending on whether one is coming from a metaphysical perspective or not, the question "What does it mean to live?," which is ultimately the question of how a body treats points, how a body confronts points, will be asked in very different ways. For the body's function is to confront points, and it is only in so doing that the body is totally alive and not just operating automatically. Well, if you're coming from a metaphysical perspective, the body's function, insofar as it treats any particular point, becomes a function transitive to the world itself. It is transitive to the world since the world inscribes or preinscribes the duality of the decision in its own makeup. Exactly like when you have to make a political decision, for example. If your perspective is ossified Marxist materialism, the decision will inevitably be predetermined by the fact that there's the socialist camp and the capitalist camp in the world, or the proletariat and the bourgeoisie, and so there's something predivided that can support your point and serve as a guide for treating it. But if you have a pure theory of points, i.e., a nonmetaphysical theory, it's another matter altogether. Because, naturally, there is a rationality to the appearance of infinity before the Two, but this rationality doesn't lie in a division of the world; it doesn't lie in a predistribution of the world itself into two possible orientations.

So, after the place, the event, and the birth of the body, I dealt with the capacity of the body. In so doing, I again took up Spinoza's excellent question, "What can a body do?," and I established the context of this question in a very positive way. What a body can do, its capacity, is to treat points in the world, that is to say, to confront the particular way infinity, from the standpoint of the body, is filtered through an essential Two, which is a Two of the decision or the choice. In the final analysis, what a body can do is, well, choose.

After this, we'd have a definition of life that does not yet answer the question "What does it mean to live?" but at least gets us a little closer to it. We could ultimately say that, conditional on a chance emergence, life is when there is the birth of a body. I must stress the fact that the birth of a body draws its materiality from the world and nowhere else. It's merely a conglomeration—with a definable inner consistency—of elements that are in a scattered state throughout the world. So there is the birth of a body, and this body can be the support for a subject-form, that is, the ability to decide about points in the world. And finally, we'll call "truth" what is created by the consequences of this treatment of points or these decisions about points, that is to say, the effectivity of the capacity of a body endowed with a subject-form, which is to decide about points, to make the world appear in the dimension of the Two. I choose the term "truth" out of fidelity to myself but also because of the line "The true life is absent." The *true* life. We, too, are trying to find out under what conditions the true life can be present. Therefore, we'll call "a truth" what results from the decisions by which a new body treats points in the world.

Once we've got all that, we'll be able to say what it means to live: to live is simply to participate in a truth. "Participate" is perhaps a bit fuzzy, you might say. Sure, but in fact what exactly does it mean for a given individual to participate in a truth? Well, there are a number of answers. For example, to be joined to the body that is the support for the subject-form. Or to be seized by the subject-form. Or to play a crucial role in treating a point. There are a number of ways for a singular individual to give meaning to the idea of participating in a truth. And I'll

340 What Does It Mean to Live?

show that these are precisely the various modes of life. Life is modal. To live "truly" will always be to participate in a truth, but there are different modes of this participation. Being joined to a body (or participating in its creation), being seized by the subject-form, or treating a point won't be the same things. All these modes of life amount to participating in a truth, but they're different from one other. Each opens up a possible answer to the question, even if the generic answer is the same.

Let's work our way back up the chain. To participate in a truth means to participate in a series of decisions about points of the world that relate to a subject-form, this subject-form being supported by a body, a body that's new, with a novelty that has been made possible by an evental rupture. Everything is obviously interrelated, and the way I'm presenting it is overly analytical. In reality, the subject-form doesn't exist without the body, the new body can't emerge without the evental rupture, and the points can't be treated if there's no body acting as a support for a subject-form. It all forms a whole. And it's when you're part of this whole, in one way or another, that you can say you are living, that this is the true life. That's why I reminded you of Rimbaud's line, "The true life is absent." The true life is absent because the true life is life lived in truth. And the fact that it's absent—this is very clear in Rimbaud—simply means: there's no truth, I can't see where the truths are, I can't see them, they're lost. This loss of truths takes all sorts of forms in Rimbaud, for example: "Science is too slow,"[3] which should be understood as: "For me, science is not practicable as truth, as life; I don't want to be a scientist, it's too slow." In saying that the true life is absent, Rimbaud is actually trying to tell us that truths, to the extent that to live would be to participate in their process, are absent. He ended up thinking that even poetry couldn't serve that purpose, that it couldn't be regarded as a truth in the sense of the possibility of life, and he would eventually call it "one of my follies."[4] Later, he became a trader. Well, he was right to, because if you're not living, you might as well be a trader, a trafficker, an arms dealer in Africa (Africa today is swarming with arms dealers)! It's very true. People who say "Nothing beats business, money, etc." are absolutely right. Of course, they're right, provided we're talking about democratic materialism, because democratic materialism, in which "there are only bodies and languages," inevitably leads to the result that there's no life,

since there's no truth. Let me remind you that, in terms of dialectical
materialism, there is only life if you add to the primordial materialist
statement the dialectical exception "except that there are truths." Otherwise, you don't have life, in the sense that Rimbaud declared its absence,
and consequently you have to come back to the fact that there are only
bodies and languages. And then, the logical decision is to be a trader. All
this makes very good sense.

My reading or interpretation of the poem will be organized along
the lines of an elucidation of these ideas. So I'll read it to you, even
though . . . I know it by heart, but I hesitate . . .

1

This quiet roof, where dove-sails saunter by,
Between the pines, the tombs, throbs visibly.
Impartial noon patterns the sea in flame—
That sea forever starting and re-starting.
When thought has had its hour, oh how rewarding
Are the long vistas of celestial calm!

2

What grace of light, what pure toil goes to form
The manifold diamond of the elusive foam!
What peace I feel begotten at that source!
When sunlight rests upon a profound sea,
Time's air is sparkling, dream is certainty—
Pure artifice both of an eternal Cause.

3

Sure treasure, simple shrine to intelligence,
Palpable calm, visible reticence,
Proud-lidded water, Eye wherein there wells
Under a film of fire such depth of sleep—
O silence! . . . Mansion in my soul, you slope
Of gold, roof of a myriad golden tiles.

4

Temple of time, within a brief sigh bounded,
To this rare height inured I climb, surrounded
By the horizons of a sea-girt eye.
And, like my supreme offering to the gods,
That peaceful coruscation only breeds
A loftier indifference on the sky.

5

Even as a fruit's absorbed in the enjoying,
Even as within the mouth its body dying
Changes into delight through dissolution,
So to my melted soul the heavens declare
All bounds transfigured into a boundless air,
And I breathe now my future's emanation.

6

Beautiful heaven, true heaven, look how I change!
After such arrogance, after so much strange
Idleness—strange, yet full of potency—
I am all open to these shining spaces;
Over the homes of the dead my shadow passes,
Ghosting along—a ghost subduing me.

7

My soul laid bare to your midsummer fire,
O just, impartial light whom I admire,
Whose arms are merciless, you have I stayed
And give back, pure, to your original place.
Look at yourself . . . But to give light implies
No less a somber moiety of shade.

8

Oh, for myself alone, mine, deep within
At the heart's quick, the poem's fount, between
The void and the pure event,[5] I beseech

[*I just have to comment here* (says a smiling Badiou, provoking laughter in
the auditorium)*: You can well imagine that I couldn't help but feel sympathetic
to someone who could write "between the void and the pure event"!*]

The intimations of my secret power.
O bitter, dark, and echoing reservoir
Speaking of depths always beyond my reach.

9

But know you—feigning prisoner of the boughs,
Gulf which eats up their slender prison-bars,
Secret which dazzles though mine eyes are closed—
What body drags me to its lingering end,
What mind draws *it* to this bone-peopled ground?
A star broods there on all that I have lost.

10

Closed, hallowed, full of insubstantial fire,
Morsel of earth to heaven's light given o'er—
This plot, ruled by its flambeaux, pleases me—
A place all gold, stone, and dark wood, where shudders
So much marble above so many shadows:
And on my tombs, asleep, the faithful sea.

11

Keep off the idolaters, bright watch-dog, while—
A solitary with the shepherd's smile—
I pasture long my sheep, my mysteries,
My snow-white flock of undisturbed graves!
Drive far away from here the careful doves,
The vain daydreams, the angels' questioning eyes!

12

Now present here, the future takes its time.
The brittle insect scrapes at the dry loam;
All is burnt up, used up, drawn up in air
To some ineffably rarefied solution . . .
Life is enlarged, drunk with annihilation,
And bitterness is sweet, and the spirit clear.

13

The dead lie easy, hidden in earth where they
Are warmed and have their mysteries burnt away.
Motionless noon, noon aloft in the blue
Broods on itself—a self-sufficient theme.
O rounded dome and perfect diadem,
I am what's changing secretly in you.

14

I am the only medium for your fears.
My penitence, my doubts, my baulked desires—
These are the flaw within your diamond pride . . .
But in their heavy night, cumbered with marble,
Under the roots of trees a shadow people
Has slowly now come over to your side.

15

To an impervious nothingness they're thinned,
For the red clay has swallowed the white kind;
Into the flowers that gift of life has passed.
Where are the dead?—their homely turns of speech,
The personal grace, the soul informing each?
Grubs thread their way where tears were once composed.

16

The bird-sharp cries of girls whom love is teasing,
The eyes, the teeth, the eyelids moistly closing,
The pretty breast that gambles with the flame,
The crimson blood shining when lips are yielded,
The last gift, and the fingers that would shield it—
All go to earth, go back into the game.

17

And you, great soul, is there yet hope in you
To find some dream without the lying hue
That gold or wave offers to fleshly eyes?
Will you be singing still when you're thin air?
All perishes. A thing of flesh and pore
Am I. Divine impatience also dies.

18

Lean immortality, all crêpe and gold,
Laurelled consoler frightening to behold,
Death is a womb, a mother's breast, you feign
The fine illusion, oh the pious trick!
Who does not know them, and is not made sick
That empty skull, that everlasting grin?

19

Ancestors deep down there, O derelict heads
Whom such a weight of spaded earth o'erspreads,
Who *are* the earth, in whom our steps are lost,
The real flesh-eater, worm unanswerable
Is not for you that sleep under the table:
Life is his meat, and I am still his host.

20

'Love,' shall we call him? 'Hatred of self,' maybe?
His secret tooth is so intimate with me
That any name would suit him well enough,
Enough that he can see, will, daydream, touch—
My flesh delights him, even upon my couch
I live but as a morsel of his life.

21

Zeno, Zeno, cruel philosopher Zeno,
Have you then pierced me with your feathered arrow
That hums and flies, yet does not fly! The sounding
Shaft gives me life, the arrow kills. Oh, sun!—
Oh, what a tortoise-shadow to outrun
My soul, Achilles' giant stride left standing!

22

No, no! Arise! The future years unfold.
Shatter, O body, meditation's mould!
And, O my breast, drink in the wind's reviving!
A freshness, exhalation of the sea,
Restores my soul . . . Salt-breathing potency!
Let's run at the waves and be hurled back to living!

23
Yes, mighty sea with such wild frenzies gifted
(The panther skin and the rent chlamys), sifted
All over with sun-images that glisten,
Creature supreme, drunk on your own blue flesh,
Who in a tumult like the deepest hush
Bite at your sequin-glittering tail—yes, listen!

24
The wind is rising! . . . We must try to live!
The huge air opens and shuts my book: the wave
Dares to explode out of the rocks in reeking
Spray. Fly away, my sun-bewildered pages!
Break, waves! Break up with your rejoicing surges
This quiet roof where sails like doves were pecking.[6]

That's it. We won't get to the end of it today. Especially since it's not just a matter of explicating it—because it's simple, after all—but of extracting from it the tools we're going to be using for this question of life.

So let me just point out a few things about the successive stages. First, I'm going to show how the poem constructs a place. This won't take us away from our problem since the question of life is always a question inscribed in or related to a figure of the world. That will be our first, brief question. Then, I'll show how the various different elements combine in the place so constructed. This is indispensable because, as I mentioned, a body is always a combination of elements, a unique coherent multiplicity. To speak about a new body is necessarily to speak about a new arrangement of certain elements of the world. It's important to know how the different constituent elements fit together in the world, in the world of the poem, in this case. Third, we'll see that, among these constituent elements, there is one that functions as the inexistent, the element that, although in the world, inexists relative to this world, or has the paradoxical status, in the world, of being the figure of what this world does away with or destroys. This is a very important point for one very simple reason, which I'm going to tell you right away since there's nothing mysterious about it . . . Actually, what is an event? Basically, an event, for a world, is something that has the ability to make exist what did not exist before in this world. But it's clear that, if an event is something that has the ability to make exist in a world what did not exist in it before, then what does not exist in a world has to mean something. That's the problem. How is it possible not to exist in a world and yet to be of this world? In other words, we have to be able to name the particular inexistent of a world, that singular element that, in a world, functions as what doesn't exist in that world.

This was the role that Marx assigned to the proletariat, to take a notable and very hypothetical example. And it's exactly what the great song *The Internationale* said: "We are nothing, let us be all!" But between the two something has to happen. Well, that's what the event is! It's when something that was nothing begins to exist maximally. The event is not that in itself; rather, it's what makes it possible for the particular inexistent of a place to come into existence in this same world, whose logic will be changed as a result. So it's crucial to identify the inexistent of the world that the poem constructs, in order to show how, in effect, when the event occurs, this inexistent is restored to existence. This is what the poem expresses as "restores my soul." The soul was lost, and something gives it back to me. But this restoring is actually the way inexistence, which takes up the whole first part of the poem, changes into an intense and maximal form of existence. So it's impossible to think the event without having a fully formed idea of what it means to inexist in a world. It's pretty intuitive, moreover. Everyone knows that when something really happens, it means that what didn't exist until then now exists. Everyone has experienced this. But if we conceptualize this experience a bit, we can see that the paradox of what is meant by not existing in a determinate world needs to be analyzed in depth. Because it's clear that the inexistent isn't nothing, that you can't reduce the inexistent to nothingness. You have to show how this inexistent is, in a certain sense, an element of the world itself that has the odd status of not existing in the world of which it is an element.

That's a key point because, ultimately, we could also say that to live means to be swept up in this new existence. If we trace the entire chain, we can clearly see that the definition of the body will be linked to the fact that the power of the event brings the inexistent to life or back to life. The new body will be what clusters around this, what is absorbed by it, what rearranges itself around this existent that emerges but that *was already* there, as an inexistent. It doesn't emerge as something absolutely new, since it was of the world and had the status of an inexistent of that world. Let's say that the inexistent had its being, but not its existence, in the worldly situation. An event is what makes a previously absent existence emerge from being. Eventality has the capacity to raise this inexistent being to maximal existence in the world. What will be called "a new body" is everything that clusters around this emergence, everything that lends an intense aura of existence to the new existent that has emerged from its previous inexistent being.

To live, when all is said and done, will mean to participate in all of this, hence to experience the effects of the coming—we might even say the coming to be—of the existence of an inexistent. Because in a determinate world there is only one inexistent. This is even one of the possible definitions of the world. If we take it the other way around, what is a world, really? It's where something doesn't exist, and it's in actual fact the inexistent that defines the world in its negative determination. And the event, hence the body, hence the treatment of points, hence truth, hence life, are entirely dependent on this logic of the inexistent.

How can all this be found in Valéry's poem? Let me give you the main reference points so you can tackle it yourselves.

The first configuration consists of the elements of the place: you'll see pretty quickly that there are three of them, the sun, the sea, and the dead. These are the elements with a positive intensity of existence; they make up the graveyard by the sea, which, I should mention, is a real place: the graveyard in the town of Sète [in the south of France]. In the poem, this real place is transformed into an allegorical place in the world by the crucial sun/sea/death relationship. Then there's an extra something, the poet's consciousness, the tiny "I" that speaks in the poem, which is faced with these three elements and will be the true inexistent term . . . because it was destroyed by Parmenides ("Zeno, Zeno, cruel philosopher Zeno / Have you then pierced me with your feathered arrow").[7] Pierced by the Eleatic arrow, it is therefore trapped in the immutability of being, in the impossibility of movement. It is captured in the place's power by Parmenidean immutability and, for this reason, as a living consciousness, it is inexistent. Thus, the place will essentially consist of three existents and one inexistent.

Next, we'll have to address the question of the event. What is its site? What happens exactly? And here we'll have to see that the event is a metamorphosis of the sea, the sea that changes from motionless sparkling, which is the pure reflection of the sun, its double, to this "mighty sea with such wild frenzies gifted." If we were to speak like the pre-Socratics, we'd say that the sea in this poem switches from the side of the sun to that of the wind. But it's still the same sea. We shall see how this, which brings the inexistent back to life, unfolds. This is why the key line is "The wind is rising! . . . We must try to live!" It's *because* the wind is rising that we must try to live. It's a causal sentence. If the wind weren't rising, it would be impossible to say that we must try to live, or even to live *tout court*. The wind is the name of the event here.

After that, we'll need to ask what body is being created. "Shatter, O body, meditation's mould!" What ingredients of the place is this body made of? Is it the biological, individuated body of the poet? It's that secondarily, but in actual fact, in the element of the place, a new body is being created, which represents a new figure of the relationship among sea, wind, sun, and the dead. There is a rearrangement of the elements of the place.

Finally, we'll ask what the points of this world are, that is, what the poem's ability is to treat the different points of this world. Now, these points are very carefully set up over the course of the poem. The poem clearly shows with respect to what issues, and in what circumstances, the world might have to be confronted with something in the form of yes or no, something in the form of a choice. There are a number of them. The world is given not just in its elements but also in its points—in the possible instances of a radical decision about the world as a whole.

Once we've found all this in the poem, well, then we'll be dealing with the promise of living ("We must try to live!"), which is the ability of this new subjectivated body, in gaining access to its own life, to treat the points of the world effectively. That's what "to try to live" means, because "to live" cannot mean the repetition of the immutability of the previous life. To try to live is something that occurs in the same place, but to live means to treat effectively, in the form of an affirmative decision, the points that were in the world but were left untreated because there was no life there.

That's what we'll extract from the poem. And in the process, we'll identify a number of categories that will be the properly philosophical categories we'll use to address the question of life comprehensively. That's what we need to start by doing if we want to answer the question "What does it mean to live?"

Session 3

December 17, 2003

There's an old phrase that has gone completely out of fashion, the phrase "ideological struggle." In the glorious period of the "red years," thirty years ago, ideological struggle was raging. I remember a worker friend of mine saying that whenever there was an ideological struggle during a meeting, the glasses would shake because everyone pounded on the table. Well, even though I'm not sure I can make anything shake, the fact is that this seminar is taking place in the general context of the ideological confrontation between two maxims, or two axioms. First, there's the axiom I propose to call that of democratic materialism: "There are only bodies and languages." It is basically the axiom of prevailing opinion. You might even say it's the axiom of the world as it is. And now there's the maxim I claim is that of dialectical materialism, in a new sense of the phrase: "There are only bodies and languages, except that there are truths." What the two maxims have in common are the major reference points of modern materialism, languages and bodies. But the "except that there are truths" dialectically adds a third term, which explicitly presents itself as a third term in a position of exception.

That's the general context. What we can then say—I'm putting this a little bit differently from the way I did in the previous sessions—is that there is naturally a retroaction of the exception on what it is an exception to. You necessarily have something of the "except that there are truths" that will retroact on "there are only bodies and languages," in the sense that the axiom must allow for the possibility of the exceptional supplement. Therefore, if you accept that there are truths, you retroactively alter the meaning of "bodies" and "languages." We obviously can't assume that the ontology is strictly the same, otherwise we wouldn't understand what is meant, in its reality, by the exception represented by the supplement called "truths." "Truths" in the plural—that's crucial. There is no one *truth*; rather, there are *truths*. But regardless of whether it's singular or multiple, an exception to the materialist bodies/languages pair must be possible. And if this exception is possible, then from the moment we first accept that that there are only bodies and languages we must think its possibility.

Let me just say a word, for now, about the retroaction of the exception of truths on the definition of languages. Actually, this retroaction is like a split. Indeed, we are now forced to admit that "languages" has two meanings. The first meaning, the meaning I'd call the classic one, "There are languages," implies that there are protocols of rules and communication, a general space of transmission. That meaning will remain. But we are at the same time forced to acknowledge another possible meaning, which will be flanked, in a way, by the question of truths and which I propose to call a subject-language. The opposition, the split, which I'm not going to elaborate on for the moment, will be between language of communication and subject-language. "Subject-language" means language associated with the emergence of a subject as such. Consequently, as we will see, subject-language is primarily in the dimension of the act, not in that of transmission or communication. Ultimately, the retroaction provokes a split between language of communication and subject-language, which itself refers back to the split between the current situation and the act, or something like that. I'm putting this as simply as possible because it's not our subject here. But you can clearly see that, in terms of its basic operation, this retroaction actually makes something emerge, within the language of communication, that is not reducible to it, something that is of course of the order of language, but as a cut rather than as continuity.

I'd like to point out that this conception of the two languages is not at all new. It's clearly explained in Mallarmé, for example. When he contrasts the inherent nature of poetic language with the nature of ordinary language, Mallarmé specifically says that, on the one hand, there is the language of communication and exchange—which he expressly calls "commercial," in the etymological sense, i.e., intended for commerce between subjects—and he compares this language to a coin that's passed from hand to hand. On the other hand, he assigns a completely different function to poetic language, a function of thought or creativity, i.e., something that will overcome absence and create new entities against a backdrop of absence. It's clear that Mallarmé's very ordinary opposition between poetic and everyday language actually refers to two different functions of language, the function of communication and the function of what might be called foundation or institution. This is something akin to what I'm saying: if you accept the exception of truths, you necessarily accept that the statement "there are languages" is a split, divided statement, which acknowledges two heterogeneous functions of language within itself and in particular acknowledges that one of them makes a cut in the function of the other.

Now what is the retroaction of our exception on the problem of bodies and their relationship with languages? This is what we'll focus on for now.

The maxim of democratic materialism as regards this issue is ultimately quite simple, simple in principle but extremely complicated in its practical intricacies. The maxim is that languages—and this is why it's actually preferable that there be a number of them—that the multiplicity of languages, then, must be such that bodies are constrained as little as possible in the development of their capacities. If we discuss this conception in detail, we'll see that it implies that a "good" nature of the body, something like a natural body, somehow exists, because otherwise there wouldn't be any universal norm for what is actually the free capacity of bodies, and we'd get embroiled in endless hairsplitting about languages and bodies. So it's absolutely necessary to make the assumption that there is an inherent nature of bodies. This makes it possible to know in what cases languages are restrictive with respect to bodies' capacities and in what cases they're not, or are less so. But let's not get into this discussion, a philosophically established one ever since the debates over natural law. We understand at any rate why, in democratic materialism, there is really one fundamental norm that is the norm of freedom, defined by the relationship between the capacities of a "natural" body and the normative and repressive dimension of languages.

If you add that there are truths, you will have both a structural and a normative change, due to the fact that this implies a regime of exception. However, every regime of exception imposes a rupture stipulation: you're no longer dealing with the simple continuity of the "there are languages and bodies" since you acknowledge that there are things that make a cut in the regime of the "there is." So there's another "there is," and calling it "truth" means that there are truths only on condition of a system of ruptures. As you know, philosophy, virtually across the entire spectrum, has chosen to call such a thing an *event*. "Event" in fact refers to the exception to the regime of the "there is," which means that something like thinking or truths are possible. "There are truths" means that we are dealing with the consequences of an event, which, indeed, refers to the discontinuity of this regime. And if it's dialectical, it's precisely because it includes the figure of discontinuity, whereas democratic material-ism is essentially continuist. That's precisely why it assumes continuous progress, which makes the extension of a democratic space possible, even if, for that to happen, it's necessary to intervene somewhat brutally from time to time, or even quite often, in the non-democratic savages' coun-tries. With my materialist dialectic, we're in a context of discontinuism that maintains that the "there is" alone does not suffice to exhaust the possible. As a result, the maxim can no longer be that languages should let bodies' capacities be, that they should let them alone as much as pos-sible (meaning: as long as they accept the "natural" value of democratic materialism). The maxim must include the element of discontinuity, an integral part of the exceptional existence of a truth.

At this point, a number of possibilities no doubt open up. The most radical one, which I think is also the most tenable one, is that, in the context of dialectical materialism, that is, with the acceptance of the eventual exception, we need to abandon the thesis that bodies' capacities should be allowed to be, in favor of the thesis that new bodies form. We end up—in close association with Deleuze's terminology—with a theory of metamorphosis. But the logic of metamorphosis does not lie in the continuity of the effects internal to the body's becoming but instead accepts that new bodies may appear. And how, very broadly, will these new bodies be characterized? Well, precisely by the fact that they will be capable of bearing a new subjective formalism. They are bodies intended for a new subject-form, which will be the subject of truth. The evental rupture makes possible the emergence of new bodies, bodies that can be the materiality, the material support, for the new subjective form, which also includes the subject-language. You can see that the procedure, in terms of bodies, actually pits the theory of a naturalness of the body, which must be left to its own capacity, against a completely different thesis, which is to let the emergence of the new bodies be. These bodies will be the material bearers of the subject-forms that will emerge under condition of the event, and these forms will in turn serve as supports for truth procedures.

In short, we could say that what the event will make possible is what, in a new vein, we will call life, because our question is still "What does it mean to live?," after all, a question that's not exactly the same in dialectical materialism as it is in democratic materialism. "What does it mean to live?" will obviously still be connected to the persistence of a body, since it is impossible to conceive of something as life without at some point assigning it to the persistence of a body. Except that, here, it will be a matter of the conditions of emergence of new bodies, and not just of the persistence, development, or "freedom" of supposedly natural bodies. So there will always be something in the "to live" *that will be akin to a second birth*—let's put it that way—a second birth co-belonging to a new body, with the proviso that "body" doesn't necessarily mean the biological body, the organic form of the body. "Body" is precisely what is able, contingent on an event, to be the support for a new figure of truth. "Body" can of course be many things, and it's true that "life" is associated with "body." Except that, here, "life" will be associated with "emergence of a new body" and therefore, at the most basically subjective level, with "second birth." A second birth for those who are lucky, a third, a fourth . . . even a twentieth birth for those who are blessed by the gods! If there *are* gods, meaning if there is an event, right? If there is an encounter . . . But in any case it will be a new birth.

This idea of a new birth is not at all a new idea; indeed, it is a very old one. As a matter of fact, it can already be found in Plato's writings or before, in old religious rites. But here it's assigned to materialism, and materialism should be taken literally, in other words: new body, new incorporation. And what is this incorporation the incorporation of? Well, the incorporation of bodies, since there are only bodies and languages. So it's really a second birth in the strictest sense, an incorporation of what already presents itself as bodies. That's why it's not incarnation, in the Christian sense, which is the becoming-body of spirit. But we're materialists: there is no spirit to be incarnated, there are only bodies and languages. We will nevertheless accept that there can be an incarnation of bodies, that is, a re-incorporation, and thus a sort of reincarnation.

Let me say that this is absolutely not an unimaginable, or mysterious, or miraculous, experience. What I'm referring to is a very common experience: the idea that we are incorporated into a new body. To take an empirical example that I often use for didactic purposes, I'm thinking about the incorporation into a political body, in its most immediate sense, i.e., the incorporation into a demonstration. A political body forms, it is more or less strong, more or less firm or resolute, it doesn't matter; it is in any case a new body that forms. As a political body, what's involved is the collective body, and your body will be incorporated into this collective body. It's clear that if there weren't any such incorporations there would be no new body. There's no need to imagine that it's a spirit: it's really bodies that make up this demonstrating collective body. And this demonstrating collective body will serve as the support for some subject-form, that is to say, some diverse and varied, or perhaps very condensed and uniform, language effects. It will contribute slogans, for example. It will say something. But you can see that when this body says something, there's a new subjective effect, supported by a new body. As there's no spirit to say the slogan, it has to be a body that expresses it.

This is an experience of many bodies being reincarnated in a new body, however ephemeral it might be. And there will be a subject-form that will somehow take hold of this body and will both form it and be supported by it. So there will indeed be a new body, which, on the one hand, can be measured by incorporations—it only consists of incorporations, so it is indeed made out of the bodies that were already there—and, on the other, will serve as the support for a subjective form, in this case a political subjective form, it being understood that this subject-form's physical reality will be the new body. If there weren't this new body, there would be no possibility of anything whatsoever.

Another empirical example is love. In love, there is also incorporation into a new body. It's not just the encounter of two bodies in exteriority. If it's really love, there will be an entity that is its own body. You're well aware of this, moreover, because it's your own body that is changed. It's it and at the same time it's not it, as everyone knows. It's a sort of enchanted body, or some such thing. This enchanted body is a new body. And this new body only exists because there is the other person's body, of course. So, the truth is, you have to consider that a new body has emerged within which there are distinctions (though there are distinctions in all bodies), a body that might be called the amorous body. And what is it the support for? It's the support for a new subjective figure, a new existential figure, a new declarative figure. Thus, also, the ability to serve as the support for new languages, new declarations. In this case as well, the real experience isn't an experience in exteriority; on a deeper level it's an experience of re-incarnation of what there is, namely, bodies and languages.

My point is that, ultimately, the question of the body is the question of "What is a new body?" provided that the "there are bodies" is the "there are" of real multiplicities, and nothing else. We're materialists, and we fully acknowledge that there are nothing but real multiplicities. Yet, under certain conditions, real multiplicities are subjectivizable bodies, bodies capable of supporting the emergence of a new subjective figure. By the way, when it comes to the subject, there are, as usual, a physics and a metaphysics. So let's take things the other way around: there's a metaphysics of the subject, of the subject of truth, which has to do with the nature of its form. Is it a political, amorous, or artistic form? This has to do with schemas that we may come across again but that concern the form that will take hold of the body and at the same time be supported by it. This is what might be called the metaphysics of the subject, its formal theory. It's the language aspect of the problem of the subject, we might say. Then, as regards the same subject of truth, there's a physics. What is the physics? It's: What is the body? What is *that* body, which is capable of serving as the support for a subject-form? Once again, we need to get a little away from the strict authority of the model of the biological body. It's important to understand that there may be other figures of the body that involve incorporation and serve as the support for a new kind of subjective formalism. But "What is the body?" is a physics, because this body is made out of what there is. It is of course contingent on a rupture or an event, contingent on something happening that is not deducible from what there is. But as a body it is made out of what there is. Let's go back to the examples I gave you a moment ago. Regardless of whether it's the amorous body, the demonstrating body, or what have you, they are all made out of the bodies that were already there. We won't give up materialism . . . The incorporation is an incorporation made out of bodies. The reincarnation is a new incarnation of the bodies. So the physics of the subject amounts to understanding how, when there's an event of some kind, new bodies emerge, with the understanding that these new bodies are combinations of what there is, i.e., bodies that are already there. They don't emerge ex nihilo. They are bodies that ultimately have other ways of connecting, combining, giving cohesion to bodies that are there. So it is indeed a physics. What I mean by "physics" is a logic of bodies in the strong sense of the term, namely, how there can appear, in the context of its new logical cohesion, a body that ultimately results from bodies that are there, bodies that exist.

Now, what quickly becomes apparent when dealing with this problem in a comprehensive way, when building a foundation for developing dialectical materialism, is that, actually, the difficult question is physics. I've already had occasion to tell you that physics is always more difficult than metaphysics. Indeed, the problem of the subject-form is a formally complex problem, but its proof process isn't terribly complicated. We can understand pretty well what the different types of subjective protocols are and the typology that distinguishes among three major types of subjects: the faithful, the reactive, and the obscure.[1] These three main examples of the subjective figure can be deduced relatively easily from what can be regarded, in a rather basic way, as operations of consequence, negation, and so on. The theory of the subject, if you will, is a formal theory. Metaphysics is formal, and this subjective formalism (which I'm not going to say anything about for now) isn't the hardest part of the work.

On the other hand, the question "What is a body?" is truly complicated. And it's easy to see why. Because, here, we're really dealing with a philosophical physics, that is, when we have to understand how something new can really be made out of the old. The subjective formalism is contingent on there being a body. In a sense, you assume that the physical problem is solved, and once you've got a body, you become involved in "What is a formalism?" It's fairly complicated but not overly so, whereas the problem of how new bodies emerge, the properly physical problem, is a more daunting and complicated one, for one very understandable reason. There's one property of the body that everyone agrees on, which is that a body that appears is, in some way, like an ultimate form of coherence or cohesiveness. So something holds together there, in a world that's been shaken by some event, which might be an encounter, a demonstration, or what have you. There's an event, there's a rupture, and it all holds together there with a visibility, an experienceability (if you'll allow me this awful word!) that wasn't there before, but it's nevertheless made out of what was already there. So you've got to think that, even though it's in a sense completely there, i.e., visible there, in this world, and not somewhere else, yet, in another sense, it's totally new. The question then arises of a new type of cohesion, of something all of whose elements, which do not emerge from the void but were already there and are combined in a new kind of visibility, are recognizable. Ultimately, the problem of the body, the problem of physics, is a problem of logic: we need to understand what the new composition or coherence of elements that were already there but were combined differently there, means. So the difficult issue is understanding the logic of the body. How are the figures of the body combined in the new postevental situation? And we've got to do this while maintaining the rigorous materialist imperative that precludes our taking the easy way out and saying that what the body is made up of wasn't there before. That would be a creationist approach. There would have to be an ex nihilo creation and thus an element totally heterogeneous to materialism.

It's from this that the question "What is a body?" arises for us. And this question requires taking a number of precautions. First, respecting the principle that the subjectivizable body is always a body that emerges. Second, this body must be identifiable as a body, so it has to have its own coherence—that's the question of logic. And third, it has to be made out of what was already there—that's the problem of materialism. Let me give you the three conditions of the physics of bodies again: (1) It's a new body and not the continuation of the capacities of a body already there. (2) Even though it's a new body, it appears as a body, has its own logic, an immanent cohesion, and is visible as a body. (3) It appears as a body inasmuch as it is made out of what was already there.

It's this triple injunction that I had decided to put to an unusual test: working through a poem. Why this test? Because this poem seems to me to be, and in fact is, as a poem, the history of the emergence of a body. As a poem, it is also in a sufficiently self-contained dimension to enable us to develop some provisional concepts. So I'm going to take up the stanzas of "The Graveyard by the Sea" again, referring to them by numbers 1–24 to make it easier for you to follow.

What is the poem about? It's ultimately pretty simple. It's the presentation of a place and therefore, in a way, the proposition of a world, of an event in this world, of a new body made possible by this event, and then of a truth for which this body serves as a support, of the subject that is incorporated into this truth, and so finally an answer to the question "What does it mean to live?"

There is, first, a theory of immobility, a continuist theory in the strictest sense of the term, that is to say, a theory of what this world would be like if it were entirely immobile, if we took its immanent immutability seriously. Then there is the theory of what I'd call the inexistent component of this world: the poet's consciousness. Next we have the evental creation, that is, the process of rupture. And, after that, directly connected with the process of rupture, the formation of the body and, retroactively, the understanding of the new body's capacities to treat points in the situation in a new way. This is the framework we're going to focus on.

So we start from a place that, I would remind you, is the town of Sète's graveyard by the sea. You can go there. You've got to see—it's strangely real. When you go there, you recognize it without any hesitation, even though, in a certain way, it's not described, or at least only in a very abstract way: there's the sea, the sun, the graves . . . Yet you're sure

362 What Does It Mean to Live?

that it's there. This is very instructive as to what a poem is when it's a complete success: it's an oxymoron, an absolutely unique generality. It's always possible, the great poems say, to express poetically with a universal power the most radically individual experience. That makes poetry an exceptional language. Poetry can start with something that might be considered untransmissible because it's an absolute singularity, and absolute singularity as such is not transmissible. And the more contemporary poetry is, the more immersed it is in absolute singularity. And yet poetry is capable of ensuring that this singularity attains a certain kind of universality without being wrested away or detached from its singularity. This is, moreover, why Plato was so worried about it. He was worried basically because, in his eyes—at least apparently, since Plato was an extremely cunning and devious character—to attain the intelligibility of the thing, you need to get away from its singularity or its immediacy. You shouldn't linger at this table but rise to the level of the table in itself. Later, you'll return to this table, but it's impossible, by clinging to it, to raise it as such to the universal. Universality is always the universality of the Idea, which, in a certain way, is nevertheless situated "elsewhere." The place of intelligibility must be distinguished from the place of immediacy. That's elementary Platonism, which ultimately has very little to do with Plato's devious subtlety. But that's what has become known as Platonism. Now, what poetry says is that it's nothing at all like that, and that, on the contrary, it's perfectly possible to universalize this particular table. Of course, to judge by the tables we have right before us here, it can't be easy! It would even be a challenge . . . But poetry, fundamentally, says that it's possible. You may not succeed, but it's not because it's impossible, it's because your poem is a failure. In the case at hand, it's very striking: there's no doubt that the starting point of the poem is the town of Sète's graveyard by the sea. The poem won't describe it, strictly speaking, and yet it never leaves it. It doesn't need to leave it to create what it has to create, namely, universal values, ultimately. So anything can be universalized by poetry, without its needing to be described in order for such an operation to be performed.

That was a little digression on poetry. Basically, the great Platonic tension runs between poetry, which makes that operation possible, and mathematics, which operates the other way around. Mathematics starts with the immediate apprehension of something that has no meaning other than its axiomatic universality, no meaning other than being affirmed in the element—not linguistic, moreover, but nearly translinguistic or directly symbolic—of its universality, that is, of its transparence. That said, it's clear that mathematics, coming from there, ends up moving, by concretions and complexifications of sorts, toward increasingly larger singularities. That's why I say it works the other way around. Actually, they are more like two intersecting movements than two opposite movements. But they're opposite in terms of their point of departure. That's what creates the tension, not just in Platonism but ultimately in thought itself, which is always poised between mathematics and poetry.

Let's return to our poem. This place, essentially, is reduced to four components. We've got the sea, the sun (which could also be called "noon"), the dead (this can also be the graves in the graveyard), and the poet's consciousness. These are the four components whose variation and interrelationship make up the whole fabric of the poem. The first three, the sea, the sun, and the dead, have a kind of undeniable existence. That is even their distinguishing feature. This point would merit a discussion in its own right, but all I'm doing is briefly describing it here. Ultimately, what is a world? Here we have a world that's the graveyard by the sea. A world consists of components associated with a certain degree of existence. But you can't just say that the world consists of components. You must also say, or make clear, what the intensity of their existence is in the world in question. A world is actually made up of components associated with a measure of existential intensity that indicates their degree of immanence to the world in question. That degree is variable. It's a variable intensity associated with the components, such that an object of the world is ultimately a couple and not a simple unit. An object of the world—and this is very general—is a component plus a value of existence, of intensity, which I, for my part, connect to something I call "the transcendental."[2] So we could say that a world consists of components with a transcendental value. I'm not going to go into the technical details. In Valéry's poem, the sun, the sea, and the dead have a maximal transcendental intensity, which simply means that their belonging to this world, their existence in this world, is absolutely indisputable. This world encompasses, contains the sea, the sun, and the dead, and all of that is the graveyard by the sea under the noonday sun. That leaves the fourth component, the poet's consciousness, whose degree of existence is less clear. It's definitely not maximal. Indeed, it borders on dissolution. It's a degree tending toward minimality. At the beginning of the poem, the poet is practically overcome by the sun and the sparkling sea. He identifies with the dead, to the point of envying them, the dead who "lie easy, hidden in earth where they / Are warmed and have their mysteries burnt away." In other words, the poet inexists.

Now, how will the poetic values work? Well, they'll work in the following way: the sun and the sea will be in a reciprocal relationship in the sense that the graveyard is the place where the sea is simply the mirror of the sun, the graveyard by the sea being the place where this relationship can be seen. As a result, we can say that, from the standpoint of the dead, of this fundamental third component, the graves, what is seen is the immobile relationship between the sun and the sea. Therefore, the world is ultimately the sun-sea-dead relationship, in which, from the standpoint of this annihilation, this earthly dissolution that is death, we see the sea and the sun as an immobile couple, each being the essence of the other. You'll find some excellent examples of all this in stanzas 10, 12, and 13, in particular.

The poet's consciousness comes in here as a question about its own degree of existence, namely, how is the consciousness positioned in relation to the dead-sun-sea triplet, that is, as you can clearly see, in relation to a fundamental principle of ontological immutability? Because, as is explained in stanzas 14 and 15, the dead are basically that dimension of the human subject that has opted for immutability, for nonlife: "To an impervious nothingness they're thinned, / For the red clay has swallowed the white kind." They are that possible aspect of consciousness that adopts the principle of immutability and, in so doing, falls on the side of the sun and the sea in their reciprocal immutability. Consequently, the consciousness is subjected to the cruel temptation of identifying with the dead, of considering that its share of the real is ultimately the people of the dead. Yet, if it identifies with the people of the dead, it will simply be the null point of the whole place. It will become that pure nullity, that "dark reservoir," which is the same as the immutability of the sun and the sea.

At bottom, the fourth component (the consciousness) is subjected to the temptation of being absorbed into the interaction of the other three, i.e., of opting for death as that which returns us to being. This isn't a speculative idea. To opt for death is actually the reason why the consciousness is ontologized, why it returns to the general destiny of being, since death is the mediation between the uncertainty of consciousness and the certainty of being. Metaphorically, poetically, the dead, the people of the dead, are the mediation between the weak existence of the consciousness and the glittering immutability of the sea-sun couple. You can see how the drama is set up. As a result, it's easy to understand why all of this concludes with a wholly speculative, or philosophical, stanza about the question of Parmenides. "Zeno, cruel philosopher Zeno!" is no doubt a bit allusive for anyone who's not familiar with this. In fact, what's at issue here is the philosophical victory of Parmenides and Zeno, that is, of these philosophers who, at the dawn of the history of philosophy, denied motion and thought that the essence of the appearance of motion was immobility. That arrow "that hums and flies, yet does not fly!" (stanza 21) is an allusion to Zeno's paradox of the arrow. Zeno attempted to show that, even though we believe the archer's arrow moves, it can actually be shown that it remains entirely motionless. There's another allusion to one of Zeno's paradoxes, the paradox of Achilles, who will never catch up with the tortoise because if the motions are broken down, it can be seen that it's impossible to catch up with another motion.

With these paradoxes that deny motion, the poem thus seems to be saying almost at its endpoint that, ultimately, death, physically present in the world, has triumphed. But it has triumphed—and this is a very important point—because it is a mediation for the immutable sovereignty of being. So it has triumphed not as an existential, nihilistic temptation but because the people of the dead have returned to that sort of immobile radiance that combines the sun and the sea. Indeed, the underlying idea is that the immutability of being is a sort of transcendence that the dead have already returned to. The consciousness is basically the absent one of this transcendence. This refers to two lines from stanza 13: "Motionless noon, noon aloft in the blue / Broods on itself—a self-sufficient theme." "Noon aloft in the blue" is transcendence, which, brooding as it should on itself, elicits the idea of a self-sufficiency of the transcendence of being. And what the poet will express right after this is that the only thing that could take exception to this immutability of being (fears, doubts, constraints, etc.) would be the consciousness, which he has say: "I am what's changing secretly in you." But this is not what the poem ultimately says: it seems to be geared toward the triumph of Parmenides and Zeno, that is, toward the triumph of the sun-sea tandem, with the help of the dead.

It's at this very moment that the "No, no!" with which stanza 22 begins comes in. Note that the line "Shatter, O body, meditation's mould!" clearly announces that the only possible recourse for avoiding this triumph of the immobility of being is the body. "Meditation's mould" is of course Parmenidean thought, thought that has succumbed to the triumph of the sun and the sea. The only means of shattering meditation's mold is the body. On the face of it, the body, here, is simply the body, meaning that the poem seems to be functioning within the opposition between the body and thought, which is further reinforced by the line "Let's run at the waves and be hurled back to living!" Yet that would be a simplistic reading of the poem, a kind of Nietzschean reading, a little like the way I said "Platonist" a moment ago, that is, a banal Nietzschean reading. It would amount to saying: Let's spark a revolt of the body and life against the sorcery of abstract thought, philosophy, and religion. This is one possible, and fairly frequent, interpretation: the reserves of the body's capabilities are appealed to, and the body is regarded as the affirmation of life against the maritime sorcery of the sun. We thus end up with a philosophy of vital spontaneity, which is contrasted with a philosophy of the capture of the mind by the immobility of being.

In fact, I think that what happens, including in the poem, is nothing at all like that. To my mind, what makes the "No, no! Arise!" possible is, on the contrary, a change in the sea's status. The sea, that fundamental component, turns out to be something different from what it was in the first part of the poem. First, we've got: "And, O my breast, drink in the wind's reviving!," which is an absolute condition. Something happens that is not just an appeal to the body against the mind. This something is the wind's reviving, which we find again a few lines later as "A freshness, exhalation of the sea." This is a surprising note, inasmuch as in all the rest of the poem, the sea was the mirror of the sun, the pure reflection of the immutable, the receptacle of transcendence. But, in reality, this heralds the last stanza, with "The wind is rising!" and "the wave / Dares to explode out of the rocks in reeking / Spray." What happened? Well, what happened was a metamorphosis of the sea, which alone will make possible the interjection "No, no!" and the chance for the emergence of the body.

Actually, there's an event in the poem itself, an event that can be very precisely described as a metamorphosis of the sea. If you think about it, you'll see that the phrase from the first stanza, the sea "forever starting and re-starting," can be interpreted in two different ways. This is an extremely interesting fact because, in a sense, it concerns the concrete dimension of all events. One interpretation might be that the sea is always self-identical, always in the process of being the same as itself. But it's also possible to interpret this to mean that the sea is nothing but perpetual difference from itself, and that this is why it is forever restarting. What happens in the poem is simply a shift from one meaning to the other. If you take "restart" [*recommencer*] in its passive sense, you will say that the fact that the sea is an ever-changing surface clearly expresses the immutability of the sea itself. It will thus become the mirror of the sun and will be made the sun's captive and a metaphor for death. Conversely, if you interpret the "forever restarted" [*toujours recommencée*] as "forever restarting" [*toujours recommençant*], you understand it to mean that the sea is ultimately eternal difference.[3] If what is imposed on visibility is the forever different, then we're dealing with a figure of the event. I propose we call this "the emergence of a site." We'll call "site" that component of a world whose transcendental value changes suddenly and absolutely. Here, the component is the sea, as a metaphor for difference. Up till this point, difference was negated by immutability, and, in consequence, the value of difference in the world of the graveyard by the sea was nil, its transcendental value was nil. And then, all of sudden, thanks to the freshness, "exhalation of the sea," "the wave / Dares to explode out of the rocks in reeking / Spray." Difference as such, i.e., the sea as the symbol of difference, assumes a decisive transcendental value.

The shift in the transcendental value of one of the constituent components of the world can be called an "event." That's what rupture is. It's not in the ex nihilo emergence of a new component; it's not creationist.

The shift is immanent to the world. It is simply the transmutation of the transcendental intensity of one of the components. What is contrived in the poem is that difference as such becomes a full-fledged component, with visible intensity, which means that metaphors of difference will proliferate and a whole metaphorics of difference, of emergence, of birth, will unfold, replacing the mirror-image metaphorics of the sun. It's the same component, "the sea," and it's even, in a way, the same word, taken in a sense that reverses its original one. It is, of course, in this evental element that you have the possibility of a body. The body that is called upon, which is without doubt the poet's body, the human body, the living body, is restored to its life only because this transformation of the sea, this switching of its transcendental meaning, has occurred. In reality, we are dealing with a new body. This body, which was explicitly said to have been attracted to the dead, this body, complicit with death, complicit with the sun's immutability, is no longer the same body as in the rest of the poem. The body that emerges is a new body, brought forth by the change and the switching of the sea's transcendental value.

That's a first, crucial point. An event is the emergence of a site in the world, hence the absolute change in the transcendental value of a component. The component remains the same, but its intensity value is radically altered, which, by the way, requires the object of the world to be a combination of the component and its intensity in order for the event to be possible. The event occurs when the intensity changes. This is exactly what an amorous encounter is: someone is already there, but the intensity changes, because of a switched, revised perception. It's clear that what is important in the eventalization of something is the change in its intensity of existence. It exists in a different way. This is very evident in the poem: the sea exists in a different way, and that's what makes it possible to say "No!" and not the other way around. Otherwise, saying "No!" would be purely rhetorical. And if this emergence of a body is not rhetorical, it's because the meaning of the sea has suddenly changed. I would add that this is a real experience for anyone who has ever been at the seashore. It's true that the sea's meaning can change. It's true that the sea is something that is constantly able to change. It can be the symbol of an annihilating glittering: you are wiped out by the sun and ultimately communicating with something that's the eternal receptacle of the sun.

But it can also be the exact opposite: the ocean swell, the storm, the excitement of living, danger. These are the two fundamental meanings of the experience of the sea. That's precisely why the sea is so fascinating. It can oscillate between two different meanings, regardless of which one is preferred. For us French, this is tantamount to the opposition between the Mediterranean and the Atlantic. But within this Mediterranean, change remains a potentiality immanent to the sea's power.

The sea has always been a philosophical subject. It's philosophical because it is essentially an immediate symbol of the opposition between Parmenides and Heraclitus, or some such thing. It is something that is shot through corporeally, so to speak, with the possibility of solar annihilation: "The sounding / Shaft gives me life, the arrow kills!" is one of the meanings of the sea, while "We must try to live!" is the other. That's why—and this is what's fascinating—it's the symbol of both the impossibility and the possibility of the event. It's the impossibility of the event because it is the immutable infinity and the pure receptacle of the sun, but, because of its heaving, its storms, its tides, its movement, it is also the symbol of the event.

"Free man, you will always cherish the sea," exclaimed Baudelaire. That's exactly right, because there is something about the sea that's like a metaphorics of the possibility of a new body. And this symbol is all the stronger because the sea is at the same time the symbol of its impossibility, something that can be understood as the endless recommencement of the sun's immobility. This can be transposed to the elements, and an elementary physics in the pre-Socratic sense can be formulated. The sea is essentially poised between the sun and the wind: there is the Parmenidean sea of the sun, and there is the Heraclitan sea of the wind. This is precisely what the poem describes, namely how the sea, which was on the side of the sun, switches over to the side of the wind at a given moment. It also describes how, provided there is a metamorphosis of the sea, a new body emerges. For the body that stands before the sea that's the receptacle of the sun is not the same body as the one that stands before the sea that has switched over to the side of the wind. It is really a new body, and this new body has capacities that the previous one didn't have.

This is what the first line of the last stanza will mean: "The wind is rising! . . . We must try to live!" With the new body, under condition of the new body, we can try to live. This is what we must now investigate. What does it mean that we must try to live? It means that the subjective imperative of the new body isn't that of the individual you were. When you have a new body, your imperatives change dramatically. Actually, with the body at the beginning of the poem, what had to be tried was to die. What had to be tried was to join the people of the dead, which is the real mediation with the immutability of being. With the new body, made possible by the eventual transformation of the seaside site, we must try to live. But what does "life" mean? Life is the new objective form appropriate to the new body, the body that opens up the possibility of a different subjective formalism, a different system of capacities, which will sediment, as it were, on this body. Which capacities? Well, the poem expresses this almost formally. A new capacity is basically a new way of saying yes and no. You'll note that stanza 22 begins with "No, no! . . . Arise!" "Arise!" is the figure in which a subjective form takes hold of the body. And stanza 23 begins with "Yes!" These are the new body's abilities: yes, we must try to live; no, it's no longer Parmenides, it's no longer the temptation of death. I reject it, and I stand facing the sea, the transformed sea, with a new body, that is to say, a new formal ability to say yes or no.

We're touching on something really important here. What I called a "point of the world" was the capacity to say yes or no to something of this world, an affirmative or a negative capacity, a capacity for the yes or no with respect to the whole world. A point of the world is the world's appearing before the capacity to decide. Formally, this means that something of the infinity of the world will go through the narrow pass of the yes or no, that is, before a tribunal of the Two. The appearance of the world before a tribunal of the Two is the infinity of the world filtered through the capacity for making a decision. And we can give a very precise definition of this capacity of the new body. It is to be able to treat new points, points that couldn't be treated before, or to treat them in a different way, and therefore to make the infinity of the world appear in a different way before the yes and no.

If we go back to the poem now, we'll be able to spot many passages that deal with this question. Will I really switch over to the side of the dead? Will I submit to the impartiality of noon? We can find this in stanza 7: "O just, impartial light whom I admire. . . ." The just, impartial light is the impartiality of noon, of this "impartial noon" [*Midi le juste*] that we encountered in the first stanza. It is Parmenidean impartiality, the impartiality that says: being is, yes, and nonbeing is not, no. And if you reread the poem, you'll find other instances of the same kind: being on the side of the "sure [*stable*] treasure" or on that of motion, being on the side of constraint or on that of freedom. In fact, all these points are taken up again at the end of the poem as pure capacities for saying yes or no, and yes or no contingent on a new body, as the capacity of a new body.

We can now reconstruct the overall plan of the poem, and this will give us a first approximation of what life is. Strictly speaking, the natural, continuous order of things does not propose life. I think Valéry has a deep, primal intuition about this issue, namely that the immediate proposition offered by a world, any world, is simply that we must comply with its fundamental disposition. That's what is meant by being of a world, being of the world, being transcendentally of the world, existing indisputably in it. And the more indisputably we exist in it, the more we are of the world. Yet what the poem is trying to tell us is that this is in some respects indistinguishable from death, that the mediation of this desire is always realized through a specific or singular figure of death. So here we have a first body that is a body of consent to the world. There's a remarkable passage in stanza 14: "But in their heavy night, cumbered with marble, / Under the roots of trees a shadow people / Has slowly now come over to your side." In Valéry's metaphorics, those who have already come over to the side of the world are the dead. More generally speaking, if you are merely the consent to the world, then death is a good metaphor for that consent. And Valéry continues in stanza 15: "To an impervious nothingness they're thinned, / For the red clay has swallowed the white kind," and he asks: "Where are the dead? [. . .] the soul informing each?," the souls of those who were willing to dissolve their singularity in the pure fact of being in the world. Therefore, if your desire is to be in the world, you'll have to reduce your singularity to the belonging to the world, and a reduction of that kind is ultimately indistinguishable from death. By "death" I mean the dissolution of a singularity, the fact of being "thinned" to "impervious nothingness." "For the red clay has swallowed the white kind" is magnificent. It's not presented as an existential drama but as an ontological figure. It's a figure of being, the resorption of singularity into being.

That's what Valéry tells us, and I'm stressing it because for us it means that life cannot be a matter of consent. Most of the time we are consenting, and that can't be called "life" in the sense that the poem is trying to ascribe to the word, not that it's, strictly speaking, something other than life, but it's a point where life is actually indistinguishable, indiscernible. Strictly speaking, it is no more death than life. It's a point of indiscernibility between life and death. The dead are ultimately the metaphor for those who came over to the side of what there is. That is a first level.

The second level is: something may nevertheless happen. In any world, something may happen, including in this world that's presented to us as the Parmenidean world, the one in which the sun, the sea, and the dead are in complete collusion with one another. And why may something happen? Well, because, when all is said and done, the transcendental values may change. If there were only what there is in the purest sense, it wouldn't be comprehensible. But what there is is always what there is combined with a value of intensity of existence in the world in question, and these transcendental values may change. Something that had a weak transcendental value may assume an intense transcendental value. That's what an event is. The event is a change in the intensity value of the existence of something in the world. I chose to call that a "site." Thus, in any world, a site may emerge, an event site. A site is something whose transcendental value becomes maximized.

It is in this sense that something may happen. And on condition that something may happen, a new body may emerge. It remains for us to ask, by way of the poem, what this new body is exactly. The answer is that it's simply everything that will subordinate its existence to the site, everything that will focus its existence on the site, that will be drawn by the site into a maximalization of its own existence. A body is a transcendental transformation. A body is everything that is required by the event. Technically, this can be put very simply: it is everything whose identity with the event is maximal. Here, too, it's formally pretty simple: you've got something that has assumed a higher transcendental value. Take all the components of the world that allow for as strong an identity as possible with this new element. Metaphorically, this is something that's mobilized by the event, something whose intensity of existence is affected by what happens and will depend on what has occurred. That is ultimately what a body is. It is something that will cluster around the eventual intensity as such and, provided that an event occurs, will form a new cohesiveness, of which the event is the referent. Let's not be too abstract, though. Let me provide an elementary phenomenology of it. A body will be, for example, what a historico-political eventality really mobilizes, namely those who become involved in the situation in a particularly strong way because of what is happening. Those who don't care aren't in the body. A new body is all the bodies that are incorporated into the site, whatever those bodies may be. So it really is an incorporation. You might say: But how does that create a new coherence? Well, it can be shown—I won't do so today because this is a very important issue that needs to be handled with care—that the components incorporated into a site have a new kind of compatibility with one another. A unique compatibility develops among all the bodies that are incorporated into a site.

Now what does the poem say about this? It says that a new compatibility develops among the wind, the sea, the poet, and, ultimately, the whole place (the rocks). Insofar as the sea's meaning has changed, because it has become the metaphor for motion, a compatibility, indeed a sort of indistinction among the poet's body, the wind, the "salt-breathing potency," and so on develops around it. And so the body of "Shatter, O body" is no longer really *my* body. It has become a part of the place, which obviously includes the "salt-breathing potency," the new meaning of the sea, the rising wind, and so on. The body is all this, all that is generated by and around the change in the meaning of the sea. That's why, in stanza 22, there's the rather terse sentence: "Let's run at the waves and be hurled back to living!" This means that the life in question, the aliveness of this new body, is in reality contained in a much larger body, that of the sea itself—the sea, the wind, and that on the basis of which there is truly life, i.e., the reason why there is a vitality and reality of the body. What the poem tells us is that we will call a "body" this new compatibility, this new coherence that forms around the event site and is a new situation internal to the world. Of course, it is this new body that will be the support for—what? Well, a new life. Life, not as it was before, but life as a new possibility of living. Because, when you think about it, "We must try to live!" is quite an extraordinary assertion. It could be said that, in order

374 What Does It Mean to Live?

to try to do anything at all, you first have to live. But this paradoxical assertion means that you have to try to use the new body's capacities. This would be impossible to understand if the capacities were the old ones, because the old capacities were already a form of life. But if we must "try" to live, it's because we have to try (i.e., try out) the new body's capacities. We have to be "hurled back to living" from a new situation.

We can now generalize and give a precise answer to the question "What does it mean to live?" To live means to always try out the capacities of a new body. And what is a capacity? I already said what it means. A capacity is the ability to treat a point. To treat a point is to summon the world to appear before the tribunal of a decision, before the yes or no. In reality, a point is a function between the transcendental of the world and a new body. It's a new compatibility, a new cohesion, that is capable of treating this type of point, capable of summoning the world to appear before the tribunal of the Two. In very basic terms, we could say that to live means a new way of confronting the bodily multiplicities that did not exist before, that suddenly emerged, and to summon them to appear as regards their capacities. But their capacities are ultimately the world caught in the net of a decision, placed in the dock before the tribunal of the Two. We might therefore say that to live always means the moment when a new body is confronted with a duality, with something that comes down to the Two of the yes or no. And what's exciting is obviously saying yes. So, in the final analysis, to live means the chance for a new body to say yes. That is what it means to live. But you all know this. Now we need to return to the general logic, and to do so in detail is not all that easy. So let's return to, and conclude with, stanza 23. Let me give you the whole stanza again:

> Yes, mighty sea with such wild frenzies gifted
> (The panther skin and the rent chlamys), sifted
> All over with sun-images that glisten . . .

By the way, you'll see that we've gone from the sun as a metaphor for the absolute One of the sea to a porous dispersal. The sea was the mirror of the sun, but now it has become the complete scattering of it. Thus, the emergence of the site is also the dispersal of what constituted One, the breakup of the One.

. . . . Creature supreme, drunk on your own blue flesh,
Who in a tumult like the deepest hush
Bite at your sequin-glittering tail—yes, listen!

And moving on to stanza 24:

The wind is rising! . . . We must try to live!

So, "yes"! Finally, the fundamental "yes" is the "yes" to the site itself, the "yes" to the new body. It is the new body accepted with its capacities. That is what it means to live. Next come all the other "yeses" that are the consequence of this original "yes." That is what it means to live.

To live basically means a new body that says yes, first of all to itself—that's the first "yes"—and then accepts the "yeses" (and also the "noes," but it's the "yeses" that matter) that are the consequences of the first "yes." This is why there's a connection between the first line of stanza 23 and the first line of stanza 24. You'll note, however, that the "We must try to live!" is not directly settled by the original "yes." The original "yes" is the accepted formation of the new body, but this does not yet settle the question of life. Life is a duration, an invention, a creation. It is what will take hold of the new body with its capacities, it is what will formalize the new body through the possibility of treating points. And it is of course the other "yeses" that will participate point by point in the consequences of the original "yes." And so what it means to live is never settled all at once; the original "yes" isn't sufficient. The fact is, to live means this random succession of "yeses," point by point, that ultimately involves the new body in the new world, the world where there is this new body. So what we'll need to investigate, once we've completely cleared up the question of points, is what the internal cohesion of these successive "yeses" is. It won't be so much the question of the body, then, as the question of the subject-form. The subject-form is what imposes the discipline of consequences on the body. A subject-form is nothing but that. It's a system of regulation of the consequences for a body, for a body that has been in a way accepted right from the start.

So there you have it.

Session 4

January 14, 2004

We are working—using everything that can help us, especially poems—from a sort of maxim that of course has no ultimate meaning other than in its effects. Remember, this maxim is: "There are only bodies and languages, except that there are truths."

We saw its significance when we analyzed it in Valéry's great poem "Le Cimetière marin."

I'd like to begin, or rather begin again, today at a more abstract level, with a few remarks about the form of this axiom. I think it's particularly important to understand the structure that's associated with the "except," i.e., with the figure of exception. I must stress that this is not the statement "There are bodies, languages, and truths," a simple assertion in which the Three would simply have been opposed to the Two through a sort of ontological supplementation. That would basically mean that whereas ordinary contemporary materialism holds that there are bodies and languages, we, for our part, just add that there are also truths. But it's not exactly additional. The "except" indicates that we're dealing with a figure of exception.

Let me remind you that the function of the exception, with its basic (including syntactic) schema ("except that," "save that," etc.), plays a key role in the poetry of Mallarmé, which is of course my main source as far as this issue is concerned. In "A Throw of the Dice Will Never Abolish Chance," for example, the final statement is "Nothing will have taken place but the place," which means that there is only what there is. Then, right after this, we read: "except on high perhaps as far as place can fuse with the beyond . . . a constellation."[1] Mallarmé recognizes that it can always be maintained that nothing will have taken place but the place, so there is only what there is. And the "except" indicates precisely that, in a certain sense, this is indeed true. The sentence "nothing will have taken place but the place" is moreover assertive, affirmative. With our maxim, it's the same thing: there are only bodies and languages, and we accept this materialist judgment or verdict. So the "except that there are truths" will in a way be an exception to the "there are only bodies and languages," including ontologically. It will let it be, but it will introduce a random exception, of absolutely the same sort, ultimately, as the constellation exception in Mallarmé's poem. That was my first remark. You can of course see how it will tie in with the theory that there ultimately have to be new bodies. Indeed, to act as a support for truths, to act as a support for what is an exception to the field of the "there is," new bodies will have to emerge, the way the constellation does.

My second remark is that, between the two statements, the democratic materialism one and the materialist dialectic one, the relation is not one of contradiction in the usual sense of the term. In other words, dialectical materialism isn't in a contradictory position in relation to democratic materialism. One is a sort of exceptional incision into the other, and it maintains the other even as it takes its distance from it. I would propose to call this, obviously echoing Deleuze, a "disjunctive relationship." Not exactly a disjunctive synthesis but a disjunctive relationship. This relationship is created through the acceptance of an exception. Why "relationship"? Well, because there is this basic relationship between them, which they both include, namely that there are only bodies and languages. As I've already had occasion to tell you, there's a materialist kinship between these two statements that shouldn't be underestimated. We're not dealing with the materialism-idealism opposition but with a split within materialism itself, with an inner division. There is indeed a relationship, therefore, but it's a disjunctive one because the second statement implies that we need to accept the exception.

If we wanted to translate this into a more Lacanian-type language, we could say that the dialectical materialism statement is explicitly a statement that cannot be the opposite of the previous one because it "is not all," it is not the totalization of its parts. In other words, it is not the totalization of "bodies," "languages," and "truths," since truths are exceptions to the first two. So we have this figure of the disjunctive relationship that ensures that the second statement is not totalizing, just as the constellation in Mallarmé's poem doesn't form a totality with the place that will have taken place. Indeed, Mallarmé says this clearly: "as far as place can fuse with the beyond." So it's neither here nor elsewhere; it's "a place" and "the beyond" fused together, it's a "here" that is elsewhere, that is neither the place nor its beyond. The same can be said about truths. The dialectical materialism statement is thus explicitly a "not-all"-style statement, which leaves totality by the wayside. By contrast, the democratic materialism statement *is* totalizing; that is even its distinguishing feature: there are only bodies and languages, and apart from bodies and languages, there's nothing. So we know what the "there is" effectively consists of. Whereas, on account of the exception, of the heterogeneous "except," there is no totalization in the other maxim. We'll therefore conclude (once again, provided we accept this Lacanian translation): dialectical materialism is on the side of the "not-all," which, as you know, is on the female side. Dialectical materialism is therefore democratic materialism's woman. I don't know if they're a couple—there's no totality in a couple, it's untotalizable, as a matter of fact—but it's something like that.

As you know, Hegel said that woman was the irony of the community. What he meant by that is that she wasn't part of the totalization of the community, that she was an exception to the totalization of the community. So he could have said something like: "There is the community, except that there are women." And this can be defended: it's a direct translation of Hegel's statement. It's sort of the same thing here: the "except that there are truths" opens a breach in the bodies-languages totalization. It is a breach, an incision. And it is what naturally prevents this statement from being on the side of dialectical totalization. This leads to a formidable consequence, namely that dialectical materialism does not represent a dialectical overcoming of democratic materialism. It's not like in the dialectical movement, where we know, or think we know, that there is a successful or positive overcoming of the miseries of the time. Here, the democratic totalization is perfectly self-sufficient, which is why it was associated with an end of history, whether you believe in such a thing or not. Indeed, the possibility of such an implication is inscribed in the totalizing nature of the statement. Furthermore, since it requires no transcendence, there isn't even any exteriority, strictly speaking. There is an immanence, but a closed immanence, which can be represented in the figure of an end. Historicity would only have to unfold, from within, this closed immanence, which, of course, in no way promises, in its inner composition, to open up. So in no way does it propose, internally, dialectical materialism as the figure of its overcoming. This means that there is no immanent logic of the exception, which is the price that has to be paid for the disjunctive nature of the relationship. If the relationship is disjunctive, there is no immanent logic of the exception, and so there is ultimately nothing but axiomatics, i.e., separate propositions neither of which is the totalization of the other. Therefore, you can always think, in effect, that today's world, as it is, is good—"good" meaning simply that it's a closed immanence—and that wanting to open it up to something else necessarily amounts to needless destruction. So it's true, in a sense, that anyone with a grudge against this world is a virtual terrorist. That's an absolutely true statement! Well, maybe not true but, let's say, consistent. Once you've got a closed immanence, you're bound to think that anyone who wants to open it up to something else is actually only working toward its destruction. This is consistent with the closed hypothesis that there are only bodies and languages and that what we need to do is adapt the languages to the bodies, i.e., as I said before, create freedom. And so the enemies of this are inherently enemies of freedom and proponents of destruction. That the war is a war on terror is, in this context, a globally relevant statement. In light of this, any other hypothesis is necessarily separate, that is to say, cannot lie within the strict immanence of the first formulation.

That's a big difference with the traditional dialectical schema, including in the orthodox Marxist tradition, which always tries to discern, in the figure of immanent totalization, the critical, dialectical, contradictory lineaments of its overcoming. Here, we have nothing like that, which is clear—I'm returning to my point of departure—from the syntactic form of the maxim. There is the same world for us as the one the democrats talk about. There's the same world, except that there's something else, but the "except that there's something else" is prescriptive, since it is not based on the recognition of the immanent virtualities of the first totalization.

As I was preparing to speak to you, I realized that there was something like that, something dialectical materialist in that sense, in the work of someone you wouldn't expect to find it in, namely Descartes. So I'd like to talk to you a bit about Descartes . . . in my own way! My starting point will be article 48 of *The Principles of Philosophy*. This work from 1644 is dedicated to Princess Elisabeth . . . Here we are, dealing with the "not-all"! The preface begins with a dedication to the princess. It's a beautiful text because it's one in which something absolutely amorous truly comes through in the flattery, in the obligatory flattery. Dedicating a book to a princess is a relatively conventional business. There are a number of things you have to say, and you're well aware of this. For that matter, if *you* had to dedicate a book to a princess, you'd be in real trouble . . . Descartes, though, had a rhetoric at his disposal. But what makes this text so remarkable, in the context of the rhetoric of dedications to the high and mighty, is the fact that there's something utterly sincere about it, something I'd call amorous in a somewhat generic, broad sense: the consideration given to Princess Elisabeth's uniqueness. Descartes considers her, not just in this text but in many others as well, as his key disciple, as someone to whom everything is ultimately addressed.

As you know, Descartes implies on several occasions that when you're a philosopher, either you address yourself to the Sorbonne or you address yourself to women. There aren't all that many other alternatives. In particular, he says: "That's why I write in French." Latin was the language of the Sorbonne people. "But the Sorbonne people have never been of any use to me," he adds, even though he also wrote a rather prudent dedication to them in the Latin text of the *Meditations*. Descartes was the first to say, before many other people, especially in the eighteenth century, that conversation with a society woman, not the Sorbonne, was the real testing ground for philosophy. That has remained the case. It's a French national invariant! If philosophy in France is different from philosophy elsewhere, it's because, ever since Descartes, it has addressed itself to women. Whereas we're not so sure if that's the case in Germany! And why is this so? Descartes explains it in the preface, and it's remarkable. Philosophy has such a position, he says, because, as a rule, the people who understand the mathematical part of his work and the people who understand the metaphysical part aren't the same people. And, in a way I think is absolutely sincere—I really don't think he's lying to us—he tells Princess Elisabeth: "You're the only one who understands both. You're the only one who approaches reading or listening in a way that doesn't specialize this listening, that doesn't systematically focus it on one aspect rather than another." You can see how this is actually a way of saying: "You accept the whole of me because you don't go in for abstract totalization and the regime of specialization, of classification, that goes with it." The Sorbonne metaphysician will understand the metaphysics because that's his own exclusive field, while someone who's exclusively a mathematician will understand the mathematical part and ignore the other. What we're dealing with there is specialized totalization, while Princess Elisabeth, by contrast, represents openness, quite simply: she doesn't need to go through the strictures of linguistic specialization to understand what Descartes is saying to her. Let's hear what he says:

> Many other people, even those of the most acumen and learning, find them [my writings] very obscure; and it generally happens with almost everyone else that if they are accomplished in Metaphysics they hate Geometry, while if they have mastered Geometry they do not grasp what I have written of First Philosophy. Your intellect is, to my knowledge, unique in finding everything equally clear; and this is why my use of the term "incomparable" is quite deserved. And when I consider that such a varied and complete knowledge of all things is to be found not in some aged pedant who has spent many years in contemplation but in a young princess whose beauty and youth call to mind one of the Graces rather than gray-eyed Minerva or any of the Muses, then I cannot but be lost in admiration.[2]

So there you have it. Of course, you could say he takes away with one hand what he gives with the other because he ends up singing the praises of femininity, but I don't think it should be understood that way . . .

Descartes was a man of the seventeenth century, of course, but as a man of the seventeenth century, he should be understood as being totally sincere in what he is saying. Ultimately, Princess Elisabeth's grace is an angle from which we can understand why she had that openness, that is, why she wasn't an "aged pedant"—the word "pedant" is very important; it is precisely opposed to that femininity he acknowledges in her. She wasn't a pedant, and because she wasn't, she was, in a way, involved in the living contemporaneity of what was being spoken about in philosophy. You need to bear this in mind when dealing with the question of whom the *Principles* was addressed to and its style.

Let's go back to article 48 now. To properly understand article 48, you need to remember the common view of Descartes, namely that he is regarded as the philosopher who made a radical distinction between two kinds of substance: extended substance and thinking substance. So there is—fundamentally, as far as the pedants are concerned—a Cartesian dualism, a radical dualism, meaning that, when the influence of one upon the other then has to be considered, it's very tricky, because the point of departure is really separation. Thought as substance and extension as a figure are really two distinct universes, almost entirely cut off from each other, and this is the foundation of Descartes's dualistic metaphysics. As is well known, it gave rise to two different traditions. On the side of the theory of bodies, there was a rigorous mechanism. This is how a host of eighteenth-century materialists would be Cartesians after their own fashion, with the animal-machine theory, and so on, hence a rigorous mechanism, since, in terms of extended substance, there was nothing but geometry. And then, on the other side, there was a spiritualist and psychologizing tradition of introspection that wholly isolated the phenomena of mind. Those are the two great post-Cartesian traditions. This is why, especially in this country, there has always been a rather strange juxtaposition of a really rigorous mechanistic scientism, on the one hand, and particularly intense forms of spiritualism, on the other. Well, the key to this riddle is very simple: it's that the two are juxtaposed in the Cartesian construction. That's why it's really our French national perspective, no doubt about it! Not just the united national perspective but, more profoundly, the national perspective of our division, of two entirely different speculative traditions.

What is so striking about article 48 of the *Principles* is that it proposes a distinction, and that this distinction is not at all the expected one. This is what suddenly struck me and what I'd like to convey to you:

> I distinguish [*this is the beginning of the article*] all the objects of our perception into two kinds: the first contains all the things (*choses*) that have some existence, and the other, all the truths that are nothing outside our thought.[3]

The unusual distinction proposed here, as more originary or fundamental than the classic distinction between thought and extension, is the distinction between things and truths. So we think, "OK, sure, but that's just another name for it: in reality there will be corporeal things, on the one hand, and the truths of the mind, on the other." Well, that's not at all the case! Because Descartes goes on to say:

> And the principal distinction that I note between created things is that some are intellectual . . . and the others are corporeal.

The great Cartesian dualistic distinction between intellectual and corporeal things is ultimately internal to the category of things. And so you have a system in which, on the one hand, there are truths, and, on the other, things. Within the things, we find the traditional dualism—intellectual and corporeal things—and then, in the third place, because he does after all have to mention them, Descartes adds mixed things, i.e., the mixtures of corporeal and intellectual, which always gave him a lot of trouble: the passions, desires, needs, and so on. But all of them are in the realm of things. So it's as though Descartes were proposing a construction within which, as you can see, the classic distinction between thought and extension, intellectual things and corporeal things, is actually subordinated to a more originary distinction, the distinction between things and truths.

So now we think: "All right! Truths must be on the side of languages, since languages are opposed to bodies." And if we look at this through modern eyes, we might say: on the one hand, there are things, that is, what simply exists, and, on the other hand, there are languages. So naturally we try to figure out what Descartes really means . . . Can we find that connection between truths and languages in his work? And, concerning language, we do find something in article 74 of the *Principles*. So what is language? Well, it's one of the causes of falsity! Not at all the container of truth! It is actually the fourth cause of our errors.

The theory of the causes of error is very fascinating. Indeed, if the basic distinction is really between truths and things, with things being themselves, in their turn, either intellectual, possibly linguistic, or corporeal, then the question of where falsity comes from, where what is truly antinomic to truths comes from, is absolutely crucial.

As you probably know, there is an almost pre-Freudian theory about this in Descartes. The main cause of falsity for him is childhood, because in childhood we acquired what he calls "prejudices." It might just as easily be said that we acquired the unconscious. It doesn't change the Cartesian system in the least. What Descartes call "prejudices" are actually primal structures that frame our experience in distinctions heterogeneous to truths. These are what he calls childhood prejudices, which are cause number 1 of our errors. So we might say, anachronistically, that cause number 1 of our errors is the unconscious as it was shaped in childhood. But why in childhood? Descartes's answer is that childhood is a time when there is a particularly intimate mixing of the intellectual and the corporeal, the time when—as he says in utterly astonishing terms—the soul and the body are in particularly close proximity to each other. So childhood has a precise definition: it is the time when the separation between the soul and the body is only just developing; it is taking shape, it is emerging. And so the soul and the body are in such close proximity that, ultimately, childhood is in a certain way the time of the body. What I mean is, it's the time of the body for the soul, a notion that is incidentally very similar to a theory of the drives. It's basically the time when the soul is wholly shot through with something that is homogeneous with the body, which it will store as what Descartes calls "prejudices," i.e., those sorts of mental dispositions we'd call primal fantasies today, which will frame our experience and are the first cause of our errors.

This is reinforced by the fact that the second cause of our errors is that these childhood prejudices are indestructible, says Descartes. This is really reminiscent of the indestructibility of unconscious formations.

And he explains that, even if we know—he practically names the unconscious—that we have childhood prejudices, it doesn't mean they'll disappear. This is really the way experience is organized, and it's very hard
to break free of it because it's a primitive corporeal imprint that can't be
removed simply by being aware of it: even if you know that that's what
childhood is like, you'll still go on structuring your experience the way
you've been structuring it.

The third cause of error is that we tire easily: concentrating the mind is
exhausting. But be careful: the concentration of the mind, mental focus,
is precisely the opposite of childhood. It's the time when you're involved
in the life of the mind as independently as possible from the pressures of
the body. To that end, Descartes explains, you have to concentrate for an
exceedingly long time on the object in question, and it's extremely tiring
to give up being a child. It's exhausting. What's more, as you know, he
himself often says that he only devotes very little time to it. He begins by
saying that he needs to get ten hours of sleep a night. And he repeats it:
if he doesn't get ten hours of sleep a night, he's a wreck. Then, he devotes
a few hours a month to mathematics, and only a few hours altogether to
metaphysics! The rest of the time he deals with things that are closer to
the body, namely, medicine, mechanics, or ethics, for example. You can
devote more time to those three because they're closer to the body. But
when you're doing mathematics or metaphysics, which are very remote
from childhood, it's exhausting. That's the third cause of our errors.

First, there's childhood as the primitive instinctual imprint; second,
there's the indestructibility of that imprint; and, in the third place,
there's the obligation to break away from all of that, which is so tiring.
Not to be a child any more is grueling, and you can't do it for very long:
you necessarily lapse back into childhood patterns. So, says Descartes, it
is language that will be the fourth cause of our errors:

Finally, because of the use of language, we tie all our concepts to the
words used to express them; and when we store concepts in our memory we always simultaneously store the corresponding words. Later on
we find the words easier to recall than the things; and because of this
it is very seldom that our concept of a thing is so distinct that we
can separate it totally from our concept of the words involved. The

thoughts of almost all people are more concerned with words than with things; and as a result people very often give their assent to words they do not understand, thinking they once understood them [*Here, he's obviously referring to childhood again: language itself comes from way back when! Long ago . . .*], or that they got them from others who did understand them correctly.[4]

As you can see, Descartes has an absolutely instrumental conception of language: language is the choice of a means of expression. It is not at all a factor in the formation of ideas as such. It's a means of transmission, and that's all. It's just that it happens to be tied to ideas, that we therefore tie ideas to their language vehicles, and, as a result, it's as though you received the things in a package and you mistook the package for the things, the box for what's inside it. Especially since you also trust the people you learned the languages from.

Therefore, we will certainly not find in language any way to distribute our terms in the great Cartesian opposition between truth and things. Actually, language is part of things. It amounts to material conventions and isn't one of the most beneficial or harmless things, if only because, generally speaking, it is deceptive. This means—and the text, moreover, shows this clearly—that there is collusion between language and childhood. Childhood is the fundamental matrix of our errors, and language itself is in cahoots with childhood because we learned it. Yet we learned it through relationships that are often completely incomprehensible. Why is such and such a word associated with such and such a thing? We have no idea! It was taught to us that way, so it's suspect, like everything that happened in childhood.

Childhood, ultimately, is the place of bodies, and the place of languages, too. And Descartes's statement could be: "There is childhood, except that there are truths," which is very profound. Indeed, I note that, as the influence of democratic materialism grows, there is rampant infantilization. That's why I think the idea of a deep connection between a universe that is limited to the relationship between things and languages, on the one hand, and to childhood, on the other, is very true. I believe that, within his own parameters, Descartes put his finger on something extremely important, which is that, when it's a matter of

eliminating the exception—which is the key issue of democratic materialism—there is not and must not be any exception. The "except that,"
the "save that," is expunged. And if you expunge that, well, in one way
or another, you lapse back into childhood. Which, once again, is not for
the time being necessarily normative, since it's possible to speak in favor
of childhood. After all, you might say that rampant infantilization is a
good thing, because if you extol the figure of the adult, you can always
be accused of being an Old World bore! As we know, there are always
polemics against the cult of youth. That debate is well known. But it's
a far-reaching one: if you've got a world in which there are only things
and languages, as Descartes with his usual perspicacity discussed, there is
effectively something childish about it. And this irreducible childishness
can be seen in the fact that what there is is the drive, the drive joined to
the object, in other words, ultimately, the compulsion to buy. The world
ends up being like a broken-down Santa Claus. It's a sack full of stuff,
and every day's a holiday, only it's a bit depressing. This image of an
endless Christmas where we'd be hanging up our stockings every night is
an image we all more or less share, and when I say as much, don't think
I'm saying it with detached irony. It's very true that there are only bodies
and languages! We ourselves are never absolutely exempt from it, that's
for sure. But the connection between this and the figure of childhood is
very important, and that's why our society is of necessity a society of the
sacralization of childhood—as the central, fantasized treatment of the
figure of the pedophile shows, it must be said. I'm not going to get into
that, which I had occasion to discuss last year . . . Even so, think about it:
the pedophile is a key figure in the public sphere, as a negative figure. And
God knows how negative a figure it is! But it's important to understand
that, if it's that figure rather than any other, it's because it corresponds to
a sacralization of childhood, a sacralization of childhood that completely
ignores the great discoveries that have been made about childhood since
the beginning of the twentieth century, starting with the great discovery
by Freud, who proved that children were anything but little saints. They
were first and foremost, as he put it, "polymorphously perverse." And
also, pretty much inherently, little criminals. Thinking of them as little
angels is rank stupidity. They're not little angels, yet, at the same time,
you can clearly see that it's important, if only in the general system of

judgments, that this should be partly the case, and that it should be this that people say or think. But it's not for an external reason, it's for a fundamental immanent reason, which is that, in a certain sense, childhood is our general norm. It's not just a question of young people, it's a question of the child, i.e., someone for whom the miracle of the world is the gift. Someone whose main occupation is playing with toys. All you have to do is walk down the street to see this . . . [*Badiou takes his cell phone out of his pocket and shows it off*]: like this, for example! [*laughter*]. I'm taking it out of my pocket; I have one too . . . Look. I have a cell phone too, I have other gadgets, toys of all sorts, too, just like everyone! But at some point, you still have to give this some serious philosophical consideration. What does it mean? I, for one, think it means that the well-nigh ontological maxim of democratic materialism is one that implies that, in the end, our general norm is the norm of childhood. This is why I was suddenly alerted by this tangential and ultimately very interesting text of Descartes's, in which the body-language-childhood connection is globally opposed to one term alone: truths. This is all the more extraordinary in that we might wonder what truths really *are* in Descartes. Well, in fact, we'll never really know. He doesn't give a definition of truths. It's not like when he defines thinking substances and extended substances, that is, traditional dualism. The opposition between truths and things is an elusive one, hard to pin down. Especially since we won't find anything to base it on in language or the linguistic medium.

Yet it's a fundamental opposition. What Descartes finally tells us is that only truths are an exception to things. And things are all there is. For, as I already mentioned, things are not just corporeal things but intellectual things as well. They're the "there is." So truths are able to stand as an exception to the "there is," which is quite enigmatic. In reality, what resists this exception with its all its might in us is childhood. Because there is indeed a theory of childhood, namely that childhood is surely not the locus of evil—that would be a pure and simple reversal of the angelic view—but it should be taken seriously in Descartes as being precisely the locus of things. It's clear that our society is a society made up of things, of a cult of things, as commodities arousing the desire of the subject for whom there are only bodies and languages. That our world is only composed of things is the thesis of Georges Perec's first book, which made his reputation and whose title, as a matter of fact, is *Things*. It's a book that can be reread today with the greatest interest. When it came out in 1965, the book made a big splash because it was the first time that the idea that our society is a society of things had been transformed into a novelistic or literary figure. But if our society is a society of things and if childhood is the locus of things, well, then there's a relationship between our society and childhood. And so, for Descartes at any rate, the figure that's an exception to this, that is bracketed off from it, will be called truths, and truths are not related to language either, which, for him, is in the realm of things. For Descartes, ultimately, there are only childish toys, except that there are truths.

I've used Descartes as an introductory overview. Let's return now to the general development of the subject, within this hypothesis, and once the position of the dialectical materialism maxim has been properly understood. I said that there had to be a retroaction of the exception on the materialist given of bodies and languages. Therefore, and this is the key to it all, there will be a transformation of the concept of body. Because if we are really materialists, we must necessarily think that this happens in connection with a split in the concept of body, in connection with the possibility of the emergence of a different body, a new body.

I also said that it's a change in the conception of freedom. In democratic materialism's conception, freedom consists in languages letting bodies be. For us, the maxim is that new bodies emerge, bodies capable of truths and of acting as the support for the subjective formalism of a truth. And I said that the meaning of "to live" also changed. Still with respect to the disjunctive relationship I was talking about, "to live," in democratic materialism, means the perpetuation of empirical bodies and their alleged desires. Living means living well. I was recently looking at an ad for one of those countless women's magazines. The name of the magazine was "Feeling Good About Your Life." Now there's a maxim for you! Feeling good about your life! I try to be on the side of women, in Lacan's sense, as the "not-all." But the magazines also try to stand resolutely and metaphysically on women's side. Because "feeling good about your life" was immediately illustrated by a fulfilled woman, a woman happy with being a woman, happy with being herself, happy with the world, happy with everything, well-adjusted and content. This woman's life can be expressed as: "feeling good about her life." Life is something that must be consistent with the positive perpetuation of human vitality, whereas, of course, in the conception that admits the exception, it might be said: to live is to participate in a new body, or some such thing. I'll suggest a precise formulation later on. But, for now, let's just say that to live is to be incorporated in the present. And to be incorporated in the present can be understood in two different ways. Either as a temporal reference, that is, the incorporation takes place in the present, here and now; it's not a pregiven, preformed, etc. incorporation. But to be incorporated into the present can also mean to enter into the body of the present. To be incorporated into the present is something urgent: it's the present that matters; the incorporation needs to happen *now*. But it's also the fact that, since this body itself is a body in the present, it is into this present that one must be incorporated, in that it offers the possibility of a new body.

After the first, as it were concrete, presentation of this question of the new body, via Valéry's poem "Le Cimetière marin," I think we can summarize things in a more abstract way. I'd say we are dealing with seven sequenced concepts, seven concepts that we can use. My aim today is just to mention all seven of them, so that everything is perfectly clear and we can move ahead and turn to the organization, the practice, of the true life.

Let me give you these seven concepts in their order of connection:

1.   *The site*, which could also be called *the evental site*. The intuitive idea, if you will—I'm not formalizing it all that much here—is that of a sudden change in meaning of one of the elements of the world. We will call "site" an element of the world, of the world in question (there's a plurality of worlds), whose meaning changes dramatically. In Valéry's poem, for example, we saw that this was the case for the sea element, "the sea forever starting and re-starting." Its meaning changed with respect to what "re-starting" meant. There was a complete change in the meaning of one of the elements of the world. We could obviously come up with many other examples. I'm taking them here in a completely abstract way. We might think, for example, of a dominated, passive segment of the people whose meaning would change dramatically because

it would become a direct, major political actor. Or of a certain type of relationship, in the work of art, between the form and the sensible world: something of the sensible world that was regarded as formless suddenly shifts over to form, is acknowledged as having form. This shift from formlessness to form, in terms of the dialectics of the sensible, is also a complete shift in the meaning of the boundary between sensible world and form. Of course, as I already mentioned, an example like this can be imagined in connection with an amorous encounter. A site is that element of the world that is exposed to a shift in its meaning and consequently appears in an absolutely different way in the world. That's why it can be identified as a site. The starting point for everything is that there must be a site.

2.   *The trace.* Naturally, this dramatic shift in meaning is, in itself, evanescent. I mean that, qua shift, it takes place, and in taking place, it passes away. The meaning has effectively changed, but the shift in meaning, that is to say, the boost in power of the shift in meaning, is evanescent. And yet it always leaves a trace. What is the trace of a site? The trace of an event? Hence the trace of a point of the world whose meaning has effectively changed? Well, this trace is always the fact that a component of the world, an element of the world, that had a very weak, almost zero or nil existential intensity—in other words, a component of the world absolutely on the point of disappearing—now has a maximal, or very great, intensity. The trace is always a change in intensity in a point. You remember how, in Valéry's poem, that zero point was the poet's consciousness, a consciousness annihilated by the world of complicity formed by the sea, the sun, and the dead. And faced with this ultimately Parmenidean world, the poet's consciousness dwindled to the point of near-nothingness. But when the seaside site revives, the poet's consciousness will instead regain a maximal intensity of existence, which will enable him to declare the "We must try to live!" Where there was, in a sense, nothingness, there is suddenly a maximal intensity. Any trace of an event appears as a change in intensity of a component that was hitherto regarded as negligible or nil, which now proves to be of exceptional intensity. This is the sign of the present, the emergence, the creation, the construction, of a new present that is the postevental present. The postevental present is a hitherto unknown intensity which is

there where there was nothing before, or only a very weak intensity. It's because of this that a present will be created. But what, incidentally, is a truth (in the sense of "except that there are truths")? Actually, a truth is the consequences of the trace. It's the general system of consequences of the trace. It's the realization of a new present and therefore the material unfolding of a new present in the world. And as the evidence of the creation of the new present is the intensity of the trace, you could also say that the unfolding of the present "in truth" is the unfolding of the consequences of the trace. It's just that these consequences have to be acted on! When we say "consequences," it doesn't mean passive determinations. These consequences have to be produced, and, to that end, there needs to be a body. Because there can be no production of consequences without the materiality of a body. So there has to be a new body, which brings us to "to be incorporated."

3.   "*To be incorporated*" is to be incorporated into the present, as I just said. And a precise definition of this can be given. To be incorporated means to exist with maximal identity with the trace, or, in other words, to exist at a very high intensity in relation to the trace, which is itself imbued with a very great intensity. To exist maximally in relation to the newness of a body. Incorporation into the present occurs when there's the emergence of an intense trace that serves as your guide for a relationship with the newness of a body, which takes possession of as much of your life or your life energy as possible. Incorporation is the process of entrance into the present. That's how you enter the new present. You enter it by existing in accordance with a model of intensity that is set by the trace. That's what incorporation is.

4.   Now, what is *the body*? Once incorporation has been defined, defining the body is quite simple. The body is all the elements of the world effectively incorporated into the present. For example, we saw in Valéry's poem that they were parts of the poet's body but also the foam, the wind, and so on. Once again, let's not conceive of this as the conventional model of the organic individual. All the elements of the world that are incorporated into the trace will constitute the identification of a body. And, of course, this is a new body, given that the figure of what is incorporated this way depends on the site and the trace and has no intrinsic consistency apart from the site and the trace, since it's the trace

that provides the measure of the incorporation intensities. The body is the product of the incorporation, the overall product of all the components incorporated into the trace of the event.

5.   After this, we need to understand *the process*, or how the body will serve as the support for the subjective formalism that unfolds the consequences of the present. How will the consequences of the trace be organized? What will the new body's process be? What will it do? To answer this, we need the concept of point. Because, basically, the answer will be: what a new body can do is treat points that were not points before. We could use a different vocabulary and say: create and solve problems that weren't problems before. But "point" seems more topological to me and therefore basically more visualizable. What is a point of the world? A point, I repeat, is a crystallization of the infinity of the world in the Two, i.e., in the tribunal of the yes or no. It's the moment when the world appears in the flash of a decision, when you have to say yes or no, when you have to decide about something. We are all familiar, in every possible sphere of experience, with those times when we can't just go along with the usual order of things, when we have to summon the world—our world, the one in which there's this experience—to appear before something that formalizes its split, that is, something that's in the radical form of consent or refusal. I suggested that it is the filtering of infinity by the Two. Technically, it's a function, that is to say, something that makes a yes or no correspond to every point of the world. You will say yes or no not to one detail or other of the world but to the world as a whole. To affirm a point, which is the essence of the subjective process of a truth and therefore the essence of the true life, is simply to say yes; it is to treat the appearance of the world in a given point with an affirmative answer. To affirm a point will be to consent to the present in the figure of a real decision, in the figure of a local consent given to a general figure.

6.   We can now define what the *efficacious part of a body* is. It can be defined for a point. Given a point, the efficacious part of a body is all the elements of the body that affirm the point. Actually, it's never the totality of the body that affirms the point, as we well know. That would be like returning to the fantasy of pure totalization, to the idea that the body has the perfect ability to fully affirm all the points. No, it's always a *part* of the body that is required by a given point, and it's this part

that will be involved in affirming the point. So the efficacious part of the body for a point will be defined as all the elements of the body that affirm the point. This is also an ordinary experience. We know very well, when we affirm a point—I mean when we decide on a global level—that it is a true decision, precisely because a part of ourselves resists it. The affirmation has to be taken seriously. The affirmation is the affirmation as a new affirmation, but an affirmation is only new if it's wrested away from something, that is, if the efficacious part of the body that affirms the point is not the totality of the body. It is the efficacious part that prevails because it's precisely it that is efficacious for the point. So we'll call "efficacious part of the body for the point" all the elements of the body that affirm this point. And you can see that as the body, in treating points, sees efficacious parts that treat these points become differentiated within it, an immanent organization of the body develops. The body is not preorganized. It becomes organized through the treatment of points. That's the constructive aspect of things. We know this from experience: we must construct. To live is to construct! It's true that life is the creative organization of life. The "living" we are talking about, the "living-in-truth," is not preorganized. On the contrary, it is the treatment of points that organizes, from within, the subjectivated body's capacity. The body is everything that is incorporated into the present; it's an inaugural gesture. But the immanent structuring of the body, its true organization, develops point by point. There's a sort of gradual sedimentation of the body's efficacy that is never global but is instead an internal organization put to the test of successive decisions. That is what an efficacious part is.

7. And now, what about *organ*, the final concept? Well, we will call "organ" the existence of a sort of synthesis of an efficacious part, i.e., what concentrates the efficacious part, what its synthetic envelope or affirmation is. Either it exists or it doesn't exist. When you've got a synthesis of the efficacious part, any point comparable to the point treated by the efficacious part will be treated by the organ, which is like a point of maximum concentration of the efficacious part. And so, little by little, the body develops organs for the points it has to treat and that are syntheses of efficacy, syntheses of affirmation of the point. The ultimate organization of the body is the internal construction of

organs appropriate for the points. It is very true that, in a certain sense, the body is born without organs—the concept of bodies without organs is, as you know, a great Deleuzian concept. We'll agree that the body is, in the first place, incorporation. Insofar as it is incorporation, it is not immediately organic; it is incorporation under the sign of the evental trace. It is a cluster of intensities, a cluster of what gives the present its existence. And it is through the development of this incorporation that it will be structured, from within, in organic form, that is to say, will acquire appropriate organs.

Take, for example, the slave revolt led by Spartacus. At first there were just a handful of gladiators—that's what the evental new body was. But what happened there? It's very clear: the site was a sudden change in meaning of the gladiators' position. The gladiators were people trained for combat as spectacle, and this "trained for combat as spectacle" changed into "trained for combat against the Roman state." In both cases, you've got the same thing, "trained for combat," except that its meaning would completely change (that was the site). The trace was a complete change in the slave subjectivity because the only statement of the slaves under Spartacus's leadership was: "We want to go back home." They weren't at all interested in making a communist revolution, only in going back home. They'd attempt to go by way of the north and then see if they could find any ships to commandeer in the south . . . Whatever the case may be, that statement was a trace because, in fact, as regards the slaves' freedom of decision, it was a total change in intensity. But the whole problem would be that, little by little, there would be war. The Roman state would send legions to fight against those people. So there would be the question of how to build up, from within, what was originally the revolt of a handful of people who just wanted to go back home . . . Little by little an army would be built up. The body was thus a military body, which would be built up from the initial revolt. And it's very clear how the organic structuring of that body would constitute the whole problem. For example, how could they confront the cavalry? How could they develop specialized organs capable of besieging cities? How could they resist this or that? How could they deal with the enormous mass of unarmed slaves following them? Et cetera. And each time, the internal structuring of things would have to follow the body's development, under the maxim that would remain unchanged: "We slaves, who normally can't do anything and don't want anything, we can and want to go back home." This is a good example of what the internal structuring of a body is, point by point, over the immanent duration of things. At first, they had had to slaughter the owners of the gladiators' circus, but later, when they had to confront legions, they had to treat points, absolutely new points. And you can see very clearly the development, point by point, of the construction of the army of the slaves, who would hold out for more than two years, which is incredible, against one legion after another sent to fight them. In this example, there's a correlation between what the original site was, what the subjectivizable trace of the site was, and what the incorporation was. Incorporation, for a slave at that time, really meant: Should I or shouldn't I join the army of rebel slaves? And you've got all the different scenarios: those who join up right away, who immediately become incorporated into the army, those who stay on the sidelines, and so on. Then there's the body of the slave army. The internal stratification of the efficacious parts develops point by point. At the very end, you've got the emergence of real organs, a slave cavalry, slave siege engines, and so on. I mentioned this because it gives a picture of how the internal organicity of the body, which is by no means a biological body in this case, is a point-by-point development. It is not preformed. An organized slave army doesn't just appear out of nowhere. There is a development, point by point, in one battle after another where limited, constructive decisions have to be made. There is an internal sedimentation of the construction of that body.

This allows us to conclude for the time being with a definition of what it means "to live." For now, we'll say: To live is to participate point by point in the organization of a body of truth. OK, I'll leave you with that.

Session 5

February 11, 2004

Suspension of Alain Badiou's seminars until next fall
(Letter read at the beginning of the session by Isabelle Vodoz,
in the absence of Alain Badiou)

Dear seminar participants and auditors,

For various reasons I have decided to suspend my regular seminars and all participation in conferences (in France, at any rate) until next fall.

This will be the case for the Wednesday night "What does it mean to live?" seminar and for the sessions scheduled for Saturday afternoons on "What is an object?" and on Deleuze. This will also be the case for my direct participation in the conference on J. T. Desanti.

I can, however, tell you three of the reasons that led to this decision.

- *My status, in any case, is going to change starting this summer, if only for reasons of age.*
- *Most of my lectures this year were focused, and were to focus, on issues developed at length in* Logics of Worlds, *the book I was writing at the same time, which will supplement the*

ideas in Being and Event. *As this book is nearing completion (sooner than I expected), I don't want to continue giving only rough ideas of what's in it.*

— *I have been asked to give lectures in foreign countries, which I consider important to do because the range of philosophical phenomena today can no longer be limited to France. And because on many issues France, as far as its intellectual composition is concerned, is even characterized by very significant reactionary tendencies (from the "New Philosophers" to the current humanitarian-imperialist movements to the overwhelming support, organized by intellectuals, for "Western" political systems).*

But don't think I'm leaving the stage or leaving you in the lurch! I intend to launch a new seminar setup in the fall, but it will be under my sole institutional responsibility, not connected with the Collège International de Philosophie. I would ask everyone who wants to continue studying with me in a new setting to let me know right away [. . .]

Thank you again so much for having made this public place of thought exist for so long. I hope I've been as helpful to you as you have been to me.

Best regards,
Alain Badiou

P.S. For those of you here who are in the degree program at Paris 8 University, I just want to mention that your second-semester credits will be certified the usual way.

Notes

About the 2001–2004 Seminar

Unless otherwise indicated, all notes are by the translator.

1. From 2014 to January 2017 the seminar was held in the Paris suburb of Auber-villiers, at the Théâtre de la Commune.

Introduction by Kenneth Reinhard

1. In what would have been the fifth session, on February 11, 2004, a letter from Badiou explaining some aspects of the situation was read aloud; this letter constitutes the final chapter of this book.

2. See the session of December 9, 2002. The previous three-year sequence of lectures on the twentieth century was reworked as the book *The Century*. Badiou argues there that one of the dominant features of the previous century is what he calls "the passion for the real." Trans. Alberto Toscano (Cambridge: Polity, 2007).

3. G. W. F. Hegel, *Outlines of the Philosophy of Right* (Revised edition), ed. Stephen Houlgate and trans. T. M. Knox (New York: Oxford University Press, 2008), 16.

4. Year 1, Session 4 (January 30, 2002).

5. Year 1, Session 4 (January 30, 2002).

6. Year 1, Session 5 (March 13, 2002).

7. Year 3, Session 1 (October 22, 2003).

8. In the last session of the first year of the seminar on May 15, 2002, Badiou describes the "naked power" behind the "emblems" or images of our present time as involving two modes of the production of "consent." The first, which makes me "believe I'm acting in accordance with my own desire, in its relation

to the image, but in reality I'm doing what is willed by the Other," he calls "alienated consent in the classical sense . . . which is closest to that described by Marxism under the name of 'ideology.' . . . The second level of consent is not consent, so to speak, to the emblems but to the need for emblems, to the fact that there have to be emblems, to the belief that I have to share in the emblematic figure. But consenting to the need for the emblematic figure is not the same thing as being alienated in the emblem."

9.   Badiou also distinguishes his concept of "images" here from Debord's notion of the "Society of the Spectacle," because democratic materialism is just as likely to suppress and delegitimize certain images as to promote other images.

10.   *Logics of Worlds*, trans. Alberto Toscano (New York: Continuum, 2009), 511. Subsequent references, unless otherwise noted, are to this edition, and page numbers will appear parenthetically in the text.

11.   While "materialist dialectic" is the expression Badiou settles on in *Logic of Worlds*, in this seminar he first proposes to call it "proletarian aristocratism": following Deleuze, exceptional truths are "aristocratic" in the sense that they are conveyed by a minority; they are "proletarian" insofar as they are produced as works that are addressed to everyone. See the session of December 3, 2001. Later in the seminar he uses the expression "dialectical materialism" until, in the final year of the seminar and in *Logics of Worlds*, finally inverting the phrase in order to mark its difference from classical Marxism.

12.   Year 3, Session 3 (December 17, 2003).

13.   Badiou gives somewhat different accounts of these analytic moments at various points in the seminar, in terms of both their makeup and their sequence, so they should be understood not as constituting a strict system or a necessary order, logical or chronological, but as points of analysis.

14.   Year 1, Session 5 (March 13, 2002).

15.   Year 1, Session 3 (December 3, 2001).

16.   Year 2, Session 1 (October 9, 2002).

17.   Badiou will return to a similar notion of "waste products" [*déchets*] in the third volume of *Being and Event*, *The Immanence of Truths* (Bloomsbury 2022), where they will be opposed to the "works" [*oeuvres*] that are the product of truth procedures.

18.   Year 1, Session 7 (May 15, 2002).

19.   Year 2, Session 1 (October 9, 2002).

20.   Badiou discusses this essay at some length in his seminar of 1987–88, *Vérité et Sujet* (Paris: Fayard, 2017), 22–82.

21.   Year 2, Session 1 (October 9, 2002).

22.   Year 3, Session 1 (October 22, 2003).

23.   Year 3, Session 2 (November 27, 2003).

24.   Year 3, Session 3 (December 17, 2003).

Session 1: November 21, 2001

1. Lacan introduced the term *hontologie*, a portmanteau word combining *honte* (shame) and *ontologie* (ontology), in the final session of his seminar XVII. See Jacques Lacan, *The Seminar, Book XVII: The Other Side of Psychoanalysis*, ed. Jacques-Alain Miller, trans. Russell Grigg (New York: Norton, 2007), 180.

2. Jacques Lacan, *The Seminar of Jacques Lacan, Book V: Formations of the Unconscious*, ed. Jacques-Alain Miller, trans. Russell Grigg (Cambridge: Polity, 2015), 246; translation slightly modified.

3. The reference here is to Félix Faure, president from 1895 to 1899.

4. *The Balcony*, trans. Barbara Wright and Terry Hands (London: Faber and Faber, 1991), xiv; translation slightly modified.

5. "The symbol first manifests itself as the killing of the thing." Jacques Lacan, *Écrits*, trans. Bruce Fink (New York: Norton, 2007), 262.

6. The italicized words in square brackets, both here and below, are Badiou's interpolated remarks.

7. Jean Genet, *The Balcony*, trans. Bernard Frechtman, in *Nine Plays of the Modern Theater* (New York: Grove, 1981), 344–45. Subsequent page references to this edition will appear in parentheses in the text.

8. Lacan, *The Seminar, Book V*, 252; translation slightly modified.

9. Henrik Ibsen, *Emperor and Galilean: A World Historical Drama*, trans. Ben Power (London: Nick Hern, 2012), 44. As noted by A. J. Bartlett and Justin Clemens in a footnote to their translation of *The Pornographic Age*, Badiou appears to have modified Ibsen's line, which actually reads: "The old beauty is no longer beautiful and the new truth is no longer true."

Session 2: December 3, 2001

1. *L'Horreur économique* is a 1996 book by Viviane Forrester, translated as *The Economic Horror* in 1999. Its title comes from Rimbaud's "Historic Evening," in *Illuminations*: "On some evening, let us say, when the innocent tourist, away from our economic horrors . . ." (Arthur Rimbaud, *Collected Poems*, trans. Martin Sorrell [Oxford: Oxford University Press, 2001], 303.)

2. "Est-ce ainsi que les hommes vivent?" [Is this the way men live?] is a line from Louis Aragon's poem "Bierstube Magie allemande" in *Le Roman inachevé* (Paris: Gallimard, 1980).

3. Jacques Lacan, *The Seminar of Jacques Lacan, Book I: Freud's Papers on Technique*, ed. Jacques-Alain Miller and trans. John Forrester (New York: Norton, 1991), 199; translation modified. Subsequent page references to this edition will appear in parentheses in the text.

4. Bertolt Brecht, "In Praise of Dialectics" (final chorus from his play *The Mother*, 1932).

Session 3: January 16, 2002

1. Friedrich Nietzsche, "Law Against Christianity," in *The Anti-Christ, Ecce Homo, Twilight of the Idols and Other Writings*, ed. Aaron Ridley and Judith Norman (Cambridge: Cambridge University Press, 2005), 25.

2. In a note, one of the translators of Nancy's essay explains that, at the author's suggestion, she invented the verb "to joy" to translate the French verb *jouir*. In the following discussion of the essay, I have retained "to joy" and "joying," the noun form of the verb, but elsewhere I have translated these more conventionally as "to enjoy" and "enjoying."

3. Jean-Luc Nancy, *The Inoperative Community*, ed. Peter Connor, trans. Peter Connor, Lisa Garbus, Michael Holland, and Simona Sawhney (Minneapolis: University of Minnesota, 1991), 106; translation modified. Subsequent page references to this edition will appear in parentheses in the text.

4. Cf. Heidegger: "The transition of coming forth into the coming forth of passing away as the *extremity of presence*." *The Event*, trans. Richard Rojcewicz (Indianapolis: Indiana University Press, 2013), 31.

5. Jean-Luc Nancy, "Changing of the World," in *A Finite Thinking*, ed. Simon Sparks, trans. Steven Miller (Stanford, CA: Stanford University Press, 2003), 322.

6. Plato, *Timaeus* and *Critias*, trans. Desmond Lee (New York: Penguin, 2008), 91; translation slightly modified to conform to the French version.

Session 4: January 30, 2002

1. Patrice de MacMahon was a French general remembered chiefly for his defeat at Sedan in the Franco-Prussian War and his suppression of the Paris Commune in 1871 when he was head of the Versailles Army. He later served as president of France from 1875 to 1879.

2. Along with Émile Picard and Adolphe Thiers, the three Juleses, after the French defeat in the Franco-Prussian War and the overthrow of the empire by largely working-class crowds, proclaimed a republic. But, as Badiou explains in *Polemics*, their only wish was to "negotiate with Bismarck in a bid to contain the working-class political insurgency" (259).

3. Here and below, the italicized text in square brackets is Badiou's interpolation.

4. Plato, *The Republic*, trans. Tom Griffith (Cambridge: Cambridge University Press, 2006), 270. Subsequent page references to this edition will appear in parentheses in the text.

5. Plato, *The Republic*, trans. Desmond Lee (New York: Penguin, 2007), 308, 569c; translation slightly modified.

6. The word for "time" and "weather" is the same in French: *le temps*. Thus, the discussion of time in this paragraph detours briefly into a discussion of (metaphorical) weather before returning to the initial subject of time.

7. Arthur Rimbaud, "Vagabonds" in *Illuminations*, trans. Louise Varèse (New York: New Directions, 1988), 64: "I, impatient to find the place and the formula . . ." Badiou cites this line in his seminar on Lacan as well as in *The Century* and in *There's No Such Thing as a Sexual Relationship: Two Essays on Lacan*, written with Barbara Cassin.

8. Jean-Pierre Chevènement held a variety of ministerial posts in France in the 1980s and 1990s. It was as Minister of the Interior in 1998 that he used the term Badiou mentions below, "little savages" (*sauvageons*), to refer to young delinquents in the *banlieue*, and introduced repressive measures to fight crime.

Session 5: March 13, 2002

1. Pierre Guyotat, *Tomb for 500,000 Soldiers*, trans. Romain Slocombe (London: Creation, 2003), 47. Subsequent page references to this edition will appear in parentheses in the text.

Session 6: March 30, 2002

1. Pierre Guyotat, *Tomb for 500,00 Soldiers*, trans. Romain Slocombe (London: Creation, 2003), 224; translation slightly modified. Subsequent page references to this edition will appear in parentheses in the text.

2. Plato, *The Republic*, ed. G. R. F. Ferrari, trans. Tom Griffith (Cambridge: Cambridge University Press, 2006), 277. Subsequent page references to this edition will appear in parentheses in the text.

Session 7: May 15, 2002

1. Michel Foucault, *Society Must Be Defended*, ed. Mauro Bertani and Alessandro Fontana, trans. David Macey (New York: Picador, 2003), 258.

2. "Only a God Can Save Us: *Der Spiegel's* Interview with Martin Heidegger," trans. Maria T. Alter and John D. Caputo, in *The Heidegger Controversy: A Critical Reader*, ed. Richard Wolin (Cambridge, MA: MIT Press, 1993), 103–4; translation slightly modified.

3. Jean Genet, *The Balcony*, trans. Bernard Frechtman, in *Nine Plays of the Modern Theater* (New York: Grove, 1981), 347–48. Subsequent page references to this edition will appear in parentheses in the text.

Session 1: October 9, 2002

1. *Après-coup* can mean a number of things, depending on whether the term is used as a noun or an adverb. As a noun, other than meaning "retroactive effect," "afterthought," "hindsight," etc., it often refers to the psychoanalytic concept of "deferred action" (*Nachträglichkeit*). When used adverbially in a sentence, it is frequently translated as "after the fact," "afterward," "retroactively," "in retrospect," etc. Badiou plays on the constitutive term *coup* (literally, "blow") in the word.

2. Saint-John Perse, "Winds," trans. Hugh Chisholm, in *Collected Poems* (Princeton, NJ: Princeton University Press, 1971), 327.

3. Bertolt Brecht, *Poems, 1913–1956*, ed. and trans. John Willett and Ralph Mannheim (London: Eyre Methuen, 1976), 169–70.

4. Victor Hugo, "What the Shadow-Mouth Said," trans. Ann Gwynn, in *European Romanticism: A Reader*, ed. Stephen Prickett and Simon Haines (London: Continuum, 2010), 677.

5. Stéphane Mallarmé, *Selected Poetry and Prose*, trans. Mary Ann Caws (New York: New Directions, 1982), 79; translation modified.

Session 2: November 20, 2002

1. Badiou's seminars from 1998 to 2001 on the twentieth century form the basis of his book *The Century*, trans. Alberto Toscano (Cambridge: Polity, 2007).

Session 3: December 4, 2002

1. The "new reactionaries" is an allusion to a book by Daniel Lindenberg, *Le Rappel à l'ordre: Enquête sur les nouveaux réactionnaires* (The call to order: an inquiry into the new reactionaries), which targeted a number of French intellectuals, Michel Houellebecq, Alain Finkielkraut, and Marcel Gauchet among them, and sparked a media-fueled controversy after its publication in 2002.

2. See *Théorie axiomatique du sujet 1996–1998* (Paris: Fayard, 2019).

3. Alexandre Dumas (1802–1870) was the popular author of, among others, *The Three Musketeers* and *The Count of Monte Cristo*.

4. Arthur Rimbaud, "Democracy," in *Illuminations and Other Prose Poems*, trans. Louise Varèse (New York: New Directions, 1957), 129; translation slightly modified.

5. "*En avant, route*" is a somewhat unusual phrase. "*En avant marche!*" is a more common formulation of "Forward, march!" It has been suggested that Rimbaud may have wanted to avoid repeating the word "*marche*," which he had just

used in "*C'est la vraie marche*" ("This is the real advance" in Varèse's translation). A more contemporary translation of "*En avant, route*" is "Let's hit the road." In any case, the road that Badiou says "has been mapped out" refers to the *route* in "*En avant, route!*"

6. Arthur Rimbaud, "War," in *Illuminations and Other Prose Poems*, 133; translation modified.

Session 4: February 26, 2003

1. In an interview given to *Time* magazine on February 16, 2003, French president Jacques Chirac justified his country's refusal to support the American military intervention in Iraq by claiming that France was not a pacifist country, as evidenced by the large number of troops it had sent to the Balkans.
2. Badiou is describing Nixon's so-called madman theory, which Chomsky analyzed in an article entitled "Rogue States" in *Z Magazine*, April 1998. Writing of a secret 1995 study of the U.S. Strategic Command (STRATCOM), Chomsky noted: "The report resurrects Nixon's 'madman theory': our enemies should recognize that we are crazed and unpredictable, with extraordinary destructive force at our command, so they will bend to our will in fear."

Session 5: March 12, 2003

1. Aside from meaning "representation," "concept," "mental image," etc., the French word *représentation* can also refer to the performance or staging of a play. Regnault points out the ambiguity a moment later.
2. François-René de Chateaubriand, *Memoirs from Beyond the Tomb*, trans. Robert Baldick (New York: Penguin, 2014), 61.
3. André Antoine (1858–1943) was the founder of the Théâtre Libre, the first Naturalist theater in France. He was considered the father of modern *mise-en-scène*. Firmin Gémier (1869–1933) was an actor, theater manager, and director, known for modernizing French theater. He created Le Théâtre National Populaire in 1920.
4. François Regnault, *Théâtre-Solstices: Écrits sur le théâtre-2* (Paris: Actes Sud, 2002), 265; my translation.
5. Serge Daney (1944–1992) was an influential French film critic who eventually also became a TV critic. He developed a critical theory of the image.
6. In the French text, this reads "*Théâââtre*," and Regnault goes on to say: "In a book about social mores that came out a few years ago, there was the following comment: 'The circumflex in the word *théâtre* is quite stylish!'" In French, a vowel with a circumflex over it can be exaggeratedly lengthened in speech, giving the word a snobbish or ridiculous—often both at once—pronunciation.

7. Mallarmé wrote: "*Le théâtre est d'essence supérieur*" ("The theater is of a superior essence"). See *Oeuvres complètes*, ed. Henri Modor and Georges-Jean Aubry (Paris: Gallimard, 1945), 312.

8. Jacques Lacan, *The Seminar of Jacques Lacan, Book VII: The Ethics of Psychoanalysis*, ed. Jacques-Alain Miller, trans. Dennis Porter (New York: Norton, 1997), 253.

9. The French verb *répéter* means both "to repeat" and "to rehearse." Although I have chosen to use "repeat" and "repetition" in this passage, both meanings should be borne in mind, as the reference to Anouilh's play *La Répétition ou l'amour puni* (translated as *The Rehearsal: Or Love Punished*) makes clear. See also below, where Badiou makes explicit reference to the two meanings of *répétition*. An additional ambiguity occurs with the use of the word *représentation* in the last line of Regnault's remarks here. Although translated here as "representation," it could also mean "performance," hence "repetition and representation" or "rehearsal and performance."

Session 6: March 26, 2003

1. "*Quelle connerie la guerre!*" is a well-known line from Jacques Prévert's moving antiwar poem "Barbara," in his collection *Paroles* (1946).

Session 7: May 14, 2003

1. Martin Heidegger, *Basic Writings*, ed. D. F. Krell (New York: HarperCollins, 1993), 443. Subsequent page references to this edition will appear in parentheses in the text.

2. What is translated here as "unconcealment" is "*l'état de non-retrait*" [the state of nonwithdrawal] in the French. In this essay, the German word *Unverborgenheit* was rendered in French by Jean Beaufret first as *l'ouvert sans retrait* [the open without withdrawal] and later as *l'état de non-retrait*. See Pierre Jacerme, "The Thoughtful Dialogue Between Martin Heidegger and Jean Beaufret: A New Way of Doing Philosophy," in *French Interpretations of Heidegger: An Exceptional Reception*, ed. David Pettigrew and François Raffoul (Albany: State University of New York Press, 2009), 70.

3. According to Daniel Fischer's transcription of the seminar online, Badiou explained what he meant by conversion as follows: "the possibility of distinguishing truth from knowledge can only be *instantaneous*—what might be called a *conversion*" (my translation). See http://www.entretemps.asso.fr/Badiou/02-03.htm.

Session 8: June 4, 2003

1. A wave of strikes engulfed France in November and December 1995. An expression of resistance to the destruction of the welfare state, the movement promoted the idea of participatory democracy, as opposed to the elitism and arrogance of the government.

2. Contrary to all expectations, in the French presidential election of 2002 the Socialist candidate, incumbent Prime Minister Lionel Jospin, came in third, behind the far-right Front National candidate Jean-Marie Le Pen. In the runoff between the much-despised Le Pen and the unpopular conservative incumbent president Jacques Chirac, the latter won by a landslide.

3. In the spring of 2003, there was a powerful movement in France against government plans to dramatically reduce retirement pensions and increase the number of years in employment required to qualify for them. Along with the attack on pensions, the so-called decentralization law, which would have led to the outsourcing of many basic public services to the private sector, threatened schools and universities in particular and incited educators at all levels to mass action.

4. Cf. Mao Zedong: "Everything under heaven is in utter chaos; the situation is excellent."

5. See Martin Heidegger, *Bremen and Freiburg Lectures: Insight Into That Which Is and Basic Principles of Thinking*, trans. Andrew J. Mitchell (Bloomington: Indiana University Press, 2012). Subsequent page references to this edition will appear in parentheses in the text.

6. The English translations of this passage do not correspond exactly to the French, which reads: *Cette liberté ressemble à celle d'un homme qui surmonte sa douleur au sens où, loin de s'en défaire et de l'oublier, il l'habite.* [This freedom is similar to that of someone who overcomes their pain, in the sense that, far from getting rid of it and forgetting about it, they inhabit it.] The German word that is translated as *liberté* in the French edition of Heidegger is *Verwinden*, which means "to get over something" or "to warp" (both in the form of nouns). Badiou repeats the sentence below.

7. Friedrich Hölderlin, *Poems of Hölderlin*, trans. James Mitchell (San Francisco: Ithuriel's Spear, 2006), 31. The French translation of the last word in the second line here is *fidélité*, which of course has a more Badiouan resonance. Hölderlin's word in the poem is *Treue*, which can mean both "loyalty" and "fidelity." Similarly, in the next citation from Hölderlin, what is translated as "loyal" in English is *fidèle* in the French and *treu* in the original German.

8. Friedrich Hölderlin, *Poems and Fragments*, trans. Michael Hamburger (London: Anvil, 2004), 307.

9. Friedrich Hölderlin, *Too Long Invisible: Poems of Friedrich Hölderlin*, trans. William A. Sigler (Carbondale, IL: Alcyone, 2020), 97.

10. Hölderlin, *Poems and Fragments*, 586.

11. G. W. F. Hegel, *Phenomenology of Spirit*, trans. A. V. Miller (Oxford: Oxford University Press, 1977), 32.

Session 1: October 22, 2003

1. Sylvain Lazarus uses the expressions "circulating category" and "circulating elements" to describe a concept that moves between heterogeneous fields (such as history and politics, or subjective and objective) without apparent contradiction. See *Anthropology of the Name*, trans. Gila Walker (Calcutta: Seagull, 2015).

2. The dialectical materialism first developed by Marx and Engels and later expanded by Plekanov and Lenin became the official version of Marxist doctrine under Stalin. It was called "diamat" for short.

3. "We must, as far as we can, make ourselves immortal." Aristotle, *Nicomachean Ethics*, trans. David Ross and Lesley Brown (Oxford: Oxford University Press, 2009), 195.

4. Friedrich Nietzsche, *Twilight of the Idols, or How to Philosophize with a Hammer*, trans. Richard Polt (Indianapolis, IN: Hackett, 1997), 13.

5. Stéphane Mallarmé, "Le vierge, le vivace et le bel aujourd'hui," in *Six French Poets of the Nineteenth Century: Lamartine, Hugo, Baudelaire, Verlaine, Rimbaud, Mallarmé*, ed. and trans. E. H. Blackmore and A. M. Blackmore (Oxford: Oxford University Press, 2000), 287.

6. Paul Valéry, "The Graveyard by the Sea," in *Selected Writings of Paul Valéry*, trans. C. Day Lewis (New York: New Directions, 1964), 49.

7. To conform with Badiou's focus below on absence, a literal translation of this line ("La vie est vaste étant ivre d'absence") seemed preferable here to C. Day Lewis's "life is enlarged, drunk with annihilation."

Session 2: November 27, 2003

1. Saint-John Perse, "Song of the Heir Presumptive," trans. Louise Varèse, in *Collected Poems* (Princeton, NJ: Princeton University Press, 1971), 93.

2. Paul Valéry, "The Graveyard by the Sea," in *Selected Writings of Paul Valéry*, trans. C. Day Lewis (New York: New Directions, 1964), 49.

3. "I know work: and science is too slow" from "Lightning," in *A Season in Hell*, in *Rimbaud Complete*, trans. Wyatt Mason (New York: Modern Library, 2003), 217.

4. From "Alchemy of the Word," in *A Season in Hell*, in *Rimbaud Complete*, 208.

5. Lewis's translation—"its pure issue"—of *"l'événement pur"* [the pure event], needed to be modified here so that Badiou's humorous interpolated comment on one of the key terms of his philosophy would make sense.

6. Valéry, "The Graveyard by the Sea," 41–49.

7. In the French, Zeno is specified as *"Zénon d'Élée!"* [Zeno of Elea], hence Badiou's reference in the next sentence to the "Eleatic arrow."

Session 3: December 17, 2003

1. See Alain Badiou, *Logics of Worlds*, trans. Alberto Toscano (New York: Continuum, 2009), 47ff.

2. In *Logics of Worlds*, Badiou discusses the appearing of an object in terms of its "transcendental indexing" in a world; see 199–230.

3. C. Day Lewis's translation ("forever starting and restarting") had to be slightly modified here to conform to Badiou's interpretation of the two French adjectives.

Session 4: January 14, 2004

1. Stéphane Mallarmé, *Collected Poems*, trans. Henry Weinfield (Berkeley: University of California Press, 1994), 144.

2. René Descartes, *Principles of Philosophy*, in *The Philosophical Writings of Descartes*, vol. 1, trans. John Cottingham, Robert Stoothoff, and Dugold Murdoch (Cambridge: Cambridge University Press, 1985), 191. Subsequent references to the *Principles of Philosophy* will be to whichever translation best corresponds to Badiou's discussion of the text.

3. René Descartes, *Principles of Philosophy*, in *Metaphysical Themes 1274–1671*, trans. Robert Pasnau (Oxford: Oxford University Press, 2013), 264.

4. René Descartes, *Principles of Philosophy*, in *The Philosophical Writings of Descartes*, vol. 1, trans. John Cottingham, Robert Stoothoff, and Dugold Murdoch (Cambridge: Cambridge University Press, 1985), 220–21.

Index

power and, 80–81, 113, 122; organ and, 394–95; pain and, 287–88; physics of, 331–32, 358–61; point and, 336, 338–40, 375, 393–94, 396; political, 357–58; prostitution and, 79–82, 84, 86, 95, 103, 105; relationship of language and, 329–31, 334; sexuality and, 329–30; Spinoza on, 226, 306, 309, 332, 339; substitutability and, 79, 103; suffering, 305–6; theater and, 226, 228; truths and, xxiii–xxiv, 309, 352–53, 355–56, 376–78, 389; Valéry on, 332, 334–36, 347, 350, 361, 366–75, 390, 392; valuation of, xxvi, 77–79, 81–83, 93; violence and, 104–7, 110; virtualities of, 329–30; world and, 336, 339, 347, 392

body, new: emergence of, xxxii, 330–31, 334–36, 349, 356, 361, 367–68, 389; event and, 355–56, 360–61, 372–73, 393, 395; *Logics of Worlds* on, xxxii–xxxiii; metamorphosis and, 355; present and, 390, 392; process of, 393; sea and, 369; site and, 373, 375, 395–96; subject-form and, 339–40, 356–60, 375, 393; trace and, 392–93; truths and, 377

Bolivia, 136

bombing, 80–81, 235, 243

Boulez, Pierre, 230

Brecht, Bertolt, 39–40, 213, 220; "Late Lamented Fame of the Giant City of New York," 137–38; on theater, 225

Brown, John, 251

Bush, George W., 193, 203, 251–52

capitalism, xxvii, xxxi, 33, 121; consent to, 126; exception to, xxvi; modernity and, 154; naked power of, 109; nihilism and, 286–87; present and, 137, 154, 285; science and, 289

categories: circulating category, 301, 408n1; democratic materialism lacking, 302–3, 305–7

catharsis, 222

cave, allegory of, xxxii, 295

Century, The (Badiou), 399n2

Century of Louis XIV (Voltaire), 212–13

"Ce que dit la bouche d'ombre" (Hugo), 139–40

change, 135, 138

Chateaubriand, François-René de, 207

Chevènement, Jean-Pierre, 72, 403n8

childhood: democratic materialism and, 386–88; Descartes on, 384–89; things and, 385–89

China, 191

Chirac, Jacques, 203; on Iraq war, 195–97, 254, 405n1; Le Pen and, 124, 126–27, 407n2; on pacifism, 195, 405n1

Chomsky, Noam, 202, 405n2

cinema, 217, 221, 223–24, 228

circulating category, 301, 408n1

circulation: contemplation and, 158, 164; creation and, 185; declaration and, xxxi, 156–58; present and, 171–72; protection from, 185–86; subject and, 167–68

city-state, Greek, 61

class war, 114–15

Clausewitz, Carl von, 189

clearing, 296; of being, 259–62, 278–79; Heidegger on, 259–63, 265, 267–68, 278–79, 281, 292; of open, 259–60, 263, 265, 278, 292; thinking and, 259–60, 263, 267–68, 281

closed immanence, 379

Cloudsplitter (Banks), 250–51

Cocteau, Jean, 225–26

Cohen, Paul, xxix

colonialism, 202; colonial war, 84–86; democracy and, 173–77, 179; Rimbaud on, 173–79, 183; Roman, 176–77. *See also* empire

comedy, 8–10, 19

commercial validation, xxvi, 78–79, 81–83

commodification: of body, 79, 93, 95, 101–7, 109, 113; destruction through, 276, 285; of present, 153

commodities, 275; body encountering, 78, 83, 93, 105; democratic subject and, xxvii, 77, 95; freedom and, 148; Marxist critique of, 276; suffering and, 287–88; as things, 388

commodity circulation. *See* circulation

common metaphysics, 301–2

communism, 220

Communist Manifesto (Marx and Engels), 154

concentration camps, 86, 115, 117–18

conditions, of philosophy. *See* philosophy

conjunctive complicity, 237

consciousness, of poet, 349–50, 364–65, 391

consent, 399n8; in democracy, 103–4, 106, 125, 127, 148–49; emblem and, xxxiii, 103–4, 124–30, 148–49; freedom and, 122–23; naked power and, 125–28, 148

constellation, 377

constructing, 280

consumption: body as consumer, 78, 107; democracy and, xxvii, 69, 77, 95, 148–49; naked power and, xxviii; passion opposed to, 166–67, 172; subject as consumer, xxvii, 77, 95, 148–49, 168; suffering of consumer, 287–88

contemplation, 150, 162, 262; of art, xxxi, 158, 163–64, 172; demonstration and, 159; eternity and, 181–82; judgment opposed to, 163–64, 167, 172; Plato on, 158–59; present and, 158, 161, 167

contemporaneity, investigating, 146–50

contractual language, 306, 308, 310

control, society of, 112

conversion, 268, 283, 331, 406n3

Copeau, Jacques, 230

Corneille, Pierre, 212–13

cosmos: Guyotat on, 88–89; Plato on, 55–57, 59, 313–15, 324–25

creation, 185; questioning and, 271–72, 279; of values, 316–17, 326

criticism, 290

Critique of Judgment (Kant), 164

Crowd, xxx, 141–44, 149

Daney, Serge, 221, 405n5

death: God and, 315; Hegel on, 325; life and, 300–301, 313–17, 324–25, 372; Plato on, 313–15, 317, 324; Valéry on, 364–66, 370–72

death penalty, 249–50

Debord, Guy, 134, 171, 400n9

Debray, Régis, 136

December 1995 movement, French, 274, 276–77, 290, 407n1

decision: point and, 336–39, 370; Two and, 336, 338–39, 370, 374; war and, 189

declaration, 151; action as political, xxxi, 159; circulation and, xxxi, 156–58; contemplation as, xxxi, 150, 158–59; criteria for, 149–50, 156; of Crowd, xxx, 141–44, 149; demonstration as, xxxi, 150, 157–59; exchange and, 156–58; of love, xxxi, 156–57; Mallarmé on, xxx, 141–44; passion

not-all, 380; dialectical materialism as, 377–78; Lacan on, 377–78, 389
number, indifference to, 186

object: democratic emblem and, 168; objectless passion, 166–67; objectless present, 167
obscure subject, xxiv–xxv, 359
One, 252–53; in philosophy, 259–60, 265; Plato on Other and, 248; of sea, 374; Two and, 291
ontological, life as, 299–300, 308
On War (Clausewitz), 189
open: Deleuze on, 259–60, 263; disconnection distinguished from, 263; Heidegger on, 259–61, 263–67, 271, 278, 283, 292; thinking and, 259–61, 263, 268
Open, The (Agamben), 259
opinion, 163–64, 167
orchestra conductor, 214, 216–17, 227
ordinary metaphysics, 301–2
Oresteia (Aeschylus), 251–52
organ, 394–95
Other: consent and, 124, 399n8; in master-slave dialectic, 247; Nancy on, 48–49; open and, 259; Plato on One and, 248; traversal of, 48–50; U.S. and, 243, 248
otherness, rejection of, 105–6

pacifism, 194–95, 253, 405n1
pain: art and, 289–90; body and, 287–88; Heidegger on, 283, 286; thinking and, 287
painting, 225, 231; museography in, 214–15, 217; past and, 220–21; in Renaissance, 211–12, 221; theater and, 211–12, 220
Parade (ballet), 225–26
Paris Commune, xxvi, xxx, 61, 164–65, 179, 402n1

Parmenides, 369; on being, 259; Valéry on, 349–50, 365–66, 370–72, 391
particularities, indifference to, 186–87
Pascal, Blaise, 4, 182, 327–28
passion, 262; consumption opposed to, 166–67, 172; as declaration, 159–60, 166; objectless, 166–67; Two in, 291
passions, fundamental, 36–38
Passions of the Soul, The (Descartes), 309
past, 134, 142, 153–54, 284–85; action and, 165; art and, 215; cinema and, 217; declaration and, 143; painting and, 220–21; reactionaries and, 169–71; stagecraft and, 218–20, 227; theater, present, and, 208–11, 214–15, 218–20, 222–23, 227, 229; theater and, 212–13
Paul (saint), 186; anti-philosophy of, 3–4; on flesh and spirit, 325
pedophilia, 82–83
Perec, Georges, 388–89
performance. *See* theater
phallus, 27, 33; in *The Balcony*, xxv, 8–9, 16–22, 28; comedy and, 8–10, 19; Lacan on, xxv, 8, 19, 23
Phèdre (Racine), 212, 219
Phenomenology of Spirit (Hegel), 325
philosophy, 234; art and, 289–90; asceticism and, 42, 46–47; conditions of, 261–63, 270–71, 278–80, 288; destiny of, 261–64, 271, 278–79; enjoyment and, 41–42, 46–47, 51–52; Heidegger on, 257–63, 271, 278, 280, 288; history of, 256–57, 322; One in, 259–60, 265; open and, 259–61, 267, 271, 278; physics and, 331–32; Plato on, 74, 154, 171; present and, 4–5, 133–34, 188, 257–58; propaganda opposed by, 171; science and, 289; sea in, 369; thinking and, 257–61, 271, 278, 288; time and, 154–55; truth in, 263–64, 270–71, 279–80; on twentieth century, 5–6

physics: of body, 331–32, 358–61;
dialectical materialism and, 359
Picasso, Pablo, 221, 225–26
place, 145, 348; of life, 318–20, 326, 335;
Mallarmé on, 376–78; present and,
151–52, 160–61; of truth, 152; Valéry
on, 347, 349–50, 361
placement, turn and, 271–72, 280
Plato, 43, 203, 248, 263; cave allegory,
xxxii, 295; on contemplation, 158–59;
on cosmos, 55–57, 59, 313–15, 324–25;
on death, 313–15, 317, 324; on detour,
74, 76, 154; on eternity, 303–4; on
forms, 303–4, 313–14; on life, 313–15,
317, 324, 335; on mathematics, 163; on
philosophy, 74, 154, 171; on poetry,
362; *Republic*, 58, 60–61, 63–64, 68,
75, 107–8, 226; *Symposium*, 158; on
theater, 226, 232; *Timaeus*, 55–57, 59,
313–14; on truth, 265; on world, xxii,
55–59, 63
Plato, on democracy, 60, 62, 64, 67, 69,
75; foreign madness and, 109–10;
Greek city-state and, 61; tyranny
and, 68, 107–9; world, absence of,
and, 58, 63; youth and, 65–66, 72
Plautus, Titus Maccius, 212–13
pleasures, substitutability of, 65, 68–69,
75
Poetics (Aristotle), 225
poetry: consciousness of poet, 349–50,
364–65, 391; language and, 317–18; on
life, 317–19, 326–28; Plato on, 362
point: affirmation of, 393–94; body
and, 336, 338–40, 375, 393–94,
396; decision and, 336–39, 370; in
metaphysics, 337–38; trace and, 391;
truth and, 339–40; Two and, 393;
Valéry on, 350–51, 391; in world,
336–39, 350–51, 370, 393
Polemics (Badiou), 402n2

politics, 338; affirmation and, 291, 333–
34; Aristotle on, 311–12, 324; body of,
357–58; of destruction, 274, 276–77;
Guyotat and, 99–100; metaphysics
of movement, 276–77, 286; naked
power and, 112, 121–22; nihilism in,
275; political pornography, 20–21;
technology and, 112; as tracing, xxvi,
25; truth in, 266; war and, 114–15
Politics (Aristotle), 311
pornography, 148; management and, 165;
political, 20–21; visual, 82–83
positionality (*Ge-stell*), 280–84, 292
possibility: freedom and, 147–48;
indifference to established, 186
post-postwar era, 191–92, 195, 197–98,
201, 204
postwar era, 191–92
power: American, 197–203, 284; in *The
Balcony*, 11, 16, 20–21, 28, 128–30;
comedy and, 8–10; emblem of, 39;
images and, 9, 16; politics and, 112,
121–22; racism and, 111–12. *See also*
biopower; naked power
presence, 402n4; enjoyment and, 48–51;
of life, 318
present, xxviii, 284; action and, 165,
167; art and, 215; *The Balcony* and,
7–8, 12–13, 17, 20–21; capitalism and,
137, 154, 285; change and, 135, 138;
circulation and, 171–72; comedy
and, 8–10; confession of, 7–8;
contemplation and, 158, 161, 167;
declaration and, xxx–xxxi, 141–43,
145–46, 149, 155–56; democratic
emblem and, 23, 75, 146; duration
of, 151–52; enjoyment and, 48,
50–51; exception and, 156, 161–63,
167, 188; false, 137, 153, 155–57, 159,
161–63, 171–72, 183, 192; Heidegger
on, 285, 291–92; images and, 13, 28,

70, 78, 206; incorporation into, xxxiii, 390, 392; Iraq war and, 190, 233; isolation structure of, 160–61; life and, xxxiii, 321, 390; Mallarmé on, xxx, 5, 141–43, 152–53, 215, 220, 285; modernity and, 135, 137–38; nihilism and, 67–69, 71, 285–86; nostalgia in, 61; objectless, 167; past and lack of, 134, 142; philosophy and, 4–6, 133–34, 188, 257–58; place and, 151–52, 160–61; reactionaries and, 169–71; real, xxiv–xxv, xxix–xxx, 12, 140, 167, 220, 257, 285–86, 305; Regnault on, 207–10, 217–18; stagecraft and, 218–20, 227; subject and, xxiv; substitutability of, 70, 75; theater, past, and, 208–11, 214–15, 218–20, 222–23, 227, 229; theater and, 207, 217, 224–25, 228, 231–32; torsion of, xxix–xxx, 145, 171–72; trace and, 391–92; tradition and lack of, 134–35, 137; twentieth century and, 4, 139; war and, 189–92, 233; worldless, xxii, 134, 188. *See also* projection; repetition; time
prime numbers, 304–5
principles, 312–13
Principles of Philosophy, The (Descartes), 380–86
projection, 150; declaration and, xxx, 142–45, 155–56; in Hugo, 143, 152; indifference to, 186; present and, xxviii–xxx, 140–43, 152–53, 155–56, 171–72, 211; reactionary critique of, 171
proletarian aristocratism, 34, 38, 400n11
proof. *See* demonstration
propaganda: *The Balcony* and, 31–32; philosophy opposing, 171; in war, 234–41
prophecy, 268–70

prostitution: in *The Balcony*, 10–11; body and, 79–82, 84, 86, 95, 103, 105; democracy and, xxvii, 79–81, 174–75; emblem and, 79–81; legalization of, 81; Rimbaud on, 174–75; suppression of, 79–82
prostitutional, xxvi; exchange and, 81–82, 89; Guyotat on, 84–86, 88–89, 93, 95; otherness rejected by, 105; pedophilia and, 82–83; substitutability of, 103; world and, 85
psychoanalysis, 146, 209; anti-philosophy of, 41–42, 51–52; *après-coup* in, 404n1; asceticism of, 36, 42; Freud, 387; Nancy on, 41, 47; Regnault and, 206, 217. *See also* Lacan, Jacques

Quechua, 136
questioning, 271–72, 279–81

Racine, Jean, 212–13, 219, 222
racism, 120; biopower and, 111–12, 115–17; Foucault on, 111–12, 114–17; technology and, 117–18; war and, 114–15
Rancière, Jacques, 174
Raphael, 211, 221, 225
reactionaries, 398; new, 169, 404n1; on projection, 171; Thermidorean, 170
reactive subject, xxiv, xxiv–xxv, 359
realization, 37–38
real tracing, xxvi, 20, 25–26, 28, 34
Regnault, François, 221–22, 226–27, 230, 405n6; *Écrits sur le théâtre*, 219–20; on painting, 211–12; on present, 207–10, 217–18; psychoanalysis and, 206, 217; on representation, 207, 231, 405n1, 406n9; on stagecraft, 207–10, 213, 216–18; *Théâtre-Solstices*, 219–20
Rehearsal, The (Anouilh), 231, 406n9
relevancies, 303–5

List of the seminars
(in chronological order)

Printed in the USA
CPSIA information can be obtained
at www.ICGtesting.com
JSHW022003260324
59977JS00003B/3